STUDY GUIDE

A PEOPLE AND A NATION
VOLUME I: TO 1877

STUDY GUIDE

A PEOPLE AND A NATION
VOLUME I: TO 1877

Fifth Edition

George C. Warren
Central Piedmont Community College

Cynthia L. Ricketson
Central Piedmont Community College

Mary Beth Norton
Cornell University

David M. Katzman
University of Kansas

Paul D. Escott
Wake Forest University

Howard P. Chudacoff
Brown University

Thomas G. Paterson
University of Connecticut

William M. Tuttle, Jr.
University of Kansas

HOUGHTON MIFFLIN COMPANY   BOSTON   NEW YORK

Senior Associate Editor: Jeffrey Greene
Manufacturing Manager: Florence Cadran
Marketing Manager: Sandra McGuire

Copyright © 1998 by Houghton Mifflin Company. All rights reserved.

No part of this work may be reproduced or transmitted in any form or by any means, electronic or mechanical, including photocopying and recording, or by any information storage or retrieval system without the prior written permission of Houghton Mifflin Company unless such use is expressly permitted by federal copyright law. Address inquiries to College Permissions, Houghton Mifflin Company, 222 Berkeley Street, Boston, MA 02116-3764.

Printed in the U.S.A.

ISBN: 0-395-78886-2

123456789-VG-01 00 99 98 97

Contents

To the Student   *vii*

To the Instructor   *ix*

Chapter 1   Three Old Worlds Create a New, 1492–1600   *1*

Chapter 2   Europeans Colonize North America, 1600–1640   *33*

Chapter 3   American Society Takes Shape, 1640–1720   *62*

Chapter 4   Growth and Diversity, 1720–1770   *82*

Chapter 5   Severing the Bonds of Empire, 1754–1774   *102*

Chapter 6   A Revolution, Indeed, 1775–1783   *138*

Chapter 7   Forging a National Republic, 1776–1789   *162*

Chapter 8   Politics and Society in the Early Republic, 1789–1800   *181*

Chapter 9   The Empire of Liberty, 1801–1824   *203*

Chapter 10   Rails, Markets, and Mills: The North and West, 1800–1860   *230*

Chapter 11   Slavery and the Growth of the South, 1800–1860   *248*

Chapter 12   The American Social Landscape, 1800–1860   *266*

Chapter 13   Reform, Politics, and Expansion, 1824–1844   *2988*

Chapter 14   Slavery and America's Future: The Road to War, 1845–1861   *312*

Chapter 15   Transforming Fire: The Civil War, 1861–1865   *330*

Chapter 16   Reconstruction: A Partial Revolution, 1865–1877   *360*

Answers   *389*

To the Student

This study guide will help you master the themes and information in the second volume of *A People and a Nation*. It won't give you a shortcut—there are no shortcuts—but it will give you direction and strategy, and if you use it conscientiously you will do well in your history course.

To get the most benefit from your study guide, you should read the introduction entitled "Taking the Mystery Out of Becoming 'Good' at History" before you do anything else. The introduction explains some of the ways of thinking about people and events that are particularly useful to history students, and it reviews the basics of good study habits applicable to a reading and writing course like history. Of course, it also tells you about how the book is arranged and what the standard chapter sections are for. You should read it carefully even before the course gets under way and you begin reading the first chapter of the textbook.

Once you get into an individual chapter in the study guide, you should do all the exercises and do them in order. It may be tempting to skip to the multiple-choice questions before you do the more time-consuming exercises or to omit the vocabulary exercise altogether. Don't yield to temptations. The less time-consuming exercises like the multiple-choice questions test the effectiveness of the work you have done on the more time-consuming exercises, such as the "Identification and Significance" and "Evaluating and Using Information" sections.

Remember as you use this book that it is working with the material that will make you understand and remember ideas and evidence. To do well requires a lot of hard work, but the right kind of hard work will make you do well. This study guide directs you toward the right kind of hard work.

To the Instructor

Looking over other study guides with all their fill-in-the-blanks, true-falses, and multiple-choices may have made you feel as though you were rifling through the files of some sorority or fraternity house on campus. But that's not how you are going to feel if you look closely at this one.

This study guide puts the objective question in its place. It does offer plenty of multiple-choice practice questions, but it places them near the ends of chapters where students can use them as culminating quizzes to find out how much they have learned. The multiple-choice section follows a series of exercises that have led students through the kind of active, mind-stretching studying you know they have to do to master the material. The answers to the multiple-choice questions in this book (at the back) are instructive, too—they explain why the right answers are right and the wrong answers are wrong. This same kind of approach to the answers section is seen in the instructive answer to the "Evaluating and Using Information" exercise for Chapter 1. Students are given a partial answer that helps them see whether they are on the right track without simply providing a whole essay written out for them to memorize.

And there's more.

Instead of the skeletal outline of each chapter that you see elsewhere, in this study guide you will see "Thematic Guides"—overviews in essay form presenting the major themes of the chapter in the textbook. The key word is *work*. Look at some of the "Identification and Significance," "Organizing Information," and "Evaluating and Using Information" exercises, for example. These call upon the student to collect and synthesize information, to organize it, and to write out answers to potential essay questions using the information they have collected.

The almost all-new "Evaluating and Using Information" exercises tackle the problem of getting students, especially freshmen, to understand what's expected of them on essay tests, what your injunction to "be concrete and specific" means. In the first several chapters, these exercises lead students through the process of creating working drafts of answers to very broad essay questions and give them advice on organizing the material for specific, commonly seen kinds of essay questions: comparison or contrast, definition, identification and significance, classification, and so forth. In later chapters, the "Evaluating and Using Information" exercises still require students to write working drafts of essay-question responses covering a lot of ground and still offer help in organizing information. However, in these later exercises, students have to shoulder more of the responsibility for determining the kind of information they need and the best way to collect it.

This study guide should help both you and your students. The exercises should awaken a lot of your students to the depth of information mastery that you expect. For many students those expectations come as a shock, and perhaps the study guide will help them to see that you are not alone in holding out such lofty expectations. In addition, if you are involved in a writing-across-the-curriculum movement, in developing a writing-intensive course on your campus, or in the renewed interest across the nation in helping students develop their critical thinking skills, you may get some ideas or even assignments from these pages.

Introduction—Taking the Mystery Out of Becoming "Good" at History

A funny short story set hundreds of years after a late twentieth-century nuclear war nearly wiped out humanity has archeologists excitedly explaining some highly polished ceramic and metallic relics from a religious shrine they have just discovered. As they describe the holy water receptacles and the fascinating devices for collecting coins for the gods, what they have found becomes clear to the story's reader: a pay toilet in New York City.

For history students, the moral of this story is that it is not just collecting some facts that is important. It's what you do with the facts that counts. History uses clues or facts to explain, or interpret, a society's events, personalities, and places; to explain why a society is as it is, why its events happened as they happened, and why its people decided as they decided and acted as they acted. But, to come up with wise interpretations, history students have to make sure both that they have collected enough useful information and that they do not let their or others' blind spots cause them to go astray.

SOME FACTORS A "GOOD" HISTORY STUDENT TAKES INTO ACCOUNT

Among the most common causes of blind spots that can get people off track are frames of reference, socialization, and, as *Star Trek*'s Mr. Spock would say, "insufficient data."

Frames of Reference

A real understanding of history will enable us to appreciate the past and apply what we learn to the problems we face today. But it will come only to those of us who can take people's *frames of reference* and *socialization* into account in judging their attitudes and behavior. Frames of reference and socialization are the emotional software that virtually forces people to think, feel, act, and react in particular, sometimes irrational, ways until they are somehow re-programmed. Frames of reference and socialization are the input; the historical events are the output.

You can think of frames of reference as constantly growing "encyclopedias" that people carry around in their heads, encyclopedias in which all their personal impressions and experiences have been and are being recorded. People refer constantly to these "encyclopedias" to make sense of what happens around them.

If you have ever smelled a particular aroma and almost immediately experienced a flood of memories, you have felt the power of your own frame of reference. Cooking aromas or the smells of the street can release a nostalgic flood that represents your own unique way of relating to or making meaning out of—interpreting—the particular smell. Your nostalgia derives from your frame of reference, your unique experiences associated with the smell. Thus the way you perceive yourself and your surroundings comes from your frame of reference. Occupation, socio-economic status, sex, race, environment, political beliefs, religious beliefs, age, nationality—all go into people's frames of reference, which determine how they interpret what goes on in their world. The people we study in history are subjected to the force of frames of reference and socialization just as we are, and their behavior must be interpreted in light of the influence of those powerful forces. Their frames of reference must be taken into account.

Socialization

A major part of people's frames of reference comes to them through *socialization,* the sum total of all the teaching done by the members of a society, in whatever way, to make sure its culture survives. In any culture young people are taught to believe that some ideas are right and others wrong, some proper and others improper. That is socialization. You can see its results in the confrontations of the English and the Indians described in Chapter 2 of *A People and a Nation.* The English had been taught to believe that people have a right to own land individually, but the North American Indians, who were socialized differently, had learned to believe that land was meant to be held communally. The differences in their socialization gave these two groups of people different frames of reference, and the resulting conflicts between the English colonists and the Indians forever changed human society on the North American continent.

Just as the attitudes and behaviors of the individuals who people the pages of history books like *A People and A Nation* result from input in the form of frames of reference and socialization, history books themselves result from input. What you see in your history textbook is the output produced by the analysis of millions of bits of raw data or *primary sources* collected over many years by thousands of people. Often writers of a history textbook study the data and analyses of earlier historians and accept their interpretations, but when they think the earlier interpretations are erroneous or when primary sources become available to them that were not available to earlier historians, they provide their own original interpretations or modifications of earlier interpretations. Always, though, primary sources are the raw material of history.

The Kind and Nature of Sources

Primary sources may be contradictory or incomplete or vague. Many primary sources are mere traces of the past, mere clues or hints that historians have to analyze to make sense of them. People in the past left the same kinds of clues that you leave as you go through your daily activities. If you carried around some carbon paper between the pages of a notepad for a few days, traces of your handling the paper in the notepad would remain, even on the sheets of paper you did not use. People from the past have left similar traces, sometimes consciously and sometimes unconsciously, whether in the form of footprints or written documents or farm implements or musical compositions. To the historian, these are like eyewitness accounts, but just as the eyewitnesses of this morning's accident do, historic eyewitnesses give conflicting accounts of what took place. Contradictory and conflicting facts make interpreting events difficult, and once historians start straightening out and interpreting the jumble of facts they have before them they inevitably give one fact more weight than another. That is when their own socialization and frames of reference begin influencing the output.

Clearly, then, if we are to understand historical events and derive meaning from them, we must recognize the importance of the kind and amount of information with which we are working, and we must attempt to be as objective as possible. We must try to prevent the biases and prejudices that emanate from our own frames of reference and socialization from blinding us to the limitations imposed upon people of earlier times and other places by their own frames of reference and socialization.

Making Interpretations Acceptable to Others

As long as you are a student rather than a professional historian, it is on tests that you will be presenting most of your interpretations of historical information. For your interpretations to be accepted as valid, you will have to show that they are based on solid information that you have studied and understood. Your explanations of how you came up with or derived your interpretations must have two qualities of effective composition: concreteness and specificity.

The Need for Concreteness

The real building blocks of the kind of interpretation that lies at the heart of history as an academic discipline are *facts*. Historians and history students must have something to interpret, and that something is a body of historical facts. So, as a history student who is expected to develop an ability to analyze and interpret data, your starting point is to master the facts themselves, facts that can be used to make an interpretation concrete and specific.

A *fact* is a bit of information that is perceived, when someone does perceive it, by means of the physical senses. It is facts that make an effective answer to an essay question. Facts are seen, heard, felt, tasted, or smelled. Facts used by history students are often actions and sounds, including the act of speaking and the sounds of speech; measurable characteristics, including dimensions, weights, distances, costs, counts; and the results of experimentation, including the raw data from polling. A fact is verifiable, confirmable either by qualified witnesses or, in the case of scientific experimentation or polling, by repetition ending in the same results. The information that the *Mayflower* landed at Plymouth could have been verified by any Indian who was around to meet the pilgrims at the shore or any pilgrim who scrambled off the ship. The truth or falsehood of the information could have been established by the visual perception of those present.

Once perceivable, a bit of information is a fact; once perceived, it is a known fact that can be reported as fact over and over again, handed down, for example, from an eyewitness to a historian and then handed on to other historians. And that brings up the problem of reliability. To decide whether a bit of information that you have gotten second- or third-hand is a fact, you have to consider its source. If the witnesses are incapable of the kind of perceiving called for or if they are dishonest, the information they call fact may not be fact, and you will need other witnesses or other forms of corroboration. Witnesses or reporters can color facts, too, through their interpretations and wording. Like lying, coloring does not really change facts, but it can certainly blur them. For example, if you and your classmates are present when your history teacher comes in the classroom and crosses from the door to the lectern, everyone in the room can perceive the movement, but some will call it *striding*, some *ambling*, some *sidling*, and some *walking*. The only thing you all will agree on is that movement has occurred. The movement is measurable. Your phrasing will affect how the fact is interpreted, but it does not affect the fact itself. The fact is the movement, not the style of movement.

The Need for Specificity

Facts are important to you as a student of history for at least two reasons. First, they are the material that you analyze to arrive at an interpretation. Second, they are essential ingredients in the presentation of the interpretation to others. The validity of an interpretation is going to be convincing only to the degree that it is perceived as having been derived logically from facts. That means that you, the interpreter, must cite the facts on which the interpretation is based (unless you are a widely known and established authority in the field). If you cite enough facts to make your interpretation clear and convincing, then you have been "concrete." However, concreteness is not enough. To be convincing, you must also be specific. The difference between

"Columbus set sail in the fifteenth century" and "Columbus set sail in 1492" is the degree of specificity. The difference between "The Tainos told Columbus about nearby islanders with strange eating habits" and "The Tainos told Columbus about the Caribs, who ate their captives" also is the degree of specificity. Usually, the more specific the evidence the more convincing it is.

The Need to Create Logical Ideas out of the Facts

Historians' and history students' interpretations are not factual, but they are arguable assertions or interpretative conclusions based on facts. They are what are called *inferences*. When you look at a series of photographs of someone in a magazine and conclude that in the first picture the individual is angry, in the second sad, and in the third embarrassed, you are making inferences. Using clues or facts in the pictures—facts such as the contortions of facial muscles, for example—you infer what the individual's emotional state is. *Inferences*, then, are ideas *created* from facts, and to be logical they must account for all the available facts on the topic.

A historian's total or final interpretation is an inference based on several narrow inferences. Facts are the building blocks of narrow inferences, and narrow inferences are the building blocks of a total interpretation, which is simply a broad inference.

An inference is not the same thing as an opinion. An inference can be thought of as a kind of educated guess—educated because it is clearly based on and derived from facts. An *opinion*, which is just as likely to be an uneducated guess as it is to be an educated guess, is a strong belief or conviction that may or may not be based on the facts. The person who offers a "mere" opinion simply does not cite the evidence that makes the basis of the opinion clear. On the other hand, a person who presents an inference is not expressing a "mere opinion."

Speculation is still another matter. A speculation is a cross between an opinion and an inference. It is a guess about the future or about a matter we can explain only with guesses either because we have inherited a shortage of facts or because the issue is such that facts alone cannot provide a clear-cut answer. Chapter 3 of your textbook, for example, presents two sets of speculation to explain the decline in church membership among New England men in the late seventeenth century.

Key to your success as a history student is your willingness to interpret, along with your willingness to master the facts on which to base your interpretations. It will be important not only in the way you read your history book and listen in class, but also in the way you share your thoughts with others and evaluate the thinking that others share with you. As you develop your interpretative approach to history, you will become more critical of your own ideas and learn to anticipate other people's objections to them or to the way you support them. Your anticipation of possible objections will force you into refining your thinking—and your interpretations.

HOW TO STUDY TO GAIN THE INFORMATION NEEDED

To master the facts you will need to develop convincing interpretations of historical data, and you must study effectively. To study effectively, you have to interact deeply with the important components of the course—the textbook, the lectures, the students, and the professor. Merely attending class is not enough. Passively reading just to get to the end of each chapter is not enough. Answering questions only when you are directly asked to is not enough.

Previewing the Text

The component of your history course with which you will have to deal most independently is your textbook. Before you do anything else, you should get a feel for the course by previewing your text. To familiarize yourself with the textbook, you need to open it and

Introduction—Taking the Mystery Out of Becoming "Good" at History xv

1. Read the title and ask what it says about the material inside. Doesn't the title *A People and a Nation* tell you that the book presents a social-cultural as well as a political history of the United States?

2. Read the preface to find out what the authors' purpose and approach are.

3. Read the biographical data about the authors to see how much authority they have and what their special interests and areas of expertise are.

4. Read the table of contents to see where the course is going to take you; compare the dates given in the titles of chapters in your book with those listed in the title of your course to determine which chapters your class will be covering.

Once you have previewed the text, you are ready to study your first chapter systematically, using both your textbook and your study guide.

Studying the Chapter Systematically

To use your textbook effectively, it is a good idea to adopt the "Survey Q 3 R" system of studying developed some forty years ago by F. P. Robinson and the learning aids and exercises in this study guide. Research confirms the effectiveness of the system's five processes: (1) *Surveying*, (2) *Questioning*, (3) *Reading*, (4) *Reciting*, and (5) *Reviewing*—SQ3R.

Surveying and Questioning. The first two steps in the system, surveying and questioning, are intimately linked. As you survey each chapter, jot down questions about the material in it. For that purpose, you need a reading notebook. Then, when you begin your close reading of the chapter, you will find that your reading is purposeful. You are looking for answers to your questions.

The surveying process itself begins with you actively reading the chapter title, making sure you understand the meaning of each word. Consider how this suggestion applies to your "survey" of Chapter 1. The word *meeting* in the title "The Meeting of Old World and New, 1492–1600" implies an interaction and might lead to the questions "What kind of interaction occurred between the Old World and the New?" and "What was its result?"

The surveying and questioning process also includes reading the headings and the chapter's introductory vignette and studying the pictures and diagrams and framing questions that they suggest. The introductory vignette (personalizes and illustrates themes covered in the chapter), headings (provide a road map of the chapter), and the illustrations (pictures, maps, diagrams, tables) all suggest questions, questions that you should ask yourself and record in your reading notebook.

Special learning aids in this study guide will help you go through the surveying and questioning process. In the chapter in the Study Guide corresponding to the chapter in your textbook that you are studying, the list of Learning Objectives tells you what your are supposed to accomplish and the Thematic Guide helps put facts and ideas within the textbook into perspective by pointing out the chapter's major themes. You can derive questions from the Learning Objectives just as you derive questions from the title, headings, vignette, and illustrations in the chapter.

The Learning Objectives are useful in another way. If you get bogged down in the details and lose your way, so to speak, all you have to do is refer to the Learning Objectives to find out where what you are reading fits into the chapter's total picture.

The Thematic Guide is designed to help you in much the same way. Chapter themes and the details in the chapter are like a long row of coat hooks and the coats hanging from them. The themes give you "hooks" on which to hang the facts. Without those hooks, you might be buried under a pile of "coats." You can refer to the Thematic Guide for help in ordering the facts in an understandable and meaningful way. The Thematic Guide can help you see whether the material you are presently reading relates to one of the major themes of the chapter. To what theme does it relate? Is the material factual information supporting one of the chapter's themes? Is it a statement of one of those themes? Is it a sub-topic or an offshoot of one of the major themes?

The Building Vocabulary section for each chapter is still another feature of this study guide that is particularly useful in the surveying and questioning steps of the SQ3R system. Each Building Vocabulary section lists words and terms that you really have to understand to understand the chapter in your textbook. When you open your dictionary and look up any words on the list that are unfamiliar to you, jot down their definitions in the space provided in your Study Guide, and you will have all the definitions you'll need when you study the chapter. Then gaps in your vocabulary will neither keep you from understanding what you are reading nor make you interrupt your reading to look up words that are new to you.

One learning aid in the Study Guide, the Finding the Main Idea exercise, appears only in its first chapter and offers you a special kind of help related to the surveying process. It is a helpful bridge between surveying the chapter and actually beginning to read the material in the chapter. If you have ever had trouble figuring out what information is really important for you to get from your textbooks, doing the Finding the Main Idea exercise in the study guide's first chapter should help you solve the problem. It will help you study all of the chapters in *A People and a Nation* more efficiently.

The exercise is closely related to the explanations of how to mark your text and find main ideas that come up later in this introduction (pages xviii–xix) and to a simple but important technique that you can use to survey each chapter in the textbook. This technique is simply to identify each of the chapter's segments, groups of usually between two and five consecutive paragraphs (occasionally a single paragraph is a segment, though) devoted to a single topic or idea. Just take a pencil and draw a line between the last paragraph of one segment and the first paragraph of the next segment. Then, when you begin "looking for the main ideas," you will be looking for the main ideas of these segments or series of paragraphs.

The number of activities involved in surveying the chapter should tell you just how important surveying is. Only after you have done all of them, which sounds more time consuming than it really is, are you ready to dive into the chapter itself.

Reading. The next step is to begin reading the body of the chapter, looking for answers to your questions. Two features of the study guide will help you with the reading part of the SQ3R system: the Learning Objectives and the Identification and Significance sections. However, three other features are also helpful: the Thematic Guide, Essay Questions, and, in some chapters, Organizing Information exercises.

As you begin this step in the SQ3R system, remember that the verb *study* is an active verb. Staring at a textbook an arm's length away, counting pages as you mentally trudge to the last page of the chapter, flipping pages with the end of a pencil—none of that is studying. Studying is successful and rewarding only when you actively, physically involve yourself in the material you are studying. That's why it is so important for you to read with a pen in your hand and use it to mark your textbook (page xix), record questions and notes in a reading notebook, and write definitions and answers to exercises in the pages of your study guide. The act of doing these things, the physical act of writing, is what makes the verb *study* an active verb

When you actually begin your close reading of a chapter, you should read manageable blocks of material rather than straight through the chapter. If in your surveying of the chapter you have drawn lines dividing the chapter into its segments, then each segment is what constitutes a manageable block.

Read a block of material and stop. Analyze the material you have read in that block and draw a box around the main idea in each paragraph unless the paragraph does no more than simply connect other paragraphs. (Such paragraphs, especially if they come at the very beginning or at the very end of the block, often state the whole point of the entire block. You might want to draw a block around such statements and mark them with asterisks.) Once you have marked the main ideas, jot them down in the margin or in your reading notebook. Then underline the supporting details and number them in the textbook margin. Figure 1 on page xix shows a paragraph that has been marked in this way.

In this reading step you should be on the lookout for information you need to compose your responses to items in the Identification and Significance exercise in the Study Guide. Once you find the information you need to identify and indicate the significance of an item on the list, write out your response to the item in your own words. (Merely copying from the textbook won't do. Copying is a rote, no-thinking-required activity as any skilled typist who routinely types long documents without having any idea what they say will tell you.) As you read the material, pay close attention to the questions you should answer to identify the item and those you need to answer to explain the item's significance. For some items, the significance section will be longer than it will be for others because some items have more consequences (significance) than others.

Relating what you are reading to the Learning Objectives listed in the Study Guide is still another important part of the reading step. If the material relates to Learning Objective 1, write in the textbook margin "OBJ. 1." That will help you find specific material later in your studying process.

Reciting. The reciting part of studying should be both mental and physical. After you find the answer to a question, STOP. Look away from your textbook and recite both the question and the answer to yourself. It is best to keep working on formulating the answer until you can do it without looking at the text. You can do the same thing physically by putting your answer in writing. After you can recite mentally, then write the question and compose your answer to it without looking at the text. If your answers are long—several pages or more—you should narrow them to keep your work manageable and the learning in bite-sized pieces.

Many of the Evaluating and Using Information exercises in this study guide will help you with the reciting step. Some of these exercises lead you through the process of gathering information from scattered parts of chapters and using the information to compose working drafts for responses to essay questions. Others simply call upon you to go through the gathering and composing process on your own. They all give you practice in using textbook information to create your own ideas about historical events, personalities, and concepts.

Reviewing. In the last stage of the SQ3R method, you review. Each day, before you begin the process of studying and learning new material, review the material you have studied and learned to that point. Go back and recite answers to the questions listed in your reading notebook; go over your underlining and reading notes; and review the Identification and Significance items to make sure you remember major ideas and main supporting details. The Ideas and Details section and the Essay Questions section at the end of each chapter of the study guide are also useful as part of the review process.

IMPROVING YOUR READING AND RECALL

No matter how systematically you work, for your studying to pay off in a history course, you have to read effectively and develop techniques that will help you remember what you read. Many students find that once they learn to pick out main ideas, insert simple and clear written reminders in their textbook as they read, and use outlining or other, less formal forms of note taking, the SQ3R method is a sure path to academic success. Why not adopt some of these techniques yourself?

Finding Main Ideas

Understanding some basic kinds of writing that you are likely to run into will help you when you set about the task of separating main ideas and finding the inferences and factual details that support them. Such understanding will also help you to see relationships among ideas and between a piece of evidence and the idea it supports. And having a strong sense of how all the information and ideas relate to one another is a tremendous help in remembering information. Let's stop and consider these basic kinds of writing.

Even though much of the paragraphing in textbooks is determined by appearance on the page rather than by the conventions of paragraph structure you learn in an English composition class, those paragraphs in a book like *A People and a Nation* that do follow the conventions fall into two categories: *developmental paragraphs* that announce ideas and then both clarify those ideas and provide evidence to support them; and *functional paragraphs* that introduce or conclude sections of chapters or shift the focus from one section or idea to another.

Each *developmental paragraph* presents one central idea and supports it either with clarifying information—such as details—definitions, and sometimes "expert" testimony, too, or with both. These paragraphs can be arranged inductively—with listed evidence followed by an interpretation of the evidence—or deductively—with the interpretive statement followed by the list of evidence. *Functional paragraphs* merely announce ideas and shifts of focus. They offer no support themselves. (Other paragraphs—developmental paragraphs—provide the support for the ideas they announce.)

What you look for when you look for main ideas may be the main idea of a single, self-contained paragraph, but it could be the one main idea of a whole group or block of paragraphs, called a *paragraph series*. Ideally, a paragraph series is introduced by a functional paragraph that announces the central idea of the whole series, very much as the introductions to most essays do. Ideally, too, another functional paragraph, a transitional-concluding paragraph, will appear at the end of the series. The appearance of functional paragraphs, then, should help you identify paragraph series, which are important, bite-size segments of the chapter. And you look for the main ideas within those bite-size pieces. Knowledge of the two basic patterns, inductive and deductive, will tell you to expect the main idea to appear near the beginning or at the end of the paragraph or paragraph series.

Because the difference between a developmental paragraph and a developmental paragraph series is primarily a matter of scale, the procedure for determining their main ideas is pretty much the same. To see how the procedure works out in practice, take a look at Figure 1. It shows a paragraph reprinted from Chapter 1 of *A People and a Nation* marked up as a student might have marked it.

If you try to decide what the main idea is before you read the whole paragraph, the first sentence can trip you up. Analysis of the whole paragraph shows that the first sentence introduces a subject, religious beliefs, and links it to another, political systems, by indicating that the two are comparable in terms of their variation. But the next two sentences focus neither on political systems nor on variations in religious beliefs. They focus on similarities, "common threads" in religious beliefs: polytheism and the relationship of the religious systems to nature. In fact, aside from the first sentence, the whole paragraph focuses on what Native Americans' religious beliefs had in common. Furthermore, most of the paragraph is devoted to examples of the second thread by naming three aspects of religion that reflected integration of tribes' economies with nature (major deities, festivals, and women's place in the religious leadership). The paragraph's main idea, then, is that polytheism and integration were two features of religion that agricultural and hunting Indian tribes shared.

MARKING YOUR TEXT

As our earlier discussion of the reading step in the SQ3R system suggests, marking the text is a very useful technique that makes it easier to remember what you have read. Not only does it help you concentrate on what you are reading but it will help you take notes on your reading. You should underline important concepts and ideas and write relevant, concise notes in the margin.

To emphasize the main idea of each paragraph or paragraph series, you can, for example, draw a box around it with a pen if the author has stated it succinctly for you. If the author takes more than one sentence to express the main idea or merely implies it, you can write it in your own words in the margin. And, finally, you can underline the supporting details in the passage and number them in the margin. What you want to avoid is overmarking or undermarking. Whether you underline just about everything or do virtually no marking at all, nothing is going to stand out to be spotted easily when you review your chapter or look through it for specific information you need.

Figure 1, below, illustrates this simple system as it might be applied to the paragraph we discussed in the previous section. Notice that in Figure 1 the student has written the main idea in the margin and underlined the three illustrations used by the writer to clarify the second sub-point (the idea that all the religions involved integration of religion and nature) and labeled them 2a, 2b, and 2c.

Figure 1. Passage in Text Marked by Student

Americans' religious beliefs varied even more than did their political systems, but all <u>the peoples were polytheistic</u>, worshipping a multitude of gods. One common thread was <u>their integration with nature</u>. Thus each group's most important <u>beliefs and rituals</u> were closely tied to its economy. The <u>major deities of agricultural peoples</u> like Pueblos and Muskogeans were associated with cultivation and their <u>chief festivals</u> centered on planting and harvest. The most important <u>gods of hunters</u> (such as those living on the Great Plains) were associated with animals, and <u>their major festivals were related to hunting. The band's economy and women's roles in it helped to determine</u> women's potential as religious leaders. Women held the most prominent positions in those agricultural societies (like the Iroquois) in which they were also the chief food producers, whereas in hunting societies men took the lead in religious as well as political affairs.	*Americans' religions had two common threads.* *1. all involved polytheism* *2. all were integrated with nature* *2a. the gods and festivals of agricultural peoples.* *2b. the gods and festivals of hunting tribes* *2c. group's economy as determiner of women's eligibility for roles as religious leaders*

OUTLINING CHAPTERS

With your reading done and passages marked, you can outline the chapter to help yourself separate the important from the unimportant and produce a guide for your practice recitations before examinations. Whether you choose to outline the whole chapter probably should depend on how effectively you can outline. You may prefer to outline key subsections of the chapter instead of outlining the whole chapter or, if you really just cannot outline very well, to replace outlining with other forms of notetaking.

The actual outlining process is one of dividing and re-dividing. You start with a "whole," and you divide it. The "whole" is the overall point of the chapter, what all the evidence supports and adds up to. Once you have read and marked the whole chapter—and, as the logic of outlining makes clear, you absolutely must do that first—you see that what you start out with is a whole idea. You have to think of that idea as a whole "thing" just as you would think of a pie as a whole thing. You then find the largest parts into which you can cut your pie, usually between two and five parts. No matter how many of these largest sub-topics you recognize, each is now to be considered an absolutely new, whole subject. You divide the first into what you recognize as its largest components and then do the same with the second and the others until you have subdivided all of your largest subtopics into their largest subtopics. You then go back and treat each of the sub-subtopics as a divisible whole subject.

How long you keep up the dividing and subdividing process depends on what you're using the outline for. If you are merely trying to identify the main themes to help you in both in-class and out-of-class notetaking, then the process does not go much past three levels of division. If you are reducing all of your out-of-class notes to outline form and plugging in information from your class notes, then you need a very thorough outline, one whose lowest-rank headings either cannot be subdivided or are enough to trigger your memory of the unnamed subdivisions. Outlines whose headings are too broad are not very helpful, but forcing unnecessary specificity into an outline wastes precious time.

It's a good idea to follow conventional outlining style in most particulars. Good headings are specific and substantive headings. They reflect the subject matter clearly and trigger recall of details. That rules out useless status headings (*Introduction, Body,* and *Conclusion*), which indicate the locations of information rather than the information itself. Good outline design includes a number-letter heading designator system and an indention system that suggest the rank and relative importance of the headings. The conventional system that you can find illustrated in almost any freshman English composition handbook is helpful but an outline's format should never take on more importance than its content.

ANTICIPATING AND PREPARING FOR TESTS

Ideally, of course, you go to all this trouble because you want to learn about the history of the United States to become a more cultured person and a better citizen or observer of American society and politics. But you probably are interested in doing well in your American history course also because how well you are deemed to have succeeded in it will become a part of your academic record. This second interest explains your desire to do well on history tests this term. How well you do on your tests will depend on how well you anticipate questions and how well you prepare yourself to answer the questions you anticipate.

GUESSING WHAT'S GOING TO BE ASKED

Obviously you can figure out some of the questions you will have to be able to answer simply by doing the exercises in this study guide. But you will want to enlarge that list of possibilities with some suggestions of your own growing out of your class notes, your supplementary reading assignments, and your familiarity with your instructor's emphases. One important way you can come up with potential essay questions that may not have occurred to you is to find subject matter in your class and textbook notes that suits some of the writing styles most commonly called for on essay tests.

Questions calling for answers written in several particular writing styles crop up on almost all essay tests. Therefore, thinking up questions that call for answers written in these styles pays off most of the time. As you are going to see, the process of developing questions to suit the particular styles is illustrated in several of the Evaluating and Using Information exercises in this Study Guide. Among the most commonly used types of questions are ones calling for exemplification, comparison, contrast, definition, causal analysis, and classification. We can add to this list a type almost peculiar to history courses, the analytical narration (or "trace the development of") question. In the exemplification type, you are to show that you can back up one of your opinions by citing examples; in the comparison type, that you can show how two or more persons, events, or concepts resemble each other; in the contrast type, that you can show how two or more persons, events, or concepts differ from each other; in the definition type, that you can explain what something is or means or who someone is; in the causal analysis type, that you can explain the causes or the effects of something; in the classification type, that you can identify the types or kinds of something; and, in the analytical narration type, that you can trace the development of something by citing and explaining the key changes it has gone through. To anticipate questions, you simply go through all of your notes and find subject matter that suits any of the particular writing styles. You might find as many as twenty or twenty-five potential matches. Once you find a match, you state the question that arises out of it. From the list of questions that results, you cull the most likely candidates, trying to create a set of questions that covers all of the material the test is to cover and providing the best style-to-subject matter matches you can produce.

Preparing Answers to Essay Questions

Once you have your list of potential essay questions, it is time to plan your answers to those questions. That's right: actual answers to the questions you have produced. Some of the Evaluating and Using Information exercises in this study guide lead you step-by-step through the whole process.

Think of it as taking an open-book, take-home test. You pore through your notes, your textbook, and your study guide to find all the relevant examples and other evidence you have been exposed to. For each of your questions, you frame your basic one-sentence response based on the sum of the evidence you collect. You then outline the material that supports your one-sentence answer (perhaps in the form of a chart like those in many of the Evaluating and Using Information exercises) or actually write out your whole answer in the form of the working draft of an essay. The one-sentence answer is the thesis of your response, whose body is the written-out evidence that you have gathered from throughout the chapter and from your class notes and have now organized. Such gathering, synthesizing, and organizing is, of course, exactly what you are asked to do in many of the Organizing Information and Evaluating and Using Information exercises in this study guide. Be warned, though: you cannot expect to be able to write out such a full answer under the time and psychological pressure of the testing situation. Such pressure will end up forcing you to select what you can hope is the best evidence from all the evidence you collected. What you really want to happen is what usually does happen. In putting together an answer, you bring together related but previously scattered material and thus make it more meaningful and more memorable.

A FINAL BIT OF ENCOURAGEMENT

So you see, becoming good at history isn't such a mysterious process after all. Yes, it takes hard work, but hard work does pay off. These techniques we've been looking at—from adopting an interpretative approach to history to marking passages in the textbook, from evaluating information to outlining, from anticipating test questions to writing out mock answers to the questions anticipated—have helped generations of young people become more interested in and knowledgeable about America's history and, yes, better history students. But, if you think that will never happen to you, here's one more technique for you: Find your own reason for being interested, not some reason your textbook's authors give you or your parents give you or your history teacher gives you, but a reason of your own. Once you want to learn, you will learn, and your success as a history student will rise dramatically. That's a promise!

CHAPTER 1
Three Old Worlds Create a New, 1492–1600

LEARNING OBJECTIVES

After you have studied Chapter 1 in your textbook and worked through this study guide chapter, you should be able to:

1. Describe the political, economic, social, and cultural characteristics of the societies of the Americas and West Africa before their contact with the Europeans.

2. Describe the political, economic, social, and cultural characteristics of European society prior to the European voyages of exploration and discovery.

3. Indicate the social, political, economic, and technological factors that made possible the European explorations of the fifteenth and sixteenth centuries, and explain the goals and motives behind those explorations.

4. Discuss the lessons learned by Europeans in the Mediterranean, Atlantic, and the North Atlantic, and explain the relationship between those lessons and European exploration, discovery, and colonization in the Americas.

5. Examine the impact of the exchange of plants, animals, diseases, peoples, and cultures resulting from European exploration, discovery, and colonization.

6. Examine the characteristics associated with Spanish colonization in the Americas, and discuss the consequences of the Spanish venture.

7. Assess fifteenth- and sixteenth-century attempts by European traders and fishermen to exploit the natural wealth of North America.

8. Indicate the motives for and explain the failure of England's first attempt to plant a permanent settlement in North America.

THEMATIC GUIDE

Chapter 1 gives us an understanding of the three main cultures that interacted with each other as a result of the European voyages of exploration and discovery of the late fifteenth and sixteenth centuries. The examination of the political, social, economic, and religious beliefs of Native Americans, West Africans, and Europeans helps us understand the interaction among the peoples of these cultures and the impact each had on the other. Although this interaction and its impact is a major theme in Chapter 1, the chapter also focuses on the impact of geography and environment on peoples and the societies they build.

The first two sections of the chapter ("American Societies" and "North America in 1492") deal primarily with the emergence and development of a variety of Native American cultures. In "American Societies" we first learn about American-Indian origins, but we are quickly introduced to the theme that geography and environment have an impact on people and the societies they build. The geography and natural environment of Mesoamerica, for example, made settled agriculture possible in that area. In turn, the practice of settled agriculture created a human-made environment conducive to the emergence of more complex civilizations. The wealth of, and the political, social, and economic complexities of, the Aztec civilization encountered by the Spanish when they invaded Mexico in 1519 were, in large measure, due to the development of agriculture in Mesoamerica thousands of years earlier.

The theme that the political, social, economic, and religious ideas of a culture directly relate to how the people of that culture obtain food necessary for survival continues in section two, "North America in 1492." The diversity of Indian cultures in North America developed when the Native Americans north of Mexico "adapted their once-similar ways of life to very different geographical settings." This, therefore, explains the emergence of small hunter-gatherer bands in areas not well suited to agriculture and the emergence of larger semi-nomadic bands that combined agriculture with hunting-and-gathering in areas with a more favorable environment. A culture's means of subsistence also serves to explain the similarities in social organization between the agricultural Pueblo society of the southwest and the agricultural societies of the East. Furthermore, the way in which each tribe obtained food affected the political structure, the gender roles, and the religious beliefs of various tribes.

Section three, "African Societies," begins with the sentence:

> Fifteenth-century Africa, like fifteenth-century America, housed a variety of cultures adapted to different geographical settings.

This statement carries the theme used in the discussion of pre-Columbian Native-American societies into the section on fifteenth-century African societies. After a brief mention of the Berbers of North Africa, the Muslim city states of the East coast, and the interior kingdoms of West Africa, our attention focuses on the societies along the Guinea coast, the area from which most slaves destined for sale in the Americas came. Here we learn of the religious beliefs and practices, the sexual division of labor, and the social systems of West African societies in the coastal area between the Senegal and Niger Rivers.

In section four our attention turns to the European societies of the fifteenth and sixteenth centuries. An explanation of the similarities and differences between European society on the one hand and American and African societies on the other hand is followed by a discussion of the devastating social, political, and economic impact of the Black Death and the Hundred Years' War on European society. That discussion returns us to the recurring theme concerning the impact of environment on peoples and their societies.

The chapter's focus then shifts to the political and technological changes in fifteenth-century Europe that paved the way for the fifteenth- and sixteenth-century voyages of exploration. But to achieve their primary goal of easy access to Asian and African goods and their secondary goal of spreading Christianity throughout the world, the early explorers had to overcome certain obstacles posed by nature. As they learned to master their environment, problems posed by the prevailing winds in the "Mediterranean Atlantic" (the Northeast Trades) led to the tactic of sailing "around the wind" and, subsequently, to discovery of the westerlies. This knowledge eventually allowed the Spanish and Portuguese to exploit for profit the islands off the coast of Africa (the Azores, the Madeiras, the Canaries, and São Tomé). In the discussion about the use of these islands and the lessons European explorers learned there, a new theme is introduced: The desire of Europeans to extract profits from the Americas led them to exploit the plants, animals, and peoples in the societies they encountered. This new theme is further developed in the discussion of Christopher Columbus's voyages and the first encounter between Europeans and Americans.

The exploitation theme continues into sections six ("Spanish Colonization and the Exchange of Plants, Animals, and Diseases") and seven ("European Traders, Fishermen, and Early Settlements"). After a general discussion of the transfer of diseases, plants, and animals between Old World and New and the impact of these transfers on the societies in question, we turn to a discussion of the elements that were part of the Spanish model of colonization and to an explanation of the consequences of the interaction between the Spanish and the Mesoamerican peoples. Our attention then shifts to attempts by the Portuguese, French, and English to exploit the natural resources of the Americas. Because they were primarily interested in profits from the natural wealth of the sea and land rather than in territorial conquest, European traders and fishermen descended upon the east coast of North America and the waters off that coast. After a discussion of the impact of the fur trade on the Europeans and Indians, the chapter turns to the reasons for England's first attempts to plant colonies in the Western Hemisphere. The chapter concludes with an explanation of why these colonization attempts by England, under the supervision of Sir Humphrey Gilbert and Sir Walter Raleigh, failed.

BUILDING VOCABULARY

Listed below are important words and terms that you need to know to get the most out of Chapter 1. They are listed in the order in which they occur in the chapter. After carefully looking through the list, refer to a dictionary and jot down the definition of words that you do not know or of which you are unsure.

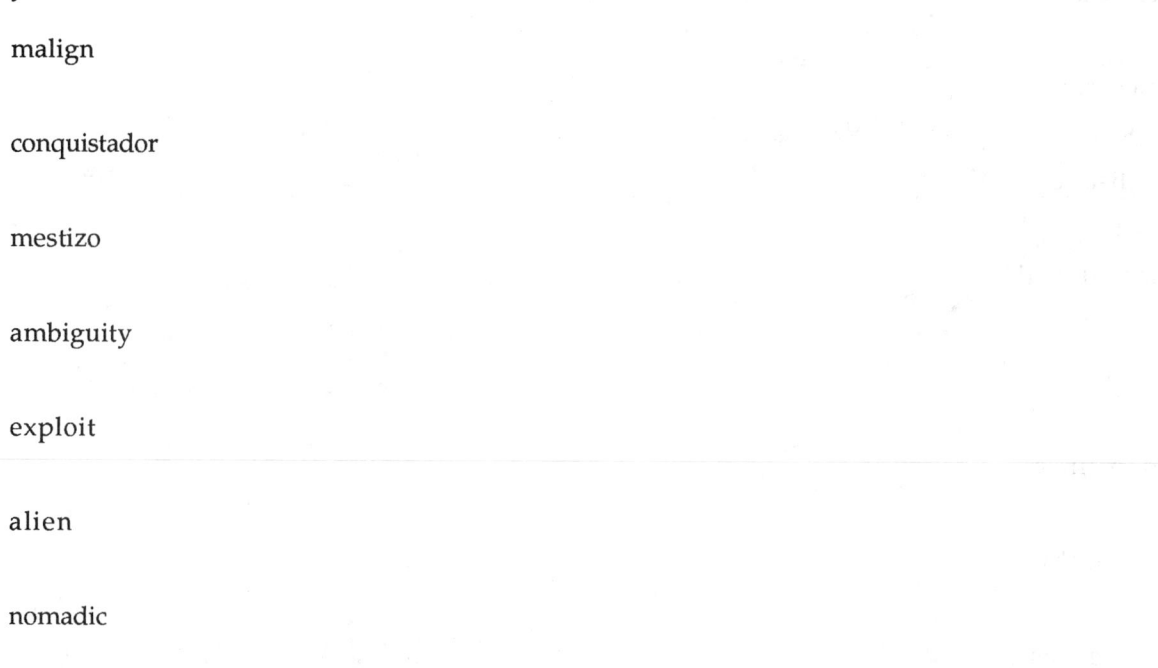

malign

conquistador

mestizo

ambiguity

exploit

alien

nomadic

band

tribe

demise

sedentary

adept

subsistence

Mesoamerica

autocratic

deity

stratified

ominous

autonomous

palisade

matrilineal

wield

patrilineal

hierarchy

consensus

autocratic

polytheistic

hereditary

elite

precept

cosmopolitan

middleman

cult

egalitarian

fallow

artisan

patriarchal

precipitous

nationalistic

circumvent

heathen

Iberia

tedious

intractable

cartographer

aesthetic

sporadic

lethal

mortality

virulent

adapt

vestige

friar

assimilate

pagan

juxtapose

pelts

insatiable

ecological

foment

manipulate

irrevocably

millennia

permeate

FINDING THE MAIN IDEA

When you begin to read material assigned to you in the textbook, it is important for you to look for (and mark) the main idea and supporting details in each paragraph or paragraph series. To see how to do so, reread "Finding Main Ideas" in the Introduction to this study guide. Then work the following three exercises and check your answers.

Exercise A

Read the paragraph on page 14 of the textbook that begins with this sentence:

> Despite their different economies and the rivalries among states, the peoples of Lower Guinea had similar social systems organized on the basis of what anthropologists have called the *dual-sex principle*.

1. What is the topic of this paragraph series?

2. What is its main idea?

3. What details support the main idea?

Exercise B

Read the paragraph on page 16 of the textbook that begins with this sentence:

> The fifteenth century also brought technological change to Europe.

1. What is the topic of this paragraph series?

2. What is its main idea?

3. What details support the main idea?

Exercise C

Read the two successive paragraphs on page 28 of the textbook, beginning with the sentence:

> European fishermen soon learned that they could supplement their profits by exchanging cloth and metal goods like pots and knives for the Native Americans' beaver pelts, which Europeans used to make fashionable hats.

1. What is the topic of this paragraph series?

2. What is its main idea?

3. What details support the main idea?

Chapter 1—Three Old Worlds Create a New, 1492–1600

IDENTIFICATION AND SIGNIFICANCE

After studying Chapter 1 of *A People and a Nation*, you should be able to identify fully *and* explain the historical significance of each item listed below.

1. Identify each item in the space provided. Give an explanation or description of the item. Answer the questions *who, what, where,* and *when*.

2. Explain the historical significance of each item in the space provided. Establish the historical context in which the item exists. Establish the item as the result of or as the cause of other factors existing in the society under study. Answer this question: *What were the political, social, economic, and/or cultural consequences of this item?*

Malinché

    Identification

    Significance

Hernán Cortés

    Identification

    Significance

Paleo-Indians

    Identification

    Significance

the Aztecs

    Identification

    Significance

Olmecs

    Identification

    Significance

the Mayas

    Identification

    Significance

Teotihuacan

    Identification

    Significance

Moundbuilders

    Identification

    Significance

the Anasazi

    Identification

    Significance

Cahokia

    Identification

    Significance

Huitzilopochtli

    Identification

    Significance

Tenochtitlan

    Identification

    Significance

sexual division of labor

    Identification

    Significance

the Pueblo, Algonkian, Iroquois, and Muskogean peoples

    Identification

    Significance

Lady of Cofitachequi

    Identification

    Significance

Upper Guinea

    Identification

    Significance

trans-Saharan trade

>Identification

>Significance

Timbuktu

>Identification

>Significance

Lower Guinea

>Identification

>Significance

dual-sex principle

>Identification

>Significance

the Sandé and Poro cults

>Identification

>Significance

the Black Death

>Identification

>Significance

Chapter 1—Three Old Worlds Create a New, 1492–1600 13

the Hundred Years War

    Identification

    Significance

the lateen sail, the astrolabe, and the quadrant

    Identification

    Significance

Ferdinand of Aragon and Isabella of Castile

    Identification

    Significance

movable type and the printing press

    Identification

    Significance

Travels by Marco Polo

    Identification

    Significance

the Mediterranean Atlantic

    Identification

    Significance

the Northeast Trades and the westerlies

    Identification

    Significance

the Azores and the Madeiras

    Identification

    Significance

the Canaries

    Identification

    Significance

Prince Henry the Navigator

    Identification

    Significance

São Tomé

    Identification

    Significance

Christopher Columbus

    Identification

    Significance

Amerigo Vespucci

    Identification

    Significance

Leif Ericsson

    Identification

    Significance

John Cabot

    Identification

    Significance

the Northwest Passage

    Identification

    Significance

killer diseases

    Identification

    Significance

tobacco and the horse

    Identification

    Significance

conquistadores

    Identification

    Significance

Francisco Pizarro

    Identification

    Significance

the Spanish model of colonization

    Identification

    Significance

the *encomienda* system

    Identification

    Significance

Spanish missionaries

    Identification

    Significance

John Hawkins and Sir Francis Drake

    Identification

    Significance

Sir Humphrey Gilbert and Sir Walter Raleigh

    Identification

    Significance

A Briefe and True Report of the New Found Land of Virginia

    Identification

    Significance

ORGANIZING INFORMATION

The clues historians gather are not important in and of themselves but in how they are used to explain the events, ideas, and personalities within a society. To use facts in this way, you need to organize them into meaningful categories. Dividing the society or topic under study into its parts, and grouping the data collected under each of the divisions, make each part simpler and easier to understand and explain.

    Consider how you can apply that approach in studying Chapter 1, which deals with interaction among several different cultures. You would organize the information about those separate cultures into meaningful categories, such as the ones used by social scientists to analyze the activities and ideas within a society.

Economic Activities and Ideas

How do people in this society produce, use, and distribute property, goods, and wealth? What skills are necessary for the production of goods? Is this society technologically advanced or is it underdeveloped? How do the economic roles of men and women differ? What ideas are used to justify the economic structure of this society?

Social Activities and Ideas

This category is the most far-reaching of the categories listed. In the questions associated with this category, you can see that social activities and ideas often relate to one of the other categories.

    What is the social organization of this society? What are the relationship patterns within the society? How are those relationship patterns determined? What are the social customs pertaining to eating, manner of dress, physical appearance? What are the relationships between the sexes, among races, and among ethnic groups? What are the relationships between parents and children? What kinship patterns exist? What social divisions exist within this society? Are privileges extended to some social groups and not to others? What ideas are used to justify the social organization of this society?

Political Activities and Ideas

How is this society governed? How is the government structured? Who participates in the decision-making process? How do the political roles of men and women differ? How are societal decisions implemented and enforced? How does this society deal with disorder and crime? What ideas are used to justify the political structure of this society?

Religious Activities and Ideas

How do the people in this society relate to what they perceive to be the mysterious, the unknown, and the supernatural? What beliefs, practices, and rituals characterize the religious activities within this society? How do the religious roles of men and women differ? What ideas are used to justify the religious belief system of this society?

Artistic Activities and Ideas

How do the people in this society express their beliefs, values, and aspirations in the realm of art, music, literature, architecture, and the like?

Although the authors mention a number of different Indian tribes in Chapters 1 and 2, they concentrate on tribes of the Algonkian, Iroquois, and Muskogean language groups, located in what is now the eastern United States, and on the Pueblos, located in what is now the southwestern United States. Tribes mentioned in the textbook fit into the Algonkian, Iroquois, and Muskogean language groups as follows:

Algonkian Tribes	*Iroquoian Tribes*	*Muskogean Tribes*
Abenakis	Six tribes of the Iroquois nation (Mohawks, Cayugas Oneidas, Onondagas, and Senecas; the Tuscaroras joined in 1722)	Chickasaws
Delawares		Choctaws
Doegs		Creeks (Lady of Cofitachique)
Illinois		Yamasees
Massachusetts		
Miamis	Cherokees	
Narragansetts	Hurons	
Nipmucks	Susquehannocks	
Pakanokets		
Pequots		
Powhatan Confederacy		
Shawnees		

Use the chart on the following page to categorize information about these major Indian cultures. Because the artistic characteristics of these societies are not examined in the textbook, that category is not included in the chart.

Make charts of your own to categorize information about African societies and European society.

CHARACTERISTICS OF INDIAN CULTURES

Indian Groups	Economic Characteristics	Social Characteristics	Political Characteristics	Religious Characteristics
Algonkian				
Iroquois				
Muskogean				
Pueblo				

Chapter 1—Three Old Worlds Create a New, 1492–1600

EVALUATING AND USING INFORMATION

Using the questions in each of the three **Evidence Sets** as your guide, collect evidence from Chapter 1 of your textbook that relates to the effect of Europe's invasion of the Western Hemisphere on the health of both Europeans and Americans.

At the end of each evidence set is a **Conclusion** section. Answer the questions in each conclusion section by stating the significance of the pieces of evidence compiled in that evidence set.

At the end of the three evidence sets is a **Thesis Question.** Answer the thesis question by stating the significance of the conclusions reached at the end of the three evidence sets. Finally, boil down what you have said to create a working draft for an essay that has the kind of specificity and concreteness that will make it suitable as a response to an essay examination question.

In writing your essay, some reordering of material is needed. Begin the whole essay with the thesis statement—your one-sentence answer to the thesis question, which is also your answer to the essay question. Use each evidence set and its conclusion as the basis for a single section or long paragraph of your essay. Use the conclusion statement to *begin* the section. The three sections are your concrete, specific support for your answer.

Notice that in doing this exercise, you have, in fact, collected and organized material that may be used to answer several different essay questions that might appear on a test on Chapter 1. You have also prepared yourself to respond correctly to dozens of objective questions.

Evidence Set 1

What happened to fourteenth-century Europeans as a result of the linking of China and Europe by way of the Silk Road?

___

___

What was the effect of European contact with the Americans on the health and size of the population of Americans of Hispaniola, Tenochtitlan, and the coastal villages north of Cape Cod?

Hispaniola (1492–1542)

___

___

Tenochtitlan, the Aztec capital (1521)

___

___

Villages along the coast north of Cape Cod (1616–1618)

___

___

What "American" disease appeared in Europe (Barcelona, Spain) for the first time in 1493? (Why would such a disease have any more or less a devastating effect on the population of Europe than smallpox and chicken pox had on American populations?)

_____

_____

What American product harmful to the health was introduced to Europe by the sixteenth century? (Why would any ill effects from use of this product have had any more or less a devastating effect on the population of Europe than smallpox and chicken pox had on American populations?)

_____

_____

Conclusion for Evidence Set 1

Which of the two civilizations, European or American, does all this evidence suggest suffered more because of the introduction of diseases and products that might undermine health as a result of the early contacts between the Old World and the New World (analogous to the effects in the fourteenth century of contacts established between non-European traders and Europeans traveling the Silk Road)?

_____

_____

Evidence Set 2

What does Christopher Columbus say about vegetation in his log?

_____

_____

What was John Cabot's report about America as a source of food products for Europe?

_____

_____

Conclusion for Evidence Set 2

What do Columbus's and Cabot's comments suggest about Europeans' awareness of the potential importance to Europe of American food products?

_____

_____

Evidence Set 3

What class of agricultural/food products was taken from America to Europe? In what ways were these products especially valuable to the health and welfare of Europeans?

_____

_____

What class of agricultural products was introduced to America by Europeans? Were these products especially valuable to the health of Americans?

_____

_____

Conclusion for Evidence Set 3

Which, if either, of the two groups, Europeans and Americans, benefited most in terms of health from the exchange of food and agricultural products in the early encounters between Europeans and Americans?

_____

_____

Thesis (Whole Point)

How did the impact on the health of the people of the Old World and the peoples of the New World caused by the early contacts between Europeans and Americans compare (appear similar) or contrast (differ)?

_____

_____

_____

_____

Essay

Working Draft for Response to an Essay Question

Respond to the question:

Compare or contrast the impact on the health of the peoples of the Old World and peoples of the New World caused by the early contacts between Europeans and peoples of the Americas. Be concrete and specific.

IDEAS AND DETAILS

Objective 1

_____ 1. It is most likely that Paleo-Indians came to the Americas
   a. by sailing a balsa-wood raft from Africa to North America.
   b. by crossing a land bridge that connected Asia and North America.
   c. by taking overland routes from Europe to Asia and then sailing across the Bering Strait.
   d. by sailing from a Nordic colony in Iceland.

Objective 1

_____ 2. Which of the following is true of the Maya civilization?
   a. It is one of the few civilizations with no known religious beliefs.
   b. Its people created the first writing system in the Americas.
   c. It was composed of city-states that remained at peace with each other for over 500 years.
   d. It had a highly advanced system of compulsory education for all Maya children.

Objective 1

_____ 3. Which of the following best explains the cultural differences between the Indian tribes of the Great Basin and the tribes living in what is now the northeastern United States?
   a. These tribes immigrated to the Americas from widely divergent parts of the world and brought their ancient cultures with them.
   b. Disagreements over political systems caused Indian groups to separate and to follow diverse cultural paths.
   c. Geographic barriers in North America made interaction between these tribes impossible.
   d. Each tribe adapted its lifestyle and culture to the environment and geography in which it settled.

Objective 1

_____ 4. The Lady of Cofitachequi is offered as evidence to support which of the following inferences?
   a. Indian religious beliefs closely resembled those of the Catholic church.
   b. Women held positions of political power in Indian tribes located in what is now the southeastern United States.
   c. The major deities of agricultural tribes were women.
   d. Social rankings within the Iroquois Confederacy were very similar to social rankings within European society.

Objective 1

_____ 5. Which of the following is true of all Indian religions?
   a. Belief in a multitude of gods
   b. A prohibition against leadership positions for women
   c. The central position of the sun and the moon in the most important rituals
   d. Belief in animism

Objectives 1 and 2

_____ 6. Which of the following provided the major link between West Africa and Europe prior to the fifteenth century?
   a. The trans-Saharan trade between Upper Guinea and the Muslim Mediterranean
   b. Long-established shipping lanes between the Mediterranean and the South Atlantic
   c. The Nile River, the source of which began just to the south of the Sahara desert
   d. The Senegal and Gambia Rivers along the coast of Upper Guinea

Objective 1

_____ 7. Which of the following was common to all of the societies of West Africa?
   a. Rice as the most important product
   b. Women as the primary local traders
   c. The same language
   d. A sense of belonging to one large tribal group

Objective 1

_____ 8. Many West African societies practiced polygyny. Which of the following best defines this practice?
   a. Males and females were not allowed to belong to the same religious cult.
   b. The male chiefs were required to have a female assistant to supervise the affairs of women.
   c. Men could have several wives and each wife lived separately with her children.
   d. Kinship was traced through the female line.

Objective 3

_____ 9. Marco Polo's *Travels,* which led many Europeans to believe that they could trade directly with China via ocean-going vessels, is evidence of which of the following?
   a. Movable type and the printing press made information more widely and readily accessible than ever before.
   b. The city-state of Venice led the way in perfecting technologically advanced navigational instruments.
   c. Most educated Europeans still believed the world was flat.
   d. Catholic missionaries took the lead in calling for European expansion.

Objective 4

_____ 10. Which of the following is true concerning interaction between Portugal and the states of West Africa?
   a. The Portuguese used force to establish trading posts along the West African coast.
   b. The African chiefdoms became the puppets of the Portuguese.
   c. The Portuguese and the West Africans found their new trade relationship mutually beneficial.
   d. The West Africans allowed the Portuguese to gain control over large estates in the interior of their states.

Objective 4

_____ 11. Which of the following is true of the island of São Tomé?
   a. It was on this island that the Portuguese established the first economy based primarily on slaves from Africa.
   b. Its native people were able to resist European encroachment and maintain their independence.
   c. Gold and silver found on this island helped the Portuguese finance most of their exploratory voyages.
   d. The natives of São Tomé taught the Portuguese how to successfully cultivate sugar cane.

Objective 3

_____ 12. Christopher Columbus differed from most other experienced sailors of his time in that he
   a. was willing to use newly developed navigational instruments.
   b. believed the earth was much smaller than others believed it to be.
   c. believed that the earth was round.
   d. was willing to redesign his ships based on information received from Arab sailors.

Objective 3

_____ 13. The Northeast Trades were to Spanish seafarers sailing to Spain from the Canary Islands as the westerlies were to
   a. Irish seafarers sailing to England from Ireland.
   b. English seafarers sailing to Iceland from England.
   c. Portuguese seafarers sailing to Italy from Portugal.
   d. Italian seafarers sailing to Morocco from Italy.

Objectives 4 and 5

_____ 14. Which of the following is a characteristic of the Spanish colonies in the New World?
   a. The Spanish government allowed its colonies a great deal of autonomy.
   b. Most settlers came to the colonies as members of family groups.
   c. The wealth of the colonies was based, in large part, on exploitation of the Indians.
   d. The colonies consisted of small agricultural units worked by independent landowners.

Objective 7

_____ 15. Queen Elizabeth supported English colonization attempts in North America because she wanted to
   a. strengthen England's alliance with Spain.
   b. establish a base for English attacks against Spanish colonies.
   c. have an outlet for England's excess population.
   d. acquire Indian slaves to work the landed estates of English nobles.

ESSAY QUESTIONS

Objective 1

1. Discuss the series of Mesoamerican civilizations that eventually gave rise to the Aztec civilization, and describe the major characteristics of Aztec culture. How did the Indian cultures that emerged in Mesoamerica differ from those that emerged in North America? What factors caused these differences?

Objective 1

2. Select several diverse North American Indian cultures to explain the impact of environment on the economic, social, political, and religious characteristics of a society.

Objectives 1 and 2

3. Discuss the similarities and differences among the gender roles in Indian cultures, West African cultures, and European culture.

Objective 3

4. Discuss the following statement: "The European explorations of the fifteenth and sixteenth centuries were made possible by technological advances and by the financial might of newly powerful national rulers."

Objective 4

5. Discuss the valuable lessons learned by European seafarers in the "Mediterranean Atlantic," and explain how these lessons prepared the way for Columbus's voyage of 1492.

Objective 6

6. Examine the Spanish model of colonization and explain the political, social, and economic impact of this model on Spain's New World colonies.

Objective 5

7. Compare and contrast the impact on the health of the people of the Old World and peoples of the New World caused by the early contacts between Europeans and peoples of the Americas. (See the Evaluating and Using Information exercise in this chapter.)

MAP EXERCISE

Exercise A

AFRICA

Refer to the map of Africa and the Mediterranean Atlantic on page 13 in the textbook and to the narrative accounts of African society in Chapters 1 and 3 (pages 12–15 and pages 68–74). You will probably find it helpful to refer to a historical map of Africa, showing the exact locations of the kingdoms dealt with in this exercise. Their original locations are considerably different from the locations of modern African states with the same names, such as Ghana and Benin.

1. On the outline map that appears on page 13, indicate the location of the following:
    a. Empire of Ghana (c. 300–1076)
    b. Empire of Mali (c. 1230–1500)

What is the geographic relationship of these ancient African empires to the Sahara and to the trans-Saharan trade routes?

2. On the outline map on page 13 indicate the location of the following:
    a. Upper Guinea
    b. Lower Guinea
    c. Rice Coast
    d. Grain Coast
    e. Ivory Coast
    f. Gold Coast

g. Slave Coast
h. kingdom of Benin (1170–1900)
i. kingdom of Dahomey (1600–1894)
j. Asante Kingdom (1695–1901)
k. Routes of the major river systems along the coast of West Africa

What is the relation between the kingdoms that emerged in the area of Lower Guinea and the major river systems extending into the interior?

3. Why do you think the kingdoms along the coast did not emerge as powerful kingdoms until well after the empires of Ghana and Mali?

4. The kingdom of Oyo also emerged along the West African coast during the period of the Atlantic slave trade. After doing some research, locate this kingdom on the map.

Exercise B

THE MEDITERRANEAN ATLANTIC

Refer to the maps of Africa and the Mediterranean Atlantic that follow. Label each of the following and use highlight pens to color each a separate color.

- Spain
- Portugal
- the Canary Islands
- the Madeiras
- the Azores
- the Cape Verde Islands
- São Tomé

Exercise C

PREVAILING WINDS

You will need five colors to complete this map exercise. (Highlight pens will work fine.)

- Trade winds (Northeast and Southeast) blow from the Horse Latitudes toward the Equator. The rotation of Earth causes these winds to blow diagonally rather than directly North or South.
- Westerlies blow from the Horse Latitudes toward the polar regions. The diagonal deflection of these winds is also caused by Earth's rotation.
- Stagnant air exists in the Horse Latitudes and in the area called the Doldrums. (The Horse Latitudes are so named because the Spanish, who frequently ferried horses across the Atlantic, often found their sailing vessels stalled in this region. As a result, they ran out of water for the horses. As the horses died from thirst, they had to be thrown overboard.)
- Polar easterlies blow from the Arctic regions toward the more temperate regions to the South.

Refer to the following map of prevailing winds.

- Use one color to highlight the area labeled *Doldrums*.
- Use a second color to highlight the Trade winds, both Northeast and Southeast.
- Use a third color to highlight the areas labeled *Horse Latitudes* (located North of the Equator and South of the Equator).
- Use a forth color to highlight the Westerlies.
- Use a fifth color to highlight the Polar Easterlies.

Indicate the location of the following on the map:

- the Azores
- the Madeiras
- the Canary Islands
- the Cape Verde Islands
- São Tomé

1. What wind-related problem did Spanish seafarers in the Atlantic have that English seafarers did not have? How did the Spanish solve their problem?

2. What problem did English seafarers in the Atlantic have that Spanish seafarers did not have? How did the English solve their problem?

— Major trade routes

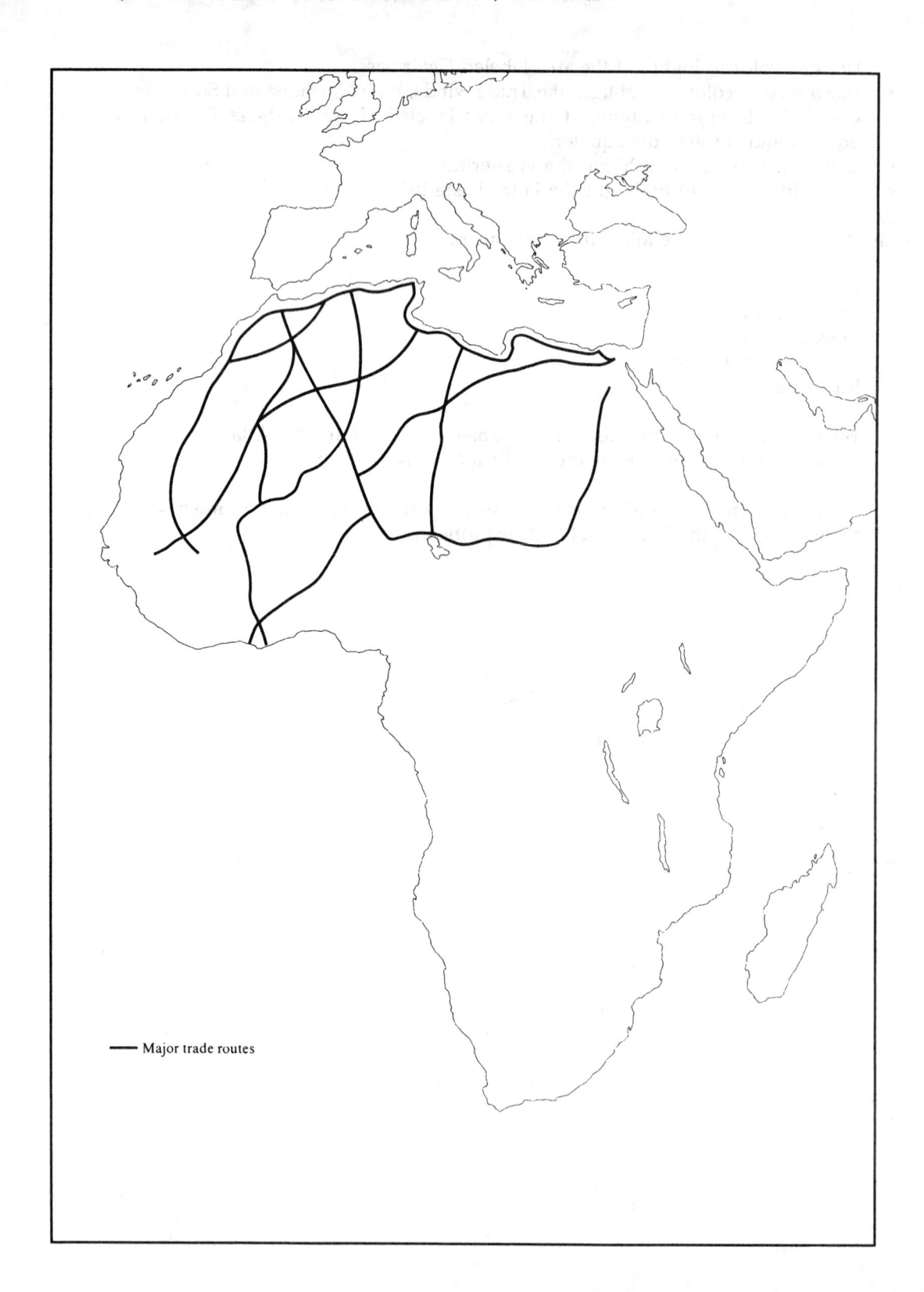

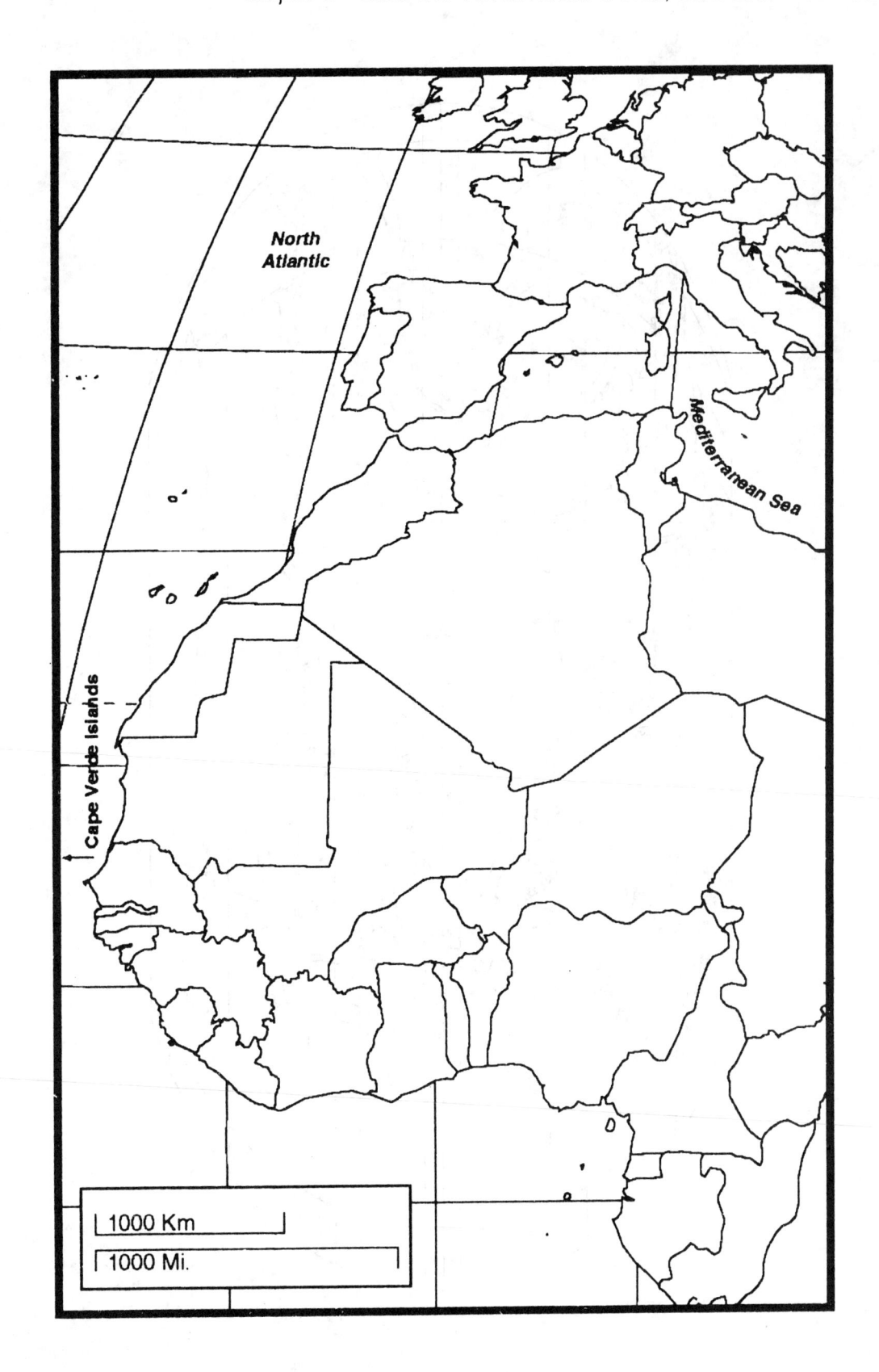

Chapter 1—Three Old Worlds Create a New, 1492–1600 31

North Atlantic

Mediterranean Sea

Cape Verde Islands

1000 Km
1000 Mi.

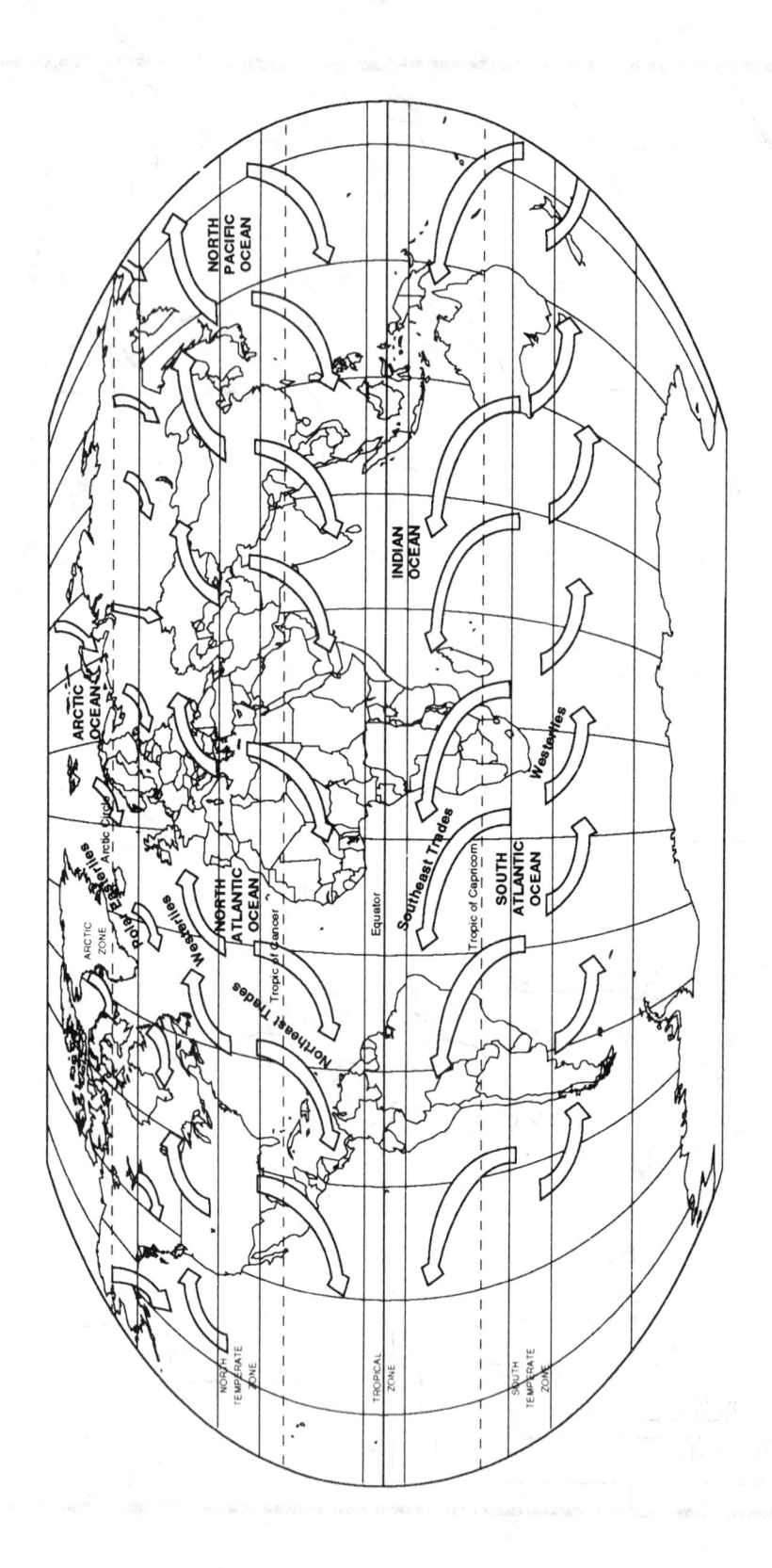

Chapter 1—Three Old Worlds Create a New, 1492–1600

CHAPTER 2
Europeans Colonize North America, 1600–1640

LEARNING OBJECTIVES

After you have studied Chapter 2 in your textbook and worked through this study guide chapter, you should be able to:

1. Discuss the characteristics of the permanent settlements established by Spain, France, and Holland on the North American mainland in the early seventeenth century.

2. Examine the seventeenth-century colonization efforts of France, Holland, and England in the Caribbean, and discuss the importance of sugar cane in those efforts.

3. Discuss the factors present in seventeenth-century England that led to colonization of the New World, and explain the goals and motives behind English colonization of the Chesapeake and New England areas.

4. Examine the relationship between the English settlers and American Indians of the Chesapeake and New England areas during the seventeenth century.

5. Assess the impact of the environment, tobacco, the headright system, and indentured servitude on the economic, social, political, and cultural development of the Chesapeake colonies.

6. Describe the beliefs of Congregationalist Puritans, and explain the impact of those beliefs on the economic, social, political, and cultural development of the New England colonies.

7. Discuss the similarities and differences in the lifestyles and in the patterns of family life of New England colonists, Chesapeake colonists, and New England Indians.

THEMATIC GUIDE

The theme of interaction among peoples of different cultures and between people and their environment begun in Chapter 1 continues in Chapter 2. In "New Spain, New France, New Netherland, and the Caribbean" we discuss the colonizing efforts of France and Holland in North America, the characteristics of the settlements they established, and the interactions between the settlers and Native Americans and between the settlers and their environment. In the latter part of the same section, the focus shifts to French, Dutch, and English efforts to gain control of the Lesser Antilles and the importance of sugar cane in those endeavors.

The second section, "England Colonizes Mainland North America," takes us from the general discussion of European colonization to the more particular case of England. A discussion of social, religious, economic, and political changes in seventeenth-century English society, changes that prompted masses of English citizens to move to North America in the seventeenth century, sets the stage for an explanation of the means, motives, and problems associated with the Jamestown settlement. We then return to the important theme of interaction—in this case the interaction between the Jamestown settlers and the Powhatan Confederacy. Here we see the development of the idea that the differences between these two cultures became the focal point of their interaction, with the economic evolution of Virginia and the subsequent spread of the tobacco culture finally leading to open warfare.

The next section, "Life in the Chesapeake: Virginia and Maryland," is a more complete discussion of the development of Chesapeake society politically, socially, and economically. Important elements are the headright system, the emergence of representative assemblies, the practice of indentured servitude, and patterns of family life. These elements interacted to produce a distinctive Chesapeake-area lifestyle.

The last two sections of the chapter, "The Founding of New England" and "Life in New England," do essentially the same thing for the New England area. Because the motives for settlement were mainly religious, the religious beliefs of the New England settlers are discussed. Examination of the impact of the interaction between settlers and Native Americans of the New England area is intertwined with a discussion of the political, social, and economic evolution of New England society. Finally, contrasts are offered between the lifestyle emerging in New England and the lifestyles of (1) the New England Indians and (2) the Chesapeake settlers.

BUILDING VOCABULARY

Listed below are important words and terms that you need to know to get the most out of Chapter 2. They are listed in the order in which they occur in the chapter. After carefully looking through the list, refer to a dictionary and jot down the definition of words that you do not know or of which you are unsure.

arduous

interloper

extort

illusory

futile

conduit

lucrative

comprise

rhetoric

fervor

piety

congenial

nominal

proximity

insatiable

altruistic

demographic

unremitting

dissenter

infatuated

schism

intermediary

omnipotence

conformity

precept

impetus

irrelevant

gentry

chronic

dissension

effeminate

unwavering

fallow

incentive

staple

forage

cohesive

incessant

convoluted

thwart

diversified

omnipotent

predestined

rudimentary

conduit

communal

transcendent

commonwealth

covenant

acquisitive

accommodate

acculturation

transitory

dowry

eccentric

malign

indelibly

IDENTIFICATION AND SIGNIFICANCE

After studying Chapter 2 of *A People and a Nation,* you should be able to identify fully *and* explain the historical significance of each item listed below.

1. Identify each item in the space provided. Give an explanation or description of the item. Answer the questions *who, what, where,* and *when.*

2. Explain the historical significance of each item in the space provided. Establish the historical context in which the item exists. Establish the item as the result of or as the cause of other factors existing in the society under study. Answer this question: *What were the political, social, economic, and or cultural consequences of this item?*

Fray Alonso de Benavides

    Identification

    Significance

Pedro Menéndez de Avilés

    Identification

    Significance

Juan de Oñate

    Identification

    Significance

Quebec and Montreal

    Identification

    Significance

the Black Robes

    Identification

    Significance

New Netherland

    Identification

    Significance

Iroquois-Huron War

    Identification

    Significance

the Greater Antilles

    Identification

    Significance

the Lesser Antilles

    Identification

    Significance

sugar

    Identification

    Significance

English population boom

    Identification

    Significance

Henry VIII

    Identification

    Significance

Martin Luther and John Calvin

    Identification

    Significance

Puritans

    Identification

    Significance

the divine right of kings

    Identification

    Significance

the Virginia Company

    Identification

    Significance

joint-stock companies

    Identification

    Significance

Jamestown

    Identification

    Significance

Captain John Smith

    Identification

    Significance

the starving time

    Identification

    Significance

the Powhatan Confederacy

    Identification

    Significance

tobacco cultivation

    Identification

    Significance

Opechancanough

    Identification

    Significance

Copyright © Houghton Mifflin Company. All rights reserved.

headright system

    Identification

    Significance

House of Burgesses

    Identification

    Significance

Maryland

    Identification

    Significance

Cecelius Calvert

    Identification

    Significance

indentured servitude

    Identification

    Significance

the "seasoning process"

    Identification

    Significance

Chesapeake families

    Identification

    Significance

the doctrine of predestination

    Identification

    Significance

Congregationalist Puritans

    Identification

    Significance

Separatists

    Identification

    Significance

Plymouth

    Identification

    Significance

Mayflower Compact

    Identification

    Significance

Massasoit

    Identification

    Significance

Squanto

    Identification

    Significance

the Massachusetts Bay Company

    Identification

    Significance

John Winthrop

    Identification

    Significance

the doctrine of the covenant

    Identification

    Significance

communal land-grant system of Massachusetts

    Identification

    Significance

Chapter 2—Europeans Colonize North America, 1600–1640   45

Pequot War

    Identification

    Significance

John Eliot

    Identification

    Significance

codes of conduct in Puritan New England

    Identification

    Significance

Roger Williams

    Identification

    Significance

Anne Marbury Hutchinson

    Identification

    Significance

ORGANIZING INFORMATION

Use the chart below to compare the cultural characteristics of one group, the Algonkians, to the two colonial societies it confronted along the eastern seaboard. The information in the Organizing Information section of Chapter 1 may be useful to you in completing this exercise.

CULTURAL COMPARISONS

	Seventeenth-Century Algonkian Culture	Seventeenth-Century New England Culture	Seventeenth-Century Chesapeake Culture
Economic Characteristics			
Social Characteristics			
Political Characteristics			
Religious Characteristics			

EVALUATING AND USING INFORMATION

As we study the material in the textbook and from lecture notes, it is important to create and answer potential test questions that can be derived from that material. This is an important study aid in that it helps us focus our attention on important information and, in turn, helps us organize that information in a meaningful way.

In this exercise, you will be dealing with pieces of information from Chapter 2 of your textbook, analyzing and organizing that information, creating a potential essay question based on that information, and writing a draft essay to answer the essay question.

Step 1

Each of the following citations comes from Chapter 2 of the textbook. In the space *following* each citation, write down the information contained in the citation *in your own words*. Be concise: you are taking notes, not copying. (The blank space preceding each citation will be used later.)

_____ "A small number of Frenchmen brought their wives and took up agriculture; even so, more than twenty-five years after Quebec's founding, it had just sixty-four resident families, along with traders and soldiers."

_____

_____

_____ "One other important group comprised part of the population of New France: missionaries of the Society of Jesus (Jesuits), a Roman Catholic order dedicated to converting nonbelievers to Christianity. The first Jesuits arrived in the colony in 1625."

_____

_____

_____ "The Jesuits, whom the Native Americans called Black Robes, initially tried to persuade indigenous peoples to live near French settlements and to adopt European agricultural methods as well as the Europeans' religion. When that effort failed, the Jesuits concluded that they could introduce Roman Catholicism to their new charges without insisting that they fundamentally alter their traditional ways of life. Accordingly, the Black Robes learned Native American languages and traveled to remote regions of the interior, where they lived in twos and threes among hundreds of potential converts."

_____

_____

Copyright © Houghton Mifflin Company. All rights reserved.

_____ "Using a variety of strategies Jesuits sought to undermine the authority of village shamans (the traditional religious leaders) and to gain the confidence of leaders who could influence others. Trained in rhetoric, they won admirers by their eloquence. Immune to smallpox (for all had survived the disease already), they explained epidemics among the Native Americans as God's punishment for sin. Their arguments were aided by the ineffectiveness of the shamans' traditional remedies against the new pestilence. Drawing on European science, the Jesuits predicted solar and lunar eclipses. Perhaps most important of all, they amazed the villagers by communicating with each other over long distances and periods of time by employing marks on paper. The Native Americans' desire to learn how to harness the extraordinary power of literacy was one of the most critical factors in making them receptive to the Jesuits' message."

_____

_____

_____ "The Netherlands, the world's dominant commercial power at the time, was interested primarily in trade rather than colonization. Thus New Netherland, like New France, remained small, and also focused on a river valley that offered easy access to its settlements. The colony's southern anchor was New Amsterdam, a town founded in 1624 on Manhattan Island, at the mouth of the Hudson River."

_____

_____

_____ "Because Puritans were challenging many of the most important precepts of the English church, the monarchs authorized the removal of Puritan clergymen from their pulpits. In the 1620s and 1630s a number of English Puritans accordingly decided to move to America, where they hoped to put their religious beliefs into practice unmolested by the Stuarts or the church hierarchy."

_____

_____

_____ "The English colonists kidnapped Powhatan's daughter, Pocahontas, holding her as a hostage in retaliation for Powhatan's seizure of several settlers. In captivity, she agreed in 1614 to marry a colonist, John Rolfe; she sailed with him to England, where she died in 1616."

_____

_____

_____ "English and Algonkian peoples had much in common: deep religious beliefs, a lifestyle oriented around agriculture, clear political and social hierarchies, and sharply defined gender roles."

_____

_____

_____ "Above all, the English settlers believed unwaveringly in the superiority of their civilization. Although in the early years of colonization they often anticipated living peacefully alongside the Native Americans, they always assumed that they would dictate the terms of such coexistence. Like Thomas Harriot at Roanoke, they expected the Native Americans to adopt English customs and to convert to Christianity."

_____

_____

_____ "Opechancanough, Powhatan's brother and successor, watched the English colonists steadily encroaching on the confederacy's lands and attempting to convert its members to Christianity. Recognizing the danger his brother had overlooked, the war leader launched coordinated attacks all along the river on March 22, 1622. By the end of the day, 347 colonists (about one-quarter of the total) lay dead, and only a timely warning from two Christian converts saved Jamestown itself from destruction."

_____

_____

_____ "Maryland, settled in 1634, [had been] given by Charles I to the Calvert family as a personal possession, proprietorship.... The Calverts intended the colony to serve as a haven for their fellow Roman Catholics, who were being persecuted in England. Cecilius Calvert, second Lord Baltimore, became the first colonizer to offer freedom of religion to all Christian settlers; he understood that protecting the Protestant majority was the only way to ensure Catholics' rights."

_____

_____

_____ "[The New England Indians] traded with the newcomers and sometimes worked with them, but for the most part they resisted acculturation or incorporation into English society."

_____

_____

_____ "Although the official seal of the Massachusetts Bay colony showed an Indian crying, 'Come over and help us,' most colonists showed little interest in converting the New England Algonkians to Christianity. Only a few Massachusetts clerics, most notably John Eliot, seriously undertook missionary activities. Eliot insisted that converts reside in towns, farm the land in English fashion, assume English names, wear European-style clothing and shoes, cut their hair, and stop observing a wide range of their own customs. Since Eliot was demanding a total cultural transformation from his adherents, he understandably met with little success. At the peak of Eliot's efforts, only eleven hundred Native Americans lived in the fourteen 'Praying Towns' he established and just 10 percent of those town residents had been formally baptized."

_____

_____

_____ "The Jesuits' successful missions in New France contrasted sharply with the Puritans' failure to win many converts.... Catholicism had several advantages over Puritanism. ... It employed attractive rituals, instructed converts that through good works they could help to earn their own salvation, and offered women ... an inspiring role model—the Virgin Mary.... [P]erhaps most important, the Jesuits understood that Christian beliefs were to some extent compatible with Native American culture. Unlike Puritans, the Jesuits were willing to accept converts who did not wholly adopt European styles of life."

_____ "[W]hat attracted Native Americans to these religious ideas? . . . Surely one primary motive was a desire to use the Europeans' religion as a means of coping with the dramatic changes the intruders had wrought."

_____ "John Winthrop's description of a smallpox epidemic that swept through southern New England in the early 1630s reveals the relationship among smallpox, conversion to Christianity, and English land claims. 'A great mortality among the Indians,' he noted in his diary in 1633. 'Divers of them, in their sickness, confessed that the Englishmen's God was a good God; and that if they recovered, they would serve him.' But most did not recover: in January 1634 an English scout reported that smallpox had spread 'as far as any Indian plantation was known to the west.' By July, Winthrop observed that most of the Indians within a 300-mile radius of Boston had died of the disease. Therefore, he declared with satisfaction, 'the Lord hathe cleared our title to what we possess.'"

_____ "Puritans objected to secular interference in religious affairs but at the same time expected the church to influence the conduct of politics and the affairs of society. They also believed that the state had an obligation to support and protect the one true church—theirs. As a result, though they came to America seeking freedom to worship as they wished, they saw no contradiction in their refusal to grant that freedom to others."

Copyright © Houghton Mifflin Company. All rights reserved.

_____ "Roger Williams, a Separatist, migrated to Massachusetts Bay in 1631. Williams soon began to express the eccentric ideas that the king of England had no right to give away land already occupied by Native Americans, that church and state should be kept entirely separate, and that Puritans should not impose their religious beliefs on others. Banished from Massachusetts in late 1635, Williams founded the town of Providence on Narragansett Bay. Because of Williams's beliefs, Providence and other towns in what became the colony of Rhode Island adopted a policy of tolerating all religions, including Judaism."

_____

_____

_____ "Europeans killed Indians with their weapons and diseases and had but limited success in converting them to European religions."

_____

_____

Step 2

Name the topic that you think is covered by all or nearly all of the evidence you have just collected from the citations.

Topic: _____

Step 3

In the short blanks preceding the citations found in Step 1, give all closely related pieces of information the same letter designation (A, B, C, D, etc.). When you finish, each citation that contributes to an understanding of the topic you named in Step 2 should have one of three or four possible letter designations. Once this is done, you will have produced three or four groups of very closely related bits of information (Groups A, B, C, and possibly D).

Step 4

Scan all the items you have put into Group A. Then, in the space below Group A, write *one* declarative sentence stating the significance of all the items in Group A. Do the same thing for each of the other groups (Group B, Group C, and, if you have a D group, Group D as well).

Group A

_____

_____

Group B

_____

_____

Group C

_____

_____

Group D

_____

_____

Step 5

Read and think about each of the sentences associated with Groups A, B, C, and D. Write *one* declarative sentence expressing the significance of all three (or four) of the sentences associated with the groups.

_____

_____

Step 6

Look at the topic you named in Step 2 and the statement you just wrote for Step 5. Compose an essay examination-type question for which the statement in Step 5 is the one-sentence answer, or *thesis statement*. Write that question in the space below.

_____

_____

Step 7

Write a draft essay answering the question in Step 6 above. You may add other bits of information from the chapter and/or from your class notes.

Begin with a one-sentence paragraph consisting of your statement of the significance of all the evidence collected (Step 5). This is your essay's introduction or *thesis paragraph*.

Using the information you collected in Step 1, organize that information into three or four paragraphs that support your one-sentence answer (*thesis statement*). Each paragraph should focus on one of the groups of information you created in Step 3 and begin with the appropriate statement of the significance of that paragraph's collection of evidence. These three or four paragraphs are the body of your essay.

Finish by writing a one- or two-sentence statement (a short paragraph) on what you have found out as a result of looking at and weighing the evidence that appears in the body of your essay. This paragraph is your essay's *conclusion*.

IDEAS AND DETAILS

Objective 1

_____ 1. North American Indians were receptive to the religious message of Jesuit missionaries in New France because
   a. the Indians wanted the powers of communication that accompanied literacy.
   b. the Jesuits allowed the village shamans to retain their role and power.
   c. the traditional religious beliefs of the Indians closely matched Catholic beliefs.
   d. the Indians became convinced that European culture was superior to their own.

Objective 1

_____ 2. Which of the following is true of the Iroquois-Huron War?
   a. The Iroquois caused a smallpox epidemic among the Hurons by intentionally infecting the tribe with the deadly disease.
   b. The Iroquois were so decisively defeated that they never again posed a serious threat to European settlers in North America.
   c. Using guns obtained from their Dutch allies, the Iroquois practically exterminated the Hurons.
   d. The war ended when European mediators arranged an equitable division of the hunting territories claimed by the two tribes.

Objective 2

_____ 3. France, Holland, and England were interested in the Lesser Antilles for which of the following reasons?
   a. They wanted to use these barren islands as penal colonies.
   b. The religious leaders in each nation insisted that missionaries convert the West Indian natives to Christianity.
   c. The islands served as important refueling stations on the way to the North American mainland.
   d. They could profit from the successful cultivation of sugar cane on these islands.

Objective 3

_____ 4. Large numbers of English citizens left their homeland in the seventeenth century because of
   a. religious differences between king and subjects.
   b. loss of economic power by the landowning elite.
   c. continued outbreaks of the Black Plague in England and throughout Europe.
   d. constant warfare between England and Holland.

Objective 4

_____ 5. The Algonkians and the English differed in which of the following ways?
   a. The agricultural orientation of Algonkian society stood in contrast to the merchant-oriented lifestyle of English society.
   b. English society had definite political hierarchies; Algonkian society was not hierarchical either politically or socially.
   c. The English had deeply held religious beliefs; the Algonkians had none.
   d. The English believed in private ownership of land; the Algonkians believed the land was held communally by the entire group.

Objective 5

_____ 6. Which of the following was, in part, a consequence of the headright system?
   a. Large land holdings in the Chesapeake colonies of Virginia and Maryland.
   b. Political stability in the Chesapeake colonies of Virginia and Maryland.
   c. The introduction of tobacco as a cash crop in the colony of Virginia.
   d. Economic success for the Virginia Company and its stockholders.

Objective 5

_____ 7. Which statement best characterizes the indentured servants who migrated to the Chesapeake in the seventeenth century?
   a. They were usually well established in England but believed there was more opportunity in America.
   b. They were usually from the dregs of English society.
   c. They were usually males between the ages of fifteen and twenty-four.
   d. They were usually married individuals who came with their families.

Objective 5

_____ 8. Ineffective government and political instability plagued the colonies of Virginia and Maryland in the late seventeenth century for which of the following reasons?
   a. The assemblies in both colonies were controlled by landless peasants.
   b. The London government attempted to rule the colonies in an autocratic manner.
   c. The assemblies in both colonies were dominated by migrants who often involved English allies in struggles for personal power.
   d. The constant threat of slave insurrections in the colonies created a climate of fear that bred political chaos.

Objectives 4 and 7

_____ 9. The Jamestown settlement and the Plymouth settlement were alike in which of the following ways?
   a. Both had representative assemblies at the time they were founded.
   b. Both settlements survived because of aid from their Indian neighbors.
   c. Both settlements were founded for religious purposes.
   d. Both settlements were located in areas under the jurisdiction of the Virginia Company.

Objective 6

_____ 10. John Winthrop's vision for the colony of Massachusetts included the
   a. building of a society in which religious liberty was extended to all people.
   b. establishment of a society in which all adults over age twenty-one had the right to vote.
   c. establishment of a commonwealth in which the good of the whole community was put ahead of the private concerns of individuals.
   d. building of a classless society in which wealth was equally distributed.

Objectives 6 and 7

_____ 11. Why did settlements in Massachusetts Bay initially tend to be compact rather than scattered?
   a. A group of families received a grant of land on which to establish a town; then each family was awarded land located around the town center.
   b. The English monarch insisted on maintaining tight control over Massachusetts and decreed that the settlements be compact.
   c. Individual settlers could receive only one fifteen-acre headright.
   d. Most of the people who settled the Massachusetts Bay colony were merchants rather than farmers.

Objectives 4 and 6

_____ 12. John Eliot met with little success in converting the New England Indians to Christianity because he
   a. allowed the Indians to blend their own religious ideas with Puritan religious ideas.
   b. insisted that converts reject traditional Indian culture and live like Europeans.
   c. preached his ideas only to Indian women.
   d. insisted that the Indians had to adhere strictly to the elaborate rituals of the Puritan church.

Objectives 1, 4, and 6

_____ 13. Jesuit missionaries in New France were more successful than Puritan missionaries in New England in converting Indians to Christianity for which of the following reasons?
   a. The Jesuits emphasized the simplicity of the worship experience; the Puritans employed elaborate rituals.
   b. The covenant of grace taught by the Jesuits was closer to Indians' religious beliefs than was the covenant of works taught by the Puritans.
   c. The Jesuits understood that Christianity and Indian culture were compatible; the Puritans did not.
   d. The large French settlements convinced the Indians of the superiority of the Christian God; the small Puritan settlements made little impression.

Objectives 5, 6, and 7

_____ 14. New Englanders were *unlike* residents of the Chesapeake in which of the following ways?
   a. The children of New England parents were generally more independent at an earlier age.
   b. New Englanders cleared new fields yearly rather than use the same fields again and again.
   c. New Englanders had smaller families.
   d. Migrants to New England usually came as part of family groups.

Objective 6

_____ 15. "You have stept out of your place, you have rather bine a Husband than a Wife and a preacher than a Hearer; and a Magistrate than a Subject." This quote is used to support the idea that the Puritan authorities
   a. allowed divorce when it could be proved that the wife had not been submissive to her husband.
   b. saw Anne Hutchinson as a threat because she challenged traditional gender roles.
   c. believed Anne Hutchinson to be a threat because she owned her own business.
   d. believed Anne Hutchinson to be a valuable asset to the community.

ESSAY QUESTIONS

Objectives 1 and 4

1. Contrast French and Spanish attempts to convert Native Americans to Christianity with similar attempts by the Puritans. Why did the Catholics succeed while the Protestants failed?

Objective 2

2. Discuss the importance of sugar cane in the colonization and development of the Lesser Antilles.

Objective 3

3. Discuss the factors that led the English to successfully colonize North America in the seventeenth century.

Objective 5

4. Describe the impact of the Chesapeake's disease and demographic environment on the colonies of Maryland and Virginia.

Objective 5

5. Examine the headright system and discuss its impact on the social, economic, and political evolution of the Chesapeake colonies.

Objective 6

6. Examine the role of Puritan theology in the political, social, and economic evolution of Massachusetts Bay society.

MAP EXERCISE

You will need six colored pens and the maps that follow to complete this exercise.

The chart below indicates the European nations that controlled the Greater and Lesser Antilles about 1698. By that date the island of Hispaniola had been divided between Spain and France. Spanish Hispaniola constituted the eastern two-thirds of the island (the modern-day Dominican Republic) and Saint-Domingue constituted the western one-third (modern-day Haiti).

Color in accordance with the following chart, using a different color to denote each European nation.

CONTROL OF THE GREATER AND LESSER ANTILLES BY EUROPEAN NATIONS, CA. 1698

Spain	England	France	Holland	Denmark
Cuba	Caicos Islands	Saint-Dominigue	St. Martin (southern portion)	St. Thomas
Spanish Hispaniola	Turks Islands	St. Croix	Saba	St. John
Puerto Rico	Jamaica	St. Martin (northern portion)	St. Eustatius	
Trinidad	British Virgin Islands	St. Kitts (NW and SE portions)	Aruba	
	Anegada	Guadeloupe	Curaçao	
	Jost van Dyke	Martinique	Bonaire	
	Tortola	St. Lucia		
	Virgin Gorda	Grenada		
	Anguilla	Tobago		
	Barbuda			
	Antigua			
	Montserrat			
	St. Kitts (central portion)			
	Nevis			
	Barbados			

The Caribs, by a 1660 treaty with France and England, remained in control of Dominica and St. Vincent. Use a separate color for these two islands to denote this fact.

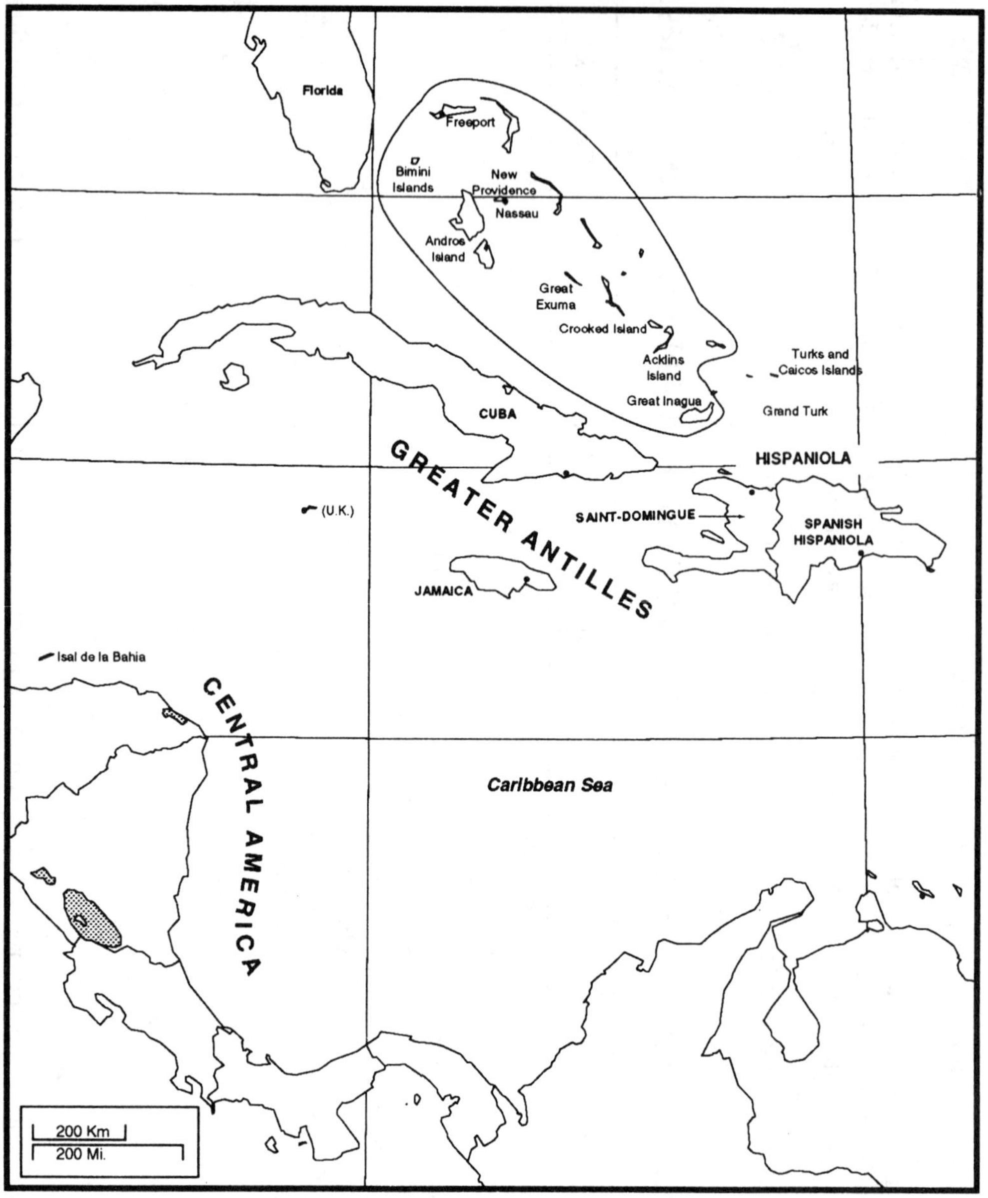
Florida
Freeport
Bimini Islands
New Providence
Nassau
Andros Island
Great Exuma
Crooked Island
Acklins Island
Great Inagua
Turks and Caicos Islands
Grand Turk
CUBA
HISPANIOLA
GREATER ANTILLES
(U.K.)
SAINT-DOMINGUE
SPANISH HISPANIOLA
JAMAICA
Isal de la Bahia
CENTRAL AMERICA
Caribbean Sea
200 Km
200 Mi.

Chapter 2—Europeans Colonize North America, 1600–1640 61

Puerto Rico
British Virgin Islands
Anguilla
St. Martin
Virgin Islands
St. Croix
Saba and St. Eustatius
St. Barthelemy
ANTIGUA AND BARBUDA
Basseterre
ST. CHRISTOPHER AND NEVIS
St. Johns
Montserrat
Guadeloupe
DOMINICA
Martinique
ST. LUCIA
BARBADOS
ST. VINCENT AND THE GRENADINES
GRENADA
Tobago
TRINIDAD AND TOBAGO
Trinidad

LESSER ANTILLES

Aruba
Curacao
Bonaire
Willemstad

SOUTH AMERICA

200 Km
200 Mi.

CHAPTER 3
American Society Takes Shape, 1640–1720

LEARNING OBJECTIVES

After you have studied Chapter 3 in your textbook and worked through this study guide chapter, you should be able to:

1. Discuss developments in England between 1640 and 1720, and explain their impact on colonial society.

2. Explain the reasons behind the new wave of English colonies founded after 1660, and identify the major characteristics of those colonies.

3. Explain the emergence of black slavery in the North American British colonies.

4. Describe the mechanics of the slave trade, the characteristics of North American slavery, and the impact of slavery on those enslaved.

5. Examine the social, political, economic, and cultural impact of slavery on American, West African, and European societies.

6. Examine the relations between white Europeans and North American Indians between 1640 and 1720.

7. Discuss the causes and consequences of Bacon's Rebellion.

8. Discuss the political, social, economic, and cultural development of the New England colonies between 1640 and 1720.

9. Explain the political and economic bases for the relationship between England and its colonies from 1640 to 1720.

10. Discuss the development of colonial political structures from 1640 to 1720.

11. Analyze the forces responsible for the Salem Village witchcraft crisis.

THEMATIC GUIDE

Chapter 3 deals with events in the British colonies in North America from 1640 to 1720. But it is important to recognize the themes and interpretations offered in this chapter and to see the facts as evidence used to support those themes.

The theme of the interaction among different cultures, important in Chapters 1 and 2, continues in Chapter 3, but the focus shifts to the period 1640 to 1720. As in the previous chapters, it is not just the fact of interaction that is important, but what the participants bring to the interaction (their frames of reference), the way in which the participants affected each other, and the way in which they change and are changed by each other.

Keeping that in mind, we deal with the impact of the English Civil War (1642–1649) and the Interregnum (1649–1660) on the relationship between England and its colonies. These periods of political turmoil were followed by the Stuart Restoration (1660–1685), which brought Charles II to the English throne. The return to political stability during Charles's reign witnessed the founding of six new proprietary colonies, known as the Restoration colonies. Discussion of the reasons for the founding of these colonies, their political, social, and economic evolution, and the interaction of peoples within them demonstrates the emergence of an even more diverse and heterogeneous colonial society.

Another interaction theme, the emergence of chattel slavery in colonial America, is considered in the section "The Forced Migration of Africans." We discuss the factors that led the English to enslave Africans, how the slave trade was organized and conducted, and the consequences of the interaction between English and Africans. These consequences include the impact of the interaction on (1) West Africa and Europe, (2) enslaved Africans, and (3) the development of colonial society and of regional differences between North and South.

We then consider a third interaction theme: relations between Europeans and Indians. The subject is complex because of the variety of Indian cultures and because of their interaction with various European countries vying for power in North America. The discussion centers on the economic uses the Europeans made of Indian cultures. The dynamics of six specific white-Indian relationships are discussed: (1) the Spanish and the Pueblos of New Mexico; (2) the colonists of South Carolina and neighboring Indian peoples; (3) the Europeans of the Northeast and the Hurons and Iroquois of that region; (4) the French colonists in the areas of the Great Lakes and Mississippi Valley and the Indians of those regions; (5) the colonists of Virginia and the Indians of that area; and (6) the colonists of the New England coastal region and the Indian tribes of that region.

In the last two sections of the chapter, we return to the relationship between England and its colonies. We discuss the interaction of forces *within* New England, the social, economic, and political evolution of New England society, and the general political evolution of the colonies. No longer did England merely *act on* its colonies, it began to *react to* colonies that were maturing socially, politically, and economically. As a consequence, those colonies became increasingly difficult to administer. In addition, the fact that England was engaged in a war with France—a war fought in Europe and in North America—was a complicating factor. At the end of the chapter, the impact of this complex set of interrelationships on New England society is discussed through an analysis of the Salem Village witchcraft crisis.

BUILDING VOCABULARY

Listed below are important words and terms that you need to know to get the most out of Chapter 3. They are listed in the order in which they occur in the chapter. After carefully looking through the list, refer to a dictionary and jot down the definition of words that you do not know or of which you are unsure.

notorious

gibbet

buccaneer

complicity

matrix

burgeoning

integral

tumultuous

cede

heterogeneous

chagrin

autocratic

backwater

contingent

intermediary

egalitarianism

sect

coreligionists

pacifist

irrevocably

categorize

qualm

rationalization

perpetual

polity

traumatic

endemic

flog

stratified

assimilate

dialect

circumstantial

indelibly

indigenous

vestiges

expropriate

avid

garrison

yeoman

autonomy

subjugate

insatiable

extirpate

dysentery

aggrieved

synod

hypothesize

onerous

cadre

barter

antagonistic

jeremiad

lament

finite

scrutinize

sanction

cataclysm

veracity

accommodate

patronage

IDENTIFICATION AND SIGNIFICANCE

After studying Chapter 3 of *A People and a Nation*, you should be able to identify fully *and* explain the historical significance of each item listed below.

1. Identify each item in the space provided. Give an explanation or description of the item. Answer the questions *who, what, where,* and *when.*

2. Explain the historical significance of each item in the space provided. Establish the historical context in which the item exists. Establish the item as the result of or as the cause of other factors existing in the society under study. Answer this question: *What were the political, social, economic, and/or cultural consequences of this item?*

Captain William Kidd

    Identification

    Significance

the English Civil War

    Identification

    Significance

the Interregnum

>Identification

>Significance

the Restoration colonies

>Identification

>Significance

James, duke of York

>Identification

>Significance

the Duke's Laws

>Identification

>Significance

Sir George Carteret and John Lord Berkeley

>Identification

>Significance

Quakers

>Identification

>Significance

William Penn

    Identification

    Significance

the Carolinas

    Identification

    Significance

the "Fundamental Constitutions of Carolina"

    Identification

    Significance

North Carolina and South Carolina

    Identification

    Significance

the slave trade

    Identification

    Significance

the Royal African Company

    Identification

    Significance

the Middle Passage

    Identification

    Significance

Olaudah Equiano

    Identification

    Significance

Gullah

    Identification

    Significance

rice and indigo cultivation

    Identification

    Significance

Eliza Lucas

    Identification

    Significance

the Pueblo revolt of 1680

    Identification

    Significance

the Indian slave trade

    Identification

    Significance

the Tuscarora War

    Identification

    Significance

the Yamasee War

    Identification

    Significance

James Oglethorpe

    Identification

    Significance

the Iroquois Confederacy

    Identification

    Significance

the Beaver Wars

    Identification

    Significance

Louis de Baude de Frontenac

    Identification

    Significance

coureurs de bois

    Identification

    Significance

le pays de Illinois

    Identification

    Significance

Bacon's Rebellion

    Identification

    Significance

King Philip's (Metacom's) War

    Identification

    Significance

New England population expansion

    Identification

    Significance

the Halfway Covenant

    Identification

    Significance

Cotton Mather

    Identification

    Significance

New England's first commercial system

    Identification

    Significance

the "triangular" trade

    Identification

    Significance

Anglican merchants

    Identification

    Significance

mercantilism

    Identification

    Significance

the Navigation Acts

    Identification

    Significance

vice-admiralty courts

    Identification

    Significance

the Board of Trade and Plantations

    Identification

    Significance

colonial political structures

    Identification

    Significance

the Dominion of New England

    Identification

    Significance

the Glorious Revolution

    Identification

    Significance

the Protestant Association

   Identification

   Significance

Jacob Leisler

   Identification

   Significance

King William's War

   Identification

   Significance

the Salem village witchcraft crisis

   Identification

   Significance

"court" parties vs. the "country interest"

   Identification

   Significance

EVALUATING AND USING INFORMATION

Using the chart "Key Parts of Definitions and Identifications" and the following hints as your guide, indicate the key information needed in a good, brief definition or identification of each of the persons, places, things, or concepts listed in the first column. When you finish, you will have the material for an effective two-sentence definition/identification of each of the items, some of which appear in the preceding and following sections. Usually on tests, students are expected to go into a little more depth—sometimes a great deal more depth—but the kind of two-sentence beginnings you are being asked to come up with in this exercise would make strong starting points.

Hints for Composing Good Definitions/Identifications

1. Begin with a formal definition, which is one declarative sentence that includes the term, class, and differentia. The sentence must include all three of the standard parts. The *term* is the name of that which you are identifying or defining. The *class* is a category or group to which the item you are defining or identifying belongs. (It answers the question, what kind of thing is this?) The *differentia* is the part of the formal definition that indicates how the item being defined or identified differs from virtually all other members of the class named.

2. The class must be both narrow and relevant to the historical significance of the item you are defining or identifying. (Instead of "a person," how about "Georgia planter"?)

3. The differentia must truly distinguish what you are defining or identifying from all other members of its class. (In the definition "Love is a strong emotion," the word *strong* is the differentia, but it does not effectively distinguish love from other emotions, such as hatred.)

4. In general, avoid writing a circular definition. Circular definitions are those in which the word being defined, or a part or a form of the word being defined, is used to do the defining. ("A wristwatch is a watch worn on the wrist.") However, if the term you are defining is a compound word like *breakdance* or is made up of two or more words, like *Duke's Laws*, repetition of part of the term being defined may be acceptable (*dance, Laws*). Use common sense to decide when such repetition is acceptable.

5. Avoid "is when" or "is where" clauses where the class should be unless what you are defining is a point in time or space. ("A sin is an infraction of Divine law," not "A sin is when you break God's commandments.")

6. Make sure that your completed response answers the question: what is _____ or who is _____? A true statement about the item in question is not necessarily a definition or identification of the item.

7. When dealing with identification/significance items, add a comment or comments after the formal definition in which you cite examples or provide other details to show that you understand the historical significance of the item. These comments should answer the question: what were the political, social, economic, and/or cultural consequences of this item? The length of these comments will depend on the item itself. Some items are more historically significant than others and, as a result, have more consequences.

Chapter 3—American Society Takes Shape, 1640–1720

Key Parts of Definitions and Identifications			
Term What is being defined or identified.	**Class** Narrow, relevant category to which the item being defined or identified belongs.	**Differentiation** What distinguishes the item being defined or identified from all other members of the category in which it has been placed.	**Additional Comment** Any additional statement needed to clarify the definition or the significance of the item being defined or identified.
notorious (page 61)			
egalitarianism (page 66)			
Quakers (pages 66–68)			
the Middle Passage (page 71)			
Gullah (page 72)			
the Pueblo revolt of 1680 (page 74)			
the Halfway Covenant (page 80)			
vice-admiralty courts (page 84)			
the Navigation Acts (page 83)			
Jacob Leisler (page 86)			

Copyright © Houghton Mifflin Company. All rights reserved.

IDEAS AND DETAILS

Objective 1

_____ 1. The Puritan migration to New England ended in the 1640s because
   a. almost all the Puritans in England had already departed.
   b. Charles I issued a decree prohibiting such migrations.
   c. news of severe hardships among the New England settlers frightened would-be immigrants.
   d. Puritans gained political dominance in England during the Civil War and Commonwealth periods.

Objective 2

_____ 2. Which of the following is a characteristic of New York, New Jersey, and Pennsylvania?
   a. All had bicameral legislative assemblies when they were founded.
   b. Upon their founding, all offered some degree of religious toleration to settlers.
   c. All were founded as royal colonies.
   d. Quakers became the dominant religious element in all three.

Objectives 2 and 6

_____ 3. Penn's enlightened policy toward American Indians failed to prevent clashes between whites and Indians in Pennsylvania for which of the following reasons?
   a. The same toleration that made the colony attractive to Indians also made it attractive to white settlers who did not share Penn's enlightened views.
   b. Most settlers who came to the colony were Quakers who believed that Indians were heathens.
   c. The dominant tribe in the region adopted a warlike attitude toward all white settlers.
   d. The Indians in the area rebelled against Penn's attempts to convert them to the Quaker religion.

Objective 3

_____ 4. The decision by English settlers in the New World to enslave Africans is explained, in part, by which of the following?
   a. Slavery was already well defined in English law and widely practiced in England.
   b. The English believed that Africans were "available" as slaves because the Spanish and the Portuguese had enslaved blacks for years.
   c. The English government issued a proclamation calling for the Christianizing of the African peoples.
   d. Leaders from the various colonies met and decided that slavery was the best way to solve their labor problems.

Objective 3

_____ 5. Black slaves supplanted white indentured servants in the Chesapeake in the 1670s for which of the following reasons?
   a. Blacks were better workers than the white indentured servants.
   b. The initial cost for black slaves was less than that for white indentured servants.
   c. Getting an adequate supply of white workers became more and more difficult.
   d. England outlawed the practice of white servitude.

Objective 4

_____ 6. Records of the slave trade reveal that
   a. the mortality rate was far greater for slaves than their white captors.
   b. slave ships were kept immaculately clean in order to reduce the incidence of disease.
   c. the slave diet during the Middle Passage consisted largely of beef, pork, and corn.
   d. black captives sometimes contemplated suicide to avoid enslavement.

Objective 5

_____ 7. The increasing reliance of the southern colonies on black slaves
   a. caused white southern society to become more egalitarian.
   b. caused a steadily widening gap between rich and poor.
   c. led to economic diversification in the South.
   d. made indentured servants affordable to most white southerners.

Objective 6

_____ 8. As a result of the Pueblo revolt in New Mexico
   a. the Spanish became more brutal and totally enslaved the Pueblos.
   b. the Pueblos were forced to adopt Spanish culture and the Christian religion.
   c. the Spanish adopted a policy of cooperation with the Pueblos.
   d. the Pueblos realized that resistance against the Spanish was futile.

Objective 6

_____ 9. Which of the following is true of the Yamasee War?
   a. The whites won partly because of an alliance with the Cherokees.
   b. The Tuscaroras and their white allies enslaved thousands of Creeks.
   c. The war demonstrated that unity among the Indians was a realizable goal.
   d. The Yamasee were massacred and ceased to exist as a tribe.

Objective 8

_____ 10. The Halfway Covenant was an attempt to deal with
   a. an increase in the number of people having the conversion experience and demanding full church membership.
   b. the Antinomian heresy, which was causing dissension within the church.
   c. the question of whether the children of non-church members could receive the sacrament of baptism.
   d. the challenge presented to Puritan authorities by the increased number of Quakers in Massachusetts.

Objectives 1 and 8

_____ 11. The collapse of New England's first economic system was caused by
   a. the new economic restrictions imposed by England.
   b. the success of a new French and Indian alliance.
   c. plant diseases, which destroyed the great timbered regions of New England.
   d. the end of the constant flow of immigrants to the colony.

Objective 9

_____ 12. Which of the following is true of the Navigation Acts?
   a. Their intent was to encourage foreign trade with the British colonies.
   b. They were an effort by England to encourage colonial assemblies to make their own decisions about colonial trade.
   c. They were designed to decrease the influence of British merchants on colonial trade.
   d. They were designed to put England at the center of American trade.

Objective 9

_____ 13. Which of the following conclusions is supported by the facts about the powers and duties of the Board of Trade?
   a. England had thoroughly centralized colonial administration by 1696.
   b. England's supervision of its colonies was haphazard.
   c. The powers of the Board of Trade could legitimately be labeled tyrannical.
   d. The Board of Trade exercised more power over the British West Indies than over the North American colonies.

Objectives 9 and 10

_____ 14. England's most drastic attempt to exert more authority over its colonies centered on New England because
   a. the Puritan-controlled area continued to support laws that ran counter to English practice.
   b. all of the New England colonies allowed religious toleration.
   c. most of the exports from New England went to England.
   d. only the New England area protested the Navigation Acts.

Objective 11

____ 15. The Salem Village witchcraft crisis is best explained as
   a. the response of an isolated village to a group of new settlers who were seen as outsiders.
   b. an isolated incident in a village of radical Puritans.
   c. a reaction to feelings of insecurity and powerlessness in an area pulled between old and new life styles.
   d. a struggle for political power between the Puritan establishment and Anglican merchants.

ESSAY QUESTIONS

Objective 2

1. Discuss the social, political, and economic development of New York from its acquisition by James, the duke of York, in 1664 to the early eighteenth century.

Objective 2

2. Explain the reasons for the founding of Pennsylvania, and discuss the social, political, and economic development of the colony from its founding in 1681 to 1720.

Objective 3

3. Explain the emergence of black slavery in the British colonies in North America.

Objective 4

4. Describe the Middle Passage, and assess its impact on cargo and crew.

Objective 5

5. Examine the social and political impact of African immigrants on South Carolina and the Chesapeake.

Objectives 6 and 7

6. Discuss the similarities and differences among the major Indian wars of this period: Bacon's Rebellion, King Philip's War, the Yamasee War, and the Tuscarora War.

Objective 8

7. Discuss the economic evolution of New England and the impact of economic changes on Puritan aims and objectives.

CHAPTER 4
Growth and Diversity, 1720–1770

LEARNING OBJECTIVES

After you have studied Chapter 4 in your textbook and worked through this study guide chapter, you should be able to:

1. Indicate the factors that contributed to population growth in the American colonies during the eighteenth century, and discuss the consequences of that growth.

2. Discuss the characteristics of the major non-English ethnic groups that came to the colonies during the period from 1720 to 1760, and explain their contributions to and impact on colonial society.

3. Discuss the economic evolution of the American colonies from 1720 to 1750.

4. Distinguish between the culture of the genteel and that of ordinary folk in eighteenth-century colonial America.

5. Identify the basic tenets of Enlightenment thought, and explain the impact of this thought on eighteenth-century American society.

6. Identify the divergent cultural traditions that emerged in eighteenth-century colonial America.

7. Discuss and explain the importance of the religious, political, economic, and intercultural rituals in which eighteenth-century colonial Americans participated.

8. Discuss the similarities and differences among Indian, mixed-race, European-American, and African-American families.

9. Examine the impact of place of residence (rural vs. urban), gender, socioeconomic status, and race on the daily lives of eighteenth-century colonial Americans.

10. Discuss the rise of colonial assemblies, and explain the characteristics of representative government in eighteenth-century colonial America.

11. Examine the causes and consequences of the Stono Rebellion, the New York conspiracy, the land riots, the Regulator movements, and the Great Awakening.

THEMATIC GUIDE

In Chapters 2 and 3, we looked at American society in its infancy. Though this society was shaped by many forces, its basic belief system and value system came from England. At the end of Chapter 3, we saw that colonial society was showing signs of evolving in its own unique direction, a fact that caused England to formulate some rules and regulations (the Navigation Acts, for example) designed to control colonial behavior.

In Chapter 4, the authors analyze the internal makeup of colonial society to show more clearly how certain forces interacted to create the unique American society.

In the first section of the chapter, "Population Growth and Ethnic Diversity," we note the reasons behind the dramatic population growth in the colonies in the eighteenth century. By examining the migration of a variety of ethnic groups that made up that migration, we see the development of the cultural pluralism that distinguishes American society. At the same time we recognize some of the internal dynamics produced by that pluralism (the question of assimilation, as well as the emergence and consequences of ethnic antagonisms).

The economic evolution of the colonies is the main theme of the second section. Although there was slow economic growth between 1720 and 1750, growth was uneven. We examine in detail the economic forces operating in (1) New England, (2) the middle colonies, (3) the Chesapeake area, and (4) the Lower South. The forces affecting the economy as a whole interacted with regional characteristics to create a separate set of economic dynamics within each region. Consequently, the colonies were not a unified whole and had no history of unity or sense of common purpose.

An examination of the characteristics of genteel and ordinary culture leads to a discussion of the religious, political, economic, and intercultural rituals in which eighteenth-century colonial residents participated and through which they forged their cultural identities. Due to differences in the historical experiences of Indians, people of mixed race, European-American, and African-Americans, different family forms emerged within each group. Ethnicity, gender, and place of residence (rural vs. urban) also affected patterns of daily life in eighteenth-century colonial America.

In the last section, "Politics and Religion: Stability and Crisis at Midcentury," we first turn to political developments—chiefly the emergence of colonial assemblies as a powerful political force. We also look at the contrasts between the ideal and the reality of representative government in eighteenth-century colonial America.

Then we return to the theme that underlies all the sections in this chapter: the seeds of tension, conflict, and crisis present within eighteenth-century American society. If you look back at the earlier sections, you can see the potential for conflict in (1) ethnic diversity; (2) the increase of urban poverty despite general economic growth, as well as the economic variations among the four regions; (3) the differences between city and rural life, between the status of men and women, and between white and black families; (4) the clashing of the older and the newer cultures and of the genteel and the ordinary; and (5) the conflict between the ideal and the reality of the role of colonial assemblies. The crises and conflicts resulting from this diversity are exemplified in the Stono Rebellion, the New York conspiracy, the land riots, and the Regulator movements.

Finally, we consider the crisis that was the most widespread because it was not confined to a particular region—the Great Awakening. This was a religious crisis, but its causes resembled those of the other crises of the period.

BUILDING VOCABULARY

Listed below are important words and terms that you need to know to get the most out of Chapter 4. They are listed in the order in which they occur in the chapter. After carefully looking through the list, refer to a dictionary and jot down the definition of words that you do not know or of which you are unsure.

extract

purloin

roust

empirical

periphery

enclaves

aversion

stagnate

indigenous

amenity

destitution

infirm

jockey (verb)

lucrative

foray

levy

hinterland

impetus

ostentatious

genteel

abstract

innate

rationalism

rudiments

communal

divergent

egalitarian

miscreant

heinous

proliferate

disparate

reciprocate

compensatory

liaison

connote

defamatory

analogy

polity

reapportion

pluralistic

malevolent

foment

vigilante

depravity

evangelical

itinerant

paradox

orthodoxy

deference

tenet

opulence

manumit

secular

volatile

IDENTIFICATION AND SIGNIFICANCE

After studying Chapter 4 of *A People and a Nation*, you should be able to identify fully *and* explain the historical significance of each item listed below.

1. Identify each item in the space provided. Give an explanation or description of the item. Answer the questions *who, what, where,* and *when.*

2. Explain the historical significance of each item in the space provided. Establish the historical context in which the item exists. Establish the item as the result of or as the cause of other factors existing in the society under study. Answer this question: *What were the political, social, economic, and/or cultural consequences of this item?*

colonial population growth

    Identification

    Significance

African immigrants

    Identification

    Significance

Scotch-Irish, Scots, and Irish immigrants

    Identification

    Significance

German immigrants

> Identification

> Significance

the Huguenots

> Identification

> Significance

Sephardic Jews

> Identification

> Significance

urban poverty

> Identification

> Significance

King George's War

> Identification

> Significance

genteel culture

> Identification

> Significance

advanced education in eighteenth-century colonial America

    Identification

    Significance

the Enlightenment

    Identification

    Significance

Essay on Human Understanding

    Identification

    Significance

John and William Bartram

    Identification

    Significance

Two Treatises of Government

    Identification

    Significance

oral cultures

    Identification

    Significance

religious rituals

> Identification

> Significance

the black family

> Identification

> Significance

civic rituals

> Identification

> Significance

rituals of consumption

> Identification

> Significance

intercultural rituals

> Identification

> Significance

colonial families

> Identification

> Significance

the "indoor" affairs of the rural household

    Identification

    Significance

the "outdoor" affairs of the rural household

    Identification

    Significance

colonial colleges

    Identification

    Significance

colonial newspapers

    Identification

    Significance

John Peter Zenger

    Identification

    Significance

eighteenth-century colonial assemblies

    Identification

    Significance

the Stono Rebellion

    Identification

    Significance

the New York conspiracy

    Identification

    Significance

the New Jersey, Vermont, and Hudson Valley land riots

    Identification

    Significance

the Regulator movements

    Identification

    Significance

the First Great Awakening

    Identification

    Significance

Jonathan Edwards

    Identification

    Significance

George Whitefield

    Identification

    Significance

"New Lights" and "Old Lights"

    Identification

    Significance

Baptists

    Identification

    Significance

the Dan River Baptist Church

    Identification

    Significance

EVALUATING AND USING INFORMATION

With the following hints as your guide, complete the four steps outlined below to produce the working draft of an essay identifying "The Enlightenment" and indicating its significance in the history of the United States, especially between 1720 and 1770. When you finish, you will have the material for either a fully developed but short essay or a response for a "quickie" identification/significance item.

    The simple identification/significance answers called for in the Evaluating and Using Information exercise for Chapter 3 suit items based on limited textbook and lecture material for which two or three sentences composed in about three minutes should suffice. (That is often the case when such items appear in a test's "short-answer" section. But the amount of detail in your response to items of this type should always be based on what your professor indicates he or she wants.)

    The kind of identification/significance answer this exercise focuses on, however, suits a question covering a large amount of information on which a well-prepared student would be expected to spend 15 or more minutes during a test. (As you work on the Identification and

Significance exercises throughout this study guide, notice that the specificity of the items themselves varies considerably. Some items ask that you deal with a person or event barely mentioned in the text, whereas other items ask you to deal with much broader and more expansive topics that are covered at some length in the chapter. As you deal with these items, decide which items call for short answers and which call for expansive answers.)

Hints for Composing Essay-Length Answers to "Significance" Questions

1. Use a statement of the item's overall impact as your one-sentence "core" answer to the question. That sentence, the thesis or whole point of your essay, can serve as the last sentence in the introductory paragraph. Or, it could be the first sentence of the essay's first body paragraph, depending on your decision about matters referred to in Hint 2. Your essay's thesis or whole point must focus on the significance of the person, place, thing, or concept; the definition merely clarifies the topic of your essay.

2. Early in your essay, include a clear, expanded definition of the item whose significance you are explaining. Use a formal definition of the type described in the previous chapter of this study guide as the first sentence of this expanded definition. In the rest of your expanded definition, answer basic questions that are most likely to make clear what or whom you are writing about. Answer a litany of questions like these: What are some examples? Who created, invented, discovered, wrote, built, etc., it? How does *the item being defined* differ from *X* (*X* being something with which people could confuse the item in question)? How is *the item being defined* like *X* (something of the same type that the essay's reader is likely to know about or expect me to know about)? What are the origins of *the item being defined*? What types or parts does *the item being defined* have? For what is *the item being defined* used? Who uses it? Under what circumstances? When and where did it exist or take place? What was its goal or purpose? How did it work? What did *the item being defined* do? What caused *the item being defined* ? In other words, answer in the definition part of your essay—whether that is in the first body paragraph or the opening of the thesis paragraph—those questions whose answers would contribute the most toward making what or who the item is clear. You have to answer only enough of the questions you come up with to accomplish that goal.

3. Once the definition/identification is taken care of, it is time to answer the real question: What is the historical significance of *the item being defined*? *Significance* implies several things. First, and usually foremost, it implies consequences or effects. Second, it implies the scope of the impact—the number and kinds of people or things affected and the duration of the effects. Decide whether one or both of these implications apply to the item you are writing about and frame your explanation of the significance accordingly (see Hints 5 and 6). Often the number of people or things affected and the duration of the effects can be covered in the expanded definition (see Hint 3).

4. How you present the specific effects representing the total significance depends on how many effects you have to name and explain.
    If there are only two or three, then either devote one paragraph to naming and explaining each effect or write one enumeration paragraph whose point is, roughly, "*the item in question* had three major effects." (The body of that kind of paragraph names and explains the first effect, names and explains the second effect, and then names and explains the third effect.)
    If there are more than two to four simple-to-explain effects, you should classify the effects (social, political, economic, religious, etc.) and devote a separate paragraph to each category. Each of these paragraphs can be either an exemplification paragraph (a

paragraph in which you assert that the item has had a particular category of effects and then provide examples of the effects it has had in that category) or an enumeration paragraph (a paragraph in which you assert that the item has had a particular number of a particular category of effects—three political effects, for example—and then name and explain each effect briefly one by one).

5. If you decide your explanation of the significance of an item should focus on who was affected and how long the effect lasted, then do more than give the bare statistics. What else you say will depend on the item. If you are saying, as you might have been on a test on Chapter 1, that the entire population of Indians who had contact with the Europeans who came to the New World were affected by the European "killer diseases" such as smallpox, some questions you might be expected to answer in your paragraph would be: Why were the Indians particularly susceptible to such diseases? How soon after the arrival of Europeans was the effect being felt? How did the number of deaths affect Indian society, their chances of resisting European incursions into their territory, and their responses to European evangelical efforts?

Step One

Complete the following chart to bring together information for your expanded definition of "The Enlightenment." For your purposes, an expanded definition is a group of sentences whose first sentence is a formal definition and whose succeeding sentences present information that clarifies the formal definition. You may want to add additional questions and answers (notes).

Step Two

Referring to the notes from the chart you created in Step One, complete the next chart by entering the three basic parts of a formal definition. (If you need to, refer to the hints in the Evaluating and Using Information exercise for Chapter 3 on pages 76–77). The results will be the material for the statement of the expanded-definition part (see Hint 2) of your finished essay, no matter whether you use it as the first sentence of the essay's thesis or introductory paragraph or as the first sentence of your essay's first body paragraph. When you finish Step Two, you will have the material for a working draft of the definition part of your answer to the identification/significance question.

Chapter 4—Growth and Diversity, 1720–1770

	Evidence: Clarifying Details for Deriving and Supporting a Formal Definition of "The Enlightenment"	
Questions	**Answers (Notes)**	**Source of Notes—(Lectures, textbook) pages or dates**
To what narrow, pertinent category of person, place, thing, or concept does "The Enlightenment" belong?		
What kinds of people are associated with "The Enlightenment"?		
What are the names of some specific individuals associated with "The Enlightenment"?		
What did those people do, say, practice, believe, or create that linked them to "The Enlightenment"?		
When did "The Enlightenment" exist? Where?		

Term	**Class**	**Differentiation**
The item being defined or identified	Narrow, relevant category to which the item being defined belongs	What distinguishes the item being defined or identified from all other members of the category in which you have placed it
The Enlightenment		

Step Three

Using the questions in the first column of the following chart as an indication of the kind of material you are looking for, search Chapter 4 of your textbook and your class notes for information about the significance of "The Enlightenment" and individuals or works associated with it. Record your notes on what you learn about the significance of "The Enlightenment" in the appropriate blanks in the chart. If your search indicates that additional questions need to be answered, enter those questions and your answers to them in the chart's last two rows.

Evidence: Clarifying Details For Deriving and Supporting an Assertion of the Overall Significance of "The Enlightenment"		
Questions	**Answers (Notes)**	**Source of Notes— (Lectures, textbook) pages or dates**
What fields of human endeavor or belief did "The Enlightenment" influence? How?		
What events, documents, inventions, creations, etc., grew out of "The Enlightenment"?		
How widespread was the influence of "The Enlightenment" (number and categories of people and works)?		
What changes in attitudes or behavior resulted from the existence of "The Enlightenment"?		

Step Four

Using the material you have gathered in Steps One through Three and the suggestions for organizing a significance essay, write (in your reading notebook) the working draft of an essay that answers the question inherent in this instruction: Identify and explain the historical significance of "The Enlightenment."

IDEAS AND DETAILS

Objective 1

_____ 1. The age at which most colonial women married was a major factor contributing to the
   a. high divorce rate in colonial America.
   b. growth of the colonial population by natural increase.
   c. unusually small size of most colonial families.
   d. high infant mortality rate in the colonies.

Objective 2

_____ 2. Which of the following is true of German immigrants?
   a. They were drawn to the urban areas of the middle colonies.
   b. They were a destabilizing force because of their radical political ideas.
   c. They contributed to the religious diversity of the middle colonies.
   d. Most were young, single men seeking economic opportunity.

Objective 2

_____ 3. For which of the following reasons were American Indians sometimes used as slave catchers?
   a. They were more fearless than white slave catchers.
   b. Such use would help prevent an anti-white alliance between blacks and Indians.
   c. Indian religious teaching portrayed blacks as a threat.
   d. They were better able than whites to lure blacks out of hiding.

Objective 3

_____ 4. Which of the following factors had a stabilizing influence on the eighteenth-century American economy?
   a. European wars
   b. The slave system
   c. The growing American population
   d. International trade

Objectives 2 and 3

_____ 5. In contrast to seventeenth-century immigrants, immigrants to the colonies in the eighteenth century
   a. had fewer opportunities for advancement.
   b. were seldom able to assimilate into Anglo-American culture.
   c. always came by choice.
   d. were primarily of English origin.

Objective 3

____ 6. The demand for foodstuffs during King George's War had a positive economic impact on
   a. Massachusetts.
   b. Pennsylvania.
   c. South Carolina.
   d. Connecticut.

Objective 5

____ 7. The Enlightenment emphasized
   a. revealed religion.
   b. faith.
   c. reason.
   d. intuitive knowledge.

Objective 5

____ 8. In his *Two Treatises of Government,* John Locke argued that
   a. government was created by God.
   b. government was created for the sole purpose of bringing order and stability to human society.
   c. the people created government and placed absolute power in the hands of the monarch.
   d. the people have the right to oust a ruler if he does not protect their rights.

Objectives 4 and 7

____ 9. The seating system in New England Congregationalist churches showed the
   a. wealth and status of church members.
   b. ethnic background of the members of the congregation.
   c. vocations of church members.
   d. marital status of church members.

Objective 7

____ 10. Tea served as a sign of status in colonial America because
   a. upper class colonists drank it hot while lower class colonists drank it cold.
   b. the drinking of tea was considered to be a lower class activity.
   c. tea was served only in salons frequented by those of genteel status.
   d. the items necessary for its "proper" consumption were expensive.

Objective 7

____ 11. Which of the following was an important component of intercultural trading rituals between Europeans and Indians?
   a. Prayer
   b. Gift-giving
   c. Cigar smoking
   d. Tea drinking

Objective 8

_____ 12. The extended family was important to blacks for which of the following reasons?
   a. It was the focus of all religious teaching.
   b. The uncertainties of slave life increased the need for a large support group.
   c. It was the basic work unit on the plantation.
   d. It was the one aspect of black culture respected by whites.

Objective 9

_____ 13. Which of the following distinguished urban life from rural life in eighteenth-century America?
   a. Work schedules in the city were governed by the sun rather than by the clock.
   b. The incidence of epidemic diseases was lower in the city.
   c. Urban dwellers had more contact with the world at large.
   d. The distance between the ordinary and the genteel was less noticeable in the city.

Objectives 10 and 11

_____ 14. The Regulator movements, the Stono Revolt, and the Hudson Valley land riots provide evidence that
   a. colonial assemblies had the means to control internal disorder.
   b. colonial assemblies did not live up to the ideal of protecting the rights of *all* the people.
   c. there were few ethnic tensions in eighteenth-century colonial America.
   d. political rights were gradually being extended to more and more people.

Objective 11

_____ 15. Which of the following was a consequence of the First Great Awakening?
   a. It brought intellectualism into religion.
   b. It created a new sense of unity between England and the colonies.
   c. It led to the founding of an established church throughout the colonies.
   d. It fostered a willingness to question traditional beliefs.

ESSAY QUESTIONS

Objective 2

1. Discuss the characteristics of the Scots-Irish, German, and Scottish immigrants to the American colonies in the eighteenth century. Why did they come? Where did they settle? How did their immigrant status affect their lives?

Objective 3

2. Examine the similarities and differences between the economic development of New England and that of the Lower South during the eighteenth century.

Objective 5

3. Discuss the ideas associated with the Enlightenment and the impact of those ideas on mid-eighteenth-century colonial society.

Objective 7

4. Discuss the importance of church attendance in the lives of eighteenth-century colonial Americans. In what way were colonial church services an expression of community values?

Objective 9

5. Examine gender roles in mid-eighteenth-century colonial America.

Objectives 2 and 8

6. Examine the characteristics of the lives of African-Americans in mid-eighteenth-century colonial America.

Objective 9

7. Discuss the similarities and differences between rural life and city life in mid-eighteenth-century colonial America.

Objective 11

8. Defend the following thesis statement:

    The Stono Rebellion and the land riots in New Jersey, Vermont, and the Hudson Valley exposed the ethnic, racial, and economic tensions in early eighteenth-century colonial America.

CHAPTER 5
Severing the Bonds of Empire, 1754–1774

LEARNING OBJECTIVES

After you have studied Chapter 5 in your textbook and worked through this study guide chapter, you should be able to:

1. Examine the relations between Europeans and North American Indians between 1701 and 1763.

2. Discuss the causes and consequences of the Seven Years' War.

3. Through an examination of Parliament's actions relating to the colonies from 1763 to 1774, explain Great Britain's approach to the crisis it faced in the post–Seven Years' War decade.

4. Through an examination of the development of the colonial resistance movement, explain the reaction of the colonists to Parliament's actions in the period from 1763 to 1774.

5. Examine the basic ideological conflict between the British and the colonists concerning (a) the nature of representative government and (b) the nature of political power.

6. Examine the ideological and constitutional arguments presented by the colonists against the Sugar Act, the Stamp Act, and the Townshend Acts.

7. Explain the role of each of the following in the development and spread of the colonial resistance movement:
   a. Pamphlets
   b. Legislative protest (e.g., Virginia Stamp Act Resolves)
   c. Crowd action
   d. Economic protest
   e. Public rituals
   f. Committees of correspondence

8. Discuss the various divisions that emerged among the colonists during the development of their resistance against the British.

9. Trace the development of the theory that Great Britain was conspiring to oppress the colonists, and explain how that theory became especially important in relation to the Tea Act, the Coercive Acts, and the Quebec Act.

THEMATIC GUIDE

The main topic of Chapter 5 is the emergence of the colonial resistance movement. The authors explain (1) the interaction of forces that determined how the American colonists and the British perceived each other between 1754 and 1774 and (2) how the actions born of those perceptions created tensions and conflicts that led to the emergence of a widespread and unified colonial resistance movement.

In the first section, "Renewed Warfare Among Europeans and Indians," we learn about the causes and outcome of the Seven Years' War and about the British attitude toward the colonists during that war. That attitude helped shape a negative colonial view of the British and so spurred the emergence of the resistance movement.

The next section, "1763: A Turning Point," presents the consequences of the French and Indian War, especially the devastating impact of the war on the southern and northwestern Indians and Pontiac's desperate attempt to regain a measure of independence for the northwestern Indians. The consequences of the war on the British, on their North American colonies, and on the relationship between the two takes up the rest of the section, and indeed the rest of the chapter. The authors explain the differing frames of reference of the British and the colonists. The British frame of reference was shaped by (1) Britain's need for additional revenue in the face of financial crisis and (2) Britain's definition of representative government, the role of Parliament, and the nature of the relationship between Parliament and colonies. The colonial frame of reference toward Great Britain was shaped by (1) a feeling of security stemming from the outcome of the French and Indian War, (2) a wariness of the British based on the influence of the Real Whigs and the Great Awakening, and (3) colonial theories about representative government. Given this frame of reference, the colonists began "to see oppressive designs behind the actions of Grenville and his successors." Out of this colonial perception grew the "conspiracy theory," considered at the end of the chapter.

Passage of the Sugar and Currency Acts in 1764 and the hesitant protest attending those acts are the topics of the third section, "The Stamp Act Crisis." The debate over constitutional issues led to widespread but relatively moderate protest at the ideological level. Involvement of the masses shifted the protest to the emotional level. Soon some internal colonial divisions appeared, caused by the tension between the "ordinary" and the "genteel" discussed in Chapter 4. Composed of merchants, lawyers, prosperous tradesmen, and the like, the Sons of Liberty attempted to capitalize on this tension, using it to create acceptable forms of resistance.

Repeal of the Stamp Act, passage of the Declaratory Act, and passage of the Townshend Acts are considered in the fourth section, "Resistance to the Townshend Acts." John Dickinson's contention that the colonists had the right to determine the intent of Parliament before deciding to obey its laws suggests that the conspiracy theory was gaining ground. British reaction to the Massachusetts Circular Letter strengthened the perception that the British were conspiring to destroy colonial rights and liberties.

In the next section, "Growing Rifts," the discussion of how the "middling sort" used public rituals to involve the "ordinary" in the resistance movement also shows the internal divisions among the colonists. The section begins with the Boston Massacre, an event that exemplified the fears of the most conservative patriots about involving the masses in the resistance movement. News of the repeal of the Townshend duties (except the tea tax), the use of the Massacre as a propaganda tool against the British, the defense of the British soldiers by two leading patriots, and the relative calm from 1770 to 1773 helped alleviate those fears. Yet both the resistance movement and the conspiracy theory continued to grow in these calm years. It was during this time that Samuel Adams used the Boston Committee of Correspondence to widen the geographic scope of the resistance movement. Both the Boston Committee's statement of rights and grievances and the response of interior Massachusetts towns to this document demonstrate the emergence of patriots more committed to American rights than to loyalty to Great Britain.

Such commitment led to definitive action by patriots, who perceived a corrupt, oppressive, tyrannical Great Britain conspiring to destroy colonial rights and liberties through passage of the Tea Act, the Coercive Acts, and the Quebec Act. As stated by the authors, "It seemed as though the full dimensions of the plot against American rights and liberties had at last been revealed." The chapter ends with the calling of delegates to the First Continental Congress for the purpose of formulating a united plan of resistance against the British.

BUILDING VOCABULARY

Listed below are important words and terms that you need to know to get the most out of Chapter 5. They are listed in the order in which they occur in the chapter. After carefully looking through the list, refer to a dictionary and jot down the definition of words that you do not know or of which you are unsure.

affluent

virtuous

resonate

obscure

coalition

provincial

nominal

demoralize

debacle

reimburse

coerce

materiel

cede

haughty

profane

vengeance

debar

tout

atrocities

portent

futile

headwaters

mediocre

erratic

status quo

hallmark

constituency

wield

dissent

inherent

perpetual

vigilance

explicitly

precedent

maritime

ideological

dilemma

contention

futile

equitably

oratorical

advocate

rescind

vassalage

effigy

mêlée

continuance

detestation

divergent

paramount

ostentatious

disfranchise

redress

grievance

vortex

intercolonial

emblazon

moratorium

ominous

assess

incentive

prerogative

satirize

harass

goad

sentry

martyr

propaganda

encompass

prudent

pernicious

confiscate

adamant

exult

intrepid

punitive

despotism

ardent

irrevocable

elicit

IDENTIFICATION AND SIGNIFICANCE

After studying Chapter 5 of *A People and a Nation*, you should be able to identify fully *and* explain the historical significance of each item listed below.

1. Identify each item in the space provided. Give an explanation or description of the item. Answer the questions *who, what, where,* and *when.*

2. Explain the historical significance of each item in the space provided. Establish the historical context in which the item exists. Establish the item as the result of or as the cause of other factors existing in the society under study. Answer this question: *What were the political, social, economic, and/or cultural consequences of this item?*

John Singleton Copley

    Identification

    Significance

Paul Revere

    Identification

    Significance

Iroquois-Catawba War

    Identification

    Significance

Albany Congress

    Identification

    Significance

George Washington

    Identification

    Significance

General Edward Braddock

    Identification

    Significance

the Seven Years' War

    Identification

    Significance

William Pitt

    Identification

    Significance

Battle of Quebec (1759)

    Identification

    Significance

Treaty of Paris of 1763

    Identification

    Significance

Pontiac's uprising

    Identification

    Significance

the Proclamation of 1763

    Identification

    Significance

George Grenville

    Identification

    Significance

George III

    Identification

    Significance

virtual representation

    Identification

    Significance

individual representation

    Identification

    Significance

the Real Whigs

    Identification

    Significance

Cato's Letters

    Identification

    Significance

the Sugar Act

    Identification

    Significance

the Currency Act

    Identification

    Significance

the Stamp Act

    Identification

    Significance

The Rights of the British Colonies Asserted and Proved

    Identification

    Significance

Patrick Henry

    Identification

    Significance

the Virginia Stamp Act Resolves

    Identification

    Significance

Considerations on the Propriety of Imposing Taxes on the British Colonies

    Identification

    Significance

the Loyal Nine

    Identification

    Significance

Andrew Oliver

    Identification

    Significance

Thomas Hutchinson

    Identification

    Significance

Ebenezer MacIntosh

    Identification

    Significance

the Sons of Liberty

    Identification

    Significance

Charleston demonstrations of October 1765 and January 1766

    Identification

    Significance

Philadelphia demonstration against Benjamin Franklin

    Identification

    Significance

the Stamp Act Congress

    Identification

    Significance

nonimportation associations of 1765

    Identification

    Significance

Lord Rockingham

    Identification

    Significance

the Declaratory Act

    Identification

    Significance

Charles Townshend

    Identification

    Significance

the Townshend Acts

    Identification

    Significance

Letters from a Farmer in Pennsylvania

    Identification

    Significance

the Massachusetts circular letter

    Identification

    Significance

the numbers 45 and 92

    Identification

    Significance

public rituals

    Identification

    Significance

the Daughters of Liberty

    Identification

    Significance

Edenton Ladies Tea Party

    Identification

    Significance

the boycott of 1768–1770

    Identification

    Significance

Lord North

    Identification

    Significance

John Hancock

    Identification

    Significance

the *Liberty* riot

    Identification

    Significance

the Boston Massacre

    Identification

    Significance

Committees of correspondence

    Identification

    Significance

Samuel Adams

    Identification

    Significance

the Boston Statement of Rights and Grievances

    Identification

    Significance

the Tea Act

    Identification

    Significance

the Boston Tea Party

> Identification

> Significance

the Coercive (Intolerable) Acts

> Identification

> Significance

the Quebec Act

> Identification

> Significance

ORGANIZING INFORMATION

According to learning objective 7, you should be able to explain the role of pamphlets, legislative protest, crowd action, economic protest, public rituals, and the committees of correspondence in the development and spread of the colonial resistance movement.

Use the following forms to organize information about pamphlets, legislative protest, and crowd action. Your professor may want to include more items than those found in this exercise, or your professor may want you to do more extensive research on these methods of protest. In such cases, add to or otherwise alter these forms to suit your purposes. If additional research is needed, the bibliographies at the end of Chapters 5 and 6 are an excellent starting point.

Major Pamphlets of the American Resistance Movement

The Rights of the British Colonies Asserted and Proved

Author: Date published:

What British actions did the pamphlet oppose?

What important ideas were presented and developed in the pamphlet?

What were Parliament's arguments against these ideas?

Considerations on the Propriety of Imposing Taxes on the British Colonies

Author: Date published:

What British actions did the pamphlet oppose?

What important ideas were presented and developed in the pamphlet?

What were Parliament's arguments against these ideas?

Do the ideas presented in this pamphlet give it a more conservative, a more radical, or about the same tone as the previous pamphlet? Explain.

Letters from a Farmer in Pennsylvania

Author: Date published:

What British actions did the pamphlet oppose?

What important ideas were presented and developed in the pamphlet?

What were Parliament's arguments against these ideas?

Do the ideas presented in this pamphlet give it a more conservative, a more radical, or about the same tone as the previous pamphlets? Explain.

Boston Statement of Rights and Grievances

Author: Date published:

What British actions did the pamphlet oppose?

What important ideas were presented and developed in the pamphlet?

What were Parliament's arguments against these ideas?

Do the ideas presented in this pamphlet give it a more conservative, a more radical, or about the same tone as the previous pamphlets? Explain.

Summary View of the Rights of British America

Author: Date published:

This pamphlet is not discussed in the textbook. Do some library research to answer the questions that follow.

What British actions did the pamphlet oppose?

What important ideas were presented and developed in the pamphlet?

What were Parliament's arguments against these ideas?

Do the ideas presented in this pamphlet give it a more conservative, a more radical, or about the same tone as the previous pamphlets? Explain.

Common Sense

Author: Date published:

This pamphlet is discussed in Chapter 6.

What British actions did the pamphlet oppose?

What important ideas were presented and developed in the pamphlet?

What were Parliament's arguments against these ideas?

Do the ideas presented in this pamphlet give it a more conservative, a more radical, or about the same tone as the previous pamphlets? Explain.

Major Legislative Resolutions of the American Resistance Movement

The Virginia Stamp Act Resolves

Author: Date adopted:

What British actions did the resolution oppose?

What important ideas were presented in the resolution? Were all of these ideas accepted by the House of Burgesses? Explain.

Do the ideas adopted match those set forth in a major pamphlet? Which pamphlet?

How were the Virginia Stamp Act Resolves reported by colonial newspapers? Why is this important?

What were Parliament's arguments against these ideas?

The Massachusetts Circular Letter

Author: Date adopted:

What British actions did the resolution oppose?

What important ideas were presented in the resolution? Do the ideas match those set forth in a major pamphlet? Which pamphlet?

What were Parliament's arguments against these ideas?

Do the ideas presented in this resolution give it a more conservative, a more radical, or about the same tone as previous legislative resolutions? Explain.

The Declaration of Rights and Grievances

Author: Date adopted:

This declaration is discussed in Chapter 6.
What British actions did the resolution oppose?

What important ideas were presented in the resolution?

What were Parliament's arguments against these ideas?

Do the ideas presented in this resolution give it a more conservative, a more radical, or about the same tone as previous legislative resolutions? Explain.

The Continental Association

Author: Date adopted:

This agreement is discussed in Chapter 6.

What British actions did the agreement oppose?

What were the details of the agreement?

What methods were recommended for enforcement of the agreement? Were these methods effective? Explain.

Do the ideas presented in this agreement give it a more conservative, a more radical, or about the same tone as previous legislative resolutions? Explain.

The Declaration of Independence

Author: Date adopted:

This declaration is discussed in Chapter 6.
What British actions did the declaration oppose?

Copyright © Houghton Mifflin Company. All rights reserved.

What important ideas were presented and developed in the declaration?

How were the ideas in this declaration and those presented by Thomas Paine in *Common Sense* important to the American Revolution and to the future American nation?

Major Crowd Action Associated with the American Resistance Movement

Boston, August 14 and 26, 1765

What British actions did the demonstrators oppose?

What course did the demonstrations take?

    August 14:

    August 26:

Did these demonstrations advance the patriot cause? Explain.

Did these demonstrations help radicalize sentiment? Explain.

Did these demonstrations reveal any divisions within the patriot ranks? Explain.

What were the consequences of these demonstrations in relation to the resistance movement and the coming of the Revolutionary War?

Charleston, October 1765 and January 1766

What British actions did the demonstrators oppose?

What course did the demonstrations take?

    October 1765:

    January 1766:

Did these demonstrations advance the patriot cause? Explain.

Did these demonstrations help radicalize sentiment? Explain.

Did these demonstrations reveal any divisions within the patriot ranks? Explain.

What were the consequences of these demonstrations in relation to the resistance movement and the coming of the Revolutionary War?

Philadelphia, September 1765

What British actions did the demonstrators oppose?

What course did the demonstration take?

Did the demonstration advance the patriot cause? Explain.

Did the demonstration help radicalize sentiment? Explain.

Did the demonstration reveal any divisions within the patriot ranks? Explain.

What were the consequences of this demonstration in relation to the resistance movement and the coming of the Revolutionary War?

Liberty *Riot*, June 1768

What British actions did the demonstrators oppose?

What course did the demonstration take?

Did the demonstration advance the patriot cause? Explain.

Did the demonstration help radicalize sentiment? Explain.

Did the demonstration reveal any divisions within the patriot ranks? Explain.

What were the consequences of this demonstration in relation to the resistance movement and the coming of the Revolutionary War?

Boston Massacre, March 1770

What British actions did the demonstrators oppose?

What course did the demonstration take?

Did the demonstration advance the patriot cause? Explain.

Did the demonstration help radicalize sentiment? Explain.

Did the demonstration reveal any divisions within the patriot ranks? Explain.

What were the consequences of this demonstration in relation to the resistance movement and the coming of the Revolutionary War?

Gaspée *Incident (Rhode Island), June 1772*

This incident is not discussed in the textbook. Do some library research to answer the questions that follow.

What British actions did the demonstrators oppose?

What course did the demonstration take?

Did the demonstration advance the patriot cause? Explain.

Did the demonstration help radicalize sentiment? Explain.

Did the demonstration reveal any divisions within the patriot ranks? Explain.

What were the consequences of this demonstration in relation to the resistance movement and the coming of the Revolutionary War?

The Boston Tea Party, December 1773

What British actions did the demonstrators oppose?

What course did the demonstration take?

Did the demonstration advance the patriot cause? Explain.

Did the demonstration help radicalize sentiment? Explain.

Did the demonstration reveal any divisions within the patriot ranks? Explain.

What were the consequences of this demonstration in relation to the resistance movement and the coming of the Revolutionary War?

EVALUATING AND USING INFORMATION

Compose the working draft of a contrast essay that answers the following question. Enter the essay in your reading notebook.

> The eleven years that led to the convening of the First Continental Congress (1763–1774) may be seen as an economic war that preceded the military war known as the American Revolution. Treating pieces of British legislation and American responses to them as skirmishes and battles in that economic war, contrast the British and American attitudes, tactics, and achievements. Remember, you are to focus on economic factors only.

Use the following questions on material in Chapter 5 and Figure 2 on page 137 of your study guide as aids in your search for the information that belongs in your essay. You will find that a great deal of the information you compiled and categorized in the Organizing Information exercise on pages 118–128 will be useful in completing this exercise.

Below you will find hints for one way of composing the kind of contrast essay called for in this exercise. If you need them, the writing-by-formula approach inherent in such hints will get you started. In any case, knowing basic formulas for composing the most common types of essay answers is quite useful to those who have to compose under the time pressure associated with tests. Experienced and confident writers have learned to go beyond the formulas when time and inspiration permit.

Hints for Writing the Contrast Essay

(Refer to Figure 1 on page 131 as you read over these hints.)

1. Think of your entire essay as a contrast of Britain and the American colonies based on the economic aspects of three characteristics or features both exhibited: (a) attitudes, (b) tactics, and (c) achievements.

2. Treat each major section in the body of your essay (see Figure 1) as a small essay contrasting Britain and the American colonies on one of the three factors, making each section of the body of your essay a long paragraph or a short paragraph series.

    Divide each of the sections into two parts, one devoted to Britain and the other devoted to the American colonies. Begin each of these parts with a statement of the point of that part. Use a contrast transitional device to connect the two parts ("In contrast, . . .", "On the other hand, . . .").

3. Write from the evidence to the sub-point it supports in the section and then from the sub-points in a section to the whole point of that section, and, finally, from the whole points of all the sections to the thesis statement. That means you should begin with Body Section One. Gather your support for Point A. Study the support (evidence) and write Point A as your interpretation of what the support adds up to or means. Then move on to Point B and go through the same process. When Points A and B are complete, revise the statement of the Whole Point of that paragraph or paragraph series (a whole section of your essay) as necessary. Then move on to Section Two of the body of your essay.

4. Unless you have strong reason to do otherwise, arrange the support for each Point A and each Point B (see Figure 1) in chronological order from the earlier skirmish/battles in the economic war (pieces of legislation) to the later ones.

Copyright © Houghton Mifflin Company. All rights reserved.

5. Make the core of the thesis statement (the statement of the point of the whole essay) that is contained in the essay's introductory paragraph a pure "contrast" statement. Do the same with the core of each of the statements of the Whole Point of each section of the body of the essay. A "pure contrast" statement is a declarative sentence made up of three components:
   a. *a naming of the members of the compound subject*—the X and Y. In this case, the X is Great Britain and the Y is the American colonies;
   b. *an indication of the logical relationship between the X and Y* that the essay is to establish. In this case, the logical relationship is, according to the question, one of difference ("differed," "contrasted with one another," or some other such phrase); and
   c. *an indication of the basis of the contrast*, the features on which the X and Y are to be shown to differ. In this case, again, according to the question, these features are economic attitudes, economic tactics, and economic achievements.

Once you get the "formula" statements of the thesis and of the sections' whole points, you should feel free to revise them, rearranging the order of the components, making their phrasing suit your own style and vocabulary, and adding any stylistic devices needed because of their positions in your essay. Expect to revise these statements as the last step in the composition process. (Only then will you know exactly what support you have used; each of the three sections' point/s and the thesis statement must interpret the support material actually used in the essay.)

Questions to Guide You in Gathering Information Needed in Your Essay

Find the answers to the questions and then select the most pertinent information you have uncovered to write the working draft of your essay. You cannot include every piece of information you find, so be selective.

1. Analyze Figure 2 on page 137 of this study guide to determine whether British legislation contributed to an already existing decline in colonial purchases of British goods or appears to have caused a decline, contributed to an upswing in American purchases of British goods, or reversed an upswing in American purchases of British goods. Remember, there will be a time lag between passage of legislation and the legislation's effect on purchases.

2. In Chapter 5 of your textbook, find any indications of how important American consumers were to the British economy.

3. Basing your answer on both Figure 2 and relevant material in Chapter 5 of your textbook, identify the turning point or the turning points in the economic war between Britain and its American colonies between 1763 and 1775. (Does this turning point or do these turning points help you to group pieces of legislation to simplify parts of your essay?)

Figure 5-1: Simple Plan for Contrast Essay

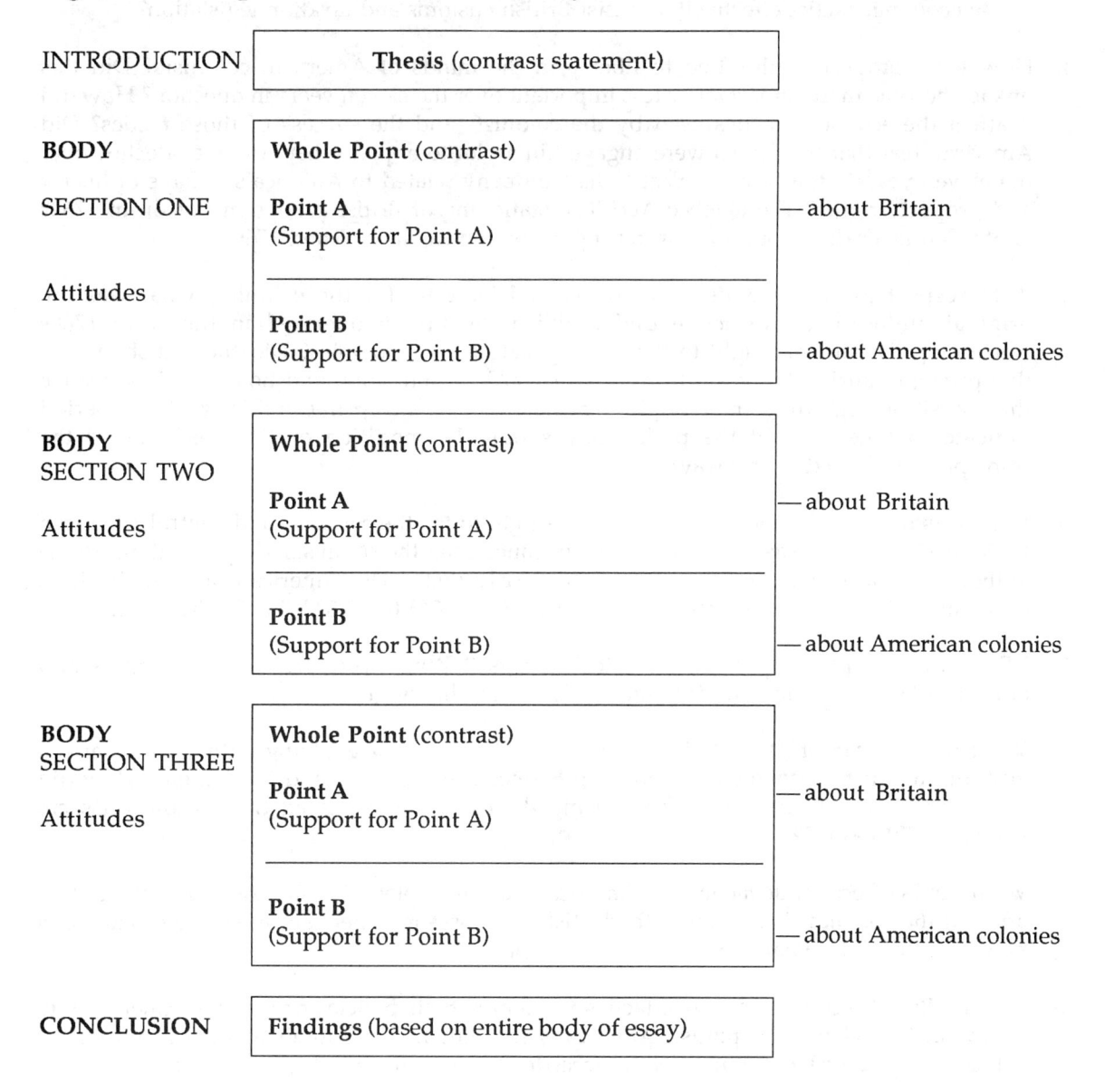

INTRODUCTION	**Thesis** (contrast statement)	
BODY SECTION ONE Attitudes	**Whole Point** (contrast) **Point A** (Support for Point A)	— about Britain
	Point B (Support for Point B)	— about American colonies
BODY SECTION TWO Attitudes	**Whole Point** (contrast) **Point A** (Support for Point A)	— about Britain
	Point B (Support for Point B)	— about American colonies
BODY SECTION THREE Attitudes	**Whole Point** (contrast) **Point A** (Support for Point A)	— about Britain
	Point B (Support for Point B)	— about American colonies
CONCLUSION	**Findings** (based on entire body of essay)	

Consider the following questions in terms of the Sugar and Currency Acts, the Stamp Act and Declaratory Act, the Townshend Acts, the Tea Act, the Coercive Acts, and the Quebec Act. Where appropriate, group pieces of legislation passed at approximately the same time.

1. What were the economic conditions in both Britain and the American colonies that influenced British efforts to raise revenue in the American colonies? . . . that influenced American resistance to such efforts? . . . that influenced the economic tactics Americans used in resisting the economic aspects of British legislation? How successful were the American campaigns against the economic aspects of British legislation? (Consider Figure 2 as well as material in Chapter 5.)

2. How did economic conditions help or hinder American use of nonimportation agreements and nonconsumption campaigns in its economic war?

3. How did unity or disunity among American socioeconomic classes affect the colonies' ability to use economic tactics effectively to resist British customs and taxation legislation?

4. How were property rights tied to liberty in the minds of American colonists? Did this linkage become more important or less important over the eleven years in question? How did it affect the economic tactics used by the colonists and the success of those tactics? Did American fear that the British were engaged in a plot to oppress them grow or decline over the eleven years? How was the East India Company related to America's linkage of liberty and property rights? The Quebec Act? The stationing of British troops in Boston in 1768? South Carolina's demonstrations protesting the Stamp Act in 1765 and 1766?

5. With respect to Parliament's right to tax and legislate for the colonies, what was the original philosophical principle under which the British operated in the early 1760s concerning Parliament's right to tax and legislate for the colonies? Did the British change this principle during the years from 1763 to 1775? When, why, and how did they change their position regarding their original principle? Did any prime minister of the period indicate that he thought the philosophy should be modified or that he believed the principle was flawed in any way?

6. What was the American view of Parliament's right to tax the colonists and control American trade in 1763? What was the American view concerning the colonists' duty to submit to the authority of Parliament and the crown in the early 1760s? Did Americans alter their views concerning either of these points over the period from 1763 to 1775? When? Why? How?

7. What was the philosophy of the "Real Whigs"? What were its basic principles and attitudes? When and how did it influence American thinking?

8. What did the pamphlets of Otis suggest about the static or evolving nature of American attitudes about the economic relationship between the colonies and Parliament? How did the ideas of the "Real Whigs" fare during the calm that followed the Boston Massacre between 1770 and 1772?

9. What kinds of economic tactics did Americans use to protest British economic policies that affected the colonies? Were any of the British responses to American resistance economic in nature? Which? In what way?

10. Did the British use any economic tactics to enforce their policies or to force Americans to accept British views? To punish Americans for refusing to submit to British authority? Which, if any, British economic tactics succeeded? How? To what degree? For how long?

11. What would make the British unwilling to drop the tax on tea when they repealed other Townshend duties? What made tea different form other products that could be taxed to raise revenues? Were the British smart in choosing tea as the one product to continue taxing? Was it any more or less difficult for Americans to participate in nonimportation and nonconsumption agreements with tea as the product to be boycotted?

12. What made Americans so resistant to the Tea Act of 1773? How would enforcement of the act affect the price of tea? What effect did the Quebec Act and the Coercive Acts have on the American theory that the British had a plot to oppress them?

Notice that in preparing to produce the working draft of the essay on the subject assigned, you have actually prepared for dozens of objective questions and for several essay questions.

IDEAS AND DETAILS

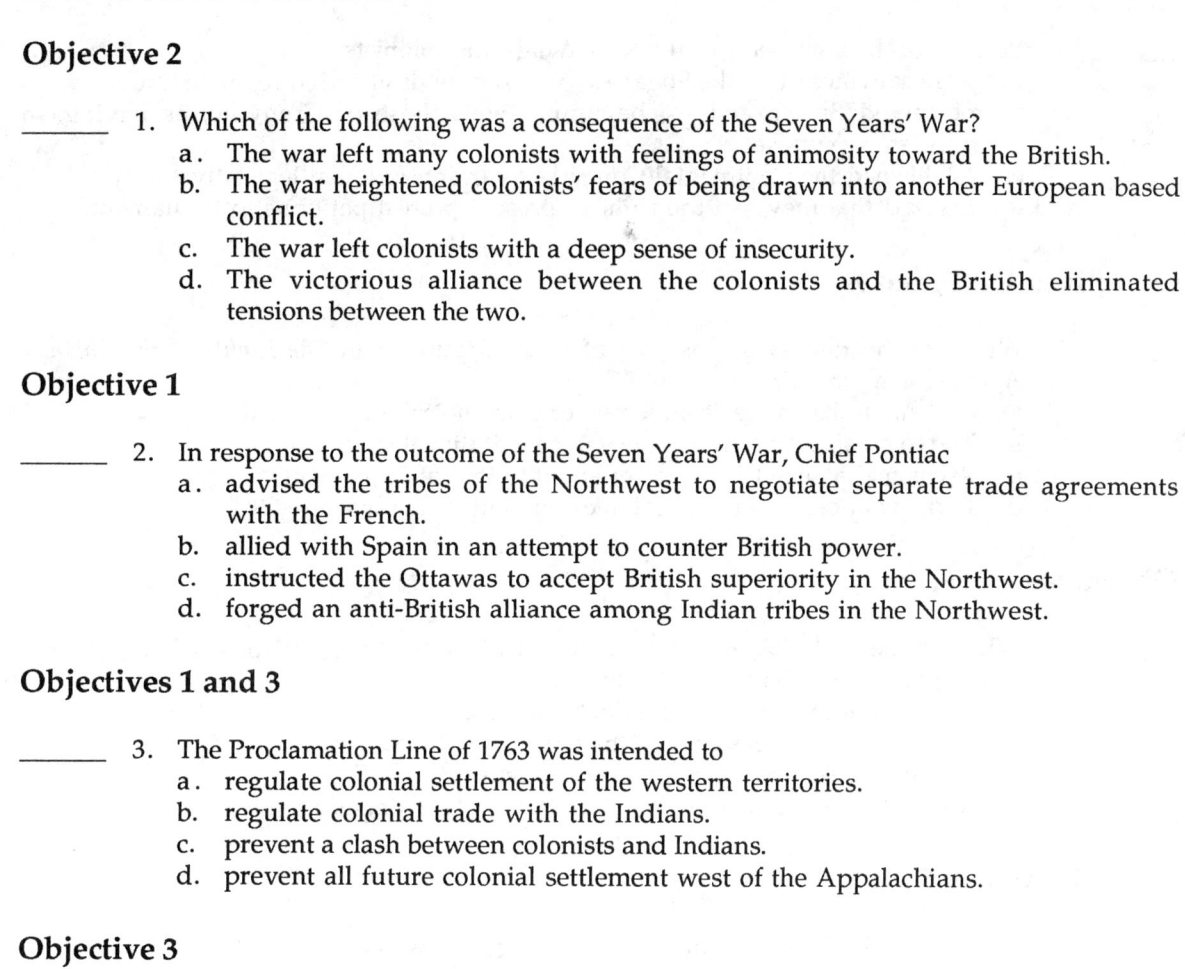

Objective 2

_____ 1. Which of the following was a consequence of the Seven Years' War?
   a. The war left many colonists with feelings of animosity toward the British.
   b. The war heightened colonists' fears of being drawn into another European based conflict.
   c. The war left colonists with a deep sense of insecurity.
   d. The victorious alliance between the colonists and the British eliminated tensions between the two.

Objective 1

_____ 2. In response to the outcome of the Seven Years' War, Chief Pontiac
   a. advised the tribes of the Northwest to negotiate separate trade agreements with the French.
   b. allied with Spain in an attempt to counter British power.
   c. instructed the Ottawas to accept British superiority in the Northwest.
   d. forged an anti-British alliance among Indian tribes in the Northwest.

Objectives 1 and 3

_____ 3. The Proclamation Line of 1763 was intended to
   a. regulate colonial settlement of the western territories.
   b. regulate colonial trade with the Indians.
   c. prevent a clash between colonists and Indians.
   d. prevent all future colonial settlement west of the Appalachians.

Objective 3

_____ 4. George Grenville's colonial policies were designed to
   a. solve Great Britain's financial crisis by raising revenue in the colonies.
   b. encourage the development of colonial manufacturing.
   c. gradually reduce the powers of the colonial assemblies by first attacking their power to tax.
   d. implement mercantilist policy by regulating colonial trade and commerce.

Objectives 4 and 5

_____ 5. In contrast to the British concept of representative government, Americans believed
   a. that each elected representative in a colonial assembly represented *all* people in the colony.
   b. in the one man, one vote concept.
   c. that an assembly could not be considered representative unless all people twenty-one years of age or over had the right to vote.
   d. that a member of the lower house of a colonial assembly represented the voters who had elected him.

Objectives 4, 5, and 9

_____ 6. Because of the arguments of the Real Whigs, the colonists
   a. were convinced that the Sugar Act was simply designed to regulate trade.
   b. perceived British actions, beginning with those of Grenville, as having an oppressive purpose.
   c. established the Continental Congress as an intercolonial legislative body.
   d. realized that they had the right to present protest petitions to Parliament.

Objectives 4, 5, 6, and 7

_____ 7. Which of the following was part of Otis's argument in *The Rights of the Colonies Asserted and Proved?*
   a. Parliament has no legislative power over the colonies.
   b. The colonists may refuse to obey unconstitutional laws.
   c. A colonial assembly has power equal to that of Parliament.
   d. Parliament cannot tax the colonies without their consent.

Objectives 4, 5, 6, and 7

_____ 8. Which of the following ideas was unacceptable to the Virginia House of Burgesses in its adoption of the Stamp Act Resolves?
   a. The American colonists are British subjects.
   b. The House of Burgesses has "the only" right to tax Virginians.
   c. Colonists enjoy the right of consent to taxation.
   d. The American colonists enjoy all of the rights of Englishmen.

Objectives 4 and 7

_____ 9. The Stamp Act ultimately could not be enforced because
   a. stamp distributors refused to perform their duties because of the widespread nature of anti-Stamp Act demonstrations.
   b. the protests of the Stamp Act Congress had created severe divisions within Parliament.
   c. Parliament realized that the tax was excessive.
   d. the tax fell heaviest on those least able to pay.

Objectives 4, 7, and 8

_____ 10. The Sons of Liberty was created to
   a. organize merchant resistance against British acts.
   b. provide a means by which leaders could control and channel the resistance movement.
   c. provide a means of distributing pamphlets throughout the colonies.
   d. organize liberty parades in major cities against the Stamp Act.

Objectives 4, 5, 6, and 7

_____ 11. Which of the following ideas was presented by John Dickinson and was unacceptable to Parliament?
   a. The colonies have the right of *virtual* representation in Parliament.
   b. English citizens have the right of consent to taxation.
   c. The colonists have the power to assess the intent of an act of Parliament.
   d. Parliament has the right to regulate trade.

Objectives 4 and 7

_____ 12. Public rituals during the revolutionary era were important because they
   a. helped refine the constitutional arguments against Parliament's actions.
   b. served as entertainment for the community.
   c. put the ideals of the revolution on a religious plane.
   d. helped to involve illiterate people in the resistance movement.

Objectives 4, 7, and 8

_____ 13. During the course of colonial resistance against the Townshend Acts, it became apparent that
   a. sentiment in favor of independence was growing.
   b. new divisions were emerging among the colonists.
   c. a new sense of equality was emerging among the colonists.
   d. Americans were beginning to question their loyalty to the king.

Objectives 4, 7, and 9

_____ 14. The response of Massachusetts towns to the Boston pamphlet of 1772 stating the rights and grievances of the colonists reveals that
   a. serious divisions existed between urban and rural colonists.
   b. most colonists favored independence in 1772.
   c. most interior Massachusetts towns agreed with ideas presented by the Boston patriots.
   d. the nonimportation movement was in serious trouble.

Objectives 4 and 9

_____ 15. Which of the following is true of the patriots' perception of the Coercive and Quebec Acts?
   a. The patriots realized that the Boston Tea Party had been a mistake and that these British measures were justified.
   b. The patriots saw the Coercive Acts as repressive but cared little about the Quebec Act because it applied to Canada.
   c. The patriots saw both measures as part of a deliberate British plot to destroy their rights.
   d. Because of divisions within their ranks, the patriots had no unified perception of these acts.

ESSAY QUESTIONS

Objective 2

1. Explain the effect of the French and Indian War on the way the colonists and the British perceived each other. What role did these perceptions play in the coming of the American Revolution?

Objective 5

2. Discuss the similarities and differences between the colonial and the British concepts of representative government.

Objectives 4, 5, 6, and 7

3. Explain the constitutional arguments presented by James Otis against the Sugar and Stamp Acts. How and why had these arguments changed by the time the Tea Act was passed in 1773?

Objectives 4, 5, 6, 7, and 8

4. Discuss the role of pamphlets and crowd action in the development and spread of the colonial resistance movement.

Figure 5-2

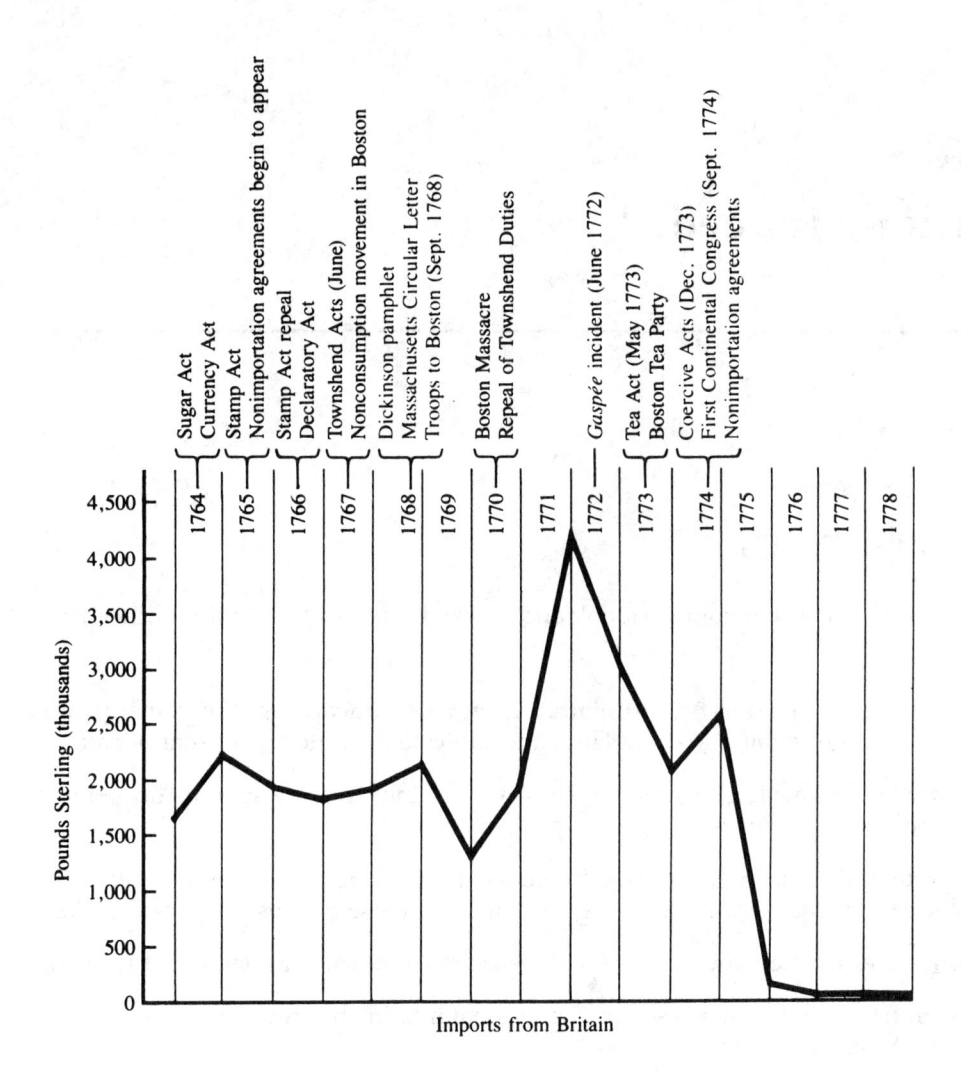

Events (left to right):
- 1764: Sugar Act; Currency Act
- 1765: Stamp Act; Nonimportation agreements begin to appear
- 1766: Stamp Act repeal; Declaratory Act
- 1767: Townshend Acts (June); Nonconsumption movement in Boston
- 1768: Dickinson pamphlet; Massachusetts Circular Letter; Troops to Boston (Sept. 1768)
- 1770: Boston Massacre; Repeal of Townshend Duties
- 1772: *Gaspée* incident (June 1772)
- 1773: Tea Act (May 1773); Boston Tea Party
- 1774: Coercive Acts (Dec. 1773); First Continental Congress (Sept. 1774); Nonimportation agreements

Y-axis: Pounds Sterling (thousands), 0 to 4,500

X-axis: Imports from Britain (1764–1778)

CHAPTER 6
A Revolution, Indeed, 1775–1783

LEARNING OBJECTIVES

After you have studied Chapter 6 in your textbook and worked through this study guide chapter, you should be able to:

1. Explain the debate at the First Continental Congress concerning the constitutional relationship between the colonies and England, and indicate the outcome of that debate.

2. Examine the process and methods by which the resistance movement was transformed into a coalition in favor of independence.

3. Discuss the reaction of African-Americans, Indians, and loyalists to the Revolutionary War, and explain the factors that limited the potential threat of these groups to the revolution.

4. Discuss the impact of the Revolutionary War on African-Americans, Indians, and loyalists.

5. Examine the strengths and weaknesses of the combatants in the Revolutionary War, and explain why the Americans were victorious.

6. Examine British strategy during the course of the Revolutionary War, and, through an examination of the northern and southern campaigns, explain how well it worked.

7. Examine American strategy during the course of the Revolutionary War, and, through an examination of the northern and southern campaigns, explain how well it worked.

8. Explain the process by which Americans gained international recognition, and assess the significance of that accomplishment.

9. Discuss the negotiations that led to the Treaty of Paris, and explain the significance of the treaty's provisions.

THEMATIC GUIDE

In Chapter 6, we consider the tasks the American patriots had to accomplish in order to achieve victory in the Revolutionary War. The first section, "Government by Congress and Committee," concerns the ideological and political task of transforming the resistance movement into a coalition supporting independence. Several factors made achievement of this task possible.

1. The process by which delegates were elected to the First Continental Congress
2. The presence of respected political figures at the Congress
3. The ability of the Congress to allow debate among divergent interest groups in the formulation of a compromise policy
4. The election of committees of observation and inspection at the local level as a means by which to enforce the Continental Association
5. The emergence of popularly elected provincial congresses to take over the reins of colonial government

The interaction of these factors leads to the conclusion that "independence was being won at the local level." Such an occurrence made American victory not only possible but likely.

Transforming the resistance movement into a coalition supporting independence also involved defeating potential internal enemies. This is the subject of the next section, "Choosing Sides: Loyalists, African-Americans, and Indians." Patriot policies, built on a broad popular base, were effective in isolating the loyalist minority and in defusing them as a potential threat. Moreover, although slaves were drawn to the British side as the side that could offer them freedom, African-Americans never became a real threat because (l) blacks did not rally to the British side as much as expected and (2) southern patriots were successful in manipulating white fears concerning a slave conspiracy. A lack of unity prevented American Indians from becoming a threat to the resistance.

In the section "War Begins," we see how the political and ideological tasks confronting the patriots converged. The British frame of reference toward the war becomes clear through the context of the early skirmishes at Lexington and Concord. At this time, the Second Continental Congress assumed responsibility for organizing the American war effort and selected George Washington as commander of the Continental Army. The discussion of Washington's background, beliefs, and war strategy (briefly outlined in the introductory vignette) suggests that his selection was an additional reason for eventual American victory.

As both sides prepared to deal with the military tasks of the war, the ideological war continued to rage. Decisive American victory in this realm was largely due to the efforts of Thomas Paine and Thomas Jefferson. These men so eloquently defined the American cause that they established principles that aided the war effort and served as a solid base on which the new republic was founded.

In the last two sections of the chapter, the military task of defeating the British takes center stage. The discussion of the northern and southern campaigns shows the importance of these factors in the patriot victory.

1. The false assumptions on which the British based their strategy
2. The battlefield errors of the British
3. The almost unlimited reservoir of man and woman power available to the American side
4. Washington's strategy of avoiding decisive losses
5. American perseverance and resourcefulness
6. American policies that effectively swayed the populace to the patriots' side
7. the Franco-American alliance of 1778

The chapter ends with a discussion of the Battle of Yorktown, the final skirmishes of the war, the impact of the war on the Indians, and the Treaty of Paris.

BUILDING VOCABULARY

Listed below are important words and terms that you need to know to get the most out of Chapter 6. They are listed in the order in which they occur in the chapter. After carefully looking through the list, refer to a dictionary and jot down the definition of words that you do not know or of which you are unsure.

compensate

disburse

consensus

coercion

prowess

extralegal

explicit

bona fide

de facto

virtuous

dissipation

dissident

malign

recant

ostracize

concurrent

cabal

anarchy

pseudonym

divergent

apathy

heinous

futile

foment

constitute

overt

avert

diehard

enmity

formidable

vanguard

contingent

mercenary

unimpeachable

inexorably

strident

exploit

conduce

desecrate

maraud

ponderous

metaphor

rendezvous

debilitate

dawdle

avenge

covertly

pacification

guerrilla

entity

IDENTIFICATION AND SIGNIFICANCE

After studying Chapter 6 of *A People and a Nation*, you should be able to identify fully *and* explain the historical significance of each item listed below.

1. Identify each item in the space provided. Give an explanation or description of the item. Answer the questions *who, what, where,* and *when.*

2. Explain the historical significance of each item in the space provided. Establish the historical context in which the item exists. Establish the item as the result of or as the cause of other factors existing in the society under study. Answer this question: *What were the political, social, economic, and/or cultural consequences of this item?*

the Committee to Aid the Black Poor

    Identification

    Significance

the First Continental Congress

    Identification

    Significance

Richard Henry Lee

    Identification

    Significance

Joseph Galloway

    Identification

    Significance

the Declaration of Rights and Grievances

    Identification

    Significance

the Continental Association

    Identification

    Significance

committees of observation and inspection

    Identification

    Significance

Reverend John Agnew

    Identification

    Significance

provincial conventions

    Identification

    Significance

Governor Josiah Martin

    Identification

    Significance

Daniel Leonard (a.k.a. Massachusettensis)

    Identification

    Significance

loyalists

    Identification

    Significance

Thomas Jeremiah

    Identification

    Significance

the British West Indian colonies

    Identification

    Significance

Lord Dunmore's proclamation

    Identification

    Significance

John Stuart, Sir William Johnson, and Guy Johnson

    Identification

    Significance

Lord Dunmore's War

    Identification

    Significance

Chief Dragging Canoe

    Identification

    Significance

William Dawes, Paul Revere, and Dr. Samuel Prescott

    Identification

    Significance

battles of Lexington and Concord

    Identification

    Significance

siege of Boston

    Identification

    Significance

Battle of Breed's (Bunker) Hill

    Identification

    Significance

Lord North and Lord George Germain

    Identification

    Significance

the Second Continental Congress

    Identification

    Significance

George Washington

    Identification

    Significance

Sir William Howe

    Identification

    Significance

Common Sense

    Identification

    Significance

Thomas Jefferson

    Identification

    Significance

the Declaration of Independence

    Identification

    Significance

New York campaign

    Identification

    Significance

New Jersey campaign

    Identification

    Significance

The Crisis

    Identification

    Significance

the battles of Trenton and Princeton

    Identification

    Significance

the Continental Army vs. the militia

    Identification

    Significance

esprit de corps among officers of the Continental Army

    Identification

    Significance

Benedict Arnold

    Identification

    Significance

Howe's Philadelphia campaign

    Identification

    Significance

the battles of Brandywine Creek and Germantown

    Identification

    Significance

Burgoyne's New York campaign

    Identification

    Significance

the Battle of Saratoga

    Identification

    Significance

the Battle of Oriskany

> Identification

> Significance

Joseph and Mary Brant

> Identification

> Significance

the retaliatory expedition of General John Sullivan

> Identification

> Significance

Benjamin Franklin

> Identification

> Significance

the Franco-American alliance

> Identification

> Significance

Sir Henry Clinton

> Identification

> Significance

the fall of Charleston

    Identification

    Significance

the Battle of Camden

    Identification

    Significance

General Nathanael Greene

    Identification

    Significance

the battles of King's Mountain, Cowpens, and Guilford Court House

    Identification

    Significance

the Battle of Yorktown

    Identification

    Significance

the Treaty of Paris

    Identification

    Significance

Chapter 6—A Revolution, Indeed, 1775–1783

ORGANIZING INFORMATION

Use the following table to compile and organize information pertaining to Revolutionary War battles and military campaigns mentioned in the textbook. More detailed information on these and other battles may be found in many of the books mentioned in the bibliography at the end of Chapter 6, especially those dealing with the military aspects of the war.

In the "Outcome" column, use A to designate an American victory, B to designate a British victory, and D to designate a draw.

Revolutionary War Battles/Campaigns

Battle	Date	Outcome	Consequences
Lexington			
Concord			
siege of Boston			
Breed's (Bunker) Hill			
Fort Ticonderoga			
patriots' Canadian campaign			
Washington's New York campaign			
Trenton			
Princeton			

Battle	Date	Outcome	Consequences
Howe's Philadelphia campaign			
Brandywine Creek			
Germantown			
Burgoyne's Northern campaign			
Fort Ticonderoga			
Bennington			
Saratoga			
Oriskany			
Charleston			
Camden			
King's Mountain			
Cowpens			
Guilford Court House			
Yorktown			

Copyright © Houghton Mifflin Company. All rights reserved.

EVALUATING AND USING INFORMATION

Some very famous documents are key examples of primary sources that historians have used to trace the development of American thought and character. One such document is the Declaration of Independence, which is referred to in Chapter 6 of your textbook. "The chief long-term importance" of the Declaration of Independence, say the authors, "lay ... in the ringing statements of principle that have served ever since as the ideal to which Americans aspire." In this exercise, you are to analyze the Declaration carefully to come to a full understanding of that assertion.

Use the following indications of the major divisions of the argument set forth in the Declaration of Independence (pages 00–00 in the appendix of your textbook) and the questions about those divisions as your guide in making your analysis. (Several questions in any set may be getting at the same point, so feel free to make one answer serve as the response to several questions whenever doing so is appropriate.)

Begin by reading the entire Declaration of Independence to get a general sense of what it says.

Section 1: The Subject and Purpose

Reread the first section of the declaration ("When . . . to the separation."). Review sections of Chapter 5 and 6 to determine the events that made up the military and political realities in the world when the declaration was written.

A. What behavior does the declaration claim people have a right to expect from the parties in a relationship between politically linked countries when one party wants to end the relationship?

B. What situation analogous to a divorce in a marriage or a breakup of a business partnership is the whole subject of the whole declaration? To which two politically linked countries do readers have to assume the declaration refers?

C. To which specific people or peoples is the declaration apparently addressed? Which people do political and military realities suggest had better be given an acceptable explanation of the rebels' reasons for seeking a dissolution of the "bonds" that have tied them to Great Britain? Who is the colonies themselves would it be desirable to convince of the legitimacy of those reasons? What major powers of the time have monarchies? Which are colonial powers? Which are friends of Britain? Which are enemies?

D. Based on your answers to questions A–C, what is the real and whole purpose of the Declaration of Independence?

Section 2: The Social and Political Assumptions

Reread the second section of the declaration ("We hold these truths . . . for their future security."). Look up the terms *assumption* and *value judgment* in one or more good dictionaries before you answer the following questions. Review the discussion of *frames of reference* in the introduction to this study guide.

A. To whom does the pronoun *we* refer? Which part of the American population is responsible for the declaration? Does the pronoun *we* embrace anyone else?

B. What does evidence about the frames of reference of those responsible for the declaration—apart from the declaration itself—suggest is meant by the words "all men are created equal"?

C. What does "endowed by their Creator with certain inalienable rights" mean? What rights do those who are issuing the declaration assume to be the birthrights of the men who are "created equal"? Does the phrasing suggest that they assume that having these rights is part of the definition of *living human being*? Of a particular kind of living human being? Does the phrasing suggest that one cannot be human (or a member of a particular group of human beings) without having the rights mentioned? What would a man of Thomas Jefferson's background and known attitudes be likely to mean by the term *Creator*?

D. What is the assumption of those issuing the declaration about each of the following subjects?
   1. The reason that governments exist
   2. Who gives a legitimate government its power
   3. When and where—if ever—rebellion is justified
   4. The willingness of people to engage in rebellion and the seriousness and duration of abuses of power before people should resort to rebellion
   5. Whether rebellion is ever the duty of a good citizen

E. What is the essential relationship between a legitimate government and those governed? Who are the principals in the relationships, and what is the responsibility of each principal? (Base your answers to these three questions on your responses to questions A–D.)

F. How do the assumptions of those responsible for issuing the declaration reflect Real Whig thinking? The views of Thomas Paine? Is it likely that the leaders of Britain, France, and Spain share most of these assumptions? Why? Why not? Are they really self-evident (in the category of "everybody knows that")?

G. Does the phrasing in this section of the document make it obvious that the truth of the ideas cannot be proved, that they differ from scientific conclusions? What is the use of listing assumptions?

Section 3: The Accusations

Reread the third section of the declaration ("Such has been . . . destruction of all ages, sexes, and conditions.") Review sections of Chapters 5 and 6 to determine which of the charges that the declaration calls *facts* you can be sure are factual or refer to facts (if you need to, review the discussion of what the term *fact* means on pages 00–00 in the introduction to this study guide.)

A. What does the declaration offer as the purpose of the British actions or types of actions listed in the charges against King George III and his government? How does the purpose given square with the idea that the British had a plot to oppress them that American colonists increasingly saw and feared between 1760 and 1775? How is it related to Real Whig philosophy?

B. For each paragraph in the section beginning with the pronoun *he*, try to cite more than one specific action on the part of the British government that illustrates the behavior of which the document is accusing the British government in the person of King George III. Would the leaders of major powers other than Britain consider many of the actions attributed to George III and his agents inappropriate? Reprehensible?

C. Would making the list of charges any more or less specific make the declaration more effective as a piece of persuasive writing than it is? Into what four to six categories can you divide the abuses with which those issuing the declaration are accusing King George III and his government? Would simplifying the list of abuses by organizing it into clearly labeled categories (military, political, commercial, etc.) make the document any easier to understand? Any more effective?

D. Does any characteristic of the declaration's American audience justify the writer's use of a shotgun (rather than selective) approach? Are the declaration's generalizations about British actions likely to bring to the minds of American readers specific instances? What part of the American public do those issuing the declaration need to convince? Are many of the charges likely to persuade such people that rebellion is justified? Would such people be likely to find all of the charges persuasive? Is it likely that all of such people would find at least one of the charges persuasive? Do the charges suggest any concern for the opinion of Indians, African-Americans, or American women or any flagrant disregard of the opinion of any of those three groups?

E. What is the psychological effect of the repetition of the personal pronoun *he* throughout the accusations section of the declaration? Are all of the actions cited in the charges attributable to King George III personally? Is the use of the personal pronoun literally appropriate? Is it appropriate as a propaganda device? What major shift in attitude toward the monarchy (as opposed to Parliament and the prime ministers) does the focus on King George III suggest those responsible for the declaration assume has occurred among the document's potential American readers? Is writing the declaration as though it is obvious that such a major shift has occurred factually appropriate? Is doing so useful as a propaganda device? What propaganda purpose is served?

F. If a reader goes along with the assumptions about the contractual relationship between the government and those who are governed and the assumption that it is the duty of citizens to rebel when the government fails to live up to its contractual responsibilities (Section 2 and your response to II.D.3), what must a reader who believes the accusations presented in Section 3 to be credible begin to realize as he or she finishes reading Section 3? (If the assumptions are valid and the accusations are true, then what?)

Section 4: Evidence of the Sincerity of Americans' Reluctance to Rebel

Reread the fourth section of the declaration ("In every stage . . . in peace friends.") Review sections of Chapters 5 and 6 to find specific actions taken by the colonists between 1760 and July of 1776 that represent their application of the methods of redress short of rebellion and separation referred to in the declaration.

A. What two methods do those issuing the declaration say they have employed to get King George III and his governments to fulfill their contractual obligations to the people in the American colonies whom they govern?

B. What, according to those issuing the declaration, has been the response of King George III and his governments to each of the two methods the American colonies have used to persuade the British government to live up to its side of the contract between those governing and those being governed?

C. If the Americans have used all reasonable means to get the British government to live up to its obligations to them and the government's abuse of power has continued for at least sixteen years, what is the only avenue left to good and dutiful citizens in the American colonies? (Look again at your response to II.D.5 above.) If the assumptions are valid, the charges are credible, and the colonists have made every effort to solve the problem without resorting to rebellion, then what?

Section 5: The Declaration

Reread the fifth section of the declaration ("We, therefore, . . . our sacred honor.")

A. What name have those issuing the declaration given to the from-this-point-on *former* American colonies of Great Britain?

B. How do those issuing the declaration indicate they are acting in accord with the assumption about the source of a government's power offered in Section 2? (Look at your response to II.D.2 above.)

C. Has the body of the declaration offered convincing support for the assertion in Section 5 that the United colonies "of right ought to be" absolved from allegiance to Britain and recognized as having all the basic powers of an independent country? Is there any indication about whether the now-former colonies think of themselves as a collection of nations or as one nation? Have Thomas Jefferson and his fellow representatives made their case?

D. Why does the actual declaration of independence come at the end of the document? Why isn't that declaration a thesis statement appearing in the introduction? If the argument were organized deductively (with the thesis preceding the supporting material) rather than inductively as it is in fact organized (the thesis following the supporting material), how would most readers whom the issuers most need to convince be likely to react?

E. To what degree is the pledge in the document's final sentence mere rhetoric and to what degree is it a reflection of a realistic appraisal of the possibilities? Is there any evidence that the participation in the rebellion cost any of the leaders' lives, fortunes, or honor?

Overview

A. List the phrases in the Declaration of Independence that you think most qualify as "ringing" statements.

B. Documents like the Declaration of Independence and "The Gettysburg Address" reflect the heart of American political philosophy, whereas a document like the Constitution reflects its brain. List several values that you see expressed or implied in the Declaration of Independence that you think represent cultural values that unite Americans and that perhaps lie behind the thinking that would later infuse the Constitution, values that are part of the American frame of reference and in whose defense virtually all Americans would make major sacrifices.

IDEAS AND DETAILS

Objective 7

1. As commander-in-chief of the Continental Army, George Washington's primary goal was to
   a. avoid decisive military losses.
   b. win a quick and decisive military victory against British forces.
   c. gain control of the urban areas.
   d. secure financial aid from foreign sources.

Objectives 1 and 2

____ 2. Measures adopted by the First Continental Congress met with widespread support because
   a. the congressional delegates took no action without first polling the populace.
   b. many colonists, through widespread open meetings, had already pledged to support the Congress's decisions.
   c. most colonists favored military action in the face of British tyranny.
   d. the measures were ambiguous and indecisive.

Objective 2

____ 3. The process by which members of the committees of observation and inspection were chosen
   a. guaranteed that the committees would have a broad popular base of support.
   b. guaranteed the election of experienced politicians.
   c. demonstrated a commitment to mass democracy.
   d. revealed divisions that could undermine the resistance movement.

Objective 3

____ 4. The question most slaves faced during the Revolutionary War was
   a. How can we best serve our masters?
   b. How can we best serve the patriot cause?
   c. Which side is morally right?
   d. Which side offers us the best chance of becoming free?

Objective 5

____ 5. Connecticut was more likely to support the revolution than was South Carolina because
   a. Connecticut had a much higher percentage of tenant farmers than did South Carolina.
   b. the Anglican church was stronger in Connecticut than in South Carolina.
   c. the Connecticut population had a much lower percentage of blacks than did the South Carolina population.
   d. there were many more Scotch-Irish in Connecticut than in South Carolina.

Objective 3

____ 6. Occasionally frontier militiamen refused to report for duty on the seaboard because they
   a. did not have adequate supplies of guns and ammunition.
   b. were reluctant to embark on such a long and treacherous journey.
   c. had no means of transportation.
   d. were afraid their absence would invite an Indian attack.

Objectives 5 and 6

_____ 7. With regard to the Revolutionary War, the British assumed that they could
   a. win the conflict by concentrating their forces in the rural areas.
   b. use the same strategy that they used in European wars.
   c. win with a small expeditionary force.
   d. wear the American forces down through a long, protracted struggle.

Objective 2

_____ 8. The pamphlet *Common Sense*
   a. argued that America would be stronger if freed from British control.
   b. argued that the colonists owed allegiance to George III.
   c. restated traditional ideas about government.
   d. was a reasoned argument in favor of reconciliation with Great Britain.

Objective 2

_____ 9. The long-term significance of the Declaration of Independence lies in its
   a. charge that the king was responsible for slavery in the colonies.
   b. charge that Parliament used excessive force in the colonies.
   c. statements of principle.
   d. commitment to strong central government.

Objectives 6 and 7

_____ 10. Which of the following is true concerning the battle for New York City?
   a. The British forces were defeated because of inadequate supplies.
   b. Washington had time to move his troops from Boston to New York because Sir William Howe delayed his attack of the city.
   c. Washington's defense was in accordance with the basic rules of military strategy.
   d. Washington's defense of the city was masterful.

Objective 5

_____ 11. Which of the following was generally true of the officers of the Continental Army?
   a. Most refused to serve for more than six months.
   b. Their primary sense of devotion was to their respective states.
   c. There was little sense of camaraderie among them.
   d. They developed an intense commitment to the patriot cause.

Objectives 4 and 6

_____ 12. The Battle of Oriskany was important because it
   a. demonstrated that loyalists were a serious threat to the American cause.
   b. resulted in British control of the Mohawk River valley.
   c. split the Iroquois Confederacy into pro-British and pro-American factions.
   d. was the first decisive American victory in the war.

Objective 8

_____ 13. France decided to actively enter the American Revolution on the American side for which of the following reasons?
   a. The establishment of a strong and independent United States was in France's best interests.
   b. France wanted to defend its Canadian colonies.
   c. The French government fully supported the republican ideals on which the American Revolution was based.
   d. The French wanted to avenge their defeat in the Seven Years' War.

Objectives 5 and 7

_____ 14. General Nathanael Greene's policies in South Carolina and Georgia included
   a. an offer of pardons to those who had fought for the British if they would join the patriot militia.
   b. destabilization of civilian governments.
   c. retaliatory strikes against the southern Indians.
   d. the seizure of loyalist property.

Objective 9

_____ 15. In the negotiations that led to the Treaty of Paris, American negotiators
   a. demonstrated that they were naive and unskilled in the art of diplomacy.
   b. relied on the French in formulating their diplomatic strategy.
   c. were so weary of the conflict that they settled for much less than they could have gotten.
   d. wisely chose to bargain separately with the British.

ESSAY QUESTIONS

Objectives 1 and 2

1. Discuss the decisions made by the First Continental Congress concerning the Galloway Plan, the Declaration of Rights and Grievances, and the Continental Association. In what way were these decisions important? What did these decisions imply about the relationship between the colonies and England?

Objective 3

2. Assess the nature and seriousness of the threat posed by loyalists, African-Americans, and Indians to the patriot war effort.

Objective 2

3. What ideas were expressed by Thomas Paine in *Common Sense* and by Thomas Jefferson in the Declaration of Independence? Assess the importance of these ideas to the patriot resistance movement.

Objectives 5 and 7

4. Explain the importance of the strategies employed by General Nathanael Green.

Objectives 5 and 8

5. Evaluate the role of the French in the Revolutionary War.

Objectives 5, 6, 7, and 8

6. Discuss the factors that led to American victory in the Revolutionary War.

CHAPTER 7
Forging a National Republic, 1776–1789

LEARNING OBJECTIVES

After you have studied Chapter 7 in your textbook and worked through this study guide chapter, you should be able to:

1. Examine the varieties of republicanism that emerged in the new American republic.

2. Examine the impact of revolutionary ideology on
   a. literature and the fine arts.
   b. educational practice.
   c. gender roles and the family.
   d. African-Americans.
   e. the development of racist theory.

3. Discuss the growth of the free African-American population and the reaction of black Americans to life in a racist society.

4. Examine the evolution of constitutional theories of government at the state level during the republic's early years.

5. Discuss the problems faced by the Confederation Congress, and assess its handling of those problems.

6. Examine the forces that led to the calling of the Constitutional Convention.

7. Discuss the characteristics of the delegates to the Constitutional Convention, and examine the role played by James Madison.

8. Discuss the major disagreements that emerged in the drafting of the Constitution, and indicate how those disagreements were resolved.

9. Explain the basic provisions and the underlying principles of the Constitution of the United States.

10. Discuss the debate over ratification of the Constitution, and explain why the Federalist forces prevailed.

THEMATIC GUIDE

After the Revolutionary War, the Americans began shaping their society to the ideals and principles of the Revolution itself. These ideals were intellectual notions, not tangible realities. They provided a visionary basis for a more nearly perfect society, but they did not automatically make such a society a reality. Therefore, the ideals had to be defined, and such definitions are born out of the frame of reference—the perceptions and prejudices—of a people existing at a particular historical time and place. In Chapter 7, we focus on the theme of ideal versus reality and examine the defining and shaping process that occurred in postrevolutionary American society.

The first section, "Creating a Virtuous Republic," presents the ideal of building a republican society and the reality of disagreement over how to define republicanism; the ideal of a "virtuous" republic and the reality of disagreement over what virtue means; the ideal of literature, painting, and architecture instilling virtue and the reality that some perceive those arts as luxuries to be avoided. Then, after dealing with educational reform, we turn to the role of women in postrevolutionary America and the interaction of the ideal of equality with the reality of sexism. From this interaction there emerged a perception that denied women a legitimate power-sharing role and stressed the differences between men and women. According to this view, men and women contributed to a republican society equally but in different ways. Moreover, it was through this perception that Americans were able "to resolve the conflict between the two most influential strands of republican thought." (See page 187 in the textbook.)

The theme of ideal versus reality recurs in the next section, "Emancipation and the Growth of Racism." Concurrent with the abolition of slavery and the dramatic growth of the free black population in the North, economic, political, and societal realities were imposed on the revolutionary ideal of equality. Consequently, a "coherent racist theory" developed in the United States, with race replacing enslavement as the determinant of the status of blacks.

In designing republican governments, the ideal called for written constitutions designed to prevent tyranny by properly distributing and limiting governmental power. At first it seemed that the ideal could be achieved by concentrating power in the hands of the legislature, but this led to the reality of weak political units. From this reality new ideas emerged, such as the concept of a balance of power among three coequal branches of government.

In the Confederation Congress, the ideal of weak central government was juxtaposed against the reality of monetary and diplomatic problems. The interaction of the two produced political impotence against which even the one "accomplishment" of the Congress, the Northwest Ordinances, must be judged.

This impotence, further emphasized symbolically by Shays's Rebellion, led to the Constitutional Convention and the writing of the Constitution. A new realism, evident in the debates among the delegates and in the compromises they reached, was present at this convention. But idealism was not dead. The delegates retained the ideal of the sovereignty of the people and embodied that ideal in the opening words of the document they wrote: "We the people of the United States." They also accepted new ideals that had emerged from experience, and these became the "key to the Constitution." However, a new realism tempered these ideals, and that, too, is apparent in the first sentence of the Constitution: "in order to form a more perfect union." This phrase suggests the delegates' realization that they had *not* created the perfect society—a realism also seen in the ratification debates.

BUILDING VOCABULARY

Listed below are important words and terms that you need to know to get the most out of Chapter 7. They are listed in the order in which they occur in the chapter. After carefully looking through the list, refer to a dictionary and jot down the definition of words that you do not know or of which you are unsure.

insurgent

fiscal

ominous

discern

polity

inculcate

concur

perpetual

homogeneous

egalitarian

frugality

lurid

reprehensible

milestone

fervent

foment

spinster

irony

abolition

emancipation

benevolence

coherent

debased

congenitally

promiscuous

specter

subjugation

antagonist

tangible

permeate

maritime

sovereignty

portent

decry

filial

impasse

paradox

impotence

exigency

invigorate

proportional

expedient

proviso

inextricable

euphemism

enumerate

circumscribe

preclude

vigilance

avert

promulgate

habeas corpus

backlash

vicissitudes

IDENTIFICATION AND SIGNIFICANCE

After studying Chapter 7 of *A People and a Nation*, you should be able to identify fully *and* explain the historical significance of each item listed below.

1. Identify each item in the space provided. Give an explanation or description of the item. Answer the questions *who, what, where,* and *when.*

2. Explain the historical significance of each item in the space provided. Establish the historical context in which the item exists. Establish the item as the result of or as the cause of other factors existing in the society under study. Answer this question: *What were the political, social, economic, and/or cultural consequences of this item?*

Shays's Rebellion

    Identification

    Significance

self-sacrificing ("Adamsian") republicanism

    Identification

    Significance

economic ("Hamiltonian") republicanism

    Identification

    Significance

egalitarian ("Painean") republicanism

    Identification

    Significance

The Power of Sympathy

    Identification

    Significance

The Contrast

    Identification

    Significance

Life of Washington

    Identification

    Significance

Gilbert Stuart, Charles Wilson Peale, and John Trumbull

    Identification

    Significance

Benjamin H. Latrobe

    Identification

    Significance

the Society of the Cincinnati

>Identification

>Significance

public elementary schools

>Identification

>Significance

Judith Sargent Murray

>Identification

>Significance

Abigail Adams

>Identification

>Significance

revolutionary ideology vs. slavery

>Identification

>Significance

growth of the free black population

>Identification

>Significance

the Brown Fellowship Society

    Identification

    Significance

the African Methodist Episcopal (AME) church

    Identification

    Significance

postrevolutionary racist theory

    Identification

    Significance

Benjamin Banneker

    Identification

    Significance

postrevolutionary state constitutions

    Identification

    Significance

the Articles of Confederation

    Identification

    Significance

Robert Morris

    Identification

    Significance

Articles 4 and 5 of the 1783 Treaty of Paris

    Identification

    Significance

the treaties of Fort Stanwix and Hopewell

    Identification

    Significance

Handsome Lake

    Identification

    Significance

the Northwest Ordinances

    Identification

    Significance

Little Turtle

    Identification

    Significance

the Battle of Fallen Timbers

    Identification

    Significance

the Treaty of Greenville

    Identification

    Significance

the Annapolis Convention

    Identification

    Significance

the Constitutional Convention

    Identification

    Significance

James Madison

    Identification

    Significance

"Vices of the Political System of the United States"

    Identification

    Significance

the principle of checks and balances

    Identification

    Significance

the Virginia Plan

    Identification

    Significance

the New Jersey Plan

    Identification

    Significance

the three-fifths compromise

    Identification

    Significance

the Constitution's slave-trade clause and fugitive-slave clause

    Identification

    Significance

the electoral college

    Identification

    Significance

the separation of powers

    Identification

    Significance

Federalists

    Identification

    Significance

Antifederalists

    Identification

    Significance

Letters of a Federal Farmer

    Identification

    Significance

The Federalist

    Identification

    Significance

EVALUATING AND USING INFORMATION

Examine the growing role of the Declaration of Independence as a source or early expression of values and assumptions that in the period between 1776 and 1789 (the period covered in Chapter 7) was uniting Americans of diverging political, social, and economic aims and contributing to the development of an identifiable American culture and character.

Use your analysis of the declaration (Evaluating and Using Information exercise for Chapter 6) and information about events, assertions, and documents found in Chapter 7 to evaluate the depth and nature of the declaration's influence.

Compile your evidence concerning the depth and nature of the influence by completing the chart headed "The Declaration of Independence as a Source of Unifying American Values." When you have finished your chart, answer the question about whether any softening of basic positions expressed in the Declaration of Independence were beginning to develop.

- In the first column, name an event or document in which an echo of the declaration's values or assumptions can be seen.

- In the second column, indicate the idea or assumption in the declaration that is being echoed.

- In the third column, indicate what in the event or document echoes the value or assumption expressed in the declaration.

- In the fourth column, indicate what specific action is being defended or what cause is being promoted and by whom it is being defended or promoted.

One entry has been made in the chart to illustrate what you are to do. Feel free to extend the chart as necessary.

Question About Any "Softening" of Positions Taken in the Declaration of Independence

Base your answer to this question on material in Chapter 7 of your textbook:

> Did any signs appear in the period from July 1776 through 1789 indicating that Americans had begun to recognize a need to soften or limit values or assumptions expressed in the Declaration of Independence because of dangers arising from their literal interpretation? List any instances you find in which people discovered that extreme language or ideals in the declaration needed to be modified for reasons of practicality or social reality.

The Declaration of Independence as a Source of Unifying American Values			
Event or Document	Idea or Assumption in the Declaration that is Being Echoed?	Specific Aspect of the Event that Echoes the Declaration?	Action or Cause Defended or Promoted in the Event? By Whom?
Shays' Rebellion (January 1787)	Duty of good citizen is to rebel when government abuses are long-term	Claim in address to Mass. government that rebelling is insurgents' duty, other means of redress having failed	Call for end to state policy of confiscating property for nonpayment of taxes Promoted by Daniel Shays' men

IDEAS AND DETAILS

Objective 1

_____ 1. Which of the following is a characteristic of "Adamsian" republicanism?
   a. It was based on the belief that republics should be large in size and diverse in population.
   b. Its adherents questioned the ability of the upper classes to speak for all people.
   c. It was based on the belief that individuals acting selfishly in their own best interest would benefit the nation.
   d. Its supporters held that in a republic individual interests should be subordinated to the good of the whole community.

Objective 2

_____ 2. Which of the following is true of the cherry tree story told by Mason Weems in his biography of George Washington?
   a. Having heard Washington tell the story in his 1792 reelection campaign, Weems assumed it to be true.
   b. Weems fabricated the story in an attempt to create a virtuous example for America's youth.
   c. Weems obtained the story while conducting extensive research on Washington's life.
   d. Weems originally used the story to discredit Alexander Hamilton, Washington's political rival.

Objective 2

_____ 3. Schooling for girls improved during the early republican period primarily because of the belief that
   a. girls had to be taught independence.
   b. girls should be prepared for jobs in the same way boys were prepared.
   c. men and women had equal intellectual abilities.
   d. would-be mothers should be properly educated in the values of republican society.

Objective 2

_____ 4. The fact that qualified women regularly voted in New Jersey in the 1780s and 1790s supports which of the following conclusions?
   a. Married women began to demand more of a voice in the making of laws.
   b. Most women actively pursued the right to vote in the early republican period.
   c. New ideas about the role of women in a republic had their greatest impact in the political arena.
   d. Some women believed they had a place in the political life of the state.

Objectives 1 and 2

_____ 5. Which of the following was true of the "ideal" republican woman during the early republican period?

a. She was free to pursue her own economic self-interest.
b. She was to pursue a public life as she aided the community.
c. She was to subordinate private interests to the good of the community.
d. She was to pursue higher education for the purpose of self-fulfillment.

Objective 3

_____ 6. The formation of the Brown Fellowship Society provides evidence that
   a. in some cases slaves worked covertly to organize abolitionist societies.
   b. free blacks often responded to life in a racist society by developing their own separate institutions.
   c. free northern blacks organized lobbying efforts to gain repeal of discriminatory laws.
   d. in the early republic some people worked to further the ideal of racial equality.

Objective 2

_____ 7. The new racist theories that developed in the postrevolutionary years
   a. emerged as a result of over ten thousand blacks having fought on the British side.
   b. were a reaction to the increasing number of slave rebellions.
   c. were an attempt to defend slavery against the revolutionary idea of equality.
   d. were an attempt to refute new scientific evidence proving blacks to be genetically equal to whites.

Objective 4

_____ 8. The first state constitutions
   a. broadened the base of government by extending the right to vote to more people.
   b. embodied the principle of checks and balances.
   c. seldom contained a written guarantee of rights.
   d. placed more power in the hands of the governor than in the legislature.

Objective 5

_____ 9. The Northwest Ordinance of 1787
   a. discouraged the future importation of slaves into the region.
   b. provided a means by which settlers could immediately apply for statehood.
   c. established the Anglican church as the favored church in the region.
   d. provided for the free distribution of land to settlers.

Objective 6

_____ 10. To many people the most frightening aspect of Shays's Rebellion was the fact that
   a. a small minority could overthrow the government of a state.
   b. poor whites and blacks had successfully forged an alliance.
   c. the rebels attempted to associate their struggle with the earlier struggle against the British.
   d. it represented a counterrevolution by the elite of Massachusetts.

Objective 7

_____ 11. James Madison is considered the most important delegate to the Constitutional Convention because
   a. he consistently argued in favor of limiting the size of the republic.
   b. he provided the delegates with a conceptual framework for the Constitution, based on his analysis of past confederacies and republics.
   c. he refused to compromise on the idea of proportional representation in the Senate.
   d. he consistently argued in favor of a written guarantee of the basic rights of the American people.

Objective 8

_____ 12. A breakdown at the Constitutional Convention over the issue of apportionment of representation in the Senate was prevented by the recommendation that
   a. states be equally represented in the Senate.
   b. senators be appointed by the state legislatures.
   c. a state's representation in the Senate be based on population.
   d. a state's two senators vote individually rather than as a unit.

Objective 9

_____ 13. Which of the following is considered to be the "key" to the Constitution?
   a. The three-fifths compromise
   b. The distribution of political authority among the three branches of government and between the state governments and the national government
   c. The inclusion of the concept of direct democracy at all levels of the new government
   d. The establishment of an elected judiciary

Objective 10

_____ 14. The Antifederalists
   a. believed that individual rights could best be protected at the state level.
   b. believed that the national government should be more powerful.
   c. were generally much younger than their opponents.
   d. were led by Thomas Jefferson.

Objective 10

_____ 15. Which of the following became the most important issue in the debate over ratification of the Constitution?
   a. The powers of the chief executive
   b. The absence of a bill of rights
   c. The extension of the vote to women
   d. The absence of any prohibitions on the powers of Congress

ESSAY QUESTIONS

Objectives 1 and 2

1. Discuss the similarities and differences between the notions concerning the "ideal" republican woman and those concerning the "ideal" republican man.

Objective 3

2. Identify the factors responsible for the dramatic growth of the free black population during the postrevolutionary years, and discuss the response of blacks to emancipation.

Objective 2

3. Examine the growth of racist theory in the late eighteenth century.

Objective 7

4. Discuss James Madison's role at the Constitutional Convention.

Objectives 8 and 9

5. Discuss the debate within the Constitutional Convention about the functions and structure of Congress, and explain the resolution of the disagreements that arose among the delegates on this issue.

CHAPTER 8
Politics and Society in the Early Republic, 1789–1800

LEARNING OBJECTIVES

After you have studied Chapter 8 in your textbook and worked through this study guide chapter, you should be able to:

1. Indicate the immediate problems faced by Congress in 1790, and explain its resolution of those problems.

2. Discuss the role of the Supreme Court from 1789 to 1800, and explain the significance of its decisions in *Ware* v. *Hylton, Hylton* v. *U.S.*, and *Chisholm* v. *Georgia*.

3. Discuss Hamilton's economic program, the opposition it aroused, and its fate in Congress.

4. Discuss the characteristics and the political, social, and economic beliefs of the Federalists and the Republicans, and explain the relationship between those beliefs and the approach of these political factions to
   a. Hamilton's economic program.
   b. the Whiskey Rebellion.
   c. the formation of Democratic-Republican societies.
   d. the Alien and Sedition Acts.
   e. the Kentucky and Virginia resolutions.

5. Examine the debate between the Federalists and the Republicans about major foreign policy issues between 1789 and 1801, and discuss the domestic impact of this debate.

6. Examine the issues in the presidential election of 1800, and explain the election's outcome.

7. Discuss the impact of westward expansion on blacks, women, and Indians.

8. Discuss the causes, characteristics, and consequences of the Second Great Awakening.

THEMATIC GUIDE

In 1790, as Americans faced the task of putting their new government into operation, they optimistically expected a future of prosperity, expansion, national unity, and independence from

Europe. In each of these areas, they experienced a measure of disappointment. Congress was able to handle the immediate problems facing the country, but as it tried to deal with the nation's financial problems, it faced the dilemma of defining the role of government in a republican society. Supporters of "self-sacrificing" republicanism, such as John Adams, and of "economic" republicanism, such as Alexander Hamilton, although seemingly at odds, became allies because of their shared belief in a strong central government. Besides, both groups were nationalist, believing that state interests and state power should be subordinated to national interests. George Washington, Alexander Hamilton, and John Adams, who were Federalists, accepted this definition of the role of government.

An opposition to this nationalist republican philosophy emerged under the leadership of James Madison and Thomas Jefferson. They took the view that the central government should have limited power, and they moved toward the democratic definition of republicanism. Believing that the elite could not speak for the masses, they opposed Hamilton's economic program and expressed a strict-constructionist view of the Constitution. Hamilton and Washington, in turn, advocated a broad interpretation of the Constitution.

The disagreement between the two groups over domestic policy soon spread to foreign policy, provoking more tension. Each group became convinced that the other was out to destroy the republic. Acting on this belief, the Federalists enacted the Alien and Sedition Acts to silence the Republicans. The Republicans responded with an extreme states' rights philosophy contained in the Kentucky and Virginia resolutions. In the midst of this disunity, the Federalists split over the republic's relations with France. This split and the reaction of the country to the Alien and Sedition Acts led to Republican triumph in the election of 1800.

During the same period, the nation experienced a dramatic migration of people into the area west of the Appalachians and, after 1795, into the Ohio country. The isolation of the settlements that emerged led to the creation of "new communities," the most meaningful of which was evangelical religion in the form of the Second Great Awakening. To some extent a continuation of the First Great Awakening, the revival movement democratized American religion by rejecting the doctrine of predestination. The chapter also explains the movement's impact on "established" state churches and on the role of women in American society. In addition, the Second Awakening is one of several factors that served to increase racial tensions. This, in turn, led to a solidifying of the institution of slavery in the South in the years after 1790.

BUILDING VOCABULARY

Listed below are important words and terms that you need to know to get the most out of Chapter 8. They are listed in the order in which they occur in the chapter. After carefully looking through the list, refer to a dictionary and jot down the definition of words that you do not know or of which you are unsure.

arduous

profane

disconcerted

presage

partisan

frugal

imbibe

preclude

mercantile

precocious

patronage

dubious

autonomy

cynicism

coalesce

compensate

disburse

infer

extralegal

subvert

vindicate

vanguard

perversion

privateering

foment

arbitration

lament

retort

impasse

sabotage

abrogate

reprobate

avarice

propaganda

states' rights

plurality

volatile

lament

congenial

evangelical

exhort

indelible

legacy

IDENTIFICATION AND SIGNIFICANCE

After studying Chapter 8 of *A People and a Nation*, you should be able to identify fully *and* explain the historical significance of each item listed below.

1. Identify each item in the space provided. Give an explanation or description of the item. Answer the questions *who, what, where,* and *when.*

2. Explain the historical significance of each item in the space provided. Establish the historical context in which the item exists. Establish the item as the result of or as the cause of other factors existing in the society under study. Answer this question: *What were the political, social, economic, and/or cultural consequences of this item?*

James Madison

    Identification

    Significance

the Revenue Act of 1789

    Identification

    Significance

the Bill of Rights

    Identification

    Significance

the Judiciary Act of 1789

    Identification

    Significance

Ware v. *Hylton* and *Hylton* v. *U.S.*

    Identification

    Significance

Chisholm v. *Georgia*

    Identification

    Significance

George Washington

    Identification

    Significance

Alexander Hamilton

    Identification

    Significance

Report on Public Credit

    Identification

    Significance

assumption of state debts

>Identification

>Significance

location of nation's capital

>Identification

>Significance

the Bank of the United States

>Identification

>Significance

strict constructionist vs. broad constructionist

>Identification

>Significance

Defense of the Constitutionality of the Bank

>Identification

>Significance

Report on Manufactures

>Identification

>Significance

the Whiskey Rebellion

    Identification

    Significance

Thomas Jefferson

    Identification

    Significance

Republicans

    Identification

    Significance

Federalists

    Identification

    Significance

the 1778 Treaty of Alliance with France

    Identification

    Significance

Citizen Edmond Genêt

    Identification

    Significance

Washington's Proclamation of Neutrality

    Identification

    Significance

Democratic-Republican societies

    Identification

    Significance

loyal opposition

    Identification

    Significance

the Jay Treaty

    Identification

    Significance

the doctrine of executive privilege

    Identification

    Significance

the Pinckney Treaty

    Identification

    Significance

Washington's Farewell Address

    Identification

    Significance

the presidential election of 1796

    Identification

    Significance

President John Adams

    Identification

    Significance

the XYZ Affair

    Identification

    Significance

the Quasi War with France

    Identification

    Significance

the Alien and Sedition Acts

    Identification

    Significance

Matthew Lyon

    Identification

    Significance

Virginia and Kentucky resolutions

    Identification

    Significance

the Convention of 1800

    Identification

    Significance

the presidential election of 1800

    Identification

    Significance

the Twelfth Amendment

    Identification

    Significance

"Ohio Fever"

    Identification

    Significance

the Second Great Awakening

    Identification

    Significance

Cane Ridge, Kentucky, camp meeting

    Identification

    Significance

Toussaint L'Ouverture

    Identification

    Significance

Gabriel's Rebellion

    Identification

    Significance

the Sancho conspiracy

    Identification

    Significance

EVALUATING AND USING INFORMATION

To see the divergence in opinion that inevitably led to the development of factions in the early years of the American republic, complete the accompanying charts about leaders and their political views using information from Chapter 8 of your textbook and from your notes on class lectures. In the spaces provided, indicate the position taken or exhibited by the named leaders or groups on the major issues of the period listed in the first column. (You will not be able to find the position of every leader or group on every issue.) When you have finished filling in the blanks in the two charts, analyze the results in terms of the differences in the frames of reference (region, socio-economic status, occupation apart from politics, etc.) of the leaders (and the groups) and in terms of the amount of agreement among the leaders within each faction.

Question or Issue Separating Factions or Revealing Splits Within Factions	LEADERS ESPOUSING VIEWS ASSOCIATED WITH FEDERALISTS		
	George Washington	Alexander Hamilton	John Adams
Should national government assume debts incurred by states during the Revolutionary War?			
Does the Constitution give Congress the authority to establish a national bank?			
Should the national government actively promote domestic manufacturing? How important is manufacturing relative to agrarian interests?			
What limits, if any, should be imposed on public protests against national laws and policies?			
How should the Alien and Sedition Acts (especially the Sedition Act) be viewed?			
What is the proper response of the national government to protest groups like the Democratic-Republican Societies?			

Chapter 8—Politics and Society in the Early Republic, 1789–1800

Question or Issue Separating Factions or Revealing Splits Within Factions	LEADERS ESPOUSING VIEWS ASSOCIATED WITH FEDERALISTS		
	George Washington	Alexander Hamilton	John Adams
What are legitimate states' rights in opposing actions of the national government?			
What is the appropriate response to the French Revolution? What relationship should the United States have with France?			
How will the growth of factionalism affect the nation?			
Should the Constitution be interpreted strictly or broadly?			
Other—			

Question or Issue Separating Factions or Revealing Splits Within Factions	LEADERS ESPOUSING VIEWS ASSOCIATED WITH REPUBLICANS		
	Thomas Jefferson	James Madison	Democratic-Republican Societies
Should national government assume debts incurred by states during the Revolutionary War?			
Does the Constitution give Congress the authority to establish a national bank?			
Should the national government actively promote domestic manufacturing? How important is manufacturing relative to agrarian interests?			
What, if any, limits should be imposed on public protests against national laws and policies?			
How should the Alien and Sedition Acts (especially the Sedition Act) be viewed?			
What is the proper response of the national government to protest groups like the Democratic-Republican Societies?			

Chapter 8—Politics and Society in the Early Republic, 1789–1800

Question or Issue Separating Factions or Revealing Splits Within Factions	LEADERS ESPOUSING VIEWS ASSOCIATED WITH REPUBLICANS		
	Thomas Jefferson	James Madison	Democratic-Republican Societies
What are legitimate states' rights in opposing actions of the national government?			
What is the appropriate response to the French Revolution? What relationship should the United States have with France?			
How will the growth of factionalism affect the nation?			
Should the Constitution be interpreted strictly or broadly?			
Other—			

EVALUATING AND USING INFORMATION

Compose the working draft for two essays, one on what the label "Federalist" had come to mean by 1800 and one on what the label "Republican" had come to mean by 1800.

Basically both essays should end up being expanded definitions (refer to the hints on expanded definitions in the Evaluating and Using Information exercise for Chapter 7). The expansions of the definitions of the two labels should cover these topics:

1. Sources of disagreement and factionalism among those people debating domestic and foreign policy during the administrations of George Washington and John Adams

2. The major leaders of the faction and their frame or frames of reference

3. The position of most of the people in the faction on the issues separating the two factions, the issues qualifying as "defining" issues.

Use the information you gathered in the Organizing Information exercise above and additional information that you find in Chapter 8 of your textbook. Then, on your own, organize and develop the points for your essay that relate to the first two of the above topics.

Developing the third topic is a bit more complex. Clearly your essay needs a major section concerning the positions that characterized the factions on the defining issues, a section that amounts to an essay within an essay. The easiest way to deal with the various positions is to classify or categorize them. Here are some hints about how to organize the categories portion of your essay, the part in which you develop the third topic listed above.

Hints for Writing about Types or Categories

1. Begin the planning process by dividing the whole plural subject into three or four categories, making sure that the categories cover all of the positions on issues that you need to cover. In the case of the essay you are working on, the whole plural subject is the positions on defining issues that divided people into factions. Could some of those issues be lumped together as "economic issues," for example? For the sake of efficiency—and to some extent logic—you should make sure the categories do not overlap. However, because a little overlapping is not going to cause serious harm here, just make sure that you assign each issue/position to the one and only category in which it best fits.

2. Introduce the major section of your essay about the categories with a transitional paragraph having about one to three sentences that serves both to connect the earlier sections of your essay to the categories section and to introduce the categories section. The main element in such a paragraph is a "classification" sentence stating the point of all the paragraphs that follow. (Example: "All the issues that defined what it was to be a Federalist fall into three categories: the A issues, the B issues, and the C issues.") If you can find one label to characterize all of the positions at once, so much the better. Being able to do that shows you can interpret the overall significance of the collection of positions. (Example: "On the major issues that divided the two factions, the Federalists were the nationalists.") However, you might have to take the time to insert a couple of sentences to explain what you mean by a unifying label like *nationalist* before you go on to your discussion of the categories themselves.

3. Devote each of the other paragraphs or sections in the categories part of your essay to one particular category. Begin each section with a definition or characterization statement about the whole category of positions. (Example: "As far as the relationship between the

states and the central government was concerned, Federalists generally stood for a strong and active central government.")

4. Within each of these sections or paragraphs, each subpoint should indicate the position on a particular proposal, action, or event that was associated with the faction. Each of these positions is one individual member of the category you are dealing with. Each of the subpoints should be supported with specific, concrete details.

IDEAS AND DETAILS

Objective 1

_____ 1. Which of the following was an important provision of the Judiciary Act of 1789?
   a. It placed limitations on the Supreme Court's power to review the constitutionality of acts of Congress.
   b. It allowed appeals from state courts to the federal court system when certain constitutional issues were raised.
   c. It gave state courts the power to declare acts of Congress unconstitutional.
   d. It allowed citizens of one state to sue another state in the federal courts.

Objective 2

_____ 2. If the Supreme Court declares a law unconstitutional, Congress may undo the court's decision by
   a. firing the justices responsible for the decision.
   b. passing a law declaring the Court's decision to be in error.
   c. adopting and gaining ratification of a constitutional amendment.
   d. persuading the president to issue an executive order contrary to the Court's decision.

Objective 3

_____ 3. Hamilton proposed that the national government assume the debts of the states for which of the following reasons?
   a. Assumption of state debts would help gain support for a national income tax by making the government's financial problems obvious.
   b. Assumption of state debts would give holders of public securities a financial stake in the success of the national government.
   c. Many of the states were on the verge of bankruptcy.
   d. Assumption of state debts would enhance the power of the states.

Objective 3

_____ 4. James Madison opposed Hamilton's proposal concerning the assumption of state debts because
   a. he believed it was unconstitutional.
   b. the plan favored large states like Virginia.
   c. he believed the proposal rewarded speculators.
   d. it was not fair to merchants involved in interstate commerce.

Objective 4

5. In his reaction to the Whiskey Rebellion, Washington demonstrated
   a. that the government would react with compassion and understanding to the plight of the disadvantaged.
   b. the national government's ability to accept criticism.
   c. that the national government would not allow violent resistance to the laws it enacted.
   d. the need for a permanent standing army.

Objective 4

6. The Democratic-Republican societies
   a. saw themselves as protectors of the people's liberties against tyranny.
   b. supported the Jay Treaty.
   c. warned against foreign alliances.
   d. were subversive organizations.

Objective 5

7. Analysis of the vote to authorize funds for carrying out the provisions of the Jay Treaty shows that
   a. merchants were opposed to the treaty.
   b. southern planters supported the treaty.
   c. Federalists and Republicans could put aside their differences when national security was at stake.
   d. the Federalist and Republican factions were becoming cohesive voting blocs.

Objective 4

8. Which of the following is generally true of the Republicans in the 1790s?
   a. They won support among non-English ethnic groups.
   b. They believed that many enemies were threatening the nation.
   c. They had serious doubts about the economic future of the United States.
   d. They usually came from urban areas.

Objective 5

9. Congress increased military spending after ratification of the Jay Treaty because
   a. England's refusal to give up its posts in the Northwest increased the likelihood of war.
   b. the treaty allowed the United States to increase its naval power in the Caribbean.
   c. France was angered by the treaty and authorized seizure of American ships carrying British goods.
   d. the treaty increased the likelihood of an Indian war by removing the Spanish from the western territories.

Objective 5

_____ 10. The XYZ affair
   a. led to undeclared war between the United States and France.
   b. caused the United States to seek a military alliance with Great Britain.
   c. was fabricated by President Adams for political reasons.
   d. was an attempt by the French to negotiate in good faith with the United States.

Objectives 4 and 5

_____ 11. The Alien and Sedition Acts were passed because
   a. foreign agents posed a serious threat to the security of the country.
   b. the Federalists wanted to crush dissent and stop the growth of the Republican party.
   c. there was a great deal of public support for restricting immigration.
   d. the country had no effective naturalization laws.

Objective 4

_____ 12. The Virginia and Kentucky resolutions supported the idea that
   a. federal law is superior to state law.
   b. a state may secede from the Union.
   c. states may resist federal laws by force of arms.
   d. a state may declare an act of Congress unconstitutional.

Objectives 5 and 6

_____ 13. President Adams's decision to reopen negotiations with France in 1800
   a. strengthened the alliance between the two countries.
   b. caused the emergence of political parties in the United States.
   c. probably caused Adams's defeat in the presidential election of the same year.
   d. created unity within the Federalist party.

Objective 8

_____ 14. One of the sources contributing to the Second Great Awakening was
   a. the serious economic depression of the 1790s.
   b. new religious ideas brought in by European immigrants.
   c. the establishment of more state-supported churches.
   d. the instability and isolation present in frontier areas.

Objectives 7 and 8

_____ 15. Which of the following may be considered a reason for increased racial tensions in the South in the late eighteenth and early nineteenth centuries?
   a. Fewer and fewer slaves were imported from Africa.
   b. The egalitarian message of the Second Great Awakening heightened the fears of planters about the possibility of a slave insurrection.
   c. White slaveowners encouraged an influx of black Haitian refugees.
   d. As economic prosperity swept through the South, white slaveowners became more secure in their control over blacks.

ESSAY QUESTIONS

Objective 4

1. Discuss the similarities and differences between the social, economic, and political philosophies of Federalists and Republicans.

Objectives 3 and 4

2. Discuss the similarities and differences between the views of Federalists and Republicans in relation to Hamilton's economic program.

Objective 5

3. Cite the provisions of the Jay Treaty, and explain the impact of this treaty on the emergence of political parties in the United States.

Objective 4

4. Discuss the causes of the Whiskey Rebellion, and explain Washington's response.

Objectives 4 and 5

5. Cite the provisions of the Alien and Sedition Acts, and explain the rationale behind their passage.

Objective 6

6. Explain the Federalist defeat in the presidential election of 1800.

CHAPTER 9
The Empire of Liberty, 1801–1824

LEARNING OBJECTIVES

After you have studied Chapter 9 in your textbook and worked through this study guide chapter, you should be able to:

1. Assess the Republicans' attempts to implement their philosophy of government.

2. By referring to specific cases, discuss the role of the Supreme Court under the direction of Chief Justice John Marshall in
   a. the strengthening of federal authority relative to state authority.
   b. the emergence of the doctrine of judicial review.
   c. the use of Federalist nationalism to protect the interests of commerce and capital.

3. Discuss Jefferson's decision to purchase the Louisiana territory, and explain the political and economic impact of this decision on the United States.

4. Examine the development of party politics in the early nineteenth century, and indicate the factors that led to the demise of the Federalist party.

5. Examine, evaluate, and discuss the consequences of United States policies from 1801 to 1812 that were designed to protect America's trading rights.

6. Discuss the causes and consequences of the War of 1812.

7. Examine the hostility between the United States and Shawnee Indians from 1801 through the war of 1812.

8. Explain the emergence of postwar nationalism, and discuss its impact on United States domestic policy.

9. Indicate the objectives of John Quincy Adams as secretary of state, and discuss the extent to which he was able to achieve his objectives.

10. Review the circumstances that led to the Monroe Doctrine, and discuss its significance.

11. Examine the erosion of nationalism and the re-emergence of sectionalism between 1815 and 1824.

THEMATIC GUIDE

Chapter 9 covers the development of the United States from 1801 to 1824. After a peaceful transition of power from the Federalists to the Republicans, the Republicans began to implement their domestic governmental philosophy by cutting taxes, reducing the army and navy budgets, reducing the size of the national debt, and allowing the Alien and Sedition Acts to expire. Furthermore, they appointed fellow Republicans to governmental offices and attacked Federalist control of the judicial branch of the government. The attack did not succeed. In fact, under the direction of Chief Justice John Marshall the Supreme Court successfully claimed the power of judicial review, which allowed the Court to develop as a coequal branch of government. The Court also asserted the supremacy of the federal government over the states.

While the Supreme Court expanded its powers and the powers of the central government, Jefferson, in the face of political reality and national interest, showed a willingness to alter his strict constructionist view of the Constitution. Seeing the possibility of doubling the size of the republic and removing major obstacles to future commercial growth, Jefferson accepted the idea of implied executive powers and agreed to the Louisiana Purchase.

These years also witnessed continued competition between Federalists and Republicans and the further development of democratic party politics. Although older Federalists remained disdainful of direct appeals to voters, Younger Federalists attempted to imitate the campaigning style and tactics of the Republicans. In those areas where Federalists and Republicans competed for voter support, party organizations emerged. This in turn brought increased voter participation in the political process and an extension of the right to vote to more people. In spite of movements in the direction of party politics, intraparty factionalism and personal rivalries prevented the emergence of political parties in the modern sense. The Hamilton-Burr duel is an excellent example of these factional forces in operation.

The United States also faced challenges from abroad during these years. Caught between two warring powers, the United States found its independence and nationhood challenged, with the greatest challenge coming from Great Britain. The adoption of the policy of "peaceable coercion" by President Thomas Jefferson and President James Madison created a situation in which the use of federal power had a tremendous economic impact on the lives of individuals and on the future economic development of the country—an ironic development in light of Jeffersonian beliefs about the role of government in society. Furthermore, the policy did not bring an end to the humiliations experienced by the young republic. Ultimately, because of continued affronts to its independence and because of the assertiveness of expansionists within the republic, the United States was drawn into the War of 1812.

Lack of preparation for war, the presence of internal divisions, and the emergence of a pan-Indian movement in the Northwest could easily have spelled disaster for the nation. Instead, defeat of the pan-Indian movement of Prophet and Tecumseh caused the collapse of Indian unity in the Old Northwest and ended effective Indian resistance to American expansion in that area, and England's preoccupation with war in Europe resulted in military stalemate with the United States and led to the status-quo ante-bellum Treaty of Ghent.

Despite the nature of the peace, the American victory at the Battle of New Orleans (fought after the signing of the peace treaty) caused most Americans to perceive the war as a major victory against the English and as a reaffirmation of the nation's independence, strength, and vitality. Therefore, the postwar years brought a mood of nationalism, which manifested itself in a renewed feeling of confidence and assertiveness domestically and internationally.

This nationalism and self-confidence brought the "Era of Good Feelings." Republicans, facing only scattered opposition from a discredited Federalist party, accepted some Federalist principles. They helped expand federal power by supporting internal improvements and economic expansion. Under the brilliant leadership of John Quincy Adams as secretary of state, the nation was also able once again to expand physically by peaceful means, and it unilaterally asserted its independence in the Western Hemisphere through the Monroe Doctrine.

However, growth and expansion brought problems in the form of economic depression and increased sectionalism. Hard economic times, which many western farm interests blamed on the Second Bank of the United States, brought east-west divisions. Physical expansion and the question of statehood for Missouri led to questions about the expansion of slavery and to north-south divisions. These divisions would shape the country over the next forty years.

BUILDING VOCABULARY

Listed below are important words and terms that you need to know to get the most out of Chapter 9. They are listed in the order in which they occur in the chapter. After carefully looking through the list, refer to a dictionary and jot down the definition of words that you do not know or of which you are unsure.

ragtag

harbingers

rout

status quo

ominous

frugal

egalitarianism

agrarian

adroitly

patronage

attrition

autocrat

avidly

disdain

demeaning

suffrage

repugnant

collusion

rudimentary

caucus

vociferously

secession

garner

repudiate

proverbial

charismatic

mettle

minuscule

flogging

astute

foil

raze

arbitration

moot

facilitate

renegade

lethal

scruples

bulwark

austere

ardent

Anglophobe

brazen

admonition

subvert

rail (*verb*)

transcend

thwart

IDENTIFICATION AND SIGNIFICANCE

After studying Chapter 9 of *A People and a Nation*, you should be able to identify fully *and* explain the historical significance of each item listed below.

1. Identify each item in the space provided. Give an explanation or description of the item. Answer the questions *who, what, where,* and *when.*

2. Explain the historical significance of each item in the space provided. Establish the historical context in which the item exists. Establish the item as the result of or as the cause of other factors existing in the society under study. Answer this question: *What were the political, social, economic, and/or cultural consequences of this item?*

the Lewis and Clark expedition

    Identification

    Significance

Sacagawea

    Identification

    Significance

President Thomas Jefferson

    Identification

    Significance

Albert Gallatin

    Identification

    Significance

Republican frugality

>Identification

>Significance

the Alien and Sedition Acts of 1798

>Identification

>Significance

the Naturalization Act of 1802

>Identification

>Significance

the Judiciary Act of 1801

>Identification

>Significance

Federal District Judge John Pickering

>Identification

>Significance

Supreme Court Justice Samuel Chase

>Identification

>Significance

Chief Justice John Marshall

>Identification

>Significance

Marbury v. Madison

>Identification

>Significance

the theory of judicial review

>Identification

>Significance

the transfer of Louisiana to France

>Identification

>Significance

the Louisiana Purchase

>Identification

>Significance

Zebulon Pike

>Identification

>Significance

Josiah Quincy

    Identification

    Significance

Younger Federalists

    Identification

    Significance

political barbecues

    Identification

    Significance

Timothy Pickering

    Identification

    Significance

Hamilton-Burr duel

    Identification

    Significance

the Burr conspiracy and trial

    Identification

    Significance

the presidential election of 1804

    Identification

    Significance

the Tripoli War

    Identification

    Significance

Stephen Decatur

    Identification

    Significance

the impressment of American sailors

    Identification

    Significance

the Non-Importation Act

    Identification

    Significance

the *Chesapeake* affair

    Identification

    Significance

the Embargo Act

> Identification

> Significance

the concept of "peaceable coercion"

> Identification

> Significance

James Madison

> Identification

> Significance

the presidential and congressional elections of 1808

> Identification

> Significance

the NonIntercourse Act of 1809

> Identification

> Significance

Macon's Bill Number 2

> Identification

> Significance

Prophet

    Identification

    Significance

Tecumseh

    Identification

    Significance

the War of 1812

    Identification

    Significance

the War Hawks

    Identification

    Significance

the invasion of Canada

    Identification

    Significance

General William Hull

    Identification

    Significance

the British naval blockade

    Identification

    Significance

the Battle of Queenstown

    Identification

    Significance

the Battle of Lake Champlain

    Identification

    Significance

the Great Lakes campaign

    Identification

    Significance

the Battle of Put-in-Bay

    Identification

    Significance

General William Henry Harrison

    Identification

    Significance

the Battle of the Thames

    Identification

    Significance

the razing of York

    Identification

    Significance

the burning of Washington, D. C.

    Identification

    Significance

the bombardment of Fort McHenry

    Identification

    Significance

Francis Scott Key

    Identification

    Significance

Andrew Jackson

    Identification

    Significance

the execution of John Woods

    Identification

    Significance

the Battle of Horseshoe Bend

    Identification

    Significance

the Treaty of Fort Jackson

    Identification

    Significance

the Battle of New Orleans

    Identification

    Significance

the Treaty of Ghent

    Identification

    Significance

the presidential and congressional elections of 1812

    Identification

    Significance

the Hartford Convention

    Identification

    Significance

Madison's nationalist program

    Identification

    Significance

the Second Bank of the United States

    Identification

    Significance

John C. Calhoun's internal-improvements bill

    Identification

    Significance

the National Road

    Identification

    Significance

the Tariff of 1816

    Identification

    Significance

James Monroe

    Identification

    Significance

the presidential election of 1816

    Identification

    Significance

the "Era of Good Feelings"

    Identification

    Significance

McCulloch v. *Maryland*

    Identification

    Significance

Fletcher v. *Peck, Dartmouth College* v. *Woodward,* and *Gibbons* v. *Ogden*

    Identification

    Significance

John Quincy Adams

    Identification

    Significance

the Rush-Bagot Treaty

    Identification

    Significance

the Convention of 1818

    Identification

    Significance

the Adams-Onís Treaty

    Identification

    Significance

the Monroe Doctrine

    Identification

    Significance

the emergence of Latin-American republics

    Identification

    Significance

the Panic of 1819

    Identification

    Significance

the Tariff of 1824

    Identification

    Significance

"stay laws"

    Identification

    Significance

Missouri's petition for statehood

    Identification

    Significance

the Tallmadge amendment

    Identification

    Significance

the Missouri Compromise

    Identification

    Significance

ORGANIZING INFORMATION

Between 1800 and 1825, both domestic and international events influenced the way Americans interpreted and implemented the plan of government embodied in the Constitution. How did those events and the guidance provided by the Constitution influence Americans' views concerning the authority and functions of the federal government?

In this exercise, you are to use the chart on the evolving picture of the functions and authority of the country's national government to help you focus on and organize the information you need to produce a complete and convincing answer to that question.

In Chapter 9 of your textbook and in your class notes, find the events, actions, or decisions relevant to each of the questions you see in the chart's first column and list them under the names of the key historical figures with whom they are associated. For now, leave the last column and the bottom row blank. (You will be asked to complete them as part of the Evaluating and Using Information exercise below.)

When you have completed columns under the key historical figures, you will have organized, both into groups of related information and in chronological order, all of the subjects you will need to cover, or at least mention, in a thorough response to the overall question.

EVALUATING AND USING INFORMATION

Using your listing of the events, actions, and decisions associated with key leaders of the period from 1800–1825, compose the working draft for the following essay question:

With regard to the period from 1800 to 1825, discuss

1. the evolution of Americans' views concerning the authority and functions of the federal government, and

2. the domestic and international events that influenced and shaped those views.

Use the chart you completed for the previous exercise (Organizing Information) as the basis for organizing your essay. By completing that chart, you have already identified the events, actions, and decisions you need to consider, and you have arranged them into groups according to the specific questions they will help you to answer. Furthermore, the historical figures on the chart are arranged in accordance with when they played their most active roles. Therefore, by listing the events, actions, and decisions relevant to each of the questions under the names of these historical figures, you have chronologically arranged the topics you need to consider to discover how the nation, through some of its key leaders, was coming to answer each of the four questions.

Once you have studied the material that your chart indicates you need to study to answer each of the four questions, enter the answers in the last column in the chart, which you left blank earlier. You can then use each answer in the last column of the chart as the main point of a major section of the body of your essay. (The specific, concrete information you will use to support each of these points will come, of course, from the information that led you to your answer.)

To arrive at the thesis or whole point of your essay, simply "add up" the answers to the four questions. "Adding up" is simply stating the meaning or significance of the four answers as a group. State this sum or overall answer in the form of the thesis statement of your essay in the essay's opening paragraph.

Following the procedure just described will produce a rough essay covering the ground you need to cover in a roughly organized way. However, it is intended as a guide to help you get started, not a straitjacket. Feel free to improve on the organization and style to make the finished essay your own and to include additional material that you think is important.

1800–1825
The Evolving Picture of the Functions and Authority of the National Government as Revealed by Events, Actions, and Decisions Associated with Key Figures

Specific Questions Being Answered	Thomas Jefferson	John Marshall (Supreme Court)	James Madison	James Monroe (John Quincy Adams)	Direction in Which Answer Is Headed
How much authority does the Supreme Court have over state laws and courts?					
To what degree is the federal government responsible for the nation's economic growth and health? Commerce?					
To what degree is the federal government responsible for defending the nation and its citizens abroad? Providing and equipping the armed forces?					
What is the responsibility of the federal government in promoting the nation's welfare and interests in international diplomacy?					
What did each individual key leader believe the overall scope and responsibility of the federal government to be?					

IDEAS AND DETAILS

Objective 1

_____ 1. The failure of the Senate to convict Supreme Court Justice Samuel Chase
   a. caused a split within the Republican party.
   b. led to legislation requiring federal judges to take annual mental competency tests.
   c. preserved the independence of the Supreme Court.
   d. caused anger among the voters and led them to return control of the Senate to the Federalists.

Objective 2

_____ 2. The case of *Marbury* v. *Madison* is important because the Court established its power to
   a. force a particular action on the president.
   b. judge the constitutionality of acts of Congress.
   c. issue a writ of mandamus.
   d. declare a state law unconstitutional.

Objective 3

_____ 3. Which of the following is true in reference to the Louisiana Purchase?
   a. Jefferson agreed to the purchase only after accepting a more flexible interpretation of the Constitution.
   b. Jefferson was angered by the fact that Monroe and Livingston had agreed to the purchase.
   c. Most Americans were angered over the purchase and thought the price too high.
   d. Jefferson, as a strict constructionist, insisted on conferring with Chief Justice Marshall before agreeing to the purchase.

Objective 3

_____ 4. Which of the following was true of the Louisiana Purchase?
   a. It angered eastern merchants but pleased western farmers.
   b. It opened the way for westward expansion across the continent.
   c. It led to Jefferson's defeat in the 1804 election.
   d. It caused Spain to ally with England against the United States.

Objective 4

_____ 5. The facts of the Burr-Hamilton duel support which of the following conclusions?
   a. Dueling was still quite common in New York in the early nineteenth century.
   b. The emergence of Younger Federalists created dissension within the Federalist party.
   c. Alexander Hamilton was an opportunist.
   d. Factionalism worked to prevent the emergence of true political parties.

Objective 5

_____ 6. Congress passed the Non-Importation Act in order to
   a. protest the British practice of impressment.
   b. correct the dangerous balance-of-payments deficit.
   c. foster the development of domestic industry.
   d. protect American virtue by preventing the influx of "decadent" European imports.

Objective 5

_____ 7. As a result of the Embargo Act of 1807,
   a. Republicans enthusiastically began to support the use of federal power.
   b. the British agreed to negotiations with the United States on the question of impressment.
   c. British warships were prevented from entering the Gulf of Mexico.
   d. exports fell dramatically, bringing depression and unemployment to the New England area.

Objective 7

_____ 8. Prophet's message to the Shawnees was that they should
   a. adapt to the white man's culture.
   b. accept the Christian religion, especially the idea of an afterlife.
   c. return to traditional Shawnee culture to achieve spritual renewal.
   d. turn to settled agriculture as a means of saving Indian culture.

Objective 6

_____ 9. Analysis of the vote in favor of a declaration of war against Great Britain in 1812 supports which of the following conclusions?
   a. Support for the war came largely from expansionists in the South and West.
   b. Congressmen representing the shipping interests in the coastal states strongly supported the war, but the South and West were opposed.
   c. Support for the war came primarily from the New England and southern states.
   d. The vote demonstrated American unity on the eve of war.

Objectives 6 and 8

_____ 10. As a result of the War of 1812,
   a. the Republicans suffered a resounding defeat in the 1812 elections.
   b. the Federalist party broadened its political base by gaining support in the South and West.
   c. the development of domestic industry in the United States was hampered.
   d. Americans experienced a new sense of nationalism and self-confidence.

Objective 8

_____ 11. That President Madison had accepted Federalist principles by 1815 is evidenced by his
   a. veto of Senator Calhoun's internal improvements bill.
   b. support for the chartering of the Second Bank of the United States.
   c. attempts to prevent passage of the protective tariff enacted in 1816.
   d. support for funds to continue the building of the National Road to Ohio.

Objective 2

_____ 12. The cases of *Fletcher* v. *Peck* and *Dartmouth College* v. *Woodward* provide evidence that
   a. the Court seldom spoke with a unified voice and often reversed its decisions.
   b. the frequency with which judges left and were replaced on the Court created confusion.
   c. the Court at an early date established the right of states to revise corporate charters.
   d. the Court under Marshall supported Federalist economic views.

Objectives 9 and 10

_____ 13. In the Monroe Doctrine, the United States
   a. joined Great Britain in a pledge to protect the independence of the states of Latin America.
   b. relinquished any future territorial ambitions in the Americas.
   c. pledged to support the anti-Spanish revolutions in Cuba, Nicaragua, and Panama.
   d. called for noncolonization of the Western Hemisphere by European nations.

Objective 11

_____ 14. As a result of the Panic of 1819,
   a. western farmers began to perceive the Second Bank of the United States as an enemy to their interests.
   b. the Federalist party regrouped and nearly defeated President Monroe in the 1820 election.
   c. the nation experienced a renewed sense of unity and purpose.
   d. the government enacted public works projects for urban workers.

Objective 11

_____ 15. The public's depth of feeling over the Missouri statehood issue stemmed primarily from
   a. fears raised in the debate about the political consequences of Missouri's admission to the Union.
   b. the possibility that repeal of the three-fifths compromise would be coupled with Missouri's admission to the Union.
   c. the passionate debate among whites over the morality of slavery.
   d. questions raised in the debate about the civil and political rights of African-Americans.

ESSAY QUESTIONS

Objective 1

1. Discuss the impeachment of Justice Chase and the significance of his acquittal.

Objective 3

2. Explain Jefferson's philosophy of government. How did the Louisiana Purchase fit into that philosophy?

Objective 5

3. Discuss the reasons for the passage of the Embargo Act of 1807, and explain its consequences.

Objectives 5 and 6

4. Explain why the United States and Great Britain went to war in 1812.

Objective 10

5. Cite the provisions of the Monroe Doctrine, and explain its significance.

Objective 11

6. Discuss the role of slavery in bringing about a North-South split, and explain the Missouri Compromise as an attempt to heal the rift.

MAP EXERCISE

1. Locate the following on the map that follows:
   - Lake Superior
   - Lake Michigan
   - Lake Huron
   - Lake Erie
   - Lake Ontario

2. Indicate the location of the following places, lakes, rivers, and battle sites on the map, and explain the significance of each in the War of 1812:

   a. the Canadian Campaign of 1812
      (1) the Western front
         - MacKinac Island and Fort Dearborn
         - Fort Detroit
         - Fort Harrison
      (2) the Niagara front
         - Fort Niagara (the Battle of Queenstown)
      (3) the offensive against Montreal

   b. the British naval blockade
      - the Chesapeake Bay
      - the Delaware Bay

   c. Campaigns of 1813
      - the Battle of Put-in-Bay
      - the Battle of the Thames
      - York

   d. Campaigns of 1814–1815
      - Washington, D.C.
      - Baltimore
      - Plattsburgh
      - Horseshoe Bend
      - Pensacola
      - the Battle of New Orleans

Chapter 9—The Empire of Liberty, 1801–1824

Map of the eastern United States showing:

- CANADA (Great Britain)
- MAINE (part of Mass.)
- VT., N.H., MASS., CONN., R.I.
- NEW YORK
- MICHIGAN TERRITORY
- ILLINOIS TERR.
- INDIANA TERR.
- OHIO
- PENNSYLVANIA
- N.J.
- MD., DEL.
- VIRGINIA
- KENTUCKY
- TENNESSEE
- NORTH CAROLINA
- SOUTH CAROLINA
- MISSISSIPPI TERRITORY
- GEORGIA
- LOUISIANA
- FLORIDA (Spain)

CHAPTER 10
Rails, Markets, and Mills: The North and West, 1800–1860

LEARNING OBJECTIVES

After you have studied Chapter 10 in your textbook and worked through this study guide chapter, you should be able to:

1. Examine the impact of the transportation and communications revolutions on the economic development of American society.

2. Identify the characteristics of a market economy, and discuss how the change from a subsistence economy to a market economy affected people's lives.

3. Examine the promotion of economic growth and geographic expansion by government from 1800 to 1860, and discuss the ideological basis for such promotion.

4. Describe the American system of manufacturing, and discuss the factors that contributed to industrial development in the United States between 1800 and 1860.

5. Discuss the development of the cotton textile industry in the United States in the first half of the nineteenth century.

6. Examine the impact of the economic growth and development of the North and West between 1800 and 1860 on women, immigrants, and non-whites.

7. Examine the development of commercial specialization in the United States during the first half of the nineteenth century and discuss its consequences.

8. Discuss the changes in the banking and insurance industries in the United States during the first half of the nineteenth century and explain how those changes affected commerce and industry.

9. Discuss the changes that occurred in the workplace and in the nature of work in the period from 1800 to 1860, and explain the impact of those changes on
   a. workers' attitudes.
   b. the relationship between employer and employee.
   c. relationships among workers.
   d. gender and work.

10. Examine the responses of workers to changes in the workplace and in the nature of work, the means by which they tried to achieve their aims and objectives, and the extent to which they were successful.

11. Explain the emergence of commercial farming in the first half of the nineteenth century and the impact of this development on the Northeast and the Old Northwest.

12. Trace the development of the frontier from fur-trading frontier to farming frontier to eventual urbanization and industrialization.

THEMATIC GUIDE

In Chapter 10, we examine the economic growth and development of the North and West in the first sixty years of the nineteenth century. During these years, the United States began changing from an agrarian society to an industrialized, urbanized society—a transformation that was not completed until the early twentieth century.

The shift from a subsistence economy to an industrialized, market-oriented economy was made possible by the presence and interaction of certain forces. For example, the transportation and communications revolutions of the nineteenth century spurred the emergence of such an economy by physically unifying the Northeast and the Old Northwest. But this unification was regional, for while the North and the West were evolving in the same economic direction, the slave South was not. The result was an economic shift from South to North and the emergence of economic links between the Northeast and the Old Northwest.

In the industrialized, market-oriented economy that had emerged in the North and West by the 1860s, crops were grown and goods were produced for sale in the marketplace. Money made from market transactions was used to purchase goods grown or produced by others. Such an economy encouraged specialization by farmers and producers, and a division of labor among workers. Although economic expansion accompanied the development of this market economy in the United States, economic growth was uneven during the period from 1800 to 1860 and was characterized by cycles of boom and bust. This market economy with its boom-and-bust cycles had differing effects on people's lives. In general, ordinary working people faced increasing insecurity; many who were accustomed to the traditional master journeyman-apprentice relationship experienced a loss of status, and women's lives were altered as many began to contribute to the family income.

Adam Smith's laissez-faire economic philosophy, largely accepted by American political leaders, created an atmosphere that encouraged the economic liberty of the individual. In addition, government at the state and federal levels accepted the idea that government could and should act as a promoter of economic growth. The federal government actively encouraged westward expansion and settlement and, in the process, promoted development of western agriculture and technological and industrial growth. Its active role in the economic life of the state was further validated by the Supreme Court. State governments, too, encouraged economic growth and provided economic aid. The combination of these factors created an economic atmosphere conducive to economic growth and development.

Industrial innovations and an available labor force for emerging factories also helped transform the economy. In the section "The Rise of Manufacturing and Commerce," we see the advent of the American system (consisting of mass production and interchangeable parts and dependent on the development of a precision machine-tool industry) and its application to the cotton textile industry and the clothing trades. We then consider the development of the Waltham (Lowell) system, which made the factory attractive to New England farm daughters. Partially as a result of these factors, the cotton textile industry became the most important industry in the country by 1860. Other factors interacting to aid the industrialization process were (1) the emergence of specialists in commercial transactions, (2) banks and other financial institutions, which made capital available, and (3) reforms that promoted the concepts of free banking and limited liability.

Growth and development in the economic sphere brought changes to the workplace and to the worker. The reality of the Waltham system never matched the ideal, for the emphasis shifted from providing decent working conditions, decent wages, and other amenities for the workers, to building an industrial empire and maximizing profits. Resulting changes in the workplace, in the nature of the work, in the relationship between owner and worker, and in relationships among workers led the New England mill women to organize and strike in the 1830s. Factory owners then began to search for a more compliant labor force. Irish women, whose work was a necessity and not merely a stage in their lives, provided the answer. Some male workers attempted to regain control over their lives by becoming more active in reform politics and by becoming involved in organized labor. But unsettled economic conditions, hostility by employers, and divisions among workers kept organized labor weak during the period. As a result, organized labor's most notable achievement during the period came when the courts relieved workers from the threat of conspiracy laws being used against them if they organized or engaged in strikes.

The chapter ends with the sections "Commercial Farming" and "Settling and Conquering the West," which discuss the adaptation of agriculture to the market economy. The first offers a brief discussion of the emergence of commercial farming and of the Old Northwest as the central agricultural region in the nation. The final section examines the rapid movement of the frontier and how quickly new areas became integrated into the market economy. In conclusion, the experience of California is discussed as an example of how rapidly frontier changed to dense settlement.

BUILDING VOCABULARY

Listed below are important words and terms that you need to know to get the most out of Chapter 10. They are listed in the order in which they occur in the chapter. After carefully looking through the list, refer to a dictionary and jot down the definition of words that you do not know or of which you are unsure.

entourage

hawker

bucolic

tangible

fervent

journeyman

subsistence

resilient

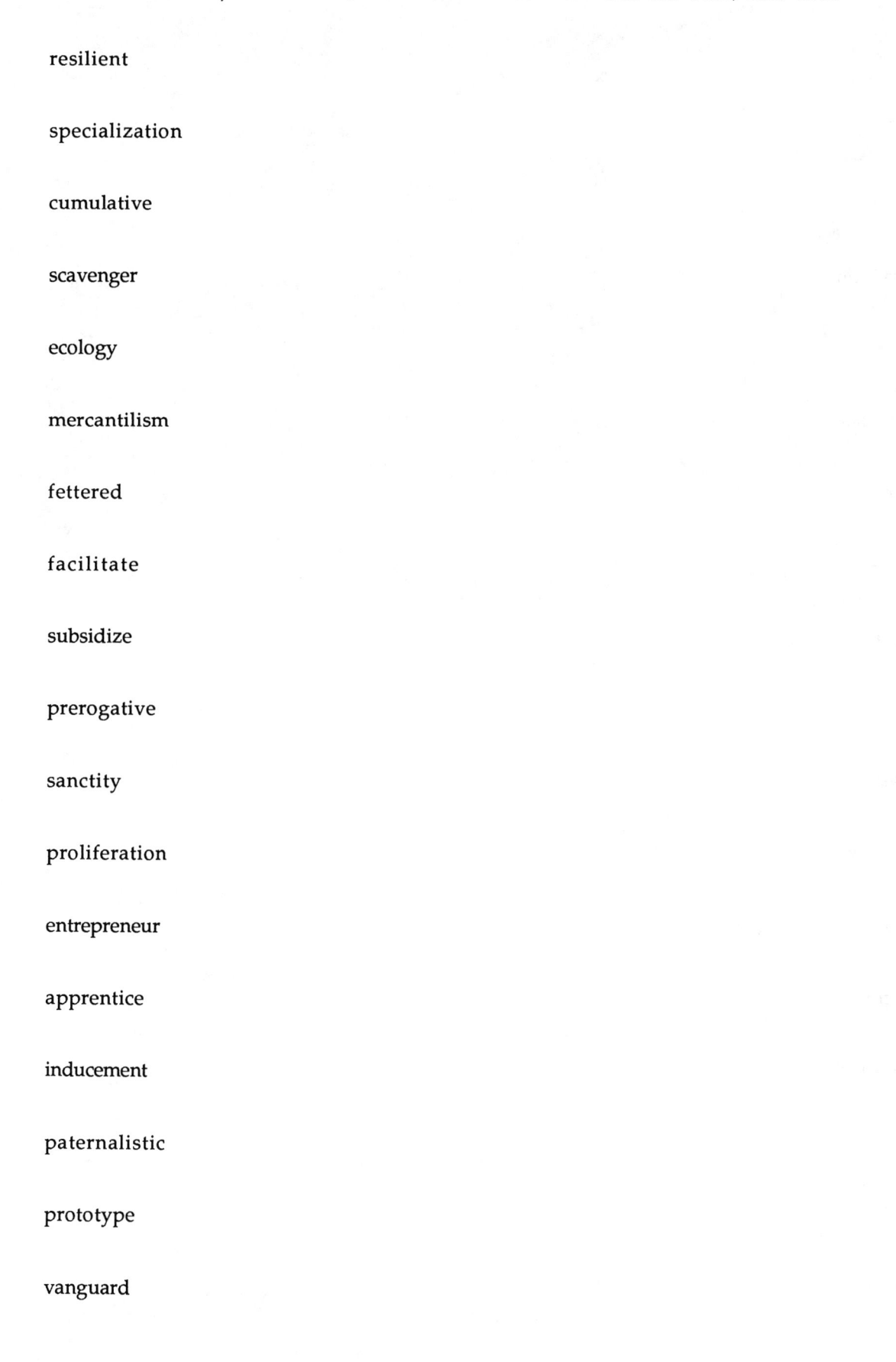

specialization

cumulative

scavenger

ecology

mercantilism

fettered

facilitate

subsidize

prerogative

sanctity

proliferation

entrepreneur

apprentice

inducement

paternalistic

prototype

vanguard

broker

din

idyllic

degradation

tenure

antithesis

maim

legions

tenuous

coercive

subserve

ethnicity

guild

integral

sporadically

impetus

lode

denude

IDENTIFICATION AND SIGNIFICANCE

After studying Chapter 10 of *A People and a Nation*, you should be able to identify fully *and* explain the historical significance of each item listed below.

1. Identify each item in the space provided. Give an explanation or description of the item. Answer the questions *who, what, where,* and *when.*

2. Explain the historical significance of each item in the space provided. Establish the historical context in which the item exists. Establish the item as the result of or as the cause of other factors existing in the society under study. Answer this question: *What were the political, social, economic, and/or cultural consequences of this item?*

the Hutchinson Family

    Identification

    Significance

the transportation revolution

    Identification

    Significance

The National Road

    Identification

    Significance

the Erie Canal

    Identification

    Significance

Chapter 10—Rails, Markets, and Mills: The North and West, 1800–1860

the railroad construction boom

    Identification

    Significance

Atlantic Ocean steamship service

    Identification

    Significance

the communications revolution

    Identification

    Significance

the magnetic telegraph

    Identification

    Significance

Samuel F. B. Morse

    Identification

    Significance

a market economy

    Identification

    Significance

Chapter 10—Rails, Markets, and Mills: The North and West, 1800–1860   **237**

boom-and-bust cycles

> Identification

> Significance

harvest and destruction

> Identification

> Significance

The Wealth of Nations

> Identification

> Significance

promotion of economic growth by federal and state governments

> Identification

> Significance

Henry Rowe Schoolcraft, Major Stephen Long, and John C. Frémont

> Identification

> Significance

Gibbons v. *Ogden*

> Identification

> Significance

the corporation and limited liability

    Identification

    Significance

Charles River Bridge v. *Warren Bridge*

    Identification

    Significance

the McCormick reaper

    Identification

    Significance

the American system of manufacturing

    Identification

    Significance

the Boston Manufacturing Company

    Identification

    Significance

the Waltham (Lowell) system

    Identification

    Significance

ready-made clothing

    Identification

    Significance

the pre–Civil War cotton textile industry

    Identification

    Significance

the Pennsylvania cotton textile industry

    Identification

    Significance

the specialization of commerce

    Identification

    Significance

free banking

    Identification

    Significance

the speed-up, the stretch-out, and the premium system

    Identification

    Significance

gender divisions in work

>Identification

>Significance

emergence of labor parties

>Identification

>Significance

the early labor movement

>Identification

>Significance

Commonwealth v. *Hunt*

>Identification

>Significance

commercial farming

>Identification

>Significance

the steel plow

>Identification

>Significance

James Fenimore Cooper

    Identification

    Significance

the California Gold Rush

    Identification

    Significance

the "forty-niners"

    Identification

    Significance

the California agricultural boom

    Identification

    Significance

frontier women

    Identification

    Significance

the Sugar Creek, Illinois, settlement

    Identification

    Significance

squatters

> Identification
>
> Significance

the Pre-emption Act

> Identification
>
> Significance

the development of frontier cities

> Identification
>
> Significance

EVALUATING AND USING INFORMATION

As an aid in focusing on the most significant facts in Chapter 10 and in organizing them to use in mock answers to likely essay questions on the chapter, complete the chart headed "Spurs to the Development of a Market Economy, 1800–1860."

In the second column of the chart, list specific changes in transportation, communication, etc., that seemed to spark a whole chain of changes in the American economy. Then, in the other columns, indicate the effects these specific changes had on the three areas named, areas usually considered important in characterizing a market economy.

When your chart is complete, use the information in it to plan and write the working drafts of responses to two of the essay questions at the end of this chapter of your study guide.

Spurs to the Development of a Market Economy, 1800-1860

Changes Introduced in Key Areas of Economic Development		Effects		
Areas That Saw Important Change	CHANGES (innovations—new activity or method, invention or discovery)	ON RELATEDNESS OF SEGMENTS OF THE POPULATION (occupational and regional interconnectedness and interdependence)	ON WORKERS AND EMPLOYMENT (new jobs, business cycle, organization of labor, etc.)	ON CONSUMERS (what consumers needed or wanted, how they paid for purchases, etc.)
Transportation				
Communications				
Production (manufacturing and farming)				
Financing and Banking				
Exploration and Discovery				

IDEAS AND DETAILS

Objective 1

_____ 1. The North became the center of American commerce because
   a. it invested heavily in canals and railroads.
   b. congressional legislation made capital more readily available in the North.
   c. the natural geographic orientation of trade routes was from west to east and from south to north.
   d. the southern terrain made the building of railroads extremely difficult.

Objective 1

_____ 2. The Erie Canal proved to be significant because it
   a. provided an example of what could be accomplished through private initiative.
   b. established an important east-west transportation link.
   c. opened new markets for wheat and corn from northeastern farms.
   d. led to wide acceptance of the funding of internal improvements by the federal government.

Objective 2

_____ 3. In a market economy
   a. the quality of merchandise is emphasized above all else.
   b. the growth of small, self-sufficient productive units is encouraged.
   c. the gap between rich and poor is narrowed as income is equalized.
   d. specialization is encouraged in agriculture, manufacturing, and finance.

Objective 3

_____ 4. Adam Smith would agree with which of the following statements?
   a. Individuals should be free to pursue their own economic self-interest.
   b. As the agent of the people, the government should regulate business and industry.
   c. The government should pass protective tariffs to foster the growth of domestic industry.
   d. Individuals should be given free land to foster the development of an egalitarian society.

Objective 3

_____ 5. Jefferson's use of government to promote economic growth is evidence that he
   a. abandoned his ideas favoring limited government.
   b. favored the wealthy and powerful.
   c. believed government should promote individual freedom.
   d. was confused over what role government should play.

Objective 3

_____ 6. The federal government encouraged the development of western agriculture by
   a. supplying farmers with the newest agricultural implements.
   b. establishing a governmental commission to design better farm tools.
   c. sponsoring irrigation projects in Minnesota and South Dakota.
   d. subsidizing railroad construction through land grants.

Objective 3

_____ 7. In the case of *Charles River Bridge* v. *Warren Bridge*, the Supreme Court
   a. paved the way for state regulation of the banking industry.
   b. for the first time declared a state law to be unconstitutional.
   c. held that decisions by state courts were not subject to review by the Supreme Court.
   d. ruled that ambiguous clauses in charter grants would be decided in favor of the public interest.

Objective 3

_____ 8. Government support and promotion of economic development was limited during the early nineteenth century primarily because of
   a. lack of funds.
   b. the philosophy of limited government.
   c. the strict-constructionist interpretation of the Constitution.
   d. hostility by financiers toward government interference.

Objective 5

_____ 9. The owners of the Boston Manufacturing Company transformed the manufacturing of textiles by
   a. organizing their workers into quality circles.
   b. personally managing their own mill.
   c. introducing the concept of the putting-out system.
   d. combining all the manufacturing processes at a single location.

Objective 5

_____ 10. When first adopted, the primary purpose of the Waltham system was to
   a. teach young women the domestic skills they would need as wives and mothers.
   b. solve the problem of a labor shortage by creating an attractive place of employment.
   c. teach virtue and morality to the young girls of New England.
   d. help women in the New England area gain financial and economic independence.

Objective 8

_____ 11. Free banking was important because
   a. by increasing the number of banks it increased the availability of credit.
   b. it made the creation of each new bank a political decision.
   c. the number of restrictions placed on banking practices was reduced.
   d. the federal government was given more control over banking and credit.

Objectives 5, 6, and 9

_____ 12. The paternalism of the Lowell system gave way to exploitation largely as a result of
   a. the change in the type of worker.
   b. a shift in emphasis from the worker and working conditions to profits.
   c. the increase in the number of spindles and looms used in textile mills.
   d. the introduction of water-powered looms.

Objectives 5, 9, and 10

_____ 13. Which of the following is true of the labor movement during the 1840s?
   a. It was made up primarily of socialists and anarchists.
   b. It was successful in getting pension plans for many workers.
   c. Its major achievement was that it gained recognition of its right to strike.
   d. It demonstrated the unity present among workers.

Objective 11

_____ 14. In the 1830s, some northeastern farmers successfully adjusted to western competition and soil exhaustion by
   a. growing more grain for the market.
   b. opening more land for cultivation.
   c. turning from commercial production of wheat to dairy farming.
   d. turning to new farm implements to increase productivity and profits.

Objective 12

_____ 15. Farm settlement and therefore the farming frontier were made possible by
   a. mechanized agriculture.
   b. the availability of land and credit.
   c. the abundance of cheap labor.
   d. high tariffs.

ESSAY QUESTIONS

Objective 2

1. Define the term *market economy* and indicate the characteristics of such an economy.

Objective 3

2. Support the contention that the Supreme Court encouraged economic growth in the early nineteenth century.

Objective 1

3. Explain the emergence of the New England and Middle Atlantic states as the center of American economic life.

Objectives 5, 6, 9, and 10

4. Discuss the changes in the New England textile mills in the years after the introduction of the Waltham system, and explain the reaction of millworkers to those changes.

Objective 12

5. Discuss the impact of the discovery of gold on the development of California.

CHAPTER 11
Slavery and the Growth of the South, 1800–1860

LEARNING OBJECTIVES

After you have studied Chapter 11 in your textbook and worked through this study guide chapter, you should be able to:

1. Explain the westward migrations of yeoman farmers and slaveowning planters from 1800 to 1860, and discuss the impact of these migrations on southern society in general and on southern blacks in particular.

2. Discuss the impact of an expansive, agrarian, slave-based economy on the development of southern society in the early nineteenth century.

3. Discuss the characteristics of the lives of yeoman farmers, landless whites, and free blacks, and explain the value system of each.

4. Discuss the characteristics of the lives of slaveowners, and explain their value system as well as their attitudes toward slavery, blacks, and women.

5. Describe the lives and attitudes of southern women in the first half of the nineteenth century.

6. Explain the conditions under which slaves lived their lives.

7. Examine the development of distinctive African-American culture.

8. Examine the attitudes of blacks toward slavery and toward whites, and discuss the extent and nature of black resistance to the institution of slavery.

9. Discuss the impact of slavery on southern values, customs, and laws.

10. Analyze the relations between planters and yeomen between 1800 and 1860.

THEMATIC GUIDE

The theme of Chapter 11 is the economic, institutional, and social development of southern society between 1800 and 1860. Within this context, we consider the belief system that emerged in the South and the impact of this belief system on southern values, customs, and laws.

In Chapter 10 we looked at the development of northern society as a diverse, market-oriented society in the period from 1800 to 1860. Chapter 11 provides an analysis of the very different southern society during this period. Material throughout the chapter elaborates and supports the idea expressed in the vignette—that the growth, change, and prosperity of southern society during those sixty years reinforced the economic, social, and institutional patterns that were already present.

The South experienced dramatic physical expansion between 1800 and 1860 as waves of yeoman farmers and slaveowning planters moved west of the Appalachians and into the Gulf region in search of economic opportunity. During this same period, the South experienced economic expansion as a result of the cotton boom. This in turn gave rise to the Cotton South and to a South in which slavery was more firmly entrenched than ever before. While this expansion gave rise to a new plantation elite, the South remained an agrarian society with a thin population distribution, weak institutions, and few urban centers or factories. Change in the South, then, was quantitative rather than qualitative—a decided contrast to the North.

In "Free Southerners: Farmers, Planters, and Free Blacks," "Slaves and the Condition of Their Servitude," and "Slave Culture and Everyday Life," we turn to a discussion of the groups that collectively made up southern society: (1) yeoman farmers, (2) landless whites, (3) free blacks, (4) slaveowners, and (5) slaves. Frequent moves characterized the lives of many yeomen, and most yeomen stressed the values of hard work, self-reliance, and personal liberty. Whether striving to become planters or content with their lives as small landowners, most yeomen derived some sense of security from land-ownership. This was not true of landless whites and free blacks.

After briefly discussing the factors that characterized the lives of landless whites and free blacks, we look at the upper end of the class spectrum. The wealthy men who dominated this group held paternalistic attitudes toward both blacks and women. These attitudes, which actually hid harsher racist and sexist assumptions, dominated the master-slave relationship as well as the male-female relationship. From the evidence presented, it is obvious that southern women had fewer choices than their northern counterparts and, therefore, less control over their lives and bodies. Within this context, slavery was, in a sexual sense, a source of trouble to women; and, since women viewed slavery differently from the way men viewed it, some women began to question the morality of the institution. Although some women began to speak out against slavery, most were silenced by the men who dominated their lives.

Next we move to a discussion of the general conditions of slave life and the emergence of slave culture. We learn about the slave diet, housing conditions, work routines, and the physical and mental abuses present in the slave system. The theme that runs through the sections on slave life and culture is the variety of ways in which slaves strove to retain a sense of mental independence and self-respect despite their bondage. For all the paternalism of the whites, tension was clearly the determining factor in the relationship between slave and master. Indeed, black culture was born of the refusal of blacks to accept slavery or to give up their struggle against it.

In the last section of the chapter, we see the impact of slavery on the South's social system, value system, and political system. Despite the distance between slaveowners and nonslaveowners, the South for a variety of reasons had been relatively free of class conflict. But between 1830 and 1860, the hardening of class lines and the widening of the gap between rich and poor began to create more tension between slaveholders and nonslaveholders, tension evidenced in white workers' protests and in the publication of *The Impending Crisis* in 1857. Nevertheless, on the eve of the Civil War, slavery seemed to be embedded securely in southern society.

BUILDING VOCABULARY

Listed below are important words and terms that you need to know to get the most out of Chapter 11. They are listed in the order in which they occur in the chapter. After carefully looking through the list, refer to a dictionary and jot down the definition of words that you do not know or of which you are unsure.

concubine

paroxysm

plaintively

obsolete

coerce

successive

lament

voracious

alluvial

density

amenity

quantitative

qualitative

autonomous

inflection

protracted

arduous

temperance

opulent

tedious

laconic

redolent

paternalistic

distemper

lucre

magnate

millinery

beriberi

pellagra

chink

wattle

daub

virulent

dysentery

noxious

lackadaisical

ply

wield

expendable

docile

subservient

retribution

motif

agility

conjuration

fervent

tenaciously

monogamous

implacable

precocious

marauding

ingratiate

ornery

impinge

scrutinize

commodity

mores

lineage

vilify

pretension

malapportionment

overt

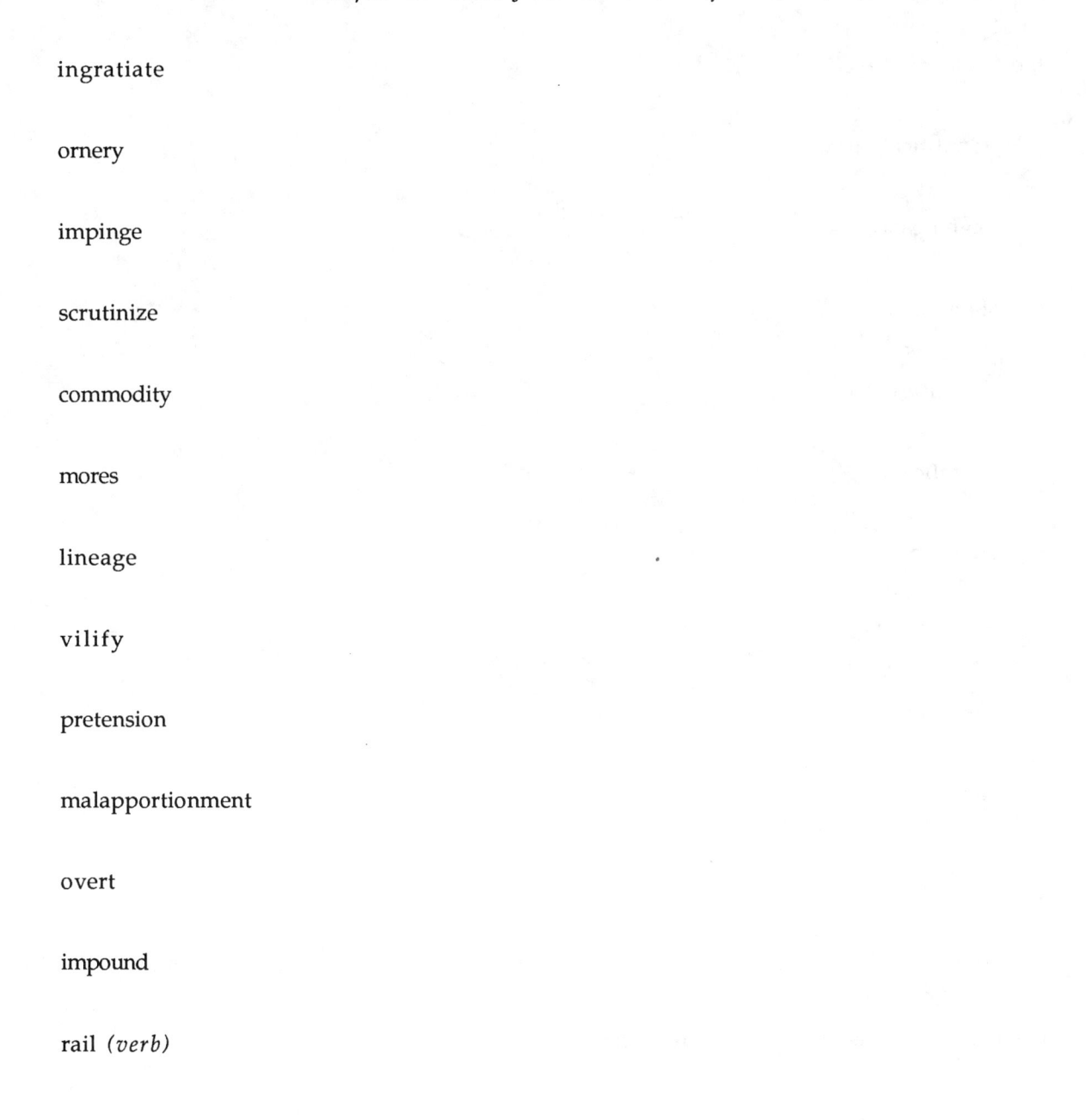

impound

rail *(verb)*

IDENTIFICATION AND SIGNIFICANCE

After studying Chapter 11 of *A People and a Nation*, you should be able to identify fully *and* explain the historical significance of each item listed below.

1. Identify each item in the space provided. Give an explanation or description of the item. Answer the questions *who, what, where,* and *when.*

2. Explain the historical significance of each item in the space provided. Establish the historical context in which the item exists. Establish the item as the result of or as the cause of other factors existing in the society under study. Answer this question: *What were the political, social, economic, and/or cultural consequences of this item?*

the "Alabama Fever"

    Identification

    Significance

the cotton boom

    Identification

    Significance

the cotton gin

    Identification

    Significance

the family of Jefferson Davis

    Identification

    Significance

the involuntary migration of black southerners

    Identification

    Significance

population distribution in the antebellum South

    Identification

    Significance

Chapter 11—Slavery and the Growth of the South, 1800–1860   **255**

antebellum southern cities

    Identification

    Significance

yeoman farmers

    Identification

    Significance

John F. Flintoff

    Identification

    Significance

Ferdinand L. Steel

    Identification

    Significance

landless whites of the antebellum South

    Identification

    Significance

free blacks of the antebellum South

    Identification

    Significance

slaveholders of the antebellum South

    Identification

    Significance

Bennet Barrow

    Identification

    Significance

noblesse oblige

    Identification

    Significance

Paul Carrington Cameron

    Identification

    Significance

upper-class women of the antebellum South

    Identification

    Significance

the ostrich game

    Identification

    Significance

the 1839 Married Women's Property Act of Mississippi

    Identification

    Significance

southern slaves

    Identification

    Significance

slaves' work routines

    Identification

    Significance

plying the lash

    Identification

    Significance

slave culture

    Identification

    Significance

slaves' religion

    Identification

    Significance

the slave family

> Identification
>
> Significance

Denmark Vesey

> Identification
>
> Significance

resistance to slavery

> Identification
>
> Significance

Nat Turner

> Identification
>
> Significance

the *code duello*

> Identification
>
> Significance

William Waightstill Avery vs. *Samuel Fleming*

> Identification
>
> Significance

democratic reform movements in the antebellum South

    Identification

    Significance

Virginia debate on slavery of 1832

    Identification

    Significance

white workers' protests in the antebellum South

    Identification

    Significance

The Impending Crisis

    Identification

    Significance

EVALUATING AND USING INFORMATION

If you look over the following statistics on southern slaveholding taken from Chapter 11, you might well wonder whether slavery as an institution would have died out even if the Civil War had not brought it to an end. After all, slaveholders—the group that could be said to have benefited the most from the institution—were a decided minority in the South.

    Gather information from Chapter 11 and, using it plus the statistics on slave-holding listed here, complete the chart "What Kept Opposition to Slaveholding in Check in the Pre–Civil War South."

    Use the information in your completed chart to guide you in planning and writing a working-draft response to this question: "What prevented the non-slaveholding majority in the South from overruling the slaveholding minority and doing away with the institution of slavery before the Civil War (between 1800 and 1860)?"

(Specifics in your chart may help you plan and write mock answers to some of the essay questions concluding this chapter of your study guide.)

1. In 1830, 36 percent of white southern families held slaves.
2. In 1860, 25 percent of white southern families held slaves.
3. In 1860, slaveholders held 90 to 95 percent of the South's agricultural wealth.
4. In 1860, the average slaveholder was fourteen times as rich as the average nonslaveholder.
5. From 25 to 40 percent of the white workers in the South were laborers who owned no land.
6. Some 88 percent of southern slaveholders had fewer than twenty slaves.
7. Slaveholders held from 50 percent to 85 percent of the South's seats in Congress.
8. Some 72 percent of southern slaveholders had fewer than ten slaves.
9. Some 50 percent of southern slaveholders had fewer than five slaves.

What Kept Opposition to Slaveholding in Check in the Pre–Civil War South

Groups that Had Reasons to Oppose Slave-Holding	Reason to Believe the Group Was a Potential Source of Opposition to Slave-Holding	Social Forces that Softened the Group's Potential Opposition	Political and/or Legal Forces that Softened the Group's Potential Opposition	Economic Forces that Softened the Group's Potential Opposition	Any Other Force that Softened the Group's Potential Opposition (such as demographics)
Female Relatives of Slaveholders					
White, Male Non-slaveholders and Their Families					
Moral Leaders Among Non-slaveholders					
Town or City-Dwellers Without Land Holdings					
The Slaves Themselves					

IDEAS AND DETAILS

Objective 1

_____ 1. Thousands of southerners migrated into the region west of the Appalachians because of
   a. overcrowding in the Old South.
   b. unsettled political conditions in the Old South.
   c. the attraction of rich, new lands.
   d. their objections to the institution of slavery.

Objective 2

_____ 2. Production of short-staple cotton was made profitable by the
   a. invention of the cotton gin.
   b. introduction of new and better farming techniques.
   c. McCormick reaper.
   d. introduction of irrigation systems.

Objective 2

_____ 3. In the period from 1800 to 1860, southern society was characterized by
   a. ethnic tensions associated with the influx of thousands of foreign immigrants.
   b. dramatic urban growth.
   c. the development of a regional transportation network.
   d. low population density.

Objective 3

_____ 4. Which of the following is true of yeoman farmers in the South between 1800 and 1860?
   a. They generally did not participate in the westward migration associated with this period.
   b. They lived their lives in a sphere separate from that of slaveowners.
   c. Their lives were transformed by the development of a market economy during this period.
   d. They became the most outspoken opponents of slavery.

Objective 3

_____ 5. Free mulattos in the cotton and Gulf regions
   a. were afforded the same privileges as whites.
   b. faced even harsher treatment than slaves.
   c. were sometimes able to gain financial backing from their white fathers.
   d. were often overseers on plantations.

Objective 4

_____ 6. The attitude of the wealthiest slaveowners toward their slaves can best be described as
   a. harsh.
   b. loving.
   c. paternalistic.
   d. accommodating.

Objective 5

_____ 7. The typical upper-class southern woman
   a. was expected to speak her views openly.
   b. was educated to think independently.
   c. had few duties in the home.
   d. was discouraged from challenging society's rules.

Objective 6

_____ 8. One of the characteristics of chattel slavery in the South was
   a. a strict division of labor by gender.
   b. frequent use of the lash.
   c. healthy and sanitary living conditions.
   d. a willingness on the part of planters to allow child slaves and elderly slaves to remain idle.

Objective 6

_____ 9. The worst evil of American slavery was the
   a. physical abuse associated with it.
   b. coercion and loss of freedom associated with one person owning another.
   c. grueling pace at which slaves were worked.
   d. fact that slaves were regarded as expendable.

Objective 8

_____ 10. The typical attitude of slaves toward whites was one of
   a. trust.
   b. kindness and respect.
   c. gratitude.
   d. antagonism and resistance.

Objective 7

_____ 11. Which of the following is true of slave culture?
   a. It contained no remnants of the African past.
   b. It helped slaves maintain their sense of identity.
   c. It stressed the idea of white superiority.
   d. It emphasized loyalty to the master.

Copyright © Houghton Mifflin Company. All rights reserved.

Objective 7

_____ 12. Which of the following is true of slave families?
  a. They did not exist.
  b. They were discouraged by slaveowners.
  c. They were a main source of support among blacks.
  d. Sexual division of labor was absent within them.

Objective 8

_____ 13. The objective of most slave resistance was to
  a. end the institution of slavery.
  b. violently overthrow the white power structure.
  c. get better housing.
  d. resist human bondage and at the same time survive.

Objective 9

_____ 14. The slave system in the South
  a. led to widespread acceptance of an aristocratic value system.
  b. caused southerners to value manual labor.
  c. caused the emergence of a relatively large and vocal abolitionist group in the South.
  d. led to serious and frequent conflicts among southern whites.

Objective 10

_____ 15. Hinton Helper's book *The Impending Crisis* indicated that
  a. the authority of slaveowners was secure in the South.
  b. tensions were increasing between slaveowners and those who did not own slaves.
  c. those who did not own slaves saw the abolition of slavery as a threat to their independence.
  d. free blacks were becoming more vocal in condemning slavery.

ESSAY QUESTIONS

Objective 4

1. Explain the attitude of slaveowners toward their slaves.

Objective 5

2. Discuss the role of planter women within southern society in general and within the marital relationship in particular.

Objective 5

3. Why was slavery a source of trouble for southern women, and what was the southern woman's perception of the institution of slavery?

Objective 9

4. Discuss the impact of slavery on the southern value system.

Objectives 6, 7, and 8

5. It seems that slaves lived in two worlds—one white and one black. Discuss this dual aspect of slaves' lives.

Objectives 6 and 7

6. Explain the methods by which slaves were able to preserve their dignity and self-respect within the institution of slavery.

CHAPTER 12
The American Social Landscape, 1800–1860

LEARNING OBJECTIVES

After you have studied Chapter 12 in your textbook and worked through this study guide chapter, you should be able to:

1. Discuss the expansion of the frontier in early nineteenth-century American society, and explain how Americans dealt with the isolation of frontier life.

2. Examine the interest in and the emergence of utopian communities in American society during the early nineteenth century, and discuss the ideas associated with these communities.

3. Discuss the expansion of urban areas in early nineteenth-century American society, the problems associated with that expansion, and the attempts to solve those problems.

4. Discuss the spread of public education in American society in the early nineteenth century.

5. Explain the changes in leisure time and in recreational activities in the urban environment of early nineteenth-century American society.

6. Explain the emergence and characteristics of each of the following, and discuss their impact on early nineteenth-century American society.
   a. Popular journalism
   b. Popular literature
   c. Theater
   d. Sports
   e. Exclusive clubs and associations

7. Indicate the nature, extent, and causes of urban conflict in American society during the first half of the nineteenth century.

8. Contrast the lives of the urban poor with the lives of the urban elite.

9. Examine the impact of economic change and urbanization during the first half of the nineteenth century on the family, gender roles, and women.

10. Discuss the similarities and differences between Irish and German immigrants' reasons for immigration, and examine the characteristics of the early nineteenth-century immigrants and their lives.

11. Discuss the policies of the United States toward the American Indians during the first half of the nineteenth century and the Indians' varying responses to those policies.

12. Examine the lives of free blacks within nineteenth-century American society, and discuss the ways in which they attempted to deal with their status.

THEMATIC GUIDE

The economic growth and development of American society in the early nineteenth century unleashed forces that changed the lives of Americans. In the process, American society became both more diverse and more divided. How the American people responded to change and increased diversity and how change affected the sense of community, the family, and individuals is the focus of Chapter 12.

The opportunities offered by the market-oriented economy led to increased mobility within American society and increased immigration into American society. Although this pushed the frontier farther west, caused the expansion of urban areas, and allowed some people to advance socially and economically, it also left many individuals with a sense of insecurity and aloneness in a changing society. At the same time, the pluralism that had been a distinctive characteristic of American society since colonial times became more pronounced. Though a great source of strength, the diversity suggested by this pluralism was also a source of tension and division. Such tension and division are natural components of a society that is a mix of ethnic, religious, and socioeconomic groups with divergent belief systems and value systems.

Some people attempted to create a sense of community in an increasingly impersonal society by experimenting with utopian communities. Whether the sexual abstention of the Shakers, the utopian socialism of New Harmony, or the transcendentalism of Brook Farm, the philosophies of these communities were usually a mix of old and new values and emphasized cooperation over competition. The search for belonging also led in new spiritual and religious directions; the Mormon movement is an example.

The rapid growth of the early nineteenth century increased distinctions between country life and city life. Urban growth brought changes in commerce and trade, transformed former villages into teeming metropolises, and brought more complexity to city institutions. Along with these changes came the urban problems of overcrowding, lack of adequate housing and sanitation, and pollution. In an effort to deal with such problems, cities began to offer the services associated with modern urban governments—garbage collection, water service, and sewer service.

Cities also began to provide education to their citizens through public schools. Because of the reform work of Horace Mann, who advocated equality of educational opportunity, the school curriculum became more secular in orientation and, therefore, more appropriate to would-be workers in a market-oriented economy. The public school curriculum no longer included direct religious indoctrination, but it did include indoctrination in moral values deemed important by the Protestant political leaders who controlled urban government and urban schools. Such indoctrination, undertaken with the intent of creating a society of like-minded citizens, was one response to the divergent belief systems brought by newcomers to the urban environment.

Life in an urban environment led to new uses of leisure time. Because the expansion of public education created a more literate public, many urban dwellers filled their leisure time by reading the newspapers, magazines, short stories, and book-length novels that abounded in the 1830s and after. Furthermore, leisure time and recreational activities became more organized within the urban environment. People became spectators of entertainment and sporting events rather than participants in such events. Again in response to the mix of peoples within the urban environment, exclusive clubs and associations emerged, allowing like-minded people a way to find and associate with each other. In many cases, involvement in sporting and entertainment events depended on membership in such clubs.

The expansive America, built on the ideal of equality, offered opportunity. But in contrast to the ideal and to the notions of some, equality of opportunity was not available to all. In early nineteenth-century America, class, ethnic, and religious divisions remained. Such divisions led to increased urban tensions and riots, which often had an ethnic or religious base. The starkness of class divisions can be seen in the contrasts between the lives of the working classes and the urban poor on the one hand and the lives of the urban elite on the other.

The family and the gender roles within it are usually affected by economic changes within society. With the shift toward job specialization in a market economy, the work of men and women diverged. In the urban environment, men left home to go to work. When women were gainfully employed, they usually sold their domestic skills rather than working in the new shops and factories. As work assumed more gender identification, the cult of domesticity emerged. It was held that women, by their nature, were more moral, virtuous, and nurturing than men. Therefore, it was believed, they should play a special role in the building of a moral, self-sacrificing, virtuous republic. Except for teaching, paid work was believed to conflict with this domestic ideal.

Economic changes and urbanization led to more family planning and a reduction in family size. With fewer children, women had more time for organized activities outside the home. Ironically, as the sphere of women shrank, they began to exercise more control over "their" domestic sphere and over their lives and bodies. They also began to engage in new activities as new roles were offered; and, as a result of their involvement in religious and community activities, they acquired organizing skills and shaped new roles for themselves. Furthermore, some women, like Louisa May Alcott, made the conscious decision to remain single in order to protect their independence.

The last three sections of the chapter focus on three additional groups that faced discrimination in American society: immigrants, Native Americans, and free people of color. The Irish and Germans were numerically the two major immigrant groups in the early nineteenth century. After considering the reasons for immigration, we look at the lives of immigrants and the prejudice they often faced in American society. During the same period, American Indians continued their struggle to retain their belief and value systems. After the defeat of the pan-Indian movement of Tecumseh and Prophet, the United States government adopted the policy of assimilation. Ultimately, however, the United States chose to remove the eastern Indians to western reservations, resulting in the Trail of Tears. A third group, free blacks, were allowed to remain within American society but were not allowed equality of economic, political, or social opportunity within that society. African-Americans, like Native Americans, struggled in various ways to maintain their dignity and self-respect in the face of the daily assaults of white racism.

BUILDING VOCABULARY

Listed below are important words and terms that you need to know to get the most out of Chapter 12. They are listed in the order in which they occur in the chapter. After carefully looking through the list, refer to a dictionary and jot down the definition of words that you do not know or of which you are unsure.

forlorn

refuge

consumption (*pathology*)

teamster

tinsmith

enclave

utopian

antipathy

pluralist

autonomy

cohesion

celibacy

perpetuate

charismatic

arid

intuitive

imbue

secular

spontaneous

ostentatious

promenade

ostracize

nativist

affront

indigent

respite

anti-Semitism

prodigious

protocol

insatiable

assimilation

proximity

irremediable

exclusionist

abject

IDENTIFICATION AND SIGNIFICANCE

After studying Chapter 12 of *A People and a Nation,* you should be able to identify fully *and* explain the historical significance of each item listed below.

1. Identify each item in the space provided. Give an explanation or description of the item. Answer the questions *who, what, where,* and *when.*

2. Explain the historical significance of each item in the space provided. Establish the historical context in which the item exists. Establish the item as the result of or as the cause of other factors existing in the society under study. Answer this question: *What were the political, social, economic, and/or cultural consequences of this item?*

farm communities

    Identification

    Significance

barn-raisings

    Identification

    Significance

country bees

    Identification

    Significance

the Shakers

    Identification

    Significance

the Mormons

    Identification

    Significance

New Harmony

    Identification

    Significance

Brook Farm

    Identification

    Significance

transcendentalism

    Identification

    Significance

the American Renaissance

    Identification

    Significance

Ralph Waldo Emerson

    Identification

    Significance

New York City

    Identification

    Significance

early nineteenth-century urban problems

    Identification

    Significance

public schools

    Identification

    Significance

Horace Mann

    Identification

    Significance

McGuffey's Eclectic Readers

    Identification

    Significance

popular literature in early nineteenth-century America

    Identification

    Significance

the theater in early nineteenth-century America

    Identification

    Significance

spectator sports in early nineteenth-century America

   Identification

   Significance

associations and clubs in early nineteenth-century America

   Identification

   Significance

the Masonic order

   Identification

   Significance

the Bowery boys and Bowery gals

   Identification

   Significance

urban riots

   Identification

   Significance

Alexis de Tocqueville

   Identification

   Significance

the Moses Brown legend

    Identification

    Significance

the new aristocracy of wealth and power

    Identification

    Significance

the urban poor

    Identification

    Significance

New York City's Five Points

    Identification

    Significance

"street rats"

    Identification

    Significance

Philip Hone

    Identification

    Significance

the urban middle class

> Identification

> Significance

the cult of domesticity

> Identification

> Significance

Catharine and Mary Beecher

> Identification

> Significance

the declining birth rate in early nineteenth-century America

> Identification

> Significance

family planning

> Identification

> Significance

methods of birth control in early nineteenth-century America

> Identification

> Significance

abortion in early nineteenth-century America

    Identification

    Significance

Louisa May Alcott

    Identification

    Significance

Castle Garden

    Identification

    Significance

Michael Gaugin

    Identification

    Significance

Irish immigrants

    Identification

    Significance

anti-Catholic sentiment in early nineteenth-century America

    Identification

    Significance

278   Chapter 12—The American Social Landscape, 1800–1860

German immigrants

    Identification

    Significance

Hispanics in early nineteenth-century America

    Identification

    Significance

removal of the Shawnees

    Identification

    Significance

the federal Indian agency system

    Identification

    Significance

the "civilization act" of 1819

    Identification

    Significance

President James Monroe's removal message of 1824

    Identification

    Significance

the "Cherokee renaissance"

    Identification

    Significance

Cherokee Nation v. *Georgia*

    Identification

    Significance

Worcester v. *Georgia*

    Identification

    Significance

the Removal Act of 1830

    Identification

    Significance

the Trail of Tears

    Identification

    Significance

the Second Seminole War

    Identification

    Significance

Osceola

> Identification

> Significance

William Medill, Commissioner of Indian Affairs

> Identification

> Significance

the legal status of free northern African-Americans

> Identification

> Significance

southern restrictions on free African-Americans

> Identification

> Significance

the "black codes"

> Identification

> Significance

Frederick Douglass

> Identification

> Significance

Harriet Tubman

    Identification

    Significance

Free-black self-help societies

    Identification

    Significance

the Negro Convention Movement

    Identification

    Significance

black nationalism

    Identification

    Significance

ORGANIZING INFORMATION

The following chart "1800–1860: Inclusionism vs. Exclusionism in America" identifies several groups focused on in Chapter 12 as well as important aspects of life in the public arena in which their inclusion or exclusion was most obvious.

    Using information that you find in Chapter 12 and in your class notes, record in the blanks in the chart specific signs indicating what each group was experiencing in terms of acceptance (inclusion) and access to power, status, and opportunity in the areas of legal and political recognition, jobs, social attitudes and practices, and education.

EVALUATING AND USING INFORMATION

Using the your filled-in Organizing Information chart, "1800–1860: Inclusionism vs. Exclusionism in America," as a guide, compose the working draft of an essay in response to this question:

How were those Americans who were themselves enjoying the benefits of full rights, power, and opportunities excluding others from enjoying the same benefits? Support your response by indicating important ways specific groups were being excluded from the power, status, and opportunities of American society.

If you develop your essay fully and familiarize yourself with its contents, you will have prepared yourself to write on any of several potential essay questions as well as dozens of objective questions.

1800–1860
Inclusionism vs. Exclusionism in America

Group	Legal Status and Political Participation and Power	Hiring and Job Opportunities	Social Attitudes and Practices	Education	Other
Women					
Free Blacks					
Irish Immigrants					
German Immigrants					
Native Americans					
Others					

IDEAS AND DETAILS

Objective 1

_____ 1. Pioneer farm families often dealt with the isolation of farm life by
   a. going to the nearest city for entertainment.
   b. having large families.
   c. gathering on each other's farms for social and work activities.
   d. living in the city during the winter months.

Objective 2

_____ 2. Most of those who organized utopian communities did so with the objective of
   a. completely withdrawing from civilized society.
   b. returning to a state of nature.
   c. establishing a cooperative, as opposed to a competitive, environment.
   d. creating a new political order based on the Bible.

Objective 3

_____ 3. In the growing urban areas of the early nineteenth century, the cost associated with construction of sewers was
   a. often covered by businessmen's associations.
   b. usually borne by individual property owners.
   c. totally covered by city tax dollars.
   d. paid for by state governments.

Objective 4

_____ 4. Horace Mann believed that
   a. moral education had no place in the public school.
   b. the public school should stand as a bastion against the secularism of the industrial age.
   c. public education should concentrate on the abolition of ignorance, not on religious indoctrination.
   d. education was a private, family concern and not the concern of the state.

Objective 6

_____ 5. In order to counteract the feeling of alienation in the urban environment, middle- and upper-class urbanites often
   a. joined clubs and voluntary associations.
   b. participated in neighborhood sports activities.
   c. joined utopian communities.
   d. ran for political office.

Objective 7

_____ 6. A common thread running through the urban riots of the 1830s and 1840s was
   a. a sense of having been unjustly treated by the authorities.
   b. white racism.
   c. anger directed against perceived political and economic rivals.
   d. greed.

Objective 8

_____ 7. Most of those who held great wealth in the 1840s and 1850s
   a. acquired their fortunes through hard work and perseverance.
   b. were very discreet about their wealth.
   c. were idle men of leisure.
   d. had inherited much of their wealth.

Objective 9

_____ 8. Most working-class women in the early nineteenth century
   a. found employment in the new factories.
   b. had to acquire specialized work skills or face unemployment.
   c. sold their domestic skills for wages.
   d. found work in urban retail shops.

Objective 9

_____ 9. According to the cult of domesticity of the nineteenth century,
   a. women were responsible for the educational, moral, and cultural functions of the family.
   b. men and women were to share family responsibilities equally.
   c. men were to concentrate on the husband-father role rather than on the wage-earner role.
   d. women were to aid their husbands by finding work outside the home.

Objective 9

_____ 10. The evidence suggests that a major reason for the decline in family size in the early nineteenth century was
   a. the use of traditional forms of birth control.
   b. the fact that men in urban areas left home to go to work.
   c. better sex education at home and at school.
   d. higher infant mortality rates.

Objective 10

_____ 11. Irish immigrants coming to America in the early nineteenth century
   a. came mainly from the Irish middle class.
   b. came mainly from the urban areas in Ireland.
   c. found work easily in the urban areas of the North.
   d. were subjected to anti-Catholic sentiment.

Copyright © Houghton Mifflin Company. All rights reserved.

Objective 11

_____ 12. Treaty negotiations between the United States and Indian tribes
   a. demonstrate the respect the United States had for Indian sovereignty.
   b. show a desire by the United States to protect the Indians' cultures.
   c. were a means by which the United States could acquire the Indians' land.
   d. usually took place in an atmosphere of friendship and cooperation.

Objective 11

_____ 13. The Indian agency system was designed to
   a. preserve the American Indian culture.
   b. make Indians dependent on government payments and thus more docile in treaty negotiations.
   c. give Indians economic independence by giving them land.
   d. starve the Indians into submission.

Objective 11

_____ 14. President Monroe's policy toward the Indians called for
   a. extermination.
   b. establishing job-training centers for Indians.
   c. removal of all Indians to the area west of the Mississippi.
   d. establishing a Bureau of Indian Affairs.

Objective 12

_____ 15. Regarding their position in American society in the 1830s and 1840s, free blacks
   a. depended upon the federal government to protect their rights.
   b. realized that the state governments could best protect their rights.
   c. attempted to improve their status by organizing self-help societies.
   d. realized they had to work primarily through white institutions to improve their status.

ESSAY QUESTIONS

Objective 2

1. Discuss the philosophy and goals of the Shaker and Mormon movements. What are the similarities and differences between the Shaker and Mormon movements on the one hand and the New Harmony and Brook Farm movements on the other hand.

Objective 3

2. Discuss the expansion of New York City during the early nineteenth century. What problems were associated with this expansion? How were these problems handled?

Objective 4

3. Discuss the contributions of Horace Mann to educational reform.

Objective 9

4. Describe the cult of domesticity, and explain its impact on women in American society.

Objective 10

5. Indicate the characteristics of the Irish and German immigrants of the 1840s and 1850s, and discuss the opportunities and hardships they encountered.

Objective 11

6. Discuss President Monroe's 1824 Indian removal policy, and describe the process by which it was carried out.

Objective 12

7. Explain the social, economic, and political characteristics of the lives of free blacks in northern society.

CHAPTER 13
Reform, Politics, and Expansion, 1824–1844

LEARNING OBJECTIVES

After you have studied Chapter 13 in your textbook and worked through this study guide chapter, you should be able to:

1. Discuss the causes, characteristics, and consequences of the Second Great Awakening.

2. Indicate the ideas, leaders, and contributions of the following reform movements in early nineteenth-century American society.
   a. The antiprostitution movement
   b. The temperance and antigambling movements
   c. The movement to establish penitentiaries, insane asylums, and other social institutions
   d. The women's movement

3. Explain the Antimasonry movement, and indicate its impact on American politics.

4. Discuss the growth of the antislavery movement, and explain its impact on American society during the first half of the nineteenth century.

5. Examine the issues in the presidential election of 1828, and explain the election's outcome.

6. Describe the characteristics of the second party system, and compare and contrast the political, social, and economic philosophies of the Jacksonian Democrats and the Whigs.

7. Examine how the political, social, and economic ideology of the Jacksonian Democrats was translated into policy during the terms of President Jackson and President Van Buren, and explain the impact of these policies on the United States.

8. Identify the domestic failures and the foreign policy accomplishments of the Tyler administration.

9. Discuss the emergence of expansionist sentiment in the 1830s and 1840s, and explain the debates over the Texas and Oregon territories.

10. Examine the issues in the presidential election of 1844, and explain the election's outcome.

THEMATIC GUIDE

Chapters 12 and 13 demonstrate that Americans responded in varied ways to the changes brought by industrialization and urbanization in the early nineteenth century. The religious revival known as the Second Great Awakening was the response of people who perceived a spiritual breakdown within society. This response, which was evangelistic and emotional in character and perfectionist in orientation, had an impact on the other reform movements of the era in that they all aimed to perfect the human condition. Some of the reform movements were attempts to cleanse society of perceived moral evils (the American Female Moral Reform Society, the Shakers, and the temperance movement). Some (the utopian communities dealt with in Chapter 12) attempted to create a sense of community in an increasingly impersonal society. And others (the movement to establish penitentiaries, insane asylums, and other social institutions) wanted to create a system by which the victims of a society perceived to be turbulent and unstable could be rehabilitated.

The reform impulse caused some Americans to redefine the ideal of equality and resulted in Antimasonry, the abolitionist movement, and the feminist movement. For many, Antimasonry served as the first bridge between reform and politics. Abolitionism, which was built on evangelical Christianity and the reform impulse, was the second bridge. Eventually territorial expansion prompted abolitionists to enter into the political arena and transformed the antislavery movement into one that consumed all other reforms.

Change in other aspects of American society was affecting the political process as well. The end of the caucus system, the trend toward choosing presidential electors by popular vote, and the election of Andrew Jackson as president all signaled the beginnings of a more open political system in which party organization and party politics were the most important ingredients in the acquisition of political power. Jackson's acquisition of power brought with it an attempt to solve the nation's problems through restoration of traditional republican values and through return to Jeffersonian concepts of limited government. It is within this context that the nullification crisis and the controversy over the rechartering of the Second Bank of the United States took place. In the former, President Jackson and Congress reaffirmed the supremacy of the federal government over what Jackson perceived to be special state privilege. In the latter, the concept of limited government was reaffirmed over what the Jacksonians perceived to be special economic privilege. However, Jackson's antibank and hard-money policies led to economic hard times, with which his successor, Martin Van Buren, was unable to deal.

Jackson's policies, his transformation of the executive branch into a more powerful arm of government, and the inching of reformists and evangelicals into politics led to the emergence of a loyal opposition in the form of the Whig party and to the emergence of the second party system. As the democratization of American society caused an expansion of the electorate, the two parties took shape and began to compete in local, state, and federal elections. In the process, disagreements between Democrats and Whigs on the fundamental issues of the age energized the political process and caused more people to become politically active. Nevertheless, the main determinants of party membership were religion and ethnicity. In the 1840 election, the Whigs capitalized on the economic hardships of the Van Buren years to capture the presidency. However, President Harrison died a month after taking office and was replaced by John Tyler, who was more a Democrat than a Whig. Tyler's achievements were confined to the area of foreign policy.

In the last section of the chapter, "Manifest Destiny and Expansionism," we consider the reasons for the emergence of the expansionist sentiment of the 1840s. Brought to fever pitch through the debates over Texas and Oregon, this sentiment, as well as the entry of abolitionists into the political arena, led to the election of James K. Polk to the presidency in 1844. This event brought momentous changes to the republic over the next fifteen years.

BUILDING VOCABULARY

Listed below are important words and terms that you need to know to get the most out of Chapter 13. They are listed in the order in which they occur in the chapter. After carefully looking through the list, refer to a dictionary and jot down the definition of words that you do not know or of which you are unsure.

austere

epitomize

crescendo

rectitude

benevolent

ardor

temperance

abolition

manifest

destiny

galvanize

spontaneous

ameliorate

catalyst

abstinence

defile

inherent

exemplify

incarceration

ribald

scathing

equivocate

forswear

rhetorical

amalgamation

garner

caucus

anomaly

inept

procure

paraphernalia

vindictive

patronage

egotism

demagogic

ostensibly

specie

intrinsic

volatile

coup de grâce

pocket veto

coalesce

arbitration

renege

mandate

imbue

IDENTIFICATION AND SIGNIFICANCE

After studying Chapter 13 of *A People and a Nation*, you should be able to identify fully *and* explain the historical significance of each item listed below.

1. Identify each item in the space provided. Give an explanation or description of the item. Answer the questions *who, what, where,* and *when.*

2. Explain the historical significance of each item in the space provided. Establish the historical context in which the item exists. Establish the item as the result of or as the cause of other factors existing in the society under study. Answer this question: *What were the political, social, economic, and/or cultural consequences of this item?*

Dorethea Dix

    Identification

    Significance

the Second Great Awakening

    Identification

    Significance

Charles G. Finney

    Identification

    Significance

the McDowall report

    Identification

    Significance

the American Female Moral Reform Society

    Identification

    Significance

the "burned-over" district

    Identification

    Significance

the American Society for the Promotion of Temperance

    Identification

    Significance

the anti-lottery movement

    Identification

    Significance

the penitentiary movement

    Identification

    Significance

the asylum movement

    Identification

    Significance

the Antimasonry movement

    Identification

    Significance

the Morgan affair

    Identification

    Significance

the convention system

    Identification

    Significance

the American Colonization Society

    Identification

    Significance

gradualists vs. immediatists

    Identification

    Significance

Black abolitionists

    Identification

    Significance

the American Anti-Slavery Society

    Identification

    Significance

William Lloyd Garrison

    Identification

    Significance

the *Liberator*

    Identification

    Significance

Elijah P. Lovejoy

    Identification

    Significance

the gag rule

    Identification

    Significance

the antislavery movement

    Identification

    Significance

women abolitionists

    Identification

    Significance

Angelina and Sarah Grimké

    Identification

    Significance

Chapter 13—Reform, Politics, and Expansion, 1824–1844   **297**

the Seneca Falls Declaration of Sentiments

    Identification

    Significance

the presidential election of 1824

    Identification

    Significance

the "corrupt bargain"

    Identification

    Significance

President John Quincy Adams

    Identification

    Significance

the presidential election of 1828

    Identification

    Significance

Andrew Jackson

    Identification

    Significance

the Jacksonian Democrats

> Identification

> Significance

the Kitchen Cabinet

> Identification

> Significance

the spoils system

> Identification

> Significance

the Maysville Road veto

> Identification

> Significance

the doctrine of nullification

> Identification

> Significance

Exposition and Protest

> Identification

> Significance

the Webster-Hayne debate

    Identification

    Significance

the Tariff of 1832

    Identification

    Significance

the nullification crisis

    Identification

    Significance

the Force Act

    Identification

    Significance

the Tariff of 1833

    Identification

    Significance

the Second Bank of the United States

    Identification

    Significance

Nicholas Biddle

    Identification

    Significance

the veto of the Second Bank rechartering bill

    Identification

    Significance

the presidential election of 1832

    Identification

    Significance

"pet" banks

    Identification

    Significance

the Deposit Act of 1836

    Identification

    Significance

the Specie Circular

    Identification

    Significance

the Second Party System

> Identification

> Significance

the Whig party

> Identification

> Significance

the presidential election of 1836

> Identification

> Significance

Martin Van Buren

> Identification

> Significance

the independent treasury system

> Identification

> Significance

the presidential election of 1840

> Identification

> Significance

William Henry Harrison

    Identification

    Significance

John Tyler

    Identification

    Significance

the *Caroline* affair

    Identification

    Significance

the Webster-Ashburton Treaty

    Identification

    Significance

Manifest Destiny

    Identification

    Significance

the Republic of Texas

    Identification

    Significance

empresarios

    Identification

    Significance

"Remember the Alamo"

    Identification

    Significance

the Texas-annexation question

    Identification

    Significance

Oregon fever

    Identification

    Significance

the Oregon-boundary question

    Identification

    Significance

the presidential election of 1844

    Identification

    Significance

James K. Polk

Identification

Significance

EVALUATING AND USING INFORMATION

Exercise A

All four of the following numbered sets of statements present facts and inferences from or related to a historical figure who played an important role in the period covered in Chapter 13.

After studying each set of statements, give one or more labels to the figure based on the statements about him or her (e. g., foe of Indians, hard-money man, Whig, Democrat).

Based on the information in the sets of statements, identify the historical figure. Then use the most significant of the labels you have come up with, especially those justified by more than one set of statements, as the subtopics for the working draft of an essay in which you present a portrait of the historical figure. Gather whatever additional information you need from your textbook and class notes.

1. He supported Georgia's position by ignoring the Supreme Court's 1831 ruling that the only way the Cherokee could lose title to their land was by voluntarily relinquishing it. . . . He and his vice president disagreed, largely over the Nullification Doctrine and what it implied. . . . At a dinner party around the time of the nullification crisis, his toast was "Our Federal Union, it *must* and *shall be* preserved."

   Label(s):

2. Angering the country's secretary of state, who was in negotiations with Spain, he led a military expedition against the Seminole in Spanish territory. . . . He ordered the removal of Indians from the Southeast to make available land for white agricultural settlement. . . . As a general, he led in the removal of the Creek from Alabama and Georgia. . . . He approved of presidents exercising their veto power to fight legislation they simply do not like. . . . He instituted an antiland speculation, anti–paper money policy like one Congress had recently rejected and then overrode Congress's efforts to repeal it.

   Label(s):

3. Being against interventionist government, he opposed the activists's advocacy of social reforms, including their calls for establishing public schools. . . . The political party that opposed him was heavily influenced by evangelical Protestantism. . . . His administration eliminated the federal surplus by giving it to the states in interest-free "loans." . . . He insisted that people use specie (or Virginia land scrip) to pay for federal lands.

Label(s):

4. Having won both the popular and the electoral college vote, he still did not win in his first attempt to gain the presidency, but he did win his second and third attempts.... He was the first president of the United States who "rose from humble beginnings."... In opposing the rechartering of the Second Bank of the United States, he attacked the special privilege and the economic power of the rich.

   Label(s):

The historical figure is: _____

Exercise B

Refer to sections of Chapter 13 outlining the political, social, and economic differences between Democrats and Whigs.

Two statements about each party are listed below. You are to support each statement with details and ideas you have collected from the textbook. Then, beginning with the name of the party (given), you are to compose a third statement about each party and support it with details and ideas that you find in the textbook. Finally, answer Questions A and B. (You may refer to earlier chapters to gather additional information about the Federalists.)

1. Democrats adhered to the ideal of a limited federal government.
   Supporting details and ideas:

2. Democrats distrusted the concentration of economic power.
   Supporting details and ideas:

3. Democrats _____.
   Supporting details and ideas:

4. Whigs believed in an activist federal government.
   Supporting details and ideas:

5. Whigs supported humanitarian and moral reform.
   Supporting details and ideas:

6. Whigs _____.
   Supporting details and ideas:

A. What were the similarities and differences between the Jeffersonian Democratic-Republicans and the Jacksonian Democrats?

B. What were the similarities and differences between the Federalists and the Whigs?

IDEAS AND DETAILS

Objective 1

_____ 1. The Second Great Awakening bred reform because it taught that
   a. the perfection of earthly society could speed the Second Coming.
   b. all people were evil and would burn in the fires of everlasting Hell.
   c. God was no longer active in human affairs.
   d. Jesus had returned to Earth and had begun the Last Judgment.

Objectives 1 and 2

_____ 2. The work of the American Female Moral Reform Society demonstrates that the Second Great Awakening
   a. was antifemale in orientation.
   b. theologically supported the concept of women's rights.
   c. was instrumental in leading women into the public and political arenas.
   d. was antiforeign in its orientation.

Objective 2

_____ 3. Which of the following is true of the temperance movement?
   a. The movement had little impact on the consumption of alcoholic beverages.
   b. Leaders of the movement simply wanted to regulate the sale of alcoholic spirits.
   c. Few women were involved in the movement.
   d. The movement was often supported by employers.

Objective 3

_____ 4. Although short-lived, Antimasonry is important because it
   a. led to the abolition of the electoral college.
   b. was the vehicle used by Andrew Jackson to gain grassroots support.
   c. demonstrated to future political candidates that moral crusades had no place in American politics.
   d. was a bridge between reform and politics.

Objective 4

_____ 5. Both the Lovejoy murder and the gag rule served to
   a. cause dissension within the antislavery movement.
   b. increase northern support for the antislavery movement.
   c. mobilize national support for the temperance movement.
   d. increase national support for government regulation of industry.

Objective 2

_____ 6. The women's movement was unlike the other reform movements of the early nineteenth century in which of the following ways?
   a. It was never able to build a broad support base from which to work.
   b. It did not arouse significant opposition.
   c. It was moral rather than social in its orientation.
   d. It was undertaken by a group that already had considerable political and economic power.

Objective 5

_____ 7. The 1828 election was important because it
   a. demonstrated that issues were more important than personalities in presidential elections.
   b. led political reformers to charge that the electoral college was obsolete.
   c. demonstrated that party organization would be very important in presidential elections.
   d. led to literacy tests for voters.

Objective 6

_____ 8. Which of the following statements best expresses Jacksonian beliefs?
   a. Strong central government is the enemy of individual liberty.
   b. Public education is essential in a democratic society.
   c. Government should be active in the economic life of the state.
   d. A strong, powerful president is to be feared.

Objective 6

_____ 9. In the Webster-Hayne debate, Webster described the Union as
   a. weak and disorderly.
   b. a collection of sovereign, independent states.
   c. the creation of God.
   d. a compact among the people rather than just the states.

Objective 7

_____ 10. As a result of the nullification crisis,
   a. federal authority was weakened because of the disagreement between Jackson and Congress.
   b. the South accepted the idea of secession.
   c. neither the federal government nor South Carolina won a clear victory.
   d. Jackson demonstrated his unwillingness to compromise.

Objective 7

_____ 11. In his veto message concerning the rechartering of the Second Bank of the United States, Jackson
   a. admitted that the bank was constitutional.
   b. denounced the bank as a symbol of special privilege and economic power.
   c. delivered a personal attack against the bank's president.
   d. attacked the bank for its tight money policies.

Objective 6

_____ 12. A person's political affiliation in the 1830s and 1840s was most closely associated with the person's
   a. social class.
   b. religious beliefs.
   c. occupation.
   d. gender.

Objective 8

_____ 13. After ascending to the presidency upon the death of President Harrison, President Tyler
   a. turned the reins of government over to Secretary of State Daniel Webster.
   b. proclaimed his opposition to Senator Calhoun's nullification theory.
   c. committed himself to the creation of an activist federal government.
   d. opposed the economic program that the deceased president had wanted enacted.

Objective 9

_____ 14. The expansionist sentiment of the 1840s emerged for which of the following reasons?
   a. The absence of threats by foreign powers caused Americans to think in expansionist terms.
   b. Such sentiment served as a release for internal conflicts caused by the economic problems of the 1840s.
   c. Spanish tyranny throughout the West was repugnant to Americans.
   d. Americans believed that it was their duty to carry their superior American civilization to inferior peoples.

Objective 10

_____ 15. James K. Polk's election to the presidency in 1844 was in large part due to
   a. fear among the voters that Henry Clay's American System would lead the nation to war.
   b. the support given him by Martin Van Buren.
   c. the presence of the Liberty party candidate on the ballot.
   d. Polk's stand against the expansion of slavery.

ESSAY QUESTIONS

Objective 2

1. Discuss the characteristics of the Second Great Awakening, and explain the impact of this religious revival on American society in the early nineteenth century.

Objective 4

2. Discuss the similarities and differences between "old" abolitionism as expressed through the American Colonization Society and "new" abolitionism as expressed through William Lloyd Garrison and the American Anti-Slavery Society.

Objective 2

3. Discuss the role of women in American society in the early nineteenth century, and explain the emergence, growth, goals, and achievements of the women's rights movement that emerged during that time.

Objectives 6 and 7

4. Discuss the social, political, and economic views of the Jacksonian Democrats, and explain how those views manifested themselves in the nullification crisis and in the controversy over rechartering the Second Bank of the United States.

Objective 9

5. Examine the expansionist sentiment that emerged in American society in the 1830s and 1840s.

MAP EXERCISE

1. On the maps that follow, label the upper map "Presidential Election, 1824," and the lower map "Presidential Election, 1828." After filling in the tables below, devise your own legend for the two maps, and indicate the states carried by each candidate in each of the two elections.

1824 Election

Candidate	Electoral Vote	% of Electoral Vote	Popular Vote	% of Popular Vote

1828 Election

Candidate	Electoral Vote	% of Electoral Vote	Popular Vote	% of Popular Vote

2. Since no candidate received a majority of electoral votes in the 1824 election, how was the president chosen? What problems did this choice present? Why?

3. Is there any discernible regional pattern in the elections? If so, explain it.

4. How were electors chosen in these elections? Why was the electoral vote in some states split among the candidates? (You will need to do some independent research to determine the answer to this question. An excellent source is *Presidential Elections Since 1789*, published by Congressional Quarterly, Inc.)

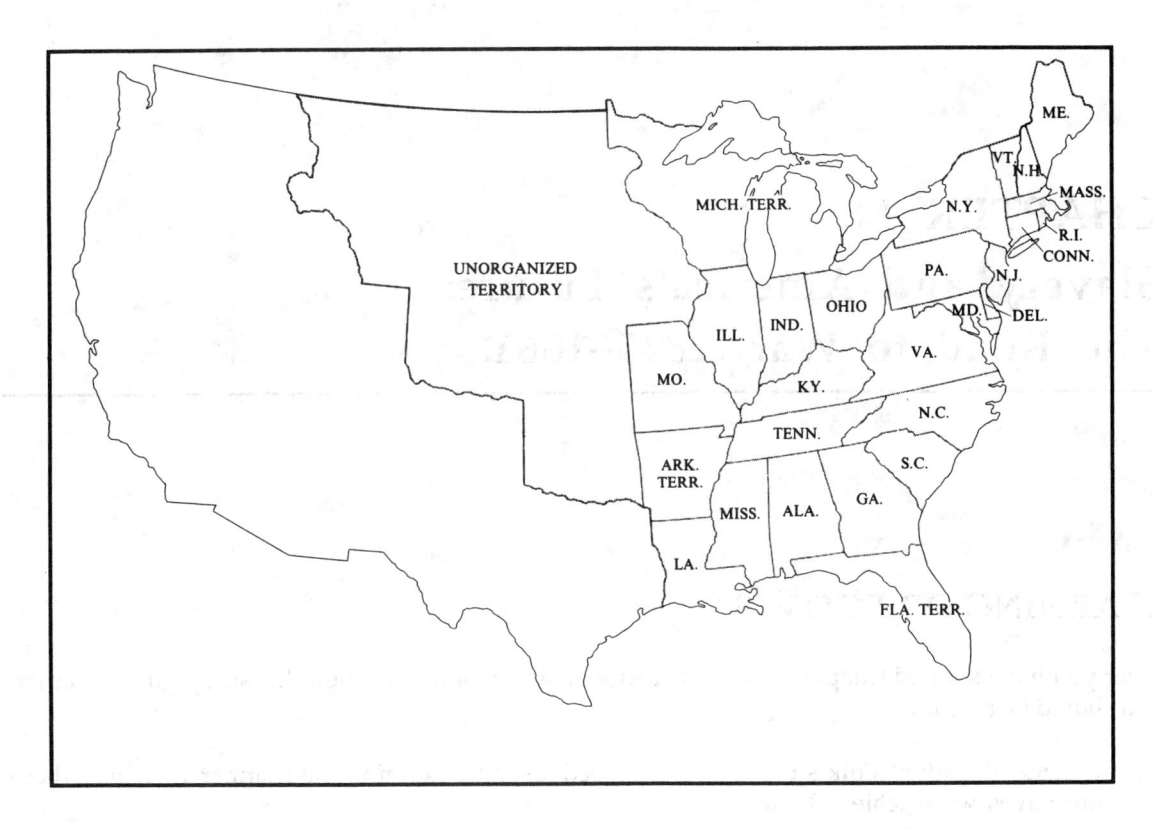

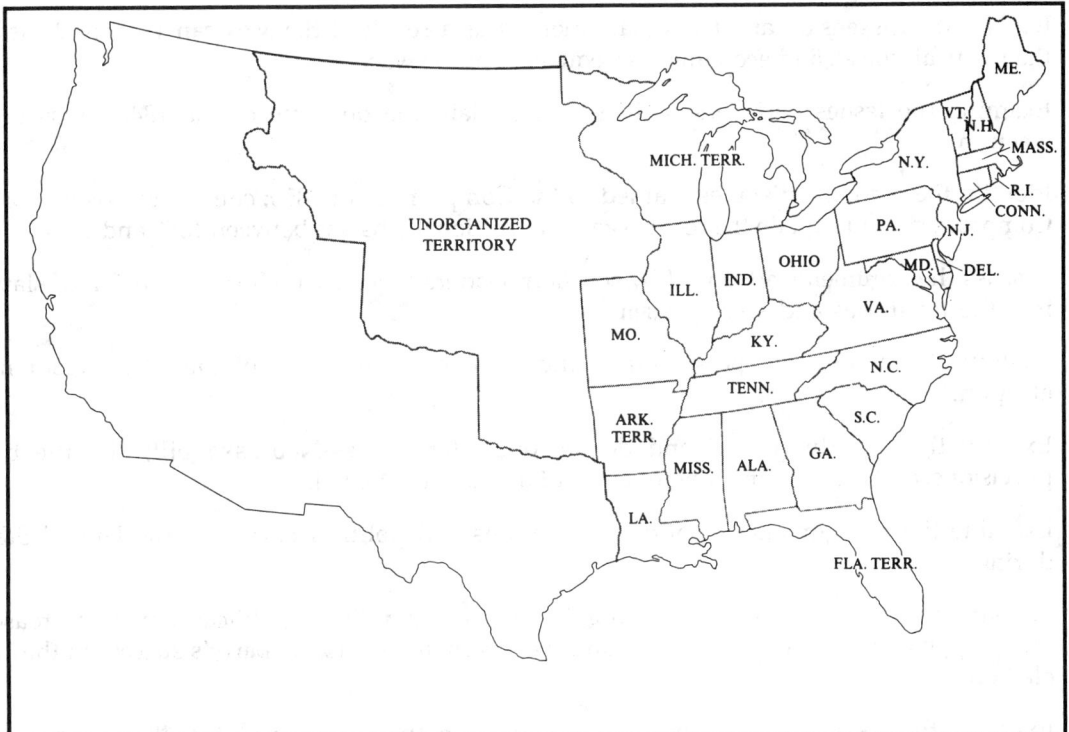

Chapter 13—Reform, Politics, and Expansion, 1824–1844

CHAPTER 14
Slavery and America's Future: The Road to War, 1845–1861

LEARNING OBJECTIVES

After you have studied Chapter 14 in your textbook and worked through this study guide chapter, you should be able to:

1. Discuss President Polk's expansionist objectives, and examine the manner in which these objectives were achieved.

2. Explain the dissension and fears that emerged as a result of the Mexican War, and discuss the political, social, and economic consequences of the war.

3. Examine the issues and personalities and explain the outcome of the 1848 presidential election.

4. Identify the sectional disputes that led to the Compromise of 1850; cite the provisions of the Compromise; and explain the re-emergence of sectional tensions between 1850 and 1854.

5. Discuss the arguments advanced by southern leaders to justify both the extension of slavery into the territories and slavery itself.

6. Examine the issues and personalities and explain the outcome of the 1852 presidential election.

7. Explain the introduction of and debate over the Kansas-Nebraska bill; cite the bill's provisions; and examine the consequences of its enactment into law.

8. Examine the realignment of political affiliations and political parties in the United States during the 1850s.

9. Explain the political, social, and economic philosophy of the Republican party, the reasons for its appeal among northern voters, and the forces that led to the party's success in the 1860 election.

10. Examine the issues and personalities and explain the outcome of the 1856 presidential election.

11. Explain the Supreme Court's decision in *Dred Scott v. Sanford,* and examine the impact of the decision on the political parties and their leaders and on northern and southern public opinion.

12. Examine the issues and personalities and explain the outcome of the 1860 presidential election.

13. Discuss the failure of attempts at compromise after the 1860 election, and explain the success of the secession movement in seven southern states between December 1860 and March 1861.

THEMATIC GUIDE

Chapter 14 has as its theme the interplay of several forces that paved the road to war in the period between 1845 and 1861. Two of the forces, territorial expansion and slavery, might at first glance seem separate, but in fact the two became inseparably intertwined. As we are told on page 376, "If slavery was the sore spot in the body politic, territorial disputes were salt rubbed into the wound." These forces became intertwined because of the addition of a third force, the perceptions (frames of reference) of the two antagonists, North and South, toward each other: "The new Republican party charged that southerners were taking over the federal government and planning to make slavery legal throughout the Union. . . . Southern leaders defended slavery and charged the North with lawless behavior in violation of the Constitution." The application of such perceptions to the twin forces of territorial expansion and slavery provided the catalyst necessary to produce sectional polarization, disunion, and war.

The Mexican War heightened northern fear of a Slave Power. This fear, present since passage of the gag rule in 1836, held that southern power and the expansion of slavery were jeopardizing the civil liberties enjoyed by whites. Northerners began to see a Slave Power conspiracy behind most of the events of the era, and since slavery was tied to the Slave Power that threatened their rights and interests, they became more and more antislavery in sentiment. The nature of northern fears and analysis of the Wilmot Proviso demonstrate that northern antislavery sentiment was racist and self-serving in its orientation.

Furthermore, the Mexican War, through introduction of the Wilmot Proviso into the House of Representatives, heightened southern fear that a hostile North was attempting to undermine and eventually abolish the institution of slavery. Southerners began to see an antislavery conspiracy behind most of the events of the era, and since such a conspiracy seemed tied to the northern abolitionist movement, southerners began to defend slavery more vociferously and, through John C. Calhoun's territorial theories, claimed slaveowners' rights were constitutionally protected.

Acquisition of territory from Mexico caused slavery to become the overriding issue in the presidential election of 1848. The Democrats and the Whigs began to fragment as a result of sectional antagonisms, and the presence of the Free-Soil party was partially responsible for Zachary Taylor's election as president. Between 1848 and 1850 several other issues emerged and caused further dissension. The most troublesome matter was the rights of settlers in the territories. The Compromise of 1850, designed to settle this and other issues, itself became a source of argument, which was further fueled by publication of *Uncle Tom's Cabin.*

As southern leaders began to feel more and more threatened by the antislavery arguments coming from the North, they developed a variety of proslavery arguments designed to explain the necessity of expanding slavery and to counter the moral arguments against slavery. Furthermore, to prevent congressional action, they continued to advance states' rights constitutional theories.

The election of Franklin Pierce to the presidency and the domestic and foreign policy decisions of his administration had the effect of further feeding northern fear that the Slave Power had captured control of the national government. Northerners saw passage of the Kansas-Nebraska Act and its repeal of the Missouri Compromise as a proslavery act inspired by the Slave

Power believed to be behind it. The shock waves from passage of this act brought the destruction of the Whig party, the birth of the Republican and American parties, and a complete realignment of the political system in the United States. In this realignment, the Republican party, by appealing to groups interested in the economic development of the West and by expounding an ideology based on the dignity of labor, became the dominant party in the North. Concurrently, the Democratic party, by arguing that slavery elevated the status of all whites, appealing to racism, and emphasizing the "rights" of southerners, became the party of the South. In addition, northerners linked Democrats with the Slave Power, while southerners linked Republicans with radical abolitionists.

Events now came in rapid succession—"Bleeding Kansas," the Sumner-Brooks affair, the *Dred Scott* decision, Stephen Douglas's Freeport Doctrine, John Brown's raid on Harpers Ferry, the splintering of the Democratic party, and Abraham Lincoln's election in 1860. Each drove the wedge more deeply between the two sections and served to further harden opinions. However, analysis of the 1860 election results indicates that the electorate did not vote in favor of extreme action. Compromise was made impossible first by Lincoln's refusal to soften his party's stand on the expansion of slavery into the territories. The situation was exacerbated by the adoption of the separate-state secession strategy by southern extremists, which led to the secession of seven southern states between the time of Lincoln's election and his inauguration. Lincoln's subsequent decision as president to reprovision the federal fort in the Charleston harbor brought the first shots of what was to be the Civil War.

BUILDING VOCABULARY

Listed below are important words and terms that you need to know to get the most out of Chapter 14. They are listed in the order in which they occur in the chapter. After carefully looking through the list, refer to a dictionary and jot down the definition of words that you do not know or of which you are unsure.

incendiary

maelstrom

heterogeneous

sinister

periphery

formidable

enmity

oligarchy

ominous

venerable

omnibus

ambiguous

anthropological

phrenology

transcontinental

cogently

perpetuity

nativist

demise

retrograde

viable

amalgamation

polarize

homogenous

hyperbole

martyr

secession

plurality

don

mantle

avert

unanimity

acquiesce

succinctly

shroud

IDENTIFICATION AND SIGNIFICANCE

After studying Chapter 14 of *A People and a Nation,* you should be able to identify fully *and* explain the historical significance of each item listed below.

1. Identify each item in the space provided. Give an explanation or description of the item. Answer the questions *who, what, where,* and *when.*

2. Explain the historical significance of each item in the space provided. Establish the historical context in which the item exists. Establish the item as the result of or as the cause of other factors existing in the society under study. Answer this question: *What were the political, social, economic, and/or cultural consequences of this item?*

James K. Polk

    Identification

    Significance

the Oregon Treaty

    Identification

    Significance

the Mexican War

    Identification

    Significance

the Treaty of Guadalupe Hidalgo

    Identification

    Significance

the Slave Power

    Identification

    Significance

the Wilmot Proviso

    Identification

    Significance

John C. Calhoun's territorial theories

    Identification

    Significance

the presidential election of 1848

    Identification

    Significance

popular sovereignty

    Identification

    Significance

the Free-Soil Party

    Identification

    Significance

the Compromise of 1850

    Identification

    Significance

the Fugitive Slave Act

    Identification

    Significance

Uncle Tom's Cabin

    Identification

    Significance

proslavery theories

    Identification

    Significance

George Fitzhugh

    Identification

    Significance

the presidential election of 1852

    Identification

    Significance

Franklin Pierce

    Identification

    Significance

Anthony Burns

    Identification

    Significance

the Ostend Manifesto

    Identification

    Significance

Stephen A. Douglas

    Identification

    Significance

the Kansas-Nebraska bill

    Identification

    Significance

personal-liberty laws

    Identification

    Significance

"Appeal of the Independent Democrats"

    Identification

    Significance

the Republican party

    Identification

    Significance

the American (Know-Nothing) party

    Identification

    Significance

"Free Soil, Free Labor, Free Men"

    Identification

    Significance

the southern version of republicanism

    Identification

    Significance

Bleeding Kansas

    Identification

    Significance

John Brown

    Identification

    Significance

the Sumner-Brooks affair

    Identification

    Significance

James Buchanan

    Identification

    Significance

the presidential election of 1856

    Identification

    Significance

the Dred Scott case

    Identification

    Significance

Lincoln's "House Divided" speech

    Identification

    Significance

the Lecompton constitution

    Identification

    Significance

the Freeport Doctrine

    Identification

    Significance

John Brown's raid on Harpers Ferry

    Identification

    Significance

the 1860 Democratic convention

    Identification

    Significance

the presidential election of 1860

    Identification

    Significance

the Crittenden Compromise

    Identification

    Significance

separate-state secession strategy

    Identification

    Significance

the Confederate States of America

    Identification

    Significance

the attack on Fort Sumter

    Identification

    Significance

324 Chapter 14—Slavery and America's Future: The Road to War, 1845–1861

EVALUATING AND USING INFORMATION

Exercise A

Below is a list of statements followed by five questions. The statements offer information to help you interpret the table about the 1860 presidential vote in Chapter 14 of your textbook and identify the members of the two sides in the Civil War to follow. Refer to both the table (see page 397 in your textbook) *and* the statements as you answer the questions.

Helpful Statements

a. The border states, which are sometimes included among the southern states, include Delaware, Kentucky, Maryland, and Missouri.

b. Slave states included Alabama, Arkansas, Delaware, Florida, Georgia, Kentucky, Louisiana, Maryland, Mississippi, Missouri, North Carolina, South Carolina, Tennessee, Texas, and Virginia.

c. The term *the North* refers to all states other than slave and border states. In 1860, *the North* meant California, Connecticut, Illinois, Indiana, Iowa, Maine, Massachusetts, Michigan, Minnesota, New Hampshire, New Jersey, New York, Ohio, Oregon, Pennsylvania, Rhode Island, Vermont, and Wisconsin.

d. In the South, in the 1860 election, Republican Abraham Lincoln received votes only in states that did not secede before the Civil War began.

e. The Confederacy included eleven states: Alabama, Arkansas, Florida, Georgia, Louisiana, Mississippi, North Carolina, South Carolina, Tennessee, Texas, and Virginia.

f. Four slave states, including Virginia, rejected secession after Lincoln's election but voted for secession after the attack on Fort Sumter.

g. In October of 1861, already disaffected by the influence of the eastern planters in Virginia politics, fifty counties west of the Alleghenies reacted to their state's vote to secede by deciding in a public referendum to secede themselves—from Virginia—and form a new state, the state of West Virginia, which was formally admitted to the Union during the war (June 20, 1863).

h. Democrat John C. Breckenridge carried nine southern states, doing especially well in the Deep South.

i. Lincoln won some of his popular votes from one of the future Confederate states that gave Tennesseean John Bell pluralities.

j. John Bell received more votes than any other candidate in Virginia, Kentucky, and Tennessee.

k. Lincoln won no popular votes in the home state of the Constitutional Union party nominee, John Bell.

l. Voting returns from eight slave states for counties in which there were few slaveholders consistently showed that a larger percentage of the voters favored Breckinridge in 1860 than favored secession in 1861.

Copyright © Houghton Mifflin Company. All rights reserved.

Questions

1. Did any slave states fight for the Union?
2. Did any free states fight for the Confederacy?
3. Which was the only state among the Confederate states to cast votes for Abraham Lincoln?
4. Which, if any, of the statements suggest that slavery was a major cause of the Civil War?
5. Formulate a rule to explain the relationship between any southern state's location and the likelihood of its opposing secession. (*Hint*: Look at a map of the United States as the nation existed at or near the Civil War period, such as the maps on p. 27 of the Atlas of American History that came with your textbook.)

Exercise B

Look at the objectives and essay questions concerning the presidential election of 1860 at the end of this chapter in your study guide. Then compose the essay question that you would ask about that election if you were the professor testing students on Chapter 14. Organize relevant information from your textbook and class notes and compose the working draft of an essay answering your own question.

In composing your answer, you may find the statistics in the Evaluating and Using Information exercise for Chapter 11 of your study guide useful.

IDEAS AND DETAILS

Objective 1

_____ 1. President Polk agreed to a negotiated settlement with Great Britain over the Oregon Territory because
   a. he wanted to avoid the possibility of simultaneous wars with Great Britain and Mexico.
   b. it was obvious that the American people would not support the use of force to gain questionable territory.
   c. public disclosures by Polk's enemies in the Senate weakened United States claims.
   d. the British were willing to grant the United States all its demands.

Objective 2

_____ 2. Both the Mexican War and the gag rule
   a. aroused fears about presidential power.
   b. aroused fears about subversive foreign influence within the United States government.
   c. made the idea of a Slave Power believable.
   d. were supported by New Englanders.

Objective 2

_____ 3. The Wilmot Proviso stipulated that
   a. slavery would be permitted in Utah and New Mexico but prohibited in California.
   b. blacks would be colonized in the territory acquired from Mexico.
   c. the civil and political rights of blacks would be guaranteed in the territory acquired from Mexico.
   d. slavery would be prohibited in all territory acquired from Mexico.

Objective 3

_____ 4. Zachary Taylor's victory in the 1848 presidential election was, in large part, due to
   a. the support he received from William Lloyd Garrison and the abolitionists.
   b. the fragmentation of the political parties over the issue of slavery in the territories.
   c. his decisive stand against the expansion of slavery into the territories.
   d. President Polk's endorsement.

Objective 4

_____ 5. One of the basic flaws in the Compromise of 1850 was the
   a. failure to abolish the slave trade in the nation's capital.
   b. admission of California as a slave state.
   c. ambiguity that surrounded the idea of popular sovereignty.
   d. extension of the Missouri Compromise line to the Pacific Ocean.

Objective 5

_____ 6. Which of the following best expresses the ideas of George Fitzhugh?
   a. He concluded that slavery should be practiced in all societies.
   b. He argued that the wage labor system was superior to the slave labor system.
   c. He relied on biblical accounts of slaveholding to defend the institution.
   d. He believed that slavery was morally wrong but economically necessary.

Objective 7

_____ 7. The Kansas-Nebraska Act
   a. rejected the concept of popular sovereignty.
   b. unified the Whig party against the Slave Power.
   c. was introduced as a proslavery measure.
   d. repealed the Missouri Compromise.

Objective 9

_____ 8. Which of the following statements best expresses the beliefs of the Republican party in the 1850s?
   a. Acceptance of the dignity of labor is essential to the future progress of the United States.
   b. The central government should remain limited in its power and should not intervene in the economic life of the states.
   c. Slavery is morally wrong and should be abolished immediately.
   d. All ethnic groups living in the United States should be afforded political, social, and economic equality.

Objective 5

_____ 9. Southern Democrats appealed to nonslaveholders in the South by
   a. promising to make slaves available to all white southerners.
   b. arguing that slavery made all white men equal.
   c. supporting a homestead bill for the western territories.
   d. supporting the use of federal funds for internal improvements in the South.

Objectives 7, 8, 9, and 10

_____ 10. Analysis of the presidential election of 1856 reveals that the
   a. Democratic party had become a purely sectional party.
   b. Republican party was partially successful in gaining support in the South.
   c. Republican party had become the dominant party in the North.
   d. voters preferred the candidate whose stand on the territorial questions was clear.

Objective 11

_____ 11. In the *Dred Scott* decision, the Court held that
   a. property rights were to be subordinated to individual rights.
   b. it was impossible for a slave to be freed.
   c. Congress could not prohibit slavery in the territories.
   d. a slave moving into a free state became a free person.

Objectives 9 and 12

_____ 12. Which of the following best expresses the beliefs of Abraham Lincoln?
   a. The territories must be open to *all* people in the United States.
   b. Slavery is morally wrong and must be abolished immediately.
   c. The question of the expansion of slavery into the territories can best be decided through the use of popular sovereignty.
   d. The Slave Power threatens the free wage labor system not only in the territories but in the free states as well.

Objective 11

_____ 13. In the Freeport Doctrine, Stephen Douglas asserted that
   a. the *Dred Scott* decision did not have the force of law and was not to be obeyed.
   b. in spite of the *Dred Scott* decision, a territorial legislature could still exclude slavery from a territory.
   c. as a result of the *Dred Scott* decision, there was no way to prevent the expansion of slavery into the territories.
   d. in spite of the *Dred Scott* decision, slavery was morally wrong and should be abolished.

Objective 12

_____ 14. In the 1860 election, John C. Breckenridge, the presidential nominee of the southern wing of the Democratic party,
   a. disavowed secession.
   b. blamed the nation's problems on Catholic immigrants.
   c. called for military preparedness in the slave states.
   d. called for repeal of the Kansas-Nebraska bill.

Objective 13

_____ 15. The Crittenden Compromise failed because
   a. the election of 1860 had so hardened sectional antagonisms that compromise was impossible.
   b. extremists gained control of southern state legislatures and made it impossible for southern congressmen to accept a compromise.
   c. northern leaders wanted the South to leave the Union.
   d. Lincoln refused to make concessions on the issue of the expansion of slavery into the territories.

ESSAY QUESTIONS

Objectives 2, 4, 7, 8, 9, 11, and 12

1. Explain what northerners meant when they referred to the Slave Power, and trace the northern fear of the Slave Power from the Mexican War through the 1860 presidential election.

Objective 4

2. Examine the fugitive slave law and its impact on relations between North and South.

Objective 5

3. Discuss the arguments used by the South to defend and justify the institution of slavery.

Objective 5

4. Discuss the constitutional arguments used by the South to defend slavery against political threats and the "scientific," sociological, and biblical arguments used to defend and justify slavery against moral threats.

Objectives 7 and 8

5. Cite the provisions of the Kansas-Nebraska bill and examine its far-reaching impact on American society.

Objective 12

6. Examine the issues and personalities in the 1860 presidential election, and explain the election's outcome and its impact on American society.

CHAPTER 15
Transforming Fire: The Civil War, 1861–1865

LEARNING OBJECTIVES

After you have studied Chapter 15 in your textbook and worked through this study guide chapter, you should be able to:

1. Explain the strategy of the combatants during the first two years of the Civil War; identify their strengths and weaknesses; and indicate the relative position of each in early 1863.

2. Examine the social, political, and economic impact of the Civil War on the South, its values, and its people.

3. Examine the social, political, and economic impact of the Civil War on the North, its values, and its people.

4. Discuss the strengths and weaknesses of the North and the South, and explain the factors that led to northern victory and southern defeat.

5. Discuss Abraham Lincoln's and Congress's approach to the slavery question during the course of the Civil War; examine their decisions on this issue; and explain the impact of those decisions on the Union and its war effort.

6. Discuss Jefferson Davis's and the Confederate Congress's approach to the slavery question, examine their decisions on this issue, and explain the impact of those decisions on the Confederacy and its war effort.

7. Discuss the impact of military life and wartime experiences on Confederate and Union soldiers during the Civil War.

8. Explain Grant's strategy in the final years of the Civil War, and describe the battles that enabled him to achieve northern victory.

9. Examine the emergence of dissent and disorder in the Confederacy and the Union in the final two years of the Civil War, and explain the impact of these forces on the two combatants.

10. Discuss the efforts of both North and South to achieve their diplomatic objectives, and indicate the outcome of those efforts.

11. Discuss the financial and human costs of the Civil War, and indicate what issues were resolved and what issues were left unresolved at war's end.

THEMATIC GUIDE

The title of Chapter 15 appropriately calls the Civil War a "transforming fire" and, in so doing, establishes the transformation of northern and southern societies as the chapter's theme. Ironically, the South, which fought to prevent change, was changed the most.

Both North and South expected the Civil War to end quickly; but, as the discussion of the military engagements of the first two years illustrates, both were mistaken. In 1862, in an attempt to adjust to the likelihood of a prolonged conflict, the Confederacy adopted the first conscription law in the history of the United States. This is the first mention of the changes brought to the South by the war. These changes also included

1. centralization of political and economic power;
2. increased urban growth;
3. increased industrialization;
4. changed roles for women;
5. mass poverty, labor shortages, food shortages, and runaway inflation; and
6. class conflict.

The theme of change continues with a discussion of the war's economic, political, and social impact on northern society.

In the midst of this change, slavery, the institution that was the underlying cause of the war, was seldom mentioned by either Jefferson Davis or Abraham Lincoln. Lincoln's silence on the issue during the first year of the war reflected both his hope that a compromise could be reached with the South and his attempt to keep intact the coalitions that constituted the Republican party. In dealing with the subject in 1862, he took a conservative and racist approach. When Congress attempted to lead on the slavery question, Lincoln refused to follow, and when abolitionists prodded him on the question, he distinguished between official duty and personal wishes. When finally he did act, it was to offer the Emancipation Proclamation—a document that was morally wanting but politically flawless. In 1864 he supported the Thirteenth Amendment, but his support wavered by 1865. It is obvious, then, that Lincoln did not lead public opinion on the race question and that preserving the Union, not ending slavery, was Lincoln's main concern.

Ultimately, Jefferson Davis also addressed the slavery issue. Dedicated to independence for the Confederacy, Davis became convinced that emancipation was a partial means to that end. Although he faced serious opposition on the issue, Davis pushed and prodded the Confederacy toward emancipation, but his actions came too late to aid the Confederate cause.

The experience of war also changed the individual soldiers who served in the Confederate and Union armies. Accustomed to living largely unrestricted lives in rural areas, many had difficulty adjusting to the military discipline that robbed them of their individuality. Subjected to deprivation and disease and surrounded by dead, dying, and wounded colleagues, the reality of war had a profound emotional impact on those who experienced it. However, the commonality of these experiences and the sense of dedication to a common task forged bonds among soldiers that they cherished for years.

The last two years of the war brought increasing antigovernment sentiment in both South and North. More widespread in the South, such sentiment involved the planters, who seemed committed only to their own selfish interests, the urban poor, and the rural masses. The deep-rooted nature of southern war resistance affected the war effort, and the internal disintegration of the Confederacy was furthered by disastrous defeats at Vicksburg and Gettysburg. It was in this atmosphere that southern peace movements emerged, more anti-Davis representatives were elected to the Confederate Congress, and secret antiwar societies began to form. Antiwar sentiment also emerged in the North; but, in large part because of Lincoln's ability to communicate with the common people, it never reached the proportions of southern opposition to the war effort. Opposition in the North was either political in nature (the Peace Democrats) or was undertaken by ordinary citizens subject to the draft (the New York draft riot).

In light of the political nature of the antiwar movement in the North, Lincoln feared for his re-election prospects in 1864. However, owing to the success of northern efforts to prevent diplomatic recognition of the Confederacy by Great Britain and France and to Sherman's successful march on Atlanta and his subsequent march to the sea, Lincoln's re-election was assured. The "transforming fire" proceeded to its conclusion with Lee's surrender at Appomattox on April 9, 1865, followed by Lincoln's assassination five days later. The era of the Civil War had ended; the era of Reconstruction began.

BUILDING VOCABULARY

Listed below are important words and terms that you need to know to get the most out of Chapter 15. They are listed in the order in which they occur in the chapter. After carefully looking through the list, refer to a dictionary and jot down the definition of words that you do not know or of which you are unsure.

scathing

crass

lucrative

eminent

obliterate

disaffection

rout

formidable

flank

incursion

notable

foil

tenacious

stoic

nonchalance

exhort

exult

privation

sparsely

mortify

rudimentary

inequity

courier

odium

entrepreneurs

blacklist

profiteering

unscrupulous

largesse

iniquity

adept

furlough

ostentation

dauntless

homoerotic

commutation

tenuous

astute

substantive

instigation

integral

onus

tedium

stupendous

vermin

pummel

citadel

beseech

respite

ominous

usurpation

atrophy

quell

austere

tacitly

melee

wantonly

protracted

IDENTIFICATION AND SIGNIFICANCE

After studying Chapter 15 of *A People and a Nation*, you should be able to identify fully *and* explain the historical significance of each item listed below.

1. Identify each item in the space provided. Give an explanation or description of the item. Answer the questions *who, what, where,* and *when*.
2. Explain the historical significance of each item in the space provided. Establish the historical context in which the item exists. Establish the item as the result of or as the cause of other factors existing in the society under study. Answer this question: *What were the political, social, economic, and/or cultural consequences of this item?*

Sam Houston and Nathaniel Banks

    Identification

    Significance

the Battle of Bull Run

    Identification

    Significance

General George McClellan

    Identification

    Significance

Union naval campaign

    Identification

    Significance

Ulysses S. Grant

    Identification

    Significance

Grant's Tennessee campaign

    Identification

    Significance

the Battle of Shiloh

    Identification

    Significance

McClellan's advance on Richmond

    Identification

    Significance

the Seven Days' battles

    Identification

    Significance

President Jefferson Davis's southern offensive

    Identification

    Significance

the Battle of Antietam

    Identification

    Significance

Jefferson Davis

    Identification

    Significance

the Confederate conscription law

> Identification

> Significance

the Confederate tax-in-kind

> Identification

> Significance

the Confederate bureaucracy

> Identification

> Significance

Josiah Gorgas

> Identification

> Significance

Janie Smith

> Identification

> Significance

inflation in the South

> Identification

> Significance

the Confederate relief program

    Identification

    Significance

the southern practice of hiring substitutes

    Identification

    Significance

the twenty-slave law

    Identification

    Significance

Jay Cooke

    Identification

    Significance

the development of heavy industry in the North

    Identification

    Significance

Cyrus and William McCormick

    Identification

    Significance

northern labor activism

    Identification

    Significance

the Union Pacific and Central Pacific Railroads

    Identification

    Significance

the Morrill Land Grant Act

    Identification

    Significance

the Tariff Act of 1864

    Identification

    Significance

Lincoln's use of presidential power

    Identification

    Significance

the National Banking Acts of 1863, 1864, and 1865

    Identification

    Significance

Walt Whitman

>   Identification

>   Significance

Lincoln's plan for gradual emancipation

>   Identification

>   Significance

the Radicals

>   Identification

>   Significance

the confiscation acts

>   Identification

>   Significance

"The Prayer of Twenty Millions"

>   Identification

>   Significance

the Emancipation Proclamations

>   Identification

>   Significance

the Thirteenth Amendment

    Identification

    Significance

the Hampton Roads Conference

    Identification

    Significance

Davis's emancipation plan

    Identification

    Significance

the U.S. Sanitary Commission

    Identification

    Significance

the "minie ball"

    Identification

    Significance

African-American soldiers in the Union army

    Identification

    Significance

the Battle of Chancellorsville

    Identification

    Significance

the Battle of Vicksburg

    Identification

    Significance

the Battle of Gettysburg

    Identification

    Significance

the Confederate constitution

    Identification

    Significance

southern food riots

    Identification

    Significance

Confederate manpower problems

    Identification

    Significance

southern peace movements

    Identification

    Significance

the Peace Democrats

    Identification

    Significance

Clement L. Vallandigham

    Identification

    Significance

Copperheads

    Identification

    Significance

New York City draft riot

    Identification

    Significance

the presidential election of 1864

    Identification

    Significance

northern diplomatic strategy

    Identification

    Significance

"king Cotton" diplomacy

    Identification

    Significance

the *Trent* affair

    Identification

    Significance

the *Alabama*

    Identification

    Significance

Sherman's southern campaign

    Identification

    Significance

Appomattox Courthouse

    Identification

    Significance

John Wilkes Booth

Identification

Significance

ORGANIZING INFORMATION

Civil War Battles and Campaigns

Using the following charts, compile and organize information pertaining to Civil War battles and military campaigns mentioned in the textbook. More detailed information on these and other battles may be found in many of the books mentioned in the bibliography at the end of Chapter 15, especially those dealing with the military aspects of the war.

In the "Outcome" column, use *C* to designate a Confederate victory, *U* to designate a Union victory, and *D* to designate a draw.

1861–1863

Battle	Date	Outcome	Consequences
Bull Run			
Union campaign along southern coast			
New Orleans			
Elkhorn Tavern			
Fort Henry and Fort Donelson			
Shiloh			
Seven Days battle			
Sharpsburg			
Antietam			
Fredericksburg			

1863–1865

Battle	Date	Outcome	Consequences
Chancellorsville			
Vicksburg			
Gettysburg			
Red River			
Mobile Bay			
Chattanooga			
Sherman's march on Atlanta			
Sherman's march to the sea			
Sherman's march through the Carolinas			
Battle of the Wilderness			
Spotsylvania			
Cold Harbor			

EVALUATING AND USING INFORMATION

As Chapter 15 suggests, the Civil War created severe hardship and stress both for the soldiers who fought it and for the citizens at home who had to endure restrictions and deprivation. In the three parts of this exercise, you are to analyze some of the stresses of both groups, first as they are discussed in Chapter 11 and then as they are reported by a soldier in a primary source.

Since Parts A and B culminate in your composing the working draft of a contrast essay, you may want to review the hints for composing such essays provided in the Evaluation and Using Information exercise in Chapter 5 of your study guide.

To add context to Parts A and B of this exercise, review the Evaluating and Using Information exercise for Chapter 11.

A: Gathering and Grouping Information for an Essay

Using the following chart as your guide, collect and organize specific, concrete information about the causes and effects of tension between (or among) classes in both the North and the South during the Civil War.

- Familiarize yourself with the topics listed in the chart.

- Find all references in Chapter 15 to the topics listed in the chart.

- Take notes on that information, recording your notes in the chart.

- To indicate how you think the information should be grouped, insert group designations (A, B, C, etc.) in the appropriate spaces in the first column. (This designation of the groups to which you are assigning related information is like what you did in the Evaluating and Using Information exercise in Chapter 2 when you wrote letters in the lead-in blanks.)

B: Interpreting Information and Using It in An Essay

- Study the groups of information related to the North and determine their main and supporting ideas and state the point that all of the main points add up to.

- Study the groups of information related to the South and determine the main and supporting ideas and state the point that all of the main points add up to.

- Combine the ideas in the two statements to create the thesis for an essay contrasting the North and the South in terms of the kind of class conflict that most characterized them.

- Compose a working draft for an essay contrasting the North and the South in terms of the kind of class conflict that most characterized each region during the war and enter it in your Reader's Notebook.

North

Group	Topics Related to Class Tension	Notes from Text
	Confiscation Acts	
	Conscription	
	Draft	
	Impressment	

North

Group	Topics Related to Class Tension	Notes from Text
	Leaders' relationship with ordinary citizens	
	Military substitutes/commutation	
	Profiteering, speculation	
	Sharing among classes of burdens of war	
	South's efforts to exploit social tensions	

South

Group	Topics Related to Class Tension	Notes from Text
	Strikes, labor unrest	
	Tariffs and/or taxes	
	Citizenry's reaction to Sherman's march	
	Draft	
	Food riots	

South

Group	Topics Related to Class Tension	Notes from Text
	Growth of government bureaucracy	
	Impressment	
	Labor force unrest	
	Military substitutes, commutation	
	North's efforts to exploit social tensions	

South

Group	Topics Related to Class Tension	Notes from Text
	Sharing among classes of burdens of war	
	Threats to "States' Rights"	
	Other (specify)	

C: Analysis of a Primary Source

The document below was first published on July 26, 1863, in the *New York Times*. Omissions to reduce its length are indicated by ellipses (three dots); insertions or changes in capitalization are indicated by brackets.

A list of ten statements follows the document. After studying the document, circle the number of every statement in the list that expresses an inference that can be derived logically from what is in the document.

> JULY 2.— Bucksville.— . . . [T]he Second brigade . . . arrived and reported that Col. JOHNSON . . . had experienced great difficulty in crossing, and that in addition to the precipitous banks and absence of all boats or others means of transportation, the enemy were hovering on the river and harassing him . . . . He was, however, quite successful in driving them back. Yesterday a young man, calling himself CHARLES ROGERS, dressed in full Confederate uniform, came into our lines and expressed a desire to join our command. . . . [A]fter a few questions I was convinced that he was a spy. I threatened to shoot him when he confessed . . . lying—in fact, he convicted himself of being a spy. I hated to shoot him, although he deserved it.

JULY 3.—My regiment behaved very gallantly in yesterday's fight . . . frequently having hand to hand encounters. Today (3d) . . . we proceeded to Columbia. They were met by detachments from three regiments (Forty-fifth Ohio, Second Ohio and First Kentucky) . . . . [In a] brief engagement . . . we drove the enemy . . . through the town capturing six prisoners, killing two . . . and wounding three. Our loss was two killed and two wounded. . . . Passed through Columbia, and camped six miles from Green River Bridge.

JULY 4.—New-Market, Ky.—A day of gloom, deep gloom. . . . [T]his morning Capt. MAGENNIS, the Adjutant-General, rode up and remarked how dreadful to reflect that we were marching on to engage in deadly strife, and how many . . . would pass into eternity before the setting of yonder sun. . . . (Before dark he was a corpse.). . . . About sunrise we drove in the enemy's pickets and were soon near their fortifications. . . . Gen. MORGAN . . . demanded the surrender, but the Colonel quietly remarked, "If it was another day he might consider the demand, *but the Fourth of July was a bad day to talk about surrender*, and he must therefore decline.". . . .

We attacked the place with two regiments, sending the remainder of our force across another ford. . . . [W]e were repulsed with severe loss—about twenty-five killed and twenty wounded. . . . Our march thus far has been very fatiguing, bad roads, little rest or sleep, little to eat and a fight every day. Yet our men are cheerful and even buoyant. . . . About three o'clock, as I rode on about forty yards in advance, I heard the General exclaim something . . . which I could not understand, and heard at the same time the report of a pistol.

I turned, and, Great God! to my horror, I saw Capt. MAGENNIS falling from his horse, with the blood gushing out of his mouth and breast. His only remark was, "Let me down easy." He was killed by Capt. MURPHY because MAGENNIS, by the direction of Gen. MORGAN, had ordered MURPHY to restore a watch taken from a prisoner. I had seen blood flow freely on many a battle-field; . . . but this caused a deeper impression and shock than any occurrence I ever witnessed. . . .

JULY 5.—Another day of gloom, fatigue and death. Moved on Lebanon at sunrise. Placed our men in line. Sent around . . . [a] brigade to the Danville road to cut off reinforcements. . . . I went in with a flag of truce. It was fired on five times. Officer apologized, saying he thought it was a man with a white coat on. Very dangerous mistake, at least for me. . . . Told Col. HANSON . . . resistance was useless. He refused to surrender. . . .

After a fight of seven hours, Gen. MORGAN, finding the town could be taken in no other way, ordered a charge. . . . Col. HANSON still held out . . . and only surrendered after we had fired the buildings. . . .

1. The forces whose activities the document describes are cavalry forces.

2. The document is part of a diary or journal.

3. The writer of the document is a Union soldier.

4. The writer of the document shot the man calling himself Charles Rogers.

5. The part of the document presented here was written around noon on July 4, 1863.

6. Capt. Murphy was executed for killing Capt. Magennis.

7. The writer is a Confederate officer.

8. The writer of the document is the commander of the forces whose activities the document describes.

9. The writer's spirits consistently rise between July 1 and July 6, 1863.

10. The officer whose men fired on the white flag lied.

IDEAS AND DETAILS

Objective 1

_____ 1. Which of the following is true of the blockade of southern ports by the Union navy?
   a. It was never completely successful in blocking the Confederacy's avenues of commerce and supply.
   b. It began an industrialization effort that caused the South's industrial capacity to match that of the North by 1865.
   c. It was the major reason for mass starvation in the Confederate states.
   d. It angered France and led to a Franco-Confederate alliance.

Objective 2

_____ 2. The Civil War changed southern society by forcing
   a. farmers to buy cotton from England.
   b. businessmen to extend loans to the army.
   c. an abandonment of the philosophy of weak central government.
   d. plantation owners to sell their estates.

Objective 3

_____ 3. The managers of northern corporations believed that
   a. the government should aid but not regulate business.
   b. business should be regulated at the state rather than at the national level.
   c. Congress should establish regulatory commissions for all industry.
   d. union leaders and corporate managers should draw up guidelines to establish fair wages and working hours.

Objectives 3 and 4

_____ 4. The mechanization of agriculture in the North caused
   a. severe depression in rural areas as farm hands lost their jobs.
   b. an expansion of the food supply for the expanding urban work force.
   c. overproduction and declining prices for farm goods.
   d. most farmers to become so heavily burdened with debt that they faced bankruptcy.

Objective 3

_____ 5. Which of the following northern groups made the highest profits during the Civil War?
   a. Ordinary citizens who invested in Erie Railroad stock
   b. Businessmen who engaged in profiteering on government contracts
   c. Union army officers who received lucrative war bonds
   d. Farm families who supplied food to the Union army

Objective 3

_____ 6. Which of the following inferences may be drawn from the facts surrounding the shipbuilding program supported by President Lincoln?
   a. Lincoln engaged in defense spending that was unnecessary and unwise.
   b. The war years witnessed an increase in presidential power.
   c. The northern press had a decided impact on military decisions made by the president.
   d. Lincoln often acted against the advice of the Joint Chiefs of Staff.

Objective 5

_____ 7. In his first mention of slavery in connection with the war, Lincoln
   a. promised to negotiate with any southern state agreeing to free its slaves.
   b. promised the large planters in the South that they would be allowed to keep twenty slaves if they freed all others.
   c. proposed that Congress promise aid to any state agreeing to gradual emancipation of its slaves.
   d. promised federal aid to all slaves who were able to escape to the North.

Objective 5

_____ 8. The Emancipation Proclamation
   a. abolished slavery in the United States.
   b. freed slaves in the border states only.
   c. provided for the gradual abolition of slavery in the Confederate states but not in the border states.
   d. freed slaves in those areas in rebellion against the United States.

Objective 5

_____ 9. Lincoln's Emancipation Proclamation was nearly flawless as a
   a. legal document.
   b. religious document.
   c. political document.
   d. humanitarian document.

Objective 6

_____ 10. To achieve the goal of independence, Jefferson Davis
   a. issued an executive order that outlawed the practice of hiring substitutes for military service.
   b. proposed that full equality be given to all southern blacks willing to actively support the Confederacy.
   c. ordered that the eligible age for Confederate recruits be lowered to twelve.
   d. proposed that emancipation be promised to slave soldiers and their families.

Objective 7

_____ 11. In the midst of the Civil War, southern planters
   a. increasingly stood in opposition to the Confederate government.
   b. demonstrated their commitment to building an independent southern nation.
   c. accepted change as a natural consequence of the revolutionary path they had chosen.
   d. did everything in their power to aid the war effort.

Objective 4

_____ 12. Abraham Lincoln, unlike Jefferson Davis, was
   a. able to reach the common people.
   b. quiet, shy, and retiring.
   c. cold and aloof.
   d. sincere in his beliefs.

Objective 10

_____ 13. The Union's primary diplomatic goal was to
   a. break the Franco-Confederate alliance.
   b. prevent recognition of the Confederacy by European nations.
   c. prevent European financiers from extending loans to the Confederacy.
   d. convince European nations to sell valuable arms and supplies to the Union.

Objective 8

_____ 14. In late 1863, General Grant decided to try the innovative strategy of
   a. repatriation of strategic southern areas under Union control.
   b. guerrilla warfare led by Union loyalists throughout the South.
   c. massive raids deep into the Confederacy.
   d. flexible response.

Objective 11

_____ 15. The crucial question that remained unanswered at the end of the Civil War was:
   a. Would the banking and transportation systems remain under federal control?
   b. Would the gains made by women be permanent?
   c. What policy would the federal government follow concerning the conscription of men into the service?
   d. What was the place of blacks in American society?

ESSAY QUESTIONS

Objectives 2, 4, and 6

1. Defend the contention that the revolutionary means chosen by secession leaders were incompatible with their conservative purpose.

Objectives 2 and 3

2. Discuss the impact of the Civil War on women in northern and southern societies.

Objectives 3, 4, and 9

3. Explain the following quote concerning northern wartime society: "It was as if there were several different wars under way, each of them serving different motives."

Objective 5

4. Discuss Lincoln's issuance of the Emancipation Proclamation. Why is it said that it was "morally wanting"? What was its impact on the war?

Objective 5

5. Defend or refute the following: "Lincoln did not lead public opinion on the race question."

Objective 9

6. Discuss the similarities and differences in antiwar sentiment in the South and in the North.

CHAPTER 16
Reconstruction by Trial and Error, 1865–1877

LEARNING OBJECTIVES

After you have studied Chapter 16 in your textbook and worked through this study guide chapter, you should be able to:

1. Discuss white northern attitudes toward blacks and black equality, and examine the impact of these attitudes on the Reconstruction process.

2. Explain the divergence between the provisions of President Johnson's Reconstruction plan and its actual operation.

3. Examine the clash between the executive and legislative branches of government over the issue of Reconstruction, and discuss the events and forces that affected the development of the congressional Reconstruction plans.

4. Cite the major provisions of the Fourteenth and Fifteenth Amendments; indicate the reasons for their passage by Congress; and explain the compromises embodied in each.

5. Cite the major provisions of the Military Reconstruction Act of 1867; indicate the reasons for its enactment by Congress; and explain why it diverged from the proposals of the Radical Republicans.

6. Discuss the political, social, and economic impact of the Reconstruction governments on southern society.

7. Examine and evaluate the means by which white southern Conservatives attempted to regain control in the South, and indicate the outcome of their efforts.

8. Examine and evaluate the Reconstruction experience for blacks.

9. Examine the events and forces that brought a weakening of the northern commitment to Reconstruction and an end to the Reconstruction era.

THEMATIC GUIDE

Reconstruction refers to the process by which the nation was rebuilt after the destruction caused by the Civil War. This rebuilding was social, political, and economic. Since there were no guidelines as to how it would be accomplished, questions and disagreements arose. Given such disagreements, as well as the emotional aftermath of four years of war and the force of individual personalities, Reconstruction proceeded by trial and error.

On the social question concerning the position of blacks within American society, events in the British Caribbean suggested that achieving black equality would require determination, commitment, and dedication by the white power structure. These characteristics were not evident in the prelude to Reconstruction played out on the Sea Islands. Instead, white paternalism and self-interest seemed paramount. In fact, it would become clear during the process of Reconstruction that Republican congressmen and their northern constituents had a limited view of equality. Although most believed in the concept of equality under the law, few believed in political, social, and economic equality.

When Congress reconvened in December 1865, it was faced with a presidential Reconstruction policy that not only allowed former Confederate leaders to regain power at the state and national levels but obviously abandoned the freedmen to hostile southern whites. Northern congressmen and the constituents they represented were unwilling to accept this outcome of the long, bitter struggle against a rebellious South. Believing that it had a constitutional right to play a role in the Reconstruction process, Congress acted. This action led to clashes with an intransigent President Johnson and to the passage of two congressional Reconstruction plans.

The first of these plans, the Fourteenth Amendment, evolved when the wrangling between President Johnson and Congress produced compromises among the conservative, moderate, and radical factions of the Republican party. Although Congress passed the Freedmen's Bureau bill and the Civil Rights Act of 1866 over the president's veto, there was concern that the Supreme Court would declare the basic provisions of the Civil Rights Act unconstitutional. Therefore, those provisions were incorporated into a constitutional amendment that was presented to the states for ratification in April 1866. The Fourteenth Amendment demonstrated that Congress wanted to guarantee equality under the law to the freedmen, but its provisions make it clear that the moderate and conservative Republicans who controlled Congress were not willing to accept the more progressive concept of equality advanced by the Radical Republicans.

When, at the urging of the president, every former Confederate state except Tennessee refused to ratify the Fourteenth Amendment, Congress passed its second Reconstruction plan—the Reconstruction Act of 1867. Although this act demonstrated some movement in the Radical direction by extending to blacks the right to vote in state elections, congressmen were still limited by the prejudices of the age. They labeled as extremist the suggestion that southern land be redistributed and so rejected the idea of giving blacks economic independence. They naively assumed that blacks would need only the ballot in their fight for a better life.

The same kinds of limitations worked within Reconstruction governments, preventing fundamental reform of southern society. Concurrently, southern Republicans adopted a policy that returned voting rights to former Confederates. These former Confederates, or Conservatives, ultimately led a campaign designed to return political and economic power to their hands by discrediting the Reconstruction governments. Adopting tactics ranging from racist charges and intimidation to organized violence, the Conservatives were able to achieve their objectives, as events in Alamance and Caswell counties in North Carolina demonstrated.

As the failures of Reconstruction revealed themselves, blacks renewed their determination to struggle for survival and true equality within American society. On one level they placed faith in education and participation in the political process as means of attaining equality, but they also turned to family and religion for strength and support. Denied the possibility of owning land, they sought economic independence through new economic arrangements such as sharecropping. However, sharecropping ultimately "proved to be a disaster for all concerned."

These setbacks indicated that northern commitment to equality had never been total. The federal government even began to retreat from partial commitment—a retreat made obvious by the policies of President Grant, the gradual erosion of congressional resolve on Reconstruction issues, the conservative decisions of the Supreme Court, and the emergence of other issues that captured the minds of white Americans. Finally, with the resolution of the disputed Hayes-Tilden election in 1876, Reconstruction ended. The promise of equality for black Americans remained unfulfilled.

BUILDING VOCABULARY

Listed below are important words and terms that you need to know to get the most out of Chapter 16. They are listed in the order in which they occur in the chapter. After carefully looking through the list, refer to a dictionary and jot down the definition of words that you do not know or of which you are unsure.

suffrage

intransigence

subvert

impeach

enfranchise

travail

tentative

amnesty

resilient

repudiate

vagrancy

servility

intransigent

titular

abridge

ambivalence

infuse

impasse

indict

exhort

disfranchise

enmity

vindictive

futile

exemption

ostracism

subjection

harassment

fiscal

philanthropy

odyssey

circumscribed

vacillate

curry

paramilitary

ominous

disparate

purport

polygamy

contraction

deference

purview

emasculate

filibuster

acquiesce

exigencies

IDENTIFICATION AND SIGNIFICANCE

After studying Chapter 16 of *A People and a Nation*, you should be able to identify fully *and* explain the historical significance of each item listed below.

1. Identify each item in the space provided. Give an explanation or description of the item. Answer the questions *who, what, where*, and *when*.

2. Explain the historical significance of each item in the space provided. Establish the historical context in which the item exists. Establish the item as the result of or as the cause of other factors existing in the society under study. Answer this question: *What were the political, social, economic, and/or cultural consequences of this item?*

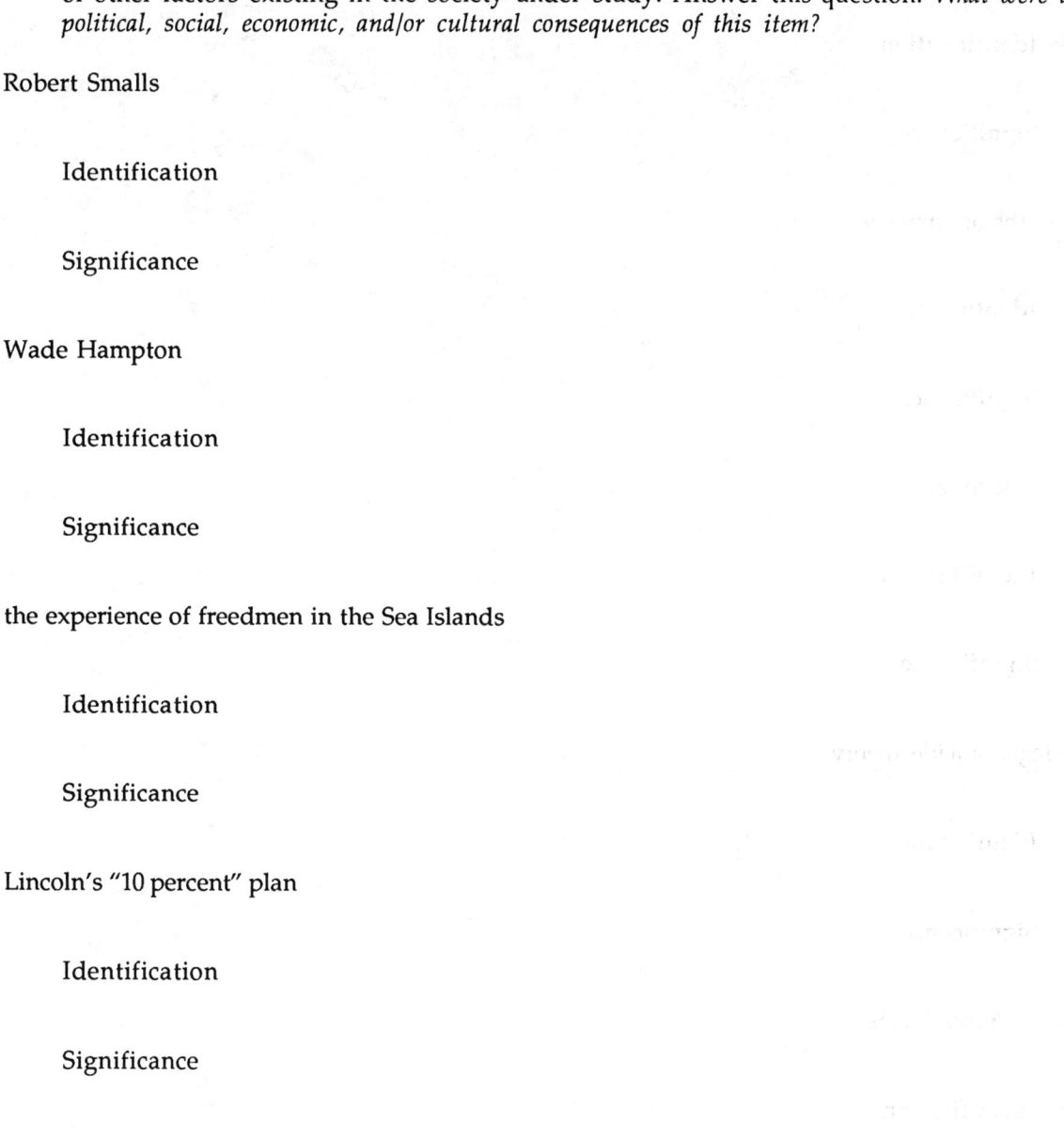

Robert Smalls

    Identification

    Significance

Wade Hampton

    Identification

    Significance

the experience of freedmen in the Sea Islands

    Identification

    Significance

Lincoln's "10 percent" plan

    Identification

    Significance

the Wade-Davis Bill

    Identification

    Significance

Johnson's Reconstruction plan

    Identification

    Significance

the oaths of amnesty

    Identification

    Significance

the black codes

    Identification

    Significance

the legal suicide theory

    Identification

    Significance

Radical Republicans

    Identification

    Significance

the Freedmen's Bureau

    Identification

    Significance

the Civil Rights Act of 1866

    Identification

    Significance

the Memphis and New Orleans riots

    Identification

    Significance

the Fourteenth Amendment

    Identification

    Significance

Johnson's "swing around the circle"

    Identification

    Significance

the congressional elections of 1866

    Identification

    Significance

the Reconstruction Act of 1867

    Identification

    Significance

Thaddeus Stevens

    Identification

    Significance

the Tenure of Office Act

    Identification

    Significance

Johnson's impeachment trial

    Identification

    Significance

the Fifteenth Amendment

    Identification

    Significance

the constitutional conventions in the former Confederate states

    Identification

    Significance

Republican governments in the former Confederate states

    Identification

    Significance

the southern Republican party

    Identification

    Significance

the southern Conservatives

    Identification

    Significance

industrialization in the former Confederate states

    Identification

    Significance

public schools in the former Confederate states

    Identification

    Significance

the charge of "Negro rule"

    Identification

    Significance

Chapter 16—Reconstruction by Trial and Error, 1865–1877

carpetbagger

    Identification

    Significance

scalawag

    Identification

    Significance

Republican tax policies in the former Confederate states

    Identification

    Significance

the Ku Klux Klan

    Identification

    Significance

Klan violence in Alamance and Caswell counties North Carolina

    Identification

    Significance

Freedmen's Bureau schools

    Identification

    Significance

the founding of black colleges

    Identification

    Significance

Francis Cardozo, P. B. S. Pinchback, Blanche K. Bruce, and Hiram Revels

    Identification

    Significance

reunification of black families

    Identification

    Significance

the founding of black churches

    Identification

    Significance

the sharecropping system

    Identification

    Significance

cotton and the southern economy

    Identification

    Significance

the presidential election of 1868

    Identification

    Significance

Ulysses S. Grant

    Identification

    Significance

the Enforcement Acts and the anti-Klan law

    Identification

    Significance

the Liberal Republican revolt

    Identification

    Significance

the Amnesty Act

    Identification

    Significance

the Civil Rights Act of 1875

    Identification

    Significance

Chapter 16—Reconstruction by Trial and Error, 1865–1877

the Panic of 1873

    Identification

    Significance

greenbacks vs. sound money

    Identification

    Significance

William H. Seward

    Identification

    Significance

Ex parte Milligan

    Identification

    Significance

the *Slaughter-House* cases

    Identification

    Significance

Bradwell v. *Illinois*

    Identification

    Significance

United States v. Cruikshank

    Identification

    Significance

United States v. Reese

    Identification

    Significance

grandfather clauses

    Identification

    Significance

the presidential election of 1876

    Identification

    Significance

the Exodusters

    Identification

    Significance

EVALUATING AND USING INFORMATION

Follow the four steps outlined below to both collect the information for and write the working draft of a rough answer to the kind of essay question that might appear on a test on Chapter 16.

Step 1 Referring to your textbook and class notes, answer the following four sets of questions.

Set 1

Upon his succession to the presidency in 1865, what led people to expect Andrew Johnson to pursue Reconstruction policies that would promote changes in voting and other political rights, and, by so doing, would attempt to alter the pre–Civil War distribution of political power in the South?

_____

_____

What feature of the "pardon" rules proposed by Andrew Johnson suggested that some southerners would be kept from regaining political power in the Reconstruction South? Looking at the pardon rules as a whole, what specific group in the South could be expected to lose power as a result of the rules?

_____

_____

According to President Johnson himself, what was his attitude toward African-American suffrage? What limitation did he put on how far he would be willing to go with this attitude?

_____

_____

What impact did President Johnson believe the Civil War had on the Union? How did this belief affect Johnson's interpretation of his power as president to issue pardons to Confederate officers and government leaders?

_____

_____

How long after taking office did Andrew Johnson control Reconstruction policy without having to deal with Congress?

_____

_____

How were the voting rights of southern whites and blacks affected by Andrew Johnson's rules about one's eligibility to serve as a delegate to a state constitutional convention and one's eligibility to vote in the election of delegates to such a convention?

_____

_____

Copyright © Houghton Mifflin Company. All rights reserved.

How was the makeup of the southern state constitutional conventions affected by the way President Johnson actually used the presidential power he thought he had to grant pardons? How did his use of this power affect the choice of representatives the southern states sent to Congress?

_____

_____

_____

How did Johnson react to Congress's effort to oppose the Black Codes and to extend the Freedman's Bureau?

_____

_____

How did Johnson react to efforts to gain passage of the Fourteenth Amendment?

_____

_____

What steps did President Johnson take regarding enforcement of provisions of the Reconstruction Act of 1867 affecting who in the South could or could not vote?

_____

_____

What step did presidential candidate Ulysses S. Grant take that indicated his attitude on the question of suffrage for African-Americans?

_____

_____

In what way did President Grant's approach to Reconstruction affect the power of the Enforcement Acts of 1870 and 1871 to stop groups such as the Ku Klux Klan from stifling citizens' rights to vote and to participate freely in politics? What was the impact of Grant's approach, and how was it felt?

_____

_____

_____

_____

Set 2

In what ways was the Civil Rights Bill of 1866 designed to affect the legal position of freedmen? What was the fate of this bill and its key provisions?

_____

_____

_____

_____

In what way did the Fourteenth and Fifteenth Amendments (especially the Fourteenth) affect Congress's plan for Reconstruction?

_____

_____

What did the Fourteenth Amendment say about (a) the responsibilities of states to protect the rights of citizens? (b) the rights of blacks to vote? and (c) the rights of women to vote?

_____

_____

a. Protection of citizens' rights

_____

_____

b. Voting rights of blacks

_____

_____

c. Voting rights of women

_____

_____

How did what the Fifteenth Amendment *prohibit* and what it *did not prohibit* influence the development of voting and related political rights?

_____

_____

Chapter 16—Reconstruction by Trial and Error, 1865–1877

What the Fifteenth Amendment *prohibited*

What the Fifteenth Amendment *did not prohibit*

What impact did Congress believe the Civil War had on the Union?

How did this belief affect Congress's interpretation of its right to inject itself into policymaking regarding Reconstruction?

How did the Reconstruction Act of 1867 affect the voting rights of Confederate leaders and freedmen?

Confederate leaders

Freedmen

Which provisions of the two Enforcement Acts and the anti-Klan law passed by Congress in the early 1870s were designed to combat the Ku Klux Klan's use of violence to intimidate potential voters? How effective were these measures?

What effect did the Amnesty Act of 1872 have on the voting or related political rights of former Confederate officers and leaders?

___

Set 3

What effects on voting and related political rights did the Supreme Court's decisions in (a) the *Slaughter-House* cases, (b) *United States v. Cruikshank,* and (c) *United States v. Reese* have?

a. *Slaughter-House* cases

___

b. *United States v. Cruikshank*

___

c. *United States v. Reese*

___

Set 4

What do (a) President Johnson's cabinet's reaction to the idea of granting voting rights to freedmen, (b) the degree of success Radical Republicans had in gaining support for African-American suffrage from outside their own ranks, (c) the voting rights of groups in the North other than native-born white males, (d) the results of votes on black suffrage, and (e) other indicators of public opinion on black suffrage in the North suggest about the North's interest in expanding voting rights in the nation as a whole?

___

a. Johnson's cabinet's reaction to the idea of black suffrage

___

b. Radical Republicans' success in enlisting support for black suffrage

c. Votes on black suffrage in the North (1865)

d. Other indicators of public opinion in the North on black suffrage

e. Groups in the North besides blacks without voting rights

When President Johnson controlled Reconstruction, what happened concerning southern elections and appointments of officeholders to influence Congress to take an active role in making Reconstruction policy? How?

How did the Fourteenth Amendment fare in the South when it was first presented by Congress?

What effects did the Fourteenth Amendment, passed because of the strong encouragement of Congress, have on the makeup of the state constitutional conventions across the South? What racial group dominated the state conventions?

How widespread was participation by freedmen in voting after the ratification of the Fourteenth Amendment? What kinds of leaders did the newly enfranchised blacks vote for?

After the state constitutional conventions revised the southern state constitutions and restructured southern state governments, how well-represented were blacks in state legislatures, appointive offices, Congress, governorships, and other high elective offices?

What provisions made the new state constitutions more democratic than the constitutions they replaced? (a) How did they change qualifications for voting? (b) Which offices would now be filled through elections? (c) How did the provisions affect women's rights?

a. Qualifications to vote

b. Elective/appointive offices

c. Women's rights

How did the South's new republican governments approach the question of voting rights for former Confederate leaders?

What group of white voters began cooperating with black voters in the South during Reconstruction? What was the basis of the cooperation between the two groups?

How common was intimidation by the Ku Klux Klan and similar groups of black, scalawag, and carpetbagger participants in political activities? How vigorously and consistently were the perpetrators prosecuted?

Copyright © Houghton Mifflin Company. All rights reserved.

How significant was political corruption in the new, Republican-dominated governments of the South? Was it more significant in the South than in the nation as a whole?

___

Step 2 Study the answers to the questions in each set and state your conclusions about the sets of answers in the following blanks. (If you need hints about the kind of conclusions you can draw, refer to the Answers section at the back of your Study Guide.

Conclusion 1

___

Conclusion 2

___

Conclusion 3

___

Conclusion 4

___

Step 3 Basing your response on the *sum* of your three conclusions, answer the following question in one declarative sentence. Write your answer in the blank.

How well served was the cause of making the United States more democratic through extension of voting and related political rights between 1865 and 1877?

___

Step 4 In your Reading Notebook, write the working draft of an essay, using the answer you wrote to complete Step 3 as its thesis, the conclusions you wrote to complete Step 2 as its major subpoints, and information in your four sets of answers as your sources of specific supporting concrete details/evidence.

IDEAS AND DETAILS

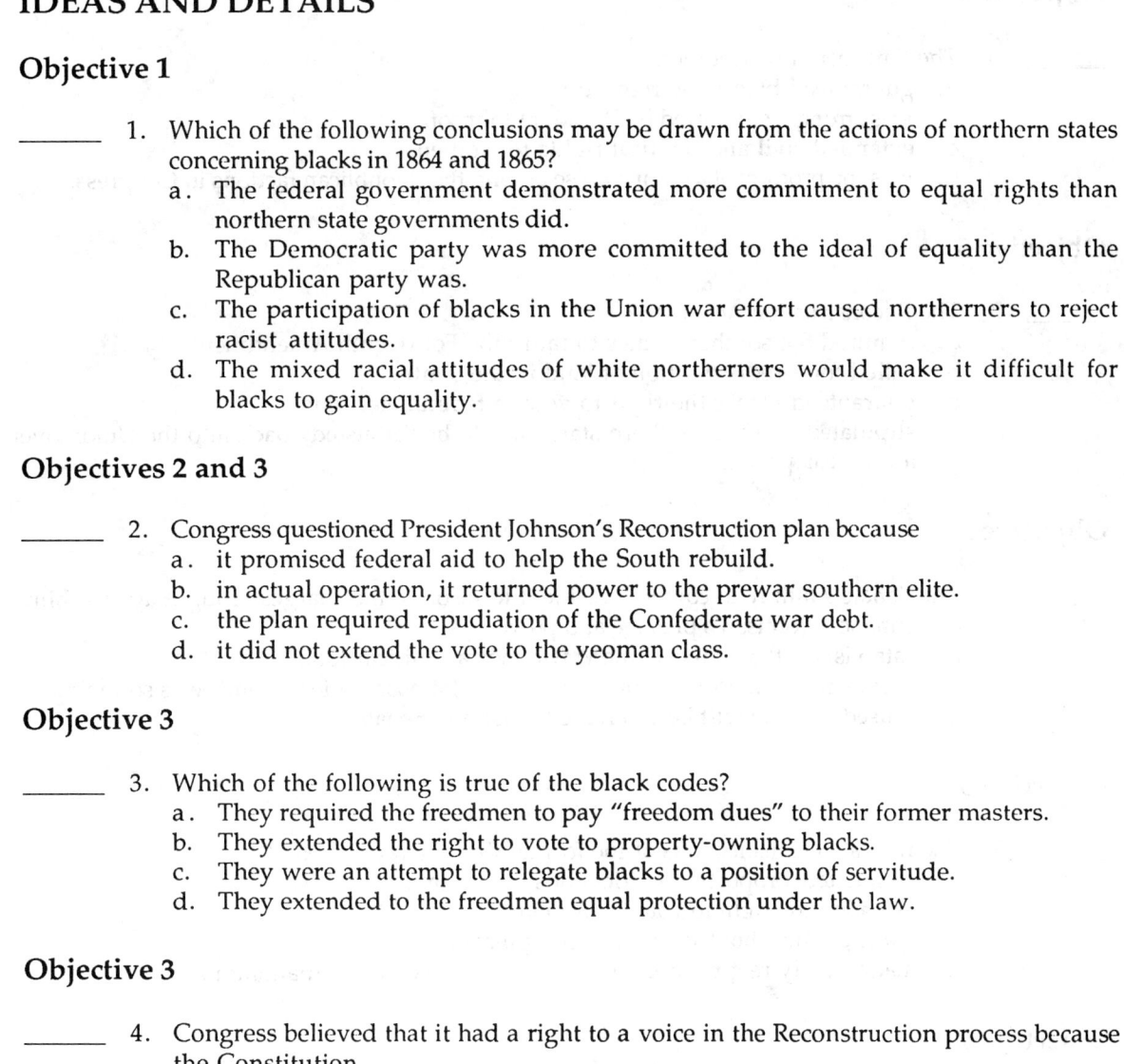

Objective 1

_____ 1. Which of the following conclusions may be drawn from the actions of northern states concerning blacks in 1864 and 1865?
   a. The federal government demonstrated more commitment to equal rights than northern state governments did.
   b. The Democratic party was more committed to the ideal of equality than the Republican party was.
   c. The participation of blacks in the Union war effort caused northerners to reject racist attitudes.
   d. The mixed racial attitudes of white northerners would make it difficult for blacks to gain equality.

Objectives 2 and 3

_____ 2. Congress questioned President Johnson's Reconstruction plan because
   a. it promised federal aid to help the South rebuild.
   b. in actual operation, it returned power to the prewar southern elite.
   c. the plan required repudiation of the Confederate war debt.
   d. it did not extend the vote to the yeoman class.

Objective 3

_____ 3. Which of the following is true of the black codes?
   a. They required the freedmen to pay "freedom dues" to their former masters.
   b. They extended the right to vote to property-owning blacks.
   c. They were an attempt to relegate blacks to a position of servitude.
   d. They extended to the freedmen equal protection under the law.

Objective 3

_____ 4. Congress believed that it had a right to a voice in the Reconstruction process because the Constitution
   a. grants treaty-making powers to Congress.
   b. grants Congress the power to declare war.
   c. assigns Congress the duty of guaranteeing republican governments in the states.
   d. assigns Congress the responsibility of "providing for the general welfare."

Objective 3

_____ 5. In order to develop a new Reconstruction program, conservative and moderate Republicans began to work with the Radical Republicans because
   a. events in the South convinced them that blacks should be given full political rights.
   b. the Radicals convinced them that black freedom depended on a redistribution of land in the South.
   c. President Johnson and the congressional Democrats refused to cooperate with them.
   d. the northern electorate clearly favored the goals of the Radical Republicans.

Objective 4

_____ 6. The Fourteenth Amendment
   a. guaranteed blacks the right to vote.
   b. was strongly supported by President Johnson.
   c. extended civil and political rights to women.
   d. was the product of a compromise among the Republican factions in Congress.

Objective 5

_____ 7. The Reconstruction Act of 1867
   a. required the southern states to ratify the Fourteenth Amendment.
   b. called for a redistribution of land in the South.
   c. guaranteed blacks the right to vote in federal elections.
   d. stipulated that the southern states would be "adjusted" back into the Union over a ten-year period.

Objective 3

_____ 8. The Senate's failure to convict President Johnson of the charges brought against him
   a. enhanced Johnson's prestige and power.
   b. established that impeachment was not a political tool.
   c. is evidence that northern opinion toward Johnson and the South was softening.
   d. caused a serious rift between the House and Senate.

Objective 6

_____ 9. The new state constitutions of the former Confederate states
   a. eliminated property qualifications for voting.
   b. extended the right to vote to women.
   c. made public school attendance compulsory.
   d. made yearly reapportionment of legislative districts mandatory.

Objective 6

_____ 10. The decision of southern Republicans to restore the voting rights of former Confederates
   a. meant that southern Republicans had to gain white support or face defeat.
   b. led to the formation of a broad-based Republican party in the South.
   c. caused the freedmen to support the more liberal southern Democrats.
   d. was politically embarrassing to congressional Republicans.

Objectives 7 and 8

_____ 11. Blacks participating in Reconstruction governments
   a. had little interest in the political process.
   b. were subjected to a racist propaganda campaign against them undertaken by the white Conservatives.
   c. insisted on social equality for blacks.
   d. displayed a vindictive attitude toward their former masters.

Objective 7

_____ 12. Activities of the Ku Klux Klan in Alamance and Caswell counties in North Carolina
   a. were disorganized and sporadic.
   b. were organized by the impoverished classes in North Carolina society.
   c. were undertaken by the former elite for the purpose of regaining political power.
   d. had little success in areas where blacks and yeoman farmers allied.

Objectives 6 and 8

_____ 13. In the final analysis, the Reconstruction governments of the South
   a. were able to alter the social structure of the South.
   b. effected a lasting alliance between blacks and whites of the yeoman class.
   c. gave blacks the means to achieve equality by giving them the right to vote.
   d. left blacks economically dependent on hostile whites.

Objective 9

_____ 14. In the *Slaughter-House* cases, the Supreme Court
   a. ruled that the Fourteenth Amendment did not protect the civil rights of individuals from state interference.
   b. protected a citizen of the United States against discrimination by an individual or a group.
   c. ruled that corporations were legal persons and were protected under the Fourteenth Amendment.
   d. ruled that national citizenship was more important than state citizenship.

Objective 9

_____ 15. From the outcome of the 1876 presidential election, it is evident that the electorate
   a. supported an inflationary monetary policy.
   b. feared that the expansionist policies of Secretary of State Seward would lead to war.
   c. had lost interest in Reconstruction.
   d. rejected government aid to business interests.

ESSAY QUESTIONS

Objective 2

1. Discuss Johnson's Reconstruction plan, and explain its actual operation. How did Congress respond to the plan? Why?

Objectives 3, 4, and 5

2. Discuss the political, social, and economic views of the Radical Republicans, and examine the role they played in the development of Congress's plans for Reconstruction.

Objective 3

3. Examine the attitudes and events that led to the impeachment of President Andrew Johnson, and assess the outcome of his trial by the Senate.

Objective 6

4. Discuss the successes and failures of the Reconstruction governments in the South.

Objective 7

5. Discuss the goals of the Conservatives and the means they used to achieve those goals.

MAP EXERCISE

1. Refer to the map on page 459 in the textbook. In the table below, list the eleven Confederate states, the date each was readmitted to the Union, the date Conservative rule was re-established in each, and the length of time the Reconstruction governments were in power in each.

Former Confederate State	Date Readmitted to Union	Date Conservative Rule Re-established	No. of Years Reconstruction Governments in Power

2. Why was Tennessee readmitted to the Union before passage of the Reconstruction Act of 1867?

3. What states were still under Reconstruction governments in 1876? What bearing did this have on the election of 1876? How was the problem resolved?

ANSWERS

CHAPTER 1

Finding the Main Idea

Exercise A

TOPIC: Characteristics of the social systems of the states of Lower Guinea.

MAIN IDEA: A characteristic common to the states of Lower Guinea was that each state's social system was organized on the basis of the dual-sex principle.

The main idea of the paragraph is stated in the paragraph's first sentence. The second sentence of the paragraph clarifies the first by offering a definition of the term *dual-sex principle*.

SUPPORTING DETAILS:

1. Dahomean kingdom—Every male official had a female counterpart (First part of sentence 3).

2. Akan States
   a. Chiefs inherited status through the female line
   b. Each chief had a female assistant who supervised the women

3. Polygyny practiced in many West African societies
   a. Each wife lived separately with her children
   b. Actions of adults scrutinized by members of own sex because of dual-sex principle.

Exercise B

TOPIC: Technological change in Europe in the fifteenth century.

MAIN IDEA: The invention of movable type and the printing press paved the way for European exploration.

The main idea is not explicitly stated in the paragraph being analyzed, but it is clearly implied and just as clearly supported by the evidence presented. In addition, it is often useful to look at the first sentence of the paragraph following the paragraph being analyzed to obtain a clearer statement of the main idea of the paragraph in question. Why? Because transition sentences, used to form bridges from one paragraph to another, often summarize the main idea or ideas of the previous paragraph or paragraphs. The first sentence of the paragraph that follows the one you were asked to analyze reads as follows:

> The European explorations of the fifteenth and sixteenth centuries were therefore made possible by technological advances and by the growing strength of newly powerful national rulers.

In this case, this sentence summarizes the ideas presented in the two previous paragraphs and explicitly states the main ideas contained in those paragraphs.

SUPPORTING DETAILS:

1. Movable type and the printing press made information more accessible to Europeans (sentence 2).
   a. *Travels* by Marco Polo was written in the thirteenth century (sentence 4).
   b. Not widely circulated until it was printed in 1477 (sentence 4).

2. Availability of information in books stimulated people's curiosity about distant places (sentence 3).
   a. *Travels* stimulated thought about trading with China by sea rather than by overland routes (sentences 5 and 6).
   b. Educated Europeans realized they could trade directly with Asia; no longer had to rely on middlemen (sentence 7).

Exercise C

TOPIC: The characteristics of and impact of the trade between Europeans and Native Americans in North America.

MAIN IDEA: The Europeans and the Native Americans along the northeastern coast of North America both derived benefits from their trade relationship, and that relationship had a significant impact on Indian societies and a negative ecological impact on certain regions.

The two paragraphs you were to read are actually the fourth and fifth paragraphs of a five-paragraph series. The main idea of the entire series is that, unlike the Spanish, some Europeans were more interested in exploiting the natural resources of America than in conquering territory. That idea is supported by a discussion of fishermen and fur traders. The two paragraphs that you were to read and analyze contain the discussion about fur traders and their impact on Indian societies and the ecology.

The first sentence in the first paragraph that you were to read is a transition sentence from the discussion about fishermen to the discussion about fur traders. The details offered about fur traders supports the idea of the five paragraph series as stated above. It also begins the development of a related idea, the main idea of the two paragraphs you were asked to read.

SUPPORTING DETAILS:

Details that support the first part of the main idea (the Europeans and the Indians both derived benefits from their trade relationship).

   a. Europeans profited from the trade in beaver pelts (paragraph 1, sentence 1).
      (1) The fur trade was so profitable that Europeans established permanent outposts on the mainland (paragraph 1, sentence 2).
      (2) The chief aim of fur traders was to acquire the largest quantity of pelts possible (paragraph 1, sentence 3).
   b. Indians wanted European goods (paragraph 2, sentence 1).
      (1) Such goods made life easier (paragraph 2, sentence 1).
      (2) Such goods helped them establish superiority over other tribes (paragraph 2, sentence 1).

Details that support the second part of the main idea (the relationship had a significant impact on Indian societies and a negative ecological impact on certain regions) are in the form of illustrations or examples.

c. Abenakis
   (1) Concentrated on trapping and selling beaver pelts to French (paragraph 2, sentence 3)
   (2) Became dependent on Massachusett tribe for food (paragraph 2, sentence 3)
d. Massachusetts
   (1) Traded food to Abenakis (paragraph 2, sentences 3 and 4)
   (2) Enabled them to obtain European metal tools from Abenakis (sentence 4)
e. Ecological impact
   (1) Beavers wiped out in some regions (paragraph 2, sentence 6)
   (2) Disappearance of beaver dams led to soil erosion; erosion further complicated by clearing of forests (paragraph 2, sentence 7)

Items a and b listed under "Supporting details" may be considered supporting *ideas* because they need factual evidence to support them. The entire five-paragraph series contains such evidence for both items.

Evaluating and Using Information

Because the value of exercises like most of the Evaluating and Using Information Exercises in this study guide lies in your working out interpretations for yourself and composing your own answers, the "answer" here is purposely incomplete. In fact, all we are going to give you is the plan for the essay implied by the questions and the way they are arranged in the exercise and the rough or working draft of the first section of the body of the essay. We're doing this to help you see whether or not you are on the right track in the process of coming up with your answer.

If you look at the information you have gathered in answering the questions in each Evidence Set, and if you look at a thesis statement that would be based on a logical interpretation of all of that information, you see that the basic plan for the working draft of your essay is something like the outline below. (The thesis statement is represented here by the essay's subject, because you need to compose your own thesis statement—a single, complete, declarative sentence expressing the whole point of the whole essay.)

Outline
(for the working draft of an essay)

Topic (substitute for *Thesis*): The effect of Europe's invasion of the Western hemisphere on the health of both Europeans and Americans

I. Indications of the possible health consequences of first contacts between two civilizations
   A. Spread of plague to Europe from China resulting from Silk Road contacts
   B. Why the Portuguese did not suffer major outbreaks of African diseases when they developed Europe's first major contacts with Africa

II. Difference in the speed and intensity of the impact of diseases and health problems introduced into Europe and the Americas as a result of the first contacts
   A. Diseases and other health problems brought back to Europe from the Americas
      1. Syphilis
      2. Health problems related to use of tobacco products
   B. European diseases that quickly devastated Indian populations
      1. Small pox
      2. Chicken pox
      3. Measles, influenza, and others

III. Recognition by early explorers of the potential value of foodstuffs from the Americas
   A. Columbus's recognition of the potential value of American vegetable products
   B. Cabot's recognition of the importance of American fish

IV. Ways exchanges of agricultural products and expertise and livestock actually benefited both Europeans and Americans
   A. Actual importance of American food resources and expertise to Europeans both in Europe and in America

1. American fish as a new and cheap source of protein in European diets
2. Nutritious, American vegetable crops such as corn, squash, beans, and potatoes as expanders of the European diet

B. Importance of horses and other livestock introduced to Americans by Europeans

Conclusion (Your interpretation, in about one to four sentences, of the overall meaning of all the specific information you have used to develop the topics in the above outline)

If you look at the plan for Section I (above) and the information you have gathered to answer the questions in Evidence Set 1 and come up with the conclusion for the section, you will see that the first section of the body of your essay probably will resemble the following paragraph. (Notice that no attempt has been made to polish the style, because we are trying only to make ourselves aware of the relevant, specific information and to understand its significance—and learn to use and spell correctly key names and terms. We are not trying to produce an essay to memorize.)

Working Draft of Section I

By the time European contacts with Americans were well under way, Europeans had had the kinds of contacts with peoples of other continents that make clear the health risk their invasion of the New World posed both for the people back home in Europe and for the Indians of the Americas. Europe had been the victim of at least one first-contact situation. When the Silk Road first linked the far reaches of Asia to Europe, traders brought with them from China the bubonic plague (1346), a disease that in three major outbreaks in the 1340s, 1360s, and 1370s wiped out up to one-third of Europe's population. Before the close of the sixteenth century, Europeans had carried diseases such as small pox and chicken pox to the Americas where they had decimated Indian populations. Earlier first-contact experiences of some Europeans, notably the Portuguese, who had initiated contact with Africa in the fifteenth century, suggest why the Indians were more vulnerable. As the first Europeans to have much contact with Africa, the Portuguese were protected by what amounts to a quarantine from African diseases that could have killed off both the travelers and large numbers of their countrymen back home. As they developed their slave trade in the late fifteenth century, for example, the Portuguese stayed on Cape Verde Island rather than mingling with large numbers of Africans on the continent itself. Both the small number of Portuguese and other European travelers who actually were in contact with Africans and later Americans plus the time and distance between them and their home ports in Europe in effect quarantined them from their fellow Europeans, an experience much different from that of the American Indians, who had no such quarantine to protect them. Most of those among the European travelers who were vulnerable to what could have been killer diseases in Africa and America would have died before they had a chance to get back home to infect others.

Multiple-Choice Questions

1a. No. In 1970, the noted Norwegian ethnologist Thor Heyerdahl and his crew successfully sailed from Africa to America in a papyrus boat. He did this in an attempt to prove that ancient Egyptians could have sailed to the Americas. However, it is extremely unlikely that Paleo-Indians came to the Americas in that way. See page 5.

1b. Correct. It is believed that the ancestors of all Native Americans migrated from Asia to North America some 15,000 years ago by way of a land bridge that connected the two continents at that time. This land bridge was located at what is now the Bering Strait. See page 5.

1c. No. It is not likely that Paleo-Indians migrated from Europe to Asia. It is even less likely that these forerunners of American Indians sailed across the Bering Strait. See page 5.

1d. No. Paleo-Indians did not have a Scandinavian (Nordic) background. They were not associated with a Nordic colony in Iceland and did not sail from such a colony to North America. See page 5.

2a. No. The Maya believed in a multitude of gods and had elaborate religious rituals in which animals, and sometimes humans, were sacrificed to the gods. The pyramids associated with Maya civilization had temples on top in which priests performed ceremonies. See page 6.

2b. Correct. The Maya developed an advanced system of writing which used pictures or symbols. Some of the Mayan hieroglyphics have been found on large stone monuments, but books of paper have also survived. See page 6.

2c. No. Mayan civilization was composed of city-states which were probably ruled by kings. However, beginning in the fifth century the rulers of these city-states vied with each other for power and engaged in constant warfare. It is very likely that this was a major factor in the decline of Mayan civilization. See page 6.

2d. No. Although the Maya did develop mathematics and astronomy, there is no evidence that they had a compulsory educational system for their children. See page 6.

3a. No. It is believed that the ancestors of all Native Americans migrated from Asia to North America some thirty thousand years ago; therefore, they were of the same ethnic and cultural stock. See page 9.

3b. No. Different political systems emerged among Indian cultures as a result of cultural divergence. They are not the reason for that cultural divergence. See page 10.

3c. No. The geographic barriers that exist in North and South America probably made interaction difficult in some instances. But such barriers are not extensive and clearly did not make interaction impossible. See page 10.

3d. Correct. After arriving in North America some thirty thousand years ago, the ancestors of Native Americans slowly spread throughout North and South America. In doing so, they encountered different geographic and environmental settings. The need and the ability to adapt to these settings led to the emergence of diverse cultural groups. See page 10.

4a. No. In the first place, Indian religious beliefs did not closely resemble those of the Catholic church. Second, the Lady of Cofitachique is not mentioned in relation to Indian religious beliefs. See pages 10–11.

4b. Correct. The Lady of Cofitachique was of the Creek tribe and governed a large group of villages in the western part of present-day South Carolina. See pages 10–11.

4c. No. The major deities of agricultural tribes were associated with cultivation, but they were not female deities. See page 11.

4d. No. The Lady of Cofitachique was not associated with one of the tribes that made up the Iroquois Confederacy and is not mentioned in relation to the social makeup of Iroquois society. See page 11.

5a. Correct. There were many differences among the religions of the various Indian tribes, but one thing they all had in common was the belief in a multitude of gods. See page 11.

5b. No. Women were allowed leadership positions in some tribes and were most likely to hold such positions in agricultural tribes. See page 11.

5c. No. Each tribe's religious ceremonies and rituals were closely tied to its economy. Therefore, it is likely that the sun and moon were central to the religious ceremonies of some tribes, but this was not true of all Indian religions. See page 11.

5d. No. Animism, the belief that everything in nature (animals, plants, stones, lakes, etc.) has a soul, was not a belief common to all Indian religions. It is a belief more closely associated with the religions of Africa and Asia. On the other hand, totemism, the belief that a clan or tribe is descended from a plant or animal, is associated with some North American Indian tribes. See page 11.

6a. Correct. The Sahara Desert acted as a great sea of sand that separated West Africa (Upper Guinea) from the societies that bordered the Mediterranean. But beginning with the Ghana Empire around 900 C.E. an organized trans-Saharan trade began to develop. This commerce was controlled by the great interior kingdoms of Ghana (ca. 900–1100 C.E.), Mali (ca. 1240–1500 C.E.), and Songhai (ca. 1460–1591) and was the major link between Europe and West Africa prior to European voyages by sea to West Africa in the fifteenth century. See page 12.

6b. No. European seafarers did not venture to the areas along the coast of West Africa until the fifteenth century, so there were no "long-established" shipping lanes between the Mediterranean and the South Atlantic. See page 12.

6c. No. The Nile is located in Northeast Africa. Although it flows into the Mediterranean, no trunk of the Nile provides a link between Europe and West Africa. See page 12.

6d. No. Both the Senegal and the Gambia Rivers are located on the bulge of West Africa and flow into the Atlantic. The Portuguese were the first Europeans to reach this area of Africa by sea and did not do so until the fifteenth century. See page 12.

7a. No. Rice was an important product of some of the West African societies, but it was not the most important product in all of those societies. See page 14.

7b. Correct. Just as men in these societies hunted and managed livestock, women cared for the children, manufactured cloth, and were the primary local traders among families, villages, and small kingdoms. See page 14.

7c. No. There are many different language groups in West Africa. See page 14.

7d. No. There were many different tribes in West Africa. The members of a tribe generally believed that they were descended from a common ancestor and saw other members of their tribe as part of their own kinship group. However, this sense of kinship and belonging did not usually transcend tribal lines. See page 14.

8a. No. In many tribes of the Lower Guinea, women belonged to the Sandé cult and men belonged to the Poro cult. However, the fact of different cults for men and women does not define the practice of polygyny. See page 14.

8b. No. Societies throughout Lower Guinea did have male political and religious leaders to govern the men and female leaders to govern the women. This is known as the dual-sex principle and does not define the practice of polygyny. See page 14.

8c. Correct. Many West African societies allowed men to have more than one wife, which was the practice of polygyny. When men had several wives, each wife lived separately with her children. See page 14.

8d. No. Matrilineal societies trade kinship through the female line. This does not define polygyny. See page 14.

9a. Correct. Marco Polo originally wrote the account of his journey to China in 1299. However, since the book had to be copied by hand, it was not widely circulated. The invention of printing by Johannes Gutenberg in 1440 changed that. Polo's book was published in 1477 and circulated widely among the educated elite in Europe. See page 16.

9b. No. Marco Polo was a merchant from Venice, but the book that Polo wrote about his journey to China in 1299 is not evidence that Venice led the way in perfecting navigational instruments. In fact, the compass was a Chinese invention that Polo may have brought back to Venice on his return. See page 16.

9c. No. At the time that Marco Polo's book was published, most educated Europeans knew that the world was round. See page 16.

9d. No. As a thirteenth-century Venetian merchant, Marco Polo was of the Catholic faith; but he was not a missionary, and his book does not give evidence that Catholic missionaries led the way in calling for European expansion. See page 16.

10a. No. By the 1490s the Portuguese had established regular trade relations with West Africa and had built their first fort, Elmina, along the Gold Coast. However, the fort was built with the consent of the African ruler, and not after Portuguese conquest of the region. See page 18.

10b. No. The Portuguese first established contact with Upper Guinea in the 1440s, and by the 1470s they had ventured down to the Gold Coast of Lower Guinea. As they developed trade relations with the coastal African kingdoms, the rulers of those kingdoms established the rules and regulations under which such trade took place. See page 18.

10c. Correct. The African rulers along the Guinea Coast welcomed trade with the Portuguese, and both parties benefited from the trade relationship that was established. See page 18.

10d. No. The rulers of the kingdoms along the Guinea Coast refused to allow the Portuguese to venture inland. Therefore, as trade relations were established between the Portuguese and West Africa, the Portuguese were confined to coastal trading posts. See page 18.

11a. Correct. The Portuguese discovered this island located in the Gulf of Guinea around 1470 and colonized the island in the 1480s. Located on the equator, the island's climate and soil proved to be ideal for the cultivation of sugar cane. To work the cane fields, the Portuguese imported slaves from the African mainland and established the first economy based primarily on the bondage of black Africans. See page 18.

11b. No. São Tomé was uninhabited when discovered by the Portuguese around 1470. See page 18.

11c. No. The Portuguese did not find gold and silver on the island of São Tomé. See page 18.

11d. No. The Portuguese had been engaged in sugar cane cultivation for some years prior to their discovery of the uninhabited island of São Tomé around 1470. See page 18.

12a. No. Most other sailors of the time willingly used the available navigational instruments. See page 19.

12b. Correct. Columbus disagreed with fellow sailors and cartographers by insisting that Japan lay just three thousand miles off the coast of southern Europe. See page 19.

12c. No. All knowledgeable seafarers knew that the world was round. See page 19.

12d. No. Columbus used the ship design that was common throughout Europe. See page 19.

13a. No. Irish seafarers sailing to England from Ireland would have the benefit of the westerlies to carry them across the Irish Sea. This situation is not analogous to the impact of the Northeast Trades on Spanish seafarers sailing to Spain from the Canary Islands. See pages 17 and 21.

13b. Correct. The Northeast Trades blow steadily toward the Southwest, causing problems for seafarers sailing from the Canary Islands to Spain. The westerlies blow steadily toward the Northeast, causing problems for seafarers sailing to Iceland from England. See pages 17 and 21.

13c. No. Portuguese seafarers sailing to Italy from Portugal would be in the area called the "horse latitudes" for most of the journey. In this area there are, for the most part, no prevailing winds; therefore, the westerlies would have no impact on their voyage and the situation is not analogous to Spanish seafarers sailing to Spain from the Canary Islands. See pages 17 and 21.

13d. No. Italian seafarers sailing to Morocco from Italy would remain within the Mediterranean. For the most part, the journey would be in the area known as the "horse latitudes" in which there are no prevailing winds. Therefore, the westerlies would have no impact on the voyage and the situation is not analogous to Spanish seafarers sailing to Spain from the Canary Islands. See pages 17 and 21.

14a. No. The Spanish government maintained tight control over its colonies, even going so far as to dictate that the colonies could only import goods from Spain. See pages 26–27.

14b. No. The Spanish government limited the number of people who could emigrate to its colonies. Those who did emigrate were usually single males. See pages 26–27.

14c. Correct. The Spanish model of colonization was based on (1) the exploitation of Native Americans and black slaves, (2) tight control of the colonies by the Spanish government, and (3) male colonists. Each characteristic had its consequences and helped shape the future of the Spanish colonies. See pages 26–27.

14d. No. Spanish conquistadors were granted great landed estates (latifundia) which were worked by Native Americans and black slaves. See pages 26–27.

15a. No. Protestant England and Catholic Spain were enemy nations in the 1580s. Spain sent the Spanish Armada against England in 1588. In other words, there was no alliance between the two nations. See page 29.

15b. Correct. Queen Elizabeth was aware of Spanish successes in the New World and was jealous of those successes. Not only did she want to match those successes by establishing English colonies, but she also wanted bases in the Americas that could conduct raids against Spanish settlements. See page 29.

15c. No. Although the English population was growing rapidly in the latter third of the sixteenth century, it is doubtful that Queen Elizabeth believed that England was overpopulated. Therefore, it is doubtful that she wanted colonies as an outlet for England's excess population. However, this was a reason that the English monarchs of the early seventeenth century supported colonization efforts. See page 29.

15d. No. There was no plan on the part of Queen Elizabeth to acquire Indian slaves to work the estates of English nobles. See page 29.

CHAPTER 2

Evaluating and Using Information

Doing this exercise gives you practice in discovering threads running through whole chapters and in developing sharply focused concrete and specific mock essays about those threads (themes). You need to judge the effectiveness of your own essay because the intellectual process of identifying themes and then finding, synthesizing, organizing, and interpreting information is even more important than of several themes in the chapter you have chosen to write about or the answer you have devised. On the other hand, you might find a review of the "answer" to the Evaluating and Using Information for Chapter One helpful.

Multiple-Choice Questions

1a. Correct. As explained on page 36, several factors explain the success of the Black Robes in converting Indians to Christianity, but the most important factor was probably their ability to communicate over long distances through the written word.

1b. No. In their efforts to convert Indians to Christianity, the Black Robes often resorted to the tactic of trying to undermine the authority of the Indians' traditional religious leaders, the village shamans. See page 36.

1c. No. In the explanation for the success of Jesuit missionaries in converting Indians to Christianity, there is no indication that the traditional beliefs of the Indians were similar to Catholic beliefs. See page 36.

1d. No. Attempts by the Jesuit missionaries to convert Indians to Christianity by first persuading them to live near French settlements and adopt European lifestyles were not very successful. This implies that the Indians did not readily accept European culture and did not believe European culture to be superior to their own. See page 36.

2a. No. Although the Hurons had been weakened by a recent epidemic, the Iroquois were not responsible and did not engage in germ warfare in their war against the Hurons. See page 38.

2b. No. The Iroquois were not "decisively defeated" in this war, and they would continue to pose a threat to European settlers for some time to come. See page 38.

2c. Correct. Again one can see the impact of the European presence in the New World on Native Americans. In addition to the goal of securing their traditional hunting territory, the Iroquois waged war in an effort to become the major supplier of pelts to the Europeans. Furthermore, the outcome of the war was in some measure decided by the weapons available to the Iroquois through their Dutch allies. See page 38.

2d. No. European negotiators did not mediate the dispute between the Iroquois and the Hurons. See page 38.

3a. No. Although many European nations established penal colonies (most notably Devil's Island by France and Australia by England), this does not explain the interest that France, Holland, and England had in the Lesser Antilles. See pages 38–40.

3b. No. Although there was some interest in converting peoples in other lands to Christianity, this does not explain the interest that France, Holland, and England had in the Lesser Antilles. Furthermore, in the three countries mentioned, "religious leaders" did not have the kind of power implied in the statement. See pages 38–40.

3c. No. It is conceivable that these islands were used, to some extent, as "resupply" stations but not as "refueling." When you are relying on wind power to "fuel" the sails of your vessel, there is no need for "refueling stations." Furthermore, even if one were dealing with a resupply station, one would expect it to be farther from the North American mainland than were these islands. See pages 38–40.

3d. Correct. Great profit could be made in the successful cultivation of sugar for sale in the European market. This lesson had been learned very early by the Spanish in the South Atlantic. See pages 38–40.

4a. Correct. English Calvinists, known as Puritans, became more and more convinced during the early seventeenth century that the Stuart monarchs, James I and Charles I, were Satan's representatives on Earth. Therefore, to accomplish their religious objectives, many Puritans decided to leave "corrupt" England and come to America. See page 42.

4b. No. Dramatic social and economic change was one of the two major developments that led many English citizens to come to the New World in the seventeenth century. However, rather than losing economic power, the landowning elite generally became wealthier as a result of this change. See page 42.

4c. No. The plague did sweep through England in 1665, leaving some 70,000 people dead in London alone, but this fact is not one of the two major developments cited in the text as an explanation for the migration of some 200,000 English citizens to the New World in the seventeenth century. See page 42.

4d. No. Although it is true that commercial rivalry between the British and the Dutch led to three Anglo-Dutch naval wars in the seventeenth century, these wars were not a major factor prompting English men and women to move to the New World. See page 42.

5a. No. Both Algonkian society and English society were oriented toward an agricultural lifestyle. See pages 44–45.

5b. No. Although it is true that there were differences in the hierarchies of the two societies, the English and Algonkian peoples both had clear political and social hierarchies. See pages 44–45.

5c. No. Although the beliefs of the Algonkians were considerably different from those of the English, both societies had deeply held religious beliefs. See pages 44–45.

5d. Correct. The Indians did not believe in individual landownership and did not believe that the land could be bought and sold absolutely. The English disagreed. See pages 44–45.

Copyright © Houghton Mifflin Company. All rights reserved.

6a. Correct. Because men who already owned land in the Chesapeake colonies could receive additional land by financing the passage of additional settlers, the headright system made it possible for Chesapeake landowners to establish large agricultural estates. See page 46.

6b. No. The establishment of a society in which private landownership was allowed did not guarantee nor did it result in political stability. See page 46.

6c. No. The cultivation and cure of tobacco was introduced into the colony in 1611 by John Rolfe before the headright system was instituted. See page 46.

6d. No. The Virginia Company introduced the headright system in 1617 in an effort to make the colony attractive to settlers and solve its financial problems, but the company continued to lose money and went bankrupt in 1624. See page 46.

7a. No. As a general rule, well-established people in the seventeenth century did not decide to leave their homeland and travel 3,000 miles to a wilderness. Furthermore, few well-established people would be willing to give up their freedom and become someone else's servant for some seven years. See page 47.

7b. No. Although those in England who chose to become indentured servants in the Chesapeake were not from the upper class, it would be a mistake to label them as the "dregs" of English society. Dregs are the least desirable part of something or the sediment left from a liquid, such as "the dregs at the bottom of the coffee pot." See page 47.

7c. Correct. Landowners in the Chesapeake wanted laborers to work their fields; and, with that in mind, they were more interested in purchasing the labor of young males than that of young women. That, in part, is one of the reasons that most migrants to the region in the seventeenth century were young males between the ages of fifteen and twenty-four. See page 47.

7d. No. In the Middle Colonies in the eighteenth century, most German immigrants came as "redemptioners." Redemptioners usually came as members of family groups. However, this was not true of the *indentured servants* who came to the Chesapeake in the seventeenth century. See page 47.

8a. No. Since adult males in all the British colonies had to meet property qualifications to be eligible to vote, the assemblies could not have been controlled by "landless peasants." See page 49.

8b. No. Both colonies had representative assemblies and were not ruled from London in an autocratic manner. See pages 49.

8c. Correct. Migrants made up a majority of the Chesapeake population throughout the seventeenth century. These migrants often looked to groups of supporters in England to help them solve their problems and fight their battles for political and economic power. This created political instability. See page 49.

8d. No. The number of slaves in the Chesapeake certainly increased in the late seventeenth century (see Chapter 3), and the fear of slave insurrections increased accordingly. However, such fear did not breed political chaos in the colonies. See page 49.

9a. No. Although the Virginia Company approved the first representative assembly for the Virginia colony in 1619, Plymouth had to wait for more towns to be founded and the population increased before it could create a representative assembly like the one in Virginia or Maryland. See page 50.

9b. Correct. The Jamestown settlers were helped by the Powhatan Confederacy, and the Pilgrims received aid from the Pokanoket Indians and from Squanto, of the Pawtuxet tribe. See page 50.

9c. No. Although the Separatists did move to Plymouth from Holland in order to isolate themselves from the corrupting influences of the world, the Virginia Company sought profit when it founded Jamestown in 1607. See page 50.

9d. No. Although the Pilgrims were supposed to settle in territory under the jurisdiction of the Virginia Company, navigational errors caused them to land in the New England region in November 1620. Rudimentary legal authority for the colony was established by the Mayflower Compact. See page 50.

10a. No. John Winthrop and other Puritans believed that the Puritan church was the one true church. In practice this meant that non-Puritans were not granted freedom of worship in Massachusetts throughout most of the seventeenth century. See pages 51–52.

10b. No. The right to vote in seventeenth-century Massachusetts was extended to adult males who were members of the Puritan church and residents of the colony. See pages 51–52.

10c. Correct. Governor Winthrop believed that God had a covenant with the Puritans and that the Puritans in turn had a covenant with each other to work together to build God's kingdom on Earth. This meant that one's individual will had to be subordinated to the good of the community of the elect. See pages 51–52.

10d. No. The Puritans believed that God had divided human beings into different socioeconomic classes. This is evident in the quotation from Winthrop's sermon found in the text. See pages 51–52.

11a. Correct. The colony of Massachusetts distributed land quite differently from the way it was distributed in the Chesapeake colonies. The land-distribution system of Massachusetts helped further the communal ideal because people living in close proximity to each other could more easily fulfill the duty of working together as the "community of the elect" to build God's kingdom on earth. See page 53.

11b. No. Charles I (1625–1649) did not issue such a decree. In fact, the Massachusetts Bay Company decided to transfer the entire company, all stockholders, and the company's charter to their new colony. Therefore, from its beginnings, Massachusetts Bay Colony enjoyed a great deal of autonomy. See page 53.

11c. No. The headright system is associated with the southern colonies and not with the New England colonies. See page 53.

11d. No. Most of the settlers who came to Massachusetts Bay colony were farmers, not merchants. See page 53.

12a. No. John Eliot expected the Indians to totally reject their own religious ideas and totally accept Puritan religious ideas. See page 54.

12b. Correct. Because John Eliot insisted that Indians undergo a total cultural transformation, his attempts to convert the New England Indians to Christianity were doomed. See page 54.

12c. No. John Eliot expressed his ideas to Indian men as well as to women. See page 54.

12d. No. Puritans associated elaborate rituals with the Catholic church, which they considered an enemy religion. Therefore, elaborate rituals were not part of the Puritan religious service. See page 54.

13a. No. The Puritan religious service tended to be far simpler than the Catholic religious service. Furthermore, the Indians were drawn to the more elaborate Catholic service rather than to the simplicity of the Puritan service. See page 54.

13b. No. The Jesuits taught that good works lead to salvation; the Puritans taught that one is saved only by the grace of God. The Indians found the Jesuit message more attractive than the Puritan message. See page 54.

13c. Correct. The Jesuits did not insist that Indians totally reject their own culture for a European lifestyle. Since the Indians did not have to go through a total cultural transformation to be considered Christians in Jesuit eyes, the Jesuits had more success in converting the Indians. See page 54.

13d. No. The French settlements were small; the Puritan settlements became large. As a result, the French did not encroach on tribal lands as much as the Puritans did. Since the French were not as intrusive, the Indians did not perceive them to be as great a threat as the Puritans. See page 54.

14a. No. For a number of reasons, New England parents were generally able to retain control over their children for a prolonged period of time; but, because of the high death rate in the Chesapeake, families there were short-lived and children were freed from parental control at an earlier age. See page 55.

14b. No. Residents of the Chesapeake cleared new fields every few years; New Englanders used fertilizer and cultivated the same fields year after year. See page 55.

14c. No. Average New England families in the seventeenth century were significantly larger than Chesapeake families. New England women raised five to seven children; Chesapeake women raised one to three. See page 55.

14d. Correct. Seventeenth-century Chesapeake migrants came to America as individuals; New England Puritan migrants came as part of family groups. See page 55.

15a. No. The quotation does not pertain to Puritan beliefs about divorce. See page 57.

15b. Correct. The quotation indicates that the Puritan authorities were disturbed not only by Anne Hutchinson's religious beliefs but by her challenge to traditional gender roles as well. See page 57.

15c. No. Anne Hutchinson was a midwife. Midwifery was an acceptable job for a woman in seventeenth-century Massachusetts. The statement is not an indication that she was seen as a threat because she "owned her own business." See page 57.

15d. No. The Puritan authorities meant their statement as a condemnation, rather than an approval, of Anne Hutchinson's actions. See page 57.

CHAPTER 3

Evaluating and Using Information

The exact phrasing of definitions/identifications is not what's important. Your own answers—in your own words—are more valuable than any canned answers we can provide for you, because it is the act of researching and creating the definitions that will make you understand and remember the concepts, events, and people you need to be able to define and identify. Nevertheless, below you will find a sampler of possible entries for your chart to help you see whether you are on the right track.

Some students find that transferring their identification/definition notes to index cards (the term on one side and the definition/identification on the other) helps for review purposes. Such cards are merely an aid they use in testing themselves on their recollection of the information, not an aid in testing themselves on how well they can memorize answers.

Key Parts of Definitions and Identifications			
Term	Class	Differentiation	Additional Comment
What's being defined or identified	Narrow, relevant category to which the item being defined or identified belongs	What distinguishes the item being defined or identified from all other members of the category in which it has been placed	Any additional statement needed to clarify the definition or the significance of the item being defined or identified.
egalitarianism	A basic assumption or doctrine	that all citizens are equal and thus entitled to the same legal, economic, and political rights.	Egalitarianism often leads to the establishment of institutions, such as schools, that promote equality of opportunity and the abandonment of overt marks of class distinctions, such as titles.
Quakers	Members of the Society of Friends, a Christian sect whose belief in the "inner light" gave them the egalitarian and pacifist attitudes	reflected in the life and policies of William Penn, the Quaker founder of Pennsylvania.	The Quaker influence in Pennsylvania led to the colony's reputation as a place where Indians could expect fair treatment but made it so popular as a haven for members of all religious groups that the colony also attracted the kind of people who would finally undermine the colony's fair-play policies.
the Pueblo revolt of 1680	Rebellion of Indians in New Mexico against the Spanish	that succeeded in getting Spanish out of New Mexico and led to debrutalizing of Spanish policies toward Indian subjects.	The Pueblo revolt was sparked primarily by Spanish attempts to force Indians to give up their religion and religious rituals and led by the shaman Popé. It was the longest, continuous North American resistance by Indians to European control in the colonial period.
Jacob Leisler	A German New Yorker hanged for treason	when he responded to news of the Glorious Revolution in England by taking over the government of his colony, assuming that William and Mary would approve American support for their ascendancy to the throne and reinstate the New England colonial charters King James II had revoked in 1684.	The American reaction to the Glorious Revolution, of which Leisler's precipitate action was a part, was only one of a whole series of crises, including the loss of New England charters, the War of the League of Augsburg, and the Salem Witchcraft Trials that show the great stress of the 1680s and 1690s.

Multiple-Choice Questions

1a. No. Although a large number of Puritans migrated to New England between 1630 and 1642, many Puritans remained in England. See pages 62–63.

1b. No. Puritans supported Parliament, not the king, in the English Civil War. Therefore, Charles would probably have been delighted to be rid of the Puritans, and he did not issue a decree prohibiting Puritan migrations to the New World. See pages 62–63.

1c. No. The Puritans always expected to encounter hardships as they undertook the task of building God's kingdom on Earth. Since they believed they were on a divine mission, they were undaunted by such hardships. Furthermore, life was not as hard for New England settlers in the 1640s as it had been in the early 1630s. See pages 62–63.

1d. Correct. Although the English Civil War, which began in 1642, was a political contest between king and Parliament, it was also a religious contest between Anglicans, who generally supported the king, and Puritans, who supported Parliament. Therefore, victory over the king was a political and religious victory for Puritans. See page 62.

2a. No. Early in the history of the Pennsylvania colony, William Penn pledged to establish a representative assembly; and, without authorization from England, New Jersey's proprietors established a representative assembly in that colony. However, New York did not have a representative assembly until 1683. See pages 65–67.

2b. Correct. Upon their founding, each of these colonies offered religious toleration to Christian settlers. See pages 65–67.

2c. No. All of these colonies were founded as proprietary colonies rather than as royal colonies. A proprietary colony was one given as a grant of land to an individual or a group. The individual or group was then responsible for governing the colony. See pages 65–67.

2d. No. Quakers were important in the early history of New Jersey but did not "become the dominant religious element." Pennsylvania was established as a Quaker colony, but because of the promise of religious toleration Quakers became a minority. Quakers were not a dominant element in New York. See pages 65–67.

3a. Correct. Penn's belief that all people are equal and his fairness toward the Indians of Pennsylvania caused Indians from other areas to move to Pennsylvania. However, many non-Quaker white migrants to the colony held prejudicial views against the Indians and repeatedly clashed with them over land titles. See page 68.

3b. No. Quakers believed in equality among all people of all races. Furthermore, these egalitarian beliefs and the policy of religious toleration to all settlers attracted many non-Quakers to Pennsylvania. See page 68.

3c. No. William Penn dealt fairly with the Delawares, the dominant tribe in Pennsylvania, by purchasing land from them before selling it to settlers. Therefore, the Delawares did not adopt a warlike attitude toward all white settlers. See page 68.

3d. No. William Penn and the Quakers believed in freedom of conscience concerning religion. He and the Quakers did not try to convert Indians to the Quaker religion. See page 68.

4a. No. The word *slavery* was not present in seventeenth-century English law, and slavery as an institution did not exist in England. See page 68.

4b. Correct. In the early seventeenth century, England had not yet established direct contact with sub-Saharan Africa. However, England knew about Spanish and Portuguese contacts with this area of Africa and knew that since the fifteenth century West Africans had been used as slaves. Therefore, in the English mind, blacks were "available" as slaves. See page 68.

4c. No. One way in which the English justified their enslavement of blacks was to say that they wanted to Christianize "heathen" peoples. However, the English government never issued a proclamation calling for the Christianizing of Africans. See page 68.

4d. No. The decision by the English colonists to enslave blacks was not the result of a meeting among leaders from the various colonies. Rather it was, as the historian Winthrop Jordan describes it, an "unthinking decision" based on the English frame of reference. See page 68.

5a. No. There is no evidence to indicate that blacks were better workers than white servants. In fact the enactment of the slave codes, which were designed to control the slave labor force, suggest that slaves presented a labor problem not posed by indentured servants. See pages 69–70.

5b. No. In the late seventeenth and early eighteenth centuries, black slaves usually cost about two-and-a-half times as much as indentured servants. See pages 69–70.

5c. Correct. The number of white servants migrating to the Chesapeake fell in the 1680s. The resulting labor shortage led Chesapeake planters to turn increasingly to black slaves to fulfill their labor needs. See pages 69–70.

5d. No. Although it was used principally in the Chesapeake colonies and the middle colonies, white indentured servitude continued in the British colonies in North America throughout the colonial period and was not outlawed by England. See pages 69–70.

6a. No. The evidence indicates that the death rate among whites involved in the slave trade was as great as, and sometimes greater than, the death rate among slaves. Why was the mortality rate sometimes greater for white Europeans than for black Africans? See pages 71–72.

6b. No. Although it was important to keep slaves healthy, seventeenth-century Europeans did not know the germ theory of disease. Although there were attempts to keep the ships clean, such attempts were not very successful because of overcrowding, sickness, and lack of proper sanitation. See pages 71–72.

6c. No. A slave diet consisting of unspoiled meat was rare. The slave diet during the Middle Passage usually consisted of beans, rice, yams, or corn cooked together to create a warm mush. See pages 71–72.

6d. Correct. Blacks resisted enslavement from the moment of capture in Africa to the moment of death. One way of resisting was suicide. See pages 71–72.

7a. No. An egalitarian society is one in which all people have social and political equality. The presence of slavery in the southern colonies created a more stratified society rather than a more egalitarian society. See page 72.

7b. Correct. The South's increasing reliance on slavery brought a corresponding decrease in the number of indentured servants. As a result, the income of poor white planters often declined because they could no longer depend on renting parts of their property to newly freed servants. See page 72.

7c. No. The South's reliance on slave labor accentuated the region's reliance on staple-crop production and did not lead to economic diversification. See page 72.

7d. No. The high demand for labor in the South during the late seventeenth century, coupled with the decrease in the number of indentured servants, means that the cost of indentured servants probably increased. Therefore, indentured servants did not become more affordable to most whites. See page 72.

8a. No. The Spanish neither became more brutal toward the Pueblos nor did they enslave them as a result of the Pueblo revolt against the Spanish in 1680. See page 74.

8b. No. As a result of their revolt against the Spanish, the Pueblos successfully resisted Spanish attempts to impose the Spanish culture and the Catholic religion on them. See page 74.

8c. Correct. When Spanish authority was restored in 1692, the Spanish stressed cooperation with the Pueblos and no longer attempted to enslave them or destroy their culture. See page 74.

8d. No. The Pueblo revolt is described as the "most successful and longest sustained Indian resistance movement in colonial North America." Therefore, resistance against the Spanish was not "futile" to the Pueblos. See page 74.

Copyright © Houghton Mifflin Company. All rights reserved.

9a. Correct. The Yamasees and their Creek allies came close to driving white settlers from South Carolina; but, because of colonial reinforcements and a Cherokee alliance with the whites, the Yamasees and Creeks were defeated. See pages 75–77.

9b. No. The Tuscaroras of North Carolina were defeated in the Tuscarora War (1711–1713) by a combined force of whites from North Carolina, South Carolina, and Virginia. Those Tuscaroras who were not sold into slavery moved northward. This happened before the Yamasee War (1715-1716), which occurred in South Carolina. See pages 75–77.

9c. No. Division and animosity among Indian tribes was a characteristic of the Yamasee War. See pages 75–77.

9d. No. The Yamasees were defeated in 1716, and they moved south to Florida to seek Spanish protection. From their southern location, they continued to cause problems, which was one reason for the chartering of Georgia in 1732. See pages 75–77.

10a. No. The number of people experiencing "saving faith," or the conversion experience, was declining in the early 1660s, as was church membership. See page 80.

10b. No. The case of Anne Hutchinson (1637) indicates problems with Antinomianism (the belief that an individual, having been assured of one's salvation by God, could know God's law and be freed from human laws), but the Halfway Covenant (1662) was not an attempt to deal with this problem. See page 80.

10c. Correct. The covenant created a kind of "halfway" membership in the church, allowing the children of parents who had been baptized but had not had the conversion experience to receive the sacrament of baptism. The goal was to bring more people under the church's authority and, in the long run, increase church membership. See page 80.

10d. No. The Puritans were intolerant of other religions and did not allow freedom of worship in Massachusetts. Quakers attempting to practice their religion in Massachusetts or acting to challenge the Puritan authorities would have been banished. See page 80.

11a. No. England did not impose economic restrictions on the New England colonies prior to the collapse of the first economic system in the 1640s. See pages 80–81.

11b. No. The first economic system collapsed around 1640. There is no indication that a French and Indian alliance was the cause of this collapse. See pages 80–81.

11c. No. Plant diseases did not destroy the New England forests and were not the reason for the collapse of the area's first economic system around 1640. See pages 80–81.

11d. Correct. New England's first economic system was based on the fur trade and the constant influx of migrants. Not only was the region's fur supply limited, but migrants stopped coming to the colony as a result of the English Civil War. These factors caused the area's first economic system to collapse in the early 1640s. See pages 80–81.

12a. No. Foreign trade with the British colonies was contrary to the mercantilist theory because it was believed such trade would aid foreign countries and enrich the colonies at England's expense. Therefore, the Navigation Acts were not designed to encourage foreign trade with the colonies. See pages 83–84.

12b. No. The Navigation Acts attempted to centralize economic decision-making in the hands of Parliament. See pages 83–84.

12c. No. British merchants were to remain important in colonial trade because, according to the theory of mercantilism, colonies are important as a market for the mother country's manufactured goods. Such goods would be supplied to the colonies by British merchants as well as by colonial merchants. See pages 83–84.

12d. Correct. Mercantilist theory held that colonies exist solely for the good of the mother country. The Navigation Acts were an attempt to apply this theory to the colonies by ensuring that England was at the center of colonial trade and profited from that trade. See pages 83–84.

13a. No. The Board of Trade was only one of several agencies and individuals within the British government that had jurisdiction over colonial affairs. This sharing of jurisdiction does not suggest that colonial administration was centralized. See page 84.

13b. Correct. The Board of Trade shared jurisdiction over the colonies with other government agencies and officials. The conclusion that may be drawn is that England governed its colonies in a decentralized and haphazard manner. See page 84.

13c. No. There is no evidence to support the inference that the Board of Trade was tyrannical in supervising the colonies. See page 84.

13d. No. The Board of Trade had no more power in the British West Indies than it had in the British colonies in North America. See page 84.

14a. Correct. James II attempted to exercise more centralized control over the colonies. Since New England was seen as an especially troublesome area, the most drastic reordering of colonial administration was attempted there in the form of the Dominion of New England. See page 85.

14b. No. The New England colonies, with the exception of Rhode Island, did not practice religious toleration. See page 85.

14c. No. Although it is true that most New England exports went to England, this was not the reason for James II's attempt to exercise more authority over the New England colonies. See page 85.

14d. No. Colonists from all regions protested enactment of the Navigation Acts. See page 85.

15a. No. Most of those accused of witchcraft were older women who had lived in the area for some time. See page 86.

15b. No. The witchcraft crisis that began at Salem Village spread throughout New England. Therefore, the crisis was not an isolated incident in a village of radical Puritans. See page 86.

15c. Correct. Many changes were occurring in Massachusetts Bay colony around 1692. These changes caused insecurity and a feeling of powerlessness among many people throughout the colony. The charge that the colony's problems were caused by Satan was attractive to many people because of its simplicity. See pages 86–87.

15d. No. Although there was a struggle for political power between the Puritan authorities and the Anglican merchants in Massachusetts Bay, this struggle does not explain the Salem Village witchcraft crisis of 1692. See page 86.

CHAPTER 4

Multiple-Choice Questions

1a. No. It was practically impossible to obtain a divorce in colonial America. See page 93.

1b. Correct. Most white women married in their early twenties, most black women in their late teens. Since married women usually became pregnant every two or three years, the young age at which women married was a factor in the rapid population growth in eighteenth-century America. See page 93.

1c. No. Women usually bore five to ten children, and a large proportion of those children reached maturity, especially in the colonies north of Virginia. Such statistics do not indicate that most colonial families were small. See page 93.

1d. No. Although the infant mortality rate was high by modern standards (women usually bore five to ten children and could expect about two-thirds of them to live to maturity), the young age at which most women married was not a major factor contributing to the infant mortality rate. See page 93.

2a. No. Although settlers of German descent were most heavily concentrated in Pennsylvania, they were not necessarily drawn to the urban areas of the colony; and during the eighteenth century they spread into the western areas of Maryland and Virginia and settled in the interior of South Carolina and Georgia. See page 94.

2b. No. Although some colonists were prejudiced against Germans and expressed a fear of them, the German immigrants were not political radicals and were not a destabilizing influence in the colonies. See pages 94–95.

2c. Correct. The German immigrants came from a variety of Protestant sects, and as they settled in the middle colonies they added to the religious diversity that already existed in that region. See page 94.

2d. No. Although the text does not indicate the gender of the German immigrants and does not indicate whether they came singly or in groups, many German immigrants came as redemptioners (a variant form of indentured servitude) and often traveled in family groups. See page 94.

3a. No. No information is given that contrasts the level of fear of white slave catchers to that of Indian slave catchers. See page 96.

3b. Correct. In colonies such as South Carolina, whites were a minority of the population and were afraid of an alliance between Indians and blacks. One way of preventing such an alliance was to promote antagonisms between the two ethnic groups by using Indians as slave catchers and blacks as soldiers in Indian wars. See page 96.

3c. No. No information is given that suggests that Indian religious teachings taught that blacks were a threat. See page 96.

3d. No. American Indians were not more adept than whites at luring runaway slaves out of hiding. See page 96.

4a. No. Rather than having a stabilizing influence on the American economy, European wars caused sharp economic fluctuations in the eighteenth-century American economy and affected different colonial regions in different ways. See pages 100–103.

4b. No. The presence of racial slavery was a source of constant tension between black slaves and white masters. In areas of the South where slaves constituted a large proportion of the total population, the fear of slave uprisings was ever present. Such tension was not a source of economic stability. See page 94.

4c. Correct. As stated in the text: "The only source of stability in the shifting economic climate was the dramatic increase in colonial population." See page 96.

4d. No. Foreign trade was the major "energizing" influence on the eighteenth-century colonial economy, but it was also a destabilizing influence. See page 98.

5a. Correct. By the mid-eighteenth century, an elite group had emerged that dominated the political, economic, and social life of the colonies. The presence of the dominant elite meant that colonial society was more stratified in the 1750s than it had been in the seventeenth century, making it more difficult for new immigrants to find advancement opportunities. See page 99.

5b. No. A variety of factors determined whether or not migrants were readily assimilated into Anglo-American culture. Huguenots were quickly absorbed, while colonial Jews were not. However, it is a misstatement to say that eighteenth-century immigrants were "seldom" able to assimilate. See page 99.

5c. No. All blacks and some whites were brought to the colonies against their will. Therefore, it is estimated that about one-third of the migrants during the colonial period came involuntarily. See page 99.

5d. No. The statistics offered in the textbook do not support the conclusion that immigrants to the colonies in the eighteenth century were primarily of English origin. See pages 99–100

6a. No. Because of the nature of the New England soil, New England farmers did not normally produce surplus farm products for the international marketplace. Therefore, wartime demand for foodstuffs did not have a positive economic impact on Massachusetts. See page 101.

6b. Correct. The fertile soil of the middle colonies, including Pennsylvania, meant that commercial farming was the norm in this area in the 1740s and 1750s. Farmers in colonies like Pennsylvania were in an excellent position to profit from the wartime demand for foodstuffs. See page 101.

6c. No. As a result of the King George's War, trade with Europe was disrupted, rice prices plummeted, and South Carolina entered a severe depression. See page 101.

6d. No. Connecticut, a New England colony, had rocky soil and relatively small landholdings. The farmers there did not normally produce a surplus of foodstuffs for the international marketplace. See page 101.

7a. No. The Enlightenment emphasized "natural religion" or, in other words, intellectual religion rather than religion based on spiritual revelation (revealed religion). See pages 103–104.

7b. No. Enlightenment thought rejected faith in favor of something else that Enlightenment thinkers believed to be much more reliable. See pages 103–104.

7c. Correct. Those who adhered to Enlightenment thought rejected spiritual revelation, faith, and intuitive knowledge as faulty and filled with superstition. All knowledge was to be based on observations of the real world and on reason. See pages 103–104.

7d. No. Those who adhered to Enlightenment thought rejected intuitive knowledge as faulty and unreliable. See pages 103–104.

8a. No. Locke believed that government was established as the result of a contract among people and between people and government. Therefore, Locke's theory of government is secular rather than religious. See page 104.

8b. No. Locke believed that people were basically good and that before the creation of government there was relative order and stability. Therefore, according to Locke, government was created for a purpose other than to impose order and stability on human society. See page 104.

8c. No. Although Locke did believe that government was created by people, he did not believe that the contract through which people established government placed absolute power in the hands of the monarch. See page 104.

8d. Correct. Locke believed that people entered into a contract with each other through which they created government. Through this contract, Locke said, government had a contractual obligation to protect the rights of the people. If government did not fulfill this obligation, the people had the right to rise in rebellion against government and institute a new government. See page 104.

9a. Correct. Seating in Congregationalist churches was determined by the wealth and social status of church members. Such status might relate to a person's ethnic background or to a person's vocation, but one's wealth and status were the basis for seating assignments. See page 105.

9b. No. It is possible that the seating system was, to some extent, a reflection of ethnic background, but the seating system showed something else much more clearly. See page 105.

9c. No. The seating system in Congregationalist churches probably did reflect, to some extent, the vocation of church members, but one's vocation did not determine where one sat. What factor did determine the seating system? See page 105.

9d. No. Seating assignments in Congregationalist churches did not indicate marital status. See page 105.

10a. No. Whether one drank tea hot or cold was not a sign of social status in colonial America. See page 107.

10b. No. People of all classes drank tea in colonial America. See page 107.

10c. No. Tea was readily available for home consumption and was not served exclusively in salons. See page 107.

10d. Correct. Although colonists of all classes drank tea, the equipment used to serve the beverage was expensive and not affordable to colonists of lower-class status. Therefore, the more elaborate one's tea service the higher one's social status. See page 107.

11a. No. Prayer was not an important component of trading rituals between Europeans and Indians. See page 107.

11b. Correct. Indians expected Europeans to present them with gifts before negotiations began over the price of furs, skins, and other items of trade. See page 107.

11c. No. Cigar smoking was not an important component of trading rituals between Europeans and Indians. See page 107.

11d. No. Tea drinking was not an important component of trading rituals between Europeans and Indians. See page 107.

12a. No. Religion was extremely important to blacks. However, most religious teaching took place within the *nuclear* family and at religious gatherings. Religious teaching was not the primary function or role of the extended family that developed among African-Americans. See pages 110–111.

12b. Correct. Slaves attempted to improve their lives and found extended kinship groups (the extended family) very important "as insurance against the uncertainties of existence under slavery." See page 110.

12c. No. The extended family was not the basic work unit on the plantation. See pages 110–111.

12d. No. White slaveowners respected few, if any, aspects of black culture and always assumed that they had absolute power over their slaves. See page 110.

13a. No. The work schedules of city workers were largely governed by the clock rather than by the sun and the seasons. See page 111.

13b. No. Because people lived in closer proximity to each other in the cities and many colonial cities were ports into which sailors and travelers brought communicable diseases, the incidence of epidemic diseases was greater in the cities than in the countryside. See page 111.

13c. Correct. Many colonial cities were port cities and subject to the influences of merchants and sailors from other parts of the world. In addition, the presence of newspapers in major cities gave urban dwellers more contact with the outside world. See page 111.

13d. No. Because people lived closer together in the cities, the differences between the ordinary and the genteel were more apparent. See page 111.

14a. No. Notice that in the Hudson Valley Land Riots of 1765 and 1766, British troops from New York City had to intervene to crush the rebellion. This does not indicate that colonial assemblies had the means to control internal disorder. See pages 113–114.

14b. Correct. Aggrieved groups were at the core of each of the crises mentioned. The presence of aggrieved groups is an indication that colonial assemblies, controlled by the genteel, did not live up to the ideal of protecting the rights of all the people. See pages 113–114.

14c. No. There was an ethnic dimension to the Regulator movements of the Carolinas and an ethnic and racial dimension to the Stono Rebellion. See pages 113–114.

14d. No. There is no indication in any of these crises that political rights were being extended to more and more people. In each crisis the aggrieved group rightly felt that it had little or no political power. See pages 113–114.

15a. No. The Enlightenment, with its emphasis on reason, gave rise to "intellectual religions" such as deism and Unitarianism. The Great Awakening was a reaction against such religious movements and emphasized emotion and faith. See pages 114–115.

15b. No. The Great Awakening was an important element in the creation of an American culture distinctively different from English culture. This and other characteristics of the Great Awakening opened the cultural distance between England and its North American colonies. See pages 114–115.

15c. No. The Great Awakening led to more religious diversity throughout the colonies, not to the founding of an established church. See pages 114–115.

15d. Correct. The Great Awakening emphasized emotion rather than learning, faith rather than reason. Those influenced by this thought began to question the people who had traditionally held positions of authority in the church and in secular society. Therefore, as a result of the Great Awakening, there was more of a willingness to question traditional beliefs. See pages 114–115.

CHAPTER 5

Multiple-Choice Questions

1a. Correct. While the coercive practices of British officers were ended by William Pitt, many colonists, especially New England soldiers who were in close contact with British soldiers, vividly remembered the British as being profane, haughty, and unfair. Therefore, they were left with feelings of animosity. See pages 124–125.

1b. No. The British victory over the French and their Indian allies was so decisive that the likelihood of the colonies being drawn into a European-based conflict seemed remote. In addition, although the war was fought to achieve European objectives, it should be remembered that the conflict began in North America. See pages 124–125.

1c. No. As a result of the war, two major sources of colonial insecurity, the French and their Indian allies, had been defeated. Therefore, colonists felt more secure than they had in years, which caused some Americans like Benjamin Franklin, to think expansively about the colonies' future. See pages 124–125.

1d. No. Although the colonists and the British ultimately cooperated and achieved victory over the French and Indians in the Seven Years' War, the alliance produced tension between the two rather than eliminating it. See pages 124, 125.

2a. No. By the Treaty of Paris, France ceded all of its territory in North America to Great Britain and Spain. In other words, since France had lost its North American empire, the Indians could not negotiate trade agreements, separate or otherwise, with the French. See pages 126, 127.

2b. No. Although France ceded all of its territory west of the Mississippi and the city of New Orleans to its ally Spain, the interior Indian tribes realized that Spain was no longer a major power and could not help them counter the power of Great Britain. See pages 126–127.

2c. No. Pontiac was not willing to accept British superiority in the Northwest and would never have advised his tribe to do so. See pages 126–127.

2d. Correct. Pontiac, realizing that British victory in the Seven Years' War placed the Indians of the Northwest in jeopardy, persuaded many Indian tribes in the area to join him in an anti-British alliance. This led to Pontiac's uprising. See pages 126–127.

3a. No. Although the proclamation did confine colonial settlements to the area east of the line, "regulation" of colonial settlement in the west was not the proclamation's major intent. See page 127.

3b. No. The proclamation did not deal with trade issues, and it was not designed to regulate colonial trade with the Indians. See page 127.

3c. Correct. The British hoped that they could prevent a clash between the colonists and the Indians by confining colonial settlements to the area east of the Appalachian Mountains. See page 127.

3d. No. The proclamation did confine colonial settlement to the area east of the Appalachians, but the British saw this as a temporary measure. See page 127.

4a. Correct. Debt burden was Britain's most pressing problem in the aftermath of the French and Indian War. Grenville's colonial policies were largely designed to solve this financial crisis by raising revenue in the colonies. See pages 128–129.

4b. No. Encouragement of colonial manufacturing would have increased competition for colonial and international markets between England and its colonies; and such encouragement would, therefore, have been contrary to mercantilist philosophy. See pages 128–129 and review the discussion of mercantilism on page 83.

4c. No. Grenville's colonial policies were not specifically or intentionally designed as an attack on the taxing powers of the colonial assemblies. See pages 128–129.

4d. No. Only in an incidental way did Grenville's policies regulate colonial trade and commerce (the Sugar Act, 1764), and this was not the primary purpose of his policies. See pages 128–129.

5a. No. The idea that each elected representative represented *all* people in the colony is a restatement, on the colonial level, of the British idea of *virtual* representation (a member of Parliament *virtually* represents every English citizen). See page 128.

5b. No. In 1765 the colonial theory of representative government had not yet reached the point of a belief in the one man, one vote concept. It was not until 1964, in the case of *Westberry* v. *Sanders*, that the Supreme Court applied the one man, one vote concept to state districts in the United States. See page 128.

5c. No. The American colonists denied the right to vote to women, blacks, and Indians. They clearly did not believe that *all* people over twenty-one years of age had to have the right to vote before a colonial assembly could be considered representative. See page 128.

5d. Correct. Whereas the British believed in *virtual* representation, the American colonists believed in *individual* or *direct* representation. This difference between the English and the colonists on how to define representative government was a major factor in the coming of the American Revolution. See page 128.

6a. No. The Real Whigs did not deal specifically with the Sugar Act in their writings and did not suggest that the intent of the Sugar Act was to regulate trade. Furthermore, one of the most influential essays written by the Real Whigs, *Cato's Letters*, was published in the 1720s, long before the Sugar Act. See page 129.

6b. Correct. In their writings, the Real Whigs warned of the tendency toward corruption and oppression inherent in powerful government. The colonists began to interpret British actions, such as the Sugar Act, in light of these warnings. See page 129.

6c. No. The arguments presented by the Real Whigs in their writings did not, in any direct way, lead to the establishment of a Continental Congress. See page 129.

6d. No. The right to petition the government for redress of grievances was a recognized right of English citizens; and English citizens regularly exercised this right concerning local matters by engaging in street demonstrations. In other words, the idea of this right was not new to the Real Whigs. In 1764 eight colonial legislatures sent separate petitions to Parliament, but the protests had no effect. See page 129.

7a. No. James Otis asserted in his pamphlet that Parliament was the supreme legislative authority in the British empire. If Otis clearly recognized Parliament's legislative power, what was the point of his pamphlet? See page 130.

7b. No. James Otis did not assert that the colonists could refuse to obey the laws of Parliament even if they knew those laws to be unconstitutional. What, according to Otis, could the colonists do about unconstitutional laws? See page 130.

7c. No. James Otis did not go so far as to say that a colonial assembly was equal in power to Parliament. See page 130.

7d. Correct. James Otis asserted by implication that Parliament did not have the right to tax the colonies without their consent. However, he further asserted that even unconstitutional laws passed by Parliament had to be obeyed because Parliament was the supreme authority in the empire. See page 130.

8a. No. In its debate relating to the Stamp Act Resolves, the Virginia House of Burgesses accepted the idea that the colonists were British subjects. It was on the basis of this idea that the colonists asserted certain rights as English citizens. See page 131.

8b. Correct. The idea that the House of Burgesses had the sole right to tax Virginians was rejected as too radical by the burgesses in 1765. See page 131.

8c. No. In their debate over the Stamp Act Resolves, the burgesses accepted the idea that the colonists enjoyed the right of consent to taxation. See page 131.

8d. No. In its debate over the resolutions presented by Patrick Henry, the House of Burgesses accepted the idea that the colonists were English citizens and enjoyed all of the rights as Englishmen. See page 131.

9a. Correct. Crowd action against the Stamp Act was so widespread and so effective that no stamp distributor was willing to enforce the law when it went into effect on November 1, 1765. See pages 132–133.

9b. No. The Stamp Act Congress was important as a show of unity on the part of the colonies, but its statements were relatively conservative and did not cause divisions within the British Parliament. See page 132.

9c. No. Parliament never viewed the tax imposed by the Stamp Act as excessive. See page 132.

9d. No. Since the Stamp Act taxed most printed materials, it had an impact on most colonists. But the genteel used printed matter more frequently than the ordinary. As a result, the tax fell most heavily on the genteel. See pages 129, 132.

10a. No. Although many merchants supported economic protest against the British by organizing nonimportation associations after passage of the Stamp Act, the Sons of Liberty was not intended to organize merchants and was not a nonimportation association. See pages 133–134.

10b. Correct. The leaders recognized that the involvement of ordinary people in crowd action could give these people a taste of power and endanger the position of those leaders within colonial society. The Sons of Liberty was formed to channel popular resistance into "acceptable forms." How successful was it in doing this? See pages 133–134.

10c. No. Although it is quite possible that members of the Sons of Liberty advanced ideas found in the pamphlets associated with the resistance movement, the organization was not created for the purpose of distributing such pamphlets. See pages 133–134.

10d. No. Popular demonstrations against the Stamp Act were already widespread, and the Sons of Liberty was not created for the purpose of organizing Liberty Parades. See pages 133–134.

11a. No. The idea of "virtual" representation was an idea advanced by Parliament and one that they found perfectly acceptable. This idea was not advanced by Dickinson in his pamphlet. See page 135. For a discussion of the idea of virtual representation, see page 128.

11b. No. Parliament accepted the idea that English citizens have the right of consent to taxation. See page 135.

11c. Correct. Parliament could never accept Dickinson's contention that colonists could determine the *intent* or motive of an act of Parliament before deciding whether to obey the act. Such an idea would undermine parliamentary supremacy. See page 135.

11d. No. Parliament totally agreed with Dickinson's contention that it had the right to regulate trade, but it disagreed with other beliefs he asserted in his essays. See page 135.

12a. No. Constitutional arguments were refined through debates in colonial assemblies and through the written word rather than through public rituals. See pages 135–136.

12b. No. Although it is true that public rituals, to some extent, served as a form of entertainment, this is not the reason that such rituals were important during the revolutionary era. See page 135.

12c. No. Public rituals were not usually religious in nature and did not serve a religious purpose in relation to the resistance movement. See pages 135–136.

12d. Correct. Illiterate colonists could not be reached through pamphlets, newspapers, and written petitions. However, through the symbols used in public rituals, they could be educated about the arguments against Parliament and drawn into the resistance movement. See pages 135–136.

13a. No. Resistance against the Townshend Acts indicated a growing willingness by the colonists to defend what they perceived to be their rights as English citizens, but it did not indicate the growth of sentiment in favor of independence. See pages 136–137.

13b. Correct. The nonimportation movement created divisions between urban merchants and artisans. In addition, continued crowd action, the use of force and violence as part of the resistance movement, and the increasing political activism of ordinary folks frightened the elite and widened the rift between these two groups. See pages 136–137.

13c. No. Analysis of the resistance to the Townshend Acts does not provide evidence that a new sense of equality was emerging among the colonists. See pages 136–137.

13d. No. Analysis of the resistance to the Townshend Acts reveals a growing rift between the colonists and Parliament but does not demonstrate that the colonists were questioning their loyalty to the king. See pages 136–137.

14a. No. Although it is true that some Massachusetts towns disagreed with some of the ideas presented in this pamphlet, the evidence does not indicate the presence of "serious divisions" between urban and rural colonists. See pages 139–140.

14b. No. This pamphlet, prepared by members of the Boston Committee of Correspondence and containing a statement of the rights and a list of the grievances of the colonists, did not advocate independence. Accordingly, response to the pamphlet did not indicate that Massachusetts colonists favored independence in 1772. See pages 139–140.

14c. Correct. The pamphlet was written in an attempt to involve people of the rural areas of Massachusetts in the resistance movement. The fact that most of the colony's towns agreed with the sentiments expressed in this document indicates widespread agreement throughout Massachusetts with the patriot position. See pages 139–140.

14d. No. Although some towns disagreed with the sentiments expressed in this pamphlet, the pamphlet did not deal directly with the nonimportation movement and reaction to the pamphlet does not provide evidence that the nonimportation movement was in serious trouble. See pages 139–140.

15a. No. Most patriots throughout the colonies approved of the Boston Tea Party and did not see the Coercive and Quebec Acts as justified. See pages 141–142.

15b. No. Although the Quebec Act was actually unrelated to the Coercive Acts, the patriots perceived the two as being linked. See pages 141–142.

15c. Correct. Although the Quebec Act (a reform measure that applied to Canada) and the Coercive Acts (laws designed to punish Massachusetts for the Boston Tea Party) were in reality unrelated, the patriots perceived a link between the two and pointed to both as further evidence that Parliament was conspiring to destroy colonial rights. See pages 141–142.

15d. No. There were divisions among the patriots, but these divisions did not prevent the patriots from having a unified view with regard to the Coercive and Quebec Acts. See pages 141–142.

CHAPTER 6

Multiple-Choice Questions

1a. Correct. Washington realized that a prolonged conflict would be to the advantage of the American forces because in such a conflict the British could be worn down. Therefore, the American army's survival to fight another battle was more important than decisively winning individual battles. See page 146.

1b. No. In light of the fact that the British had a well-trained, well-equipped, and well-disciplined army, Washington realized that a quick and decisive military victory against the British was practically impossible to achieve. See page 146.

1c. No. Washington realized that since the vast majority of the American people lived in the countryside, not in urban areas, the loss of urban areas would not seriously damage the American cause. See page 146.

1d. No. Although Washington realized that shortage of funds was a serious American weakness, the task of financing the war was largely left to the Second Continental Congress. See page 146.

2a. No. Although members of the First Continental Congress tried to represent their constituents, this was not an age in which polls were taken to judge the mood and desires of the electorate. See page 147.

2b. Correct. During the summer of 1774, people throughout the colonies had participated in open meetings in which they pledged to support decisions made at the First Continental Congress. See page 147.

2c. No. Although many colonists labeled parliamentary actions as tyrannical, most colonists wanted reconciliation with the mother country. These sentiments were reflected among the delegates to the First Continental Congress. See page 147.

2d. No. The measures adopted by the First Continental Congress were decisive. Therefore, widespread support for these measures was not due to their ambiguity. See pages 147–148.

3a. Correct. The First Continental Congress stipulated that members of the committees of observation and inspection were to be chosen by all people qualified to vote for delegates to the lower houses of the colonial assemblies. This stipulation was extremely important because it guaranteed the committees a broad popular base. See page 148.

3b. No. The process by which members of the committees were chosen did, in some instances, lead to the election of experienced local officeholders, but the process also led to the election of many people who had never before held public office. See page 148.

3c. No. Members of these committees were to be chosen by all people qualified to vote for delegates to the lower houses of the colonial assemblies—that is, adult males, twenty-one years of age or older, who met certain property qualifications. This was not "mass democracy." See page 148.

3d. No. The process by which members of these committees were chosen was the same process used to elect delegates to the lower houses of the colonial assemblies. Although there were divisions in the resistance movement, this process did not, in and of itself, reveal those divisions. See page 148.

4a. No. In normal times, how they could best serve their masters was not the primary question on the minds of slaves. These were not normal times, and this particular question was even less important. See pages 151–152.

4b. No. In the eyes of many slaves, the patriot cause was a cause associated with white Americans. Although some slaves decided to join that cause, they, along with other slaves, had to deal with another question before choosing sides. See pages 151–152.

4c. No. Deciding the moral rightness of the combatants was not the question faced by most slaves during the Revolutionary War. See pages 151–152.

4d. Correct. Since slaves wanted freedom, deciding which side offered the best chance of achieving that goal was the dilemma faced by most slaves during the Revolution. This question transcends the moral question concerning the combatants, just as it transcends how best slaves could serve their masters or the patriot cause. See pages 151–152.

5a. No. There is no evidence provided that suggests that Connecticut had a higher percentage of tenant farmers than did South Carolina. In addition, tenant farmers, especially those whose landlords were patriots, tended to be loyalists. See page 152.

5b. No. The Anglican church tended to be stronger in the southern colonies than in the New England colonies. Furthermore, Anglicans in the north tended to be loyalists. See page 152. See also page 150.

5c. Correct. In colonies such as South Carolina and Georgia, where blacks constituted at least 50 percent of the population, whites were afraid that involvement in the resistance movement would increase the likelihood of (1) a slave revolt and (2) the British use of slaves against patriot masters. See page 152.

5d. No. People of Scotch-Irish descent constituted a much lower percentage of the Connecticut population than of the South Carolina population. Furthermore, Scotch-Irish settlers often remained neutral in the conflict. See page 152. See also page 150.

6a. No. Life in the colonial frontier was such that muskets were considered a necessity by frontier dwellers and were not usually in short supply. See page 153.

6b. No. American militiamen, including those on the frontier, were not eager to travel far from home to fight, but when their homes were threatened they would rally to the cause. See page 153.

6c. No. The occasional refusal of frontier militiamen to report for duty on the seaboard was not due to the length of the journey, and such a journey was generally not considered treacherous. See page 153.

6d. Correct. The Indian threat seldom seriously hampered the patriot cause, but occasionally frontier militia refused to turn out for duty on the seaboard because they feared Indians would attack in their absence. See page 153.

7a. No. Rather than concentrating their forces in the countryside, the British concentrated on capturing major American cities. See page 155.

7b. Correct. This was one of the three major assumptions about the war made by the British. The other two were that (1) patriot forces could not withstand the assaults of British troops and (2) the allegiance of the colonies could be retained by a military victory. All three assumptions proved to be false. See page 155.

7c. No. In the belief that overwhelming military force would guarantee a swift victory, Great Britain sent to the colonies the largest single force it had ever assembled anywhere. See page 155.

7d. No. The British assumed that they could win a quick, decisive military victory. See page 155.

8a. Correct. One of the beliefs challenged by Paine in his pamphlet was the belief that an independent America would be weak. See page 157.

8b. No. The fact that Paine called for the establishment of a republic indicates that he rejected the idea that Americans owed allegiance to the English king. See page 157.

8c. No. Paine questioned traditional ideas about government and even called for the establishment of a republic. See page 157.

8d. No. Notice that the words "strident" and "stirring" are used to describe Paine's pamphlet. These are not descriptive of a "reasoned" presentation. In addition, Paine was not attempting to bring about a reconciliation between England and the colonies. See page 157.

9a. No. Thomas Jefferson originally included this charge in his list of grievances against the king. However, the charge was deleted from the document before its acceptance by Congress because of objections from southern delegates. In addition, the grievances against the king would not prove to be that significant in the long run. See page 158.

9b. No. Since Americans no longer saw themselves as subjects of Parliament, the document did not mention their specific grievances against Parliament's actions. See page 158.

9c. Correct. At the time it was adopted, the document was important because it identified George III as the villain. However, its list of grievances against the king were, in the long run, less important than its statements of principle. See page 158.

9d. No. The Declaration of Independence did not provide an outline for a central government and did not support the idea of strong central government. Instead, it contended that government exists for the limited purpose of protecting the rights of the people. See page 158.

10a. No. Sir William Howe did not suffer defeat at the hands of Washington's forces, and the British forces were not inadequately supplied. See pages 158–159.

10b. Correct. Sir William Howe's troops landed on Long Island on July 2, 1776, but Howe waited until August to begin his attack against New York City. This delay gave Washington time to move his troops from Boston to New York. See page 158.

10c. No. In his defense of New York City, Washington divided his force in the face of a superior enemy. In so doing, he broke a basic rule of military strategy. See page 159.

10d. No. Since Washington divided his force in the face of a superior enemy and exposed his army to the danger of entrapment, his defense cannot be described as masterful. See page 159.

11a. No. Enlistments in the Continental Army were for periods ranging from one year to the duration of the war. By way of contrast, most enlistments in state militias were usually for three-, six-, or nine-month periods. See pages 160–161.

11b. No. The officers in the Continental Army developed a tremendous sense of devotion to the revolutionary cause. See page 160.

11c. No. Due to their shared experiences and hardships, a sense of comradeship did develop among the officers of the Continental Army. See page 160.

11d. Correct. Those officers in the Continental Army who fought together for a long period of time developed a sense of pride and commitment to the revolutionary cause. See page 160.

12a. No. Although the British force at the Battle of Oriskany was composed of a loyalist contingent, the battle did not indicate that loyalists posed a serious threat to the American cause. See page 162.

12b. No. Although the British claimed victory at the battle, in fact they broke off the engagement at Oriskany, and Colonel Barry St. Leger abandoned his siege of Fort Stanwix, returning to Niagara. See pages 162–163.

12c. Correct. The Battle of Oriskany was the most important battle of the northern campaign for the Indians. During this battle, tribes that had belonged to the Iroquois Confederacy fought against each other, ending a league of friendship that had lasted for three hundred years. See page 163.

12d. No. The Battle of Trenton (December 26, 1776) was the first American victory in the Revolutionary War. See page 163.

13a. No. France did not foresee nor desire the creation of a "strong and independent" United States. See pages 163, 168.

13b. No. In the Treaty of Alliance in 1778, France abandoned all its claims to Canada. See page 163.

13c. No. France was, in many respects, the center of the intellectual movement known as the Enlightenment. As a result, many people in France found the American Revolution attractive because of the principles expressed in the Declaration of Independence. But this was not true of the French government. See page 163.

13d. Correct. France wanted revenge against the British because of the French defeat in 1763. Convinced by the Battle of Saratoga that American victory was possible, France hoped that a formal alliance with the United States would hasten Britain's defeat and make that defeat more embarrassing. See pages 163, 168.

14a. Correct. In an effort to restore some semblance of stability in a South devastated by years of guerrilla warfare, Nathanael Greene adopted a policy of conciliation toward loyalists in that region. See pages 165–166.

14b. No. When Greene assumed command of the southern campaign in 1780, the provincial congresses of South Carolina and Georgia had already been shattered by years of guerrilla warfare. See page 165.

14c. No. In an attempt to turn the tide in favor of the patriots in the South, Nathanael Greene adopted a conciliatory policy toward the southern Indians. See pages 165–166.

14d. No. After assuming command of the southern forces in 1780, Greene specifically ordered his troops to respect the property rights of loyalists in the South. See page 165.

15a. No. American negotiators demonstrated their intelligence and skill. See page 168.

15b. No. American negotiators were instinctively wary of French advice. See page 168.

15c. No. It was the British negotiators, not the Americans, who were weary of the war. American negotiators proved adept at playing the game of power politics and gained their main goal, which was independence as a united nation. See page 168.

15d. Correct. American negotiators chose to disobey their instructions to be guided by the French. They seemed to instinctively recognize that what was in the best interests of the United States was not necessarily in the best interests of France. As a result, they bargained separately with the British. See page 168.

CHAPTER 7

Multiple-Choice Questions

1a. No. None of the three definitions of *republicanism* specifically held that republics should be large and have a diverse population. In fact, "Adamsian" republicanism specifically held that republics had to be small and have a homogeneous population. See page 174.

1b. No. Democratic republicanism, rather than "Adamsian" republicanism, tended to be egalitarian in its approach. Therefore, it advocated widespread political participation and questioned the notion that the upper classes could speak for all people. See page 174.

1c. No. Economic republicanism, rather than "Adamsian" republicanism, emphasized the idea that individuals actively pursuing their own economic self-interest would enrich not only themselves but the nation as well. See page 174.

1d. Correct. Self-sacrificing republicanism stressed the idea that individuals within a republic should be willing to sacrifice their private interest for the good of the whole. Notice that this is similar to the Puritan notion of the godly commonwealth. See page 174.

2a. No. As far as is known, Washington never told such a story either in his 1792 bid for the presidency or otherwise. See page 175.

2b. Correct. Weems was not a historian in the modern sense of the word and did not feel bound to base his conclusions on fact. The cherry tree story indicates that he was less interested in the truth than in imparting certain moral principles to his readers. See page 175.

2c. No. Weems was not a historian in the modern sense of the word and did not engage in extensive research in the writing of his biography of Washington. See page 175.

2d. No. The cherry tree story is not an attempt by Weems to discredit Alexander Hamilton. Furthermore, Washington and Hamilton were not political rivals. See page 175.

3a. No. Judith Sargent Murray's belief that girls should be taught to be economically independent was not a belief held by most Americans and cannot be said to have been the primary reason that schooling for girls improved during the early republic. See pages 176–177.

3b. No. Most Americans of the late eighteenth century did not believe that girls should receive the same education as boys. Nor did they believe that young women should be prepared for jobs in the same way that young men were prepared. See pages 176–177.

3c. No. Judith Sargent Murray's belief that men and women had equal intellectual abilities was held by few Americans and cannot be said to have been the primary reason that schooling for girls improved during the early republic. See pages 176–177.

3d. Correct. Eighteenth-century Americans believed that women were primarily responsible for teaching the virtues necessary for the new republic's survival. As a result, more emphasis was placed on properly educating future mothers. See pages 176–177.

4a. No. The New Jersey law that allowed some women to claim the right to vote applied only to unmarried white women who met certain property qualifications. See pages 177–178.

4b. No. The information about voting rights for women in New Jersey in the 1780s and 1790s does not provide evidence that *most* women actively pursued the right to vote. See pages 177–178.

4c. No. The re-evaluation of the role of women in American society that occurred during the early republican period had more of an impact on women's private lives than on their political role in society. See pages 177–178.

4d. Correct. Although most women believed they could best serve the republic in their roles as wives and mothers, some women actively sought a more public role. The fact that some New Jersey women successfully claimed the right to vote in the 1780s and 1790s is evidence of this. See pages 177–178.

5a. No. The "republican man," rather than the "republican woman," was free to pursue his own economic self-interest. See page 178.

5b. No. Although the "republican woman" was supposed to aid the community, she was also supposed to remain primarily a private being, bound to home and family. See page 178.

5c. Correct. The "ideal republican woman" was to be the perfect embodiment of self-sacrificing republicanism. In other words, she was to sacrifice her individual will to the common good. See page 178.

5d. No. This would be seen as far too selfish a notion for the "ideal republican woman." See page 178.

6a. No. This society was not formed by slaves and was not an abolitionist society. See page 181.

6b. Correct. Free blacks continued to face the political, social, and economic discrimination that accompanied white racism. To help themselves, they often formed separate institutions such as the Brown Fellowship Society. See page 181.

6c. No. Although there were instances of free northern blacks working to gain repeal of discriminatory laws, the Brown Fellowship Society is not an example of such efforts. See page 181.

6d. No. Although some people did work to advance racial equality during the years of the early republic, most notably the Quakers, the Brown Fellowship Society is not an example of such efforts. See page 181.

7a. No. The exact number of slaves who left their masters to fight for the British is not known, but it was considerably less that ten thousand. Furthermore, British recruitment of slaves led to acceptance of blacks in the Continental Army and in most state militias (Georgia and South Carolina were exceptions). See page 181. See also page 151.

7b. No. There is no evidence in the text to suggest that the number of slave rebellions increased in the period immediately after the Revolutionary War. See pages 181–182.

7c. Correct. The questioning of slavery that accompanied the American Revolution led to the gradual abolition of slavery in the North. However, southern slaveholders, in order to defend the practice of holding blacks in bondage, developed new racist notions that made the concept that "all men are created equal" inapplicable to blacks. See pages 181–182.

7d. No. Although such evidence is available today, the scientific community of the late eighteenth century presented no such evidence and had little knowledge of genetic theory. See pages 181–182.

8a. Correct. Most states lowered property qualifications for voting and, as a result, broadened the base of American government. See page 182.

8b. No. The first state constitutions did not attempt to control governmental power through a system of checks and balances. Such an idea developed in response to the failures of the first constitutions, was included in some revised constitutions during the 1780s, and was finally included in the national constitution drafted in 1787. See pages 182–183.

8c.   No. As is stated in the text: "Seven of the constitutions contained formal bills of rights, and the others had similar clauses." See page 182.

8d.   No. During the colonial period Americans had learned to fear colonial governors as agents of the king. This fear led them to put little power in the hands of governors in the first state constitutions. See page 182.

9a.   Correct. The Northwest Ordinance of 1787 discouraged the future importation of slaves into the Northwest Territory. Therefore the ordinance "prevented slavery from taking deep root" in the region, and slavery was abolished in the Old Northwest in 1848. See page 188.

9b.   No. A process was established by which settlers in the Northwest Territory could eventually apply for statehood, but first they had to go through successive stages of territorial government. See page 188.

9c.   No. The Northwest Ordinance of 1787 guaranteed freedom of religion to settlers in the Northwest Territory and did not create an established church. See page 188.

9d.   No. The Ordinance of 1785 established that each township would be divided into thirty-six sections of 640 acres each. Price per acre was one dollar, and the minimum sale was 640 acres. See page 188.

10a.   No. The rebels involved in Shays's Rebellion were able to halt court proceedings briefly, but they never seriously threatened the Massachusetts government and were dispersed by militiamen in 1787. See pages 171–172 and 190.

10b.   No. Shays's Rebellion did not involve an alliance between poor whites and blacks. See pages 171–172 and 190.

10c.   Correct. The rebels asserted that since they did not have adequate representation in the Massachusetts legislature they had not been afforded the "right of consent to taxation." In addition, they often referred to their experience as revolutionary soldiers and used many of the slogans of the revolutionary era See pages 172 and 190.

10d.   No. The rebellion was undertaken by farmers in Massachusetts angered by the state's fiscal policies and was not a counterrevolutionary movement by the Massachusetts elite. See pages 171–172 and 190.

11a.   No. Madison rejected the prevailing idea that republics had to be small to survive. Instead, he contended that in a large republic there would be so many interest groups vying for power that no one group would be able to control the government. See pages 191–192.

11b.   Correct. Madison's thorough analysis of past confederacies and republics led him to advance the principle of checks and balances as the route to political stability. This principle, to a great extent, was the conceptual framework from which the delegates to the Constitutional Convention worked. See pages 191–192.

11c.   No. Madison agreed to the compromise by which each state had equal representation in the Senate, and he was one of the 42 delegates to sign the Constitution. See pages 191–192.

11d.   No. Madison did not insist on a bill of rights during the Constitutional Convention. It was only during the ratification campaign in New York that he promised in the *Federalist Papers* that a bill of rights would be added. See pages 191–192, 196.

12a.   No. Even after a committee created to work out a compromise suggested equal representation of the states in the Senate, the deadlock continued. See pages 192–193.

12b.   No. It was generally agreed that members of the House would be popularly elected and senators would be elected by the state legislatures. Therefore, this suggestion did not break a deadlock at the convention. See pages 192–193.

12c. No. The committee appointed to work out a compromise concerning the question of whether the states would be equally represented or proportionately represented in the Senate recommended equal representation. See page 193.

12d. Correct. Even though a partial compromise over the issue of representation in the Senate had been worked out in committee, the key to breaking the deadlock was Roger Sherman's suggestion that a state's two senators be allowed to vote individually and not as a unit. See page 193.

13a. No. The three-fifths compromise was important in resolving a potentially divisive issue, but it is not considered the "key" to the Constitution. See page 194.

13b. Correct. This distribution of political power, with its elaborate system of checks and balances, is considered the key to the Constitution. What are the strengths and weaknesses of this system? See page 194.

13c. No. The Constitution did not embody the concept of direct democracy at all levels of government. The only part of government to be elected directly by the people was the House of Representatives. Why do you think the founding fathers made this decision? See page 194.

13d. No. The Constitution does not provide for an elected federal judiciary. Federal judges are appointed by the president with the advice and consent of the Senate. What was the rationale for this? See page 194.

14a. Correct. The Antifederalists believed that constant vigilance by the people was necessary to prevent oppression by the government. They believed that such vigilance was possible at the state level but that it was considerably more difficult at the national level. See page 195.

14b. No. The Antifederalists were fearful of a powerful central government. See page 195.

14c. No. The Antifederalists tended to be older Americans whose political ideas had been shaped during the earlier period of the resistance movement against Great Britain. See page 195.

14d. No. Thomas Jefferson favored ratification of the Constitution and was not the leader of the Antifederalists. See page 195.

15a. No. The powers of the chief executive were not the most important issue in the debate over ratification of the Constitution. See page 195.

15b. Correct. The absence of a bill of rights became the most important issue in the debate over ratification of the Constitution. Why did the founding fathers not include a bill of rights in the original document? See page 195.

15c. No. The Constitution did not extend the vote to women, and those wanting such an extension were a decided minority. Why do you think they were a minority? See page 195.

15d. No. By enumerating the powers of Congress, the Constitution did place restrictions on Congress's powers. How does such an enumeration of powers place restrictions? In what way was the "necessary and proper" clause important? See page 195.

CHAPTER 8

Multiple-Choice Questions

1a. No. The Judiciary Act of 1789 did not limit the Supreme Court's power of judicial review. See page 203.

1b. Correct. In Section 25 of the Judiciary Act of 1789, Congress attempted to implement a broad interpretation of Article VI of the Constitution by allowing the right of appeal from state to federal courts. See page 203 and the second paragraph of Article VI in the Appendix.

1c. No. The Judiciary Act of 1789 dealt with the federal court system, not with state courts or their powers. Within the confines of the Constitution, the supreme law of the land, the powers of state courts were established at the state level. See page 203.

1d. No. This right was established by the Supreme Court in 1793 in the case of *Chisholm* v. *Georgia* and was later overturned by the Eleventh Amendment to the Constitution. See page 203.

2a. No. Supreme Court justices are appointed for life and may be removed from office through the impeachment process for treason, bribery, or other "high crimes and misdemeanors." Formal impeachment charges must be brought by the House; the trial based on those charges must take place in the Senate. See page 203.

2b. No. When the Court declares a law to be unconstitutional, its decision is based on the Court's interpretation of the Constitution. Since the Court has the ultimate power of judicial review, such a decision may not be undone by a law declaring the Court's decision—its interpretation of the Constitution—to be in error. See page 203.

2c. Correct. If the Court declares a law to be unconstitutional, Congress may undo or overrule the Court's decision by amending the Constitution itself. This, then, is Congress's check on the Court's power of judicial review. See page 203.

2d. No. When the Court declares a law to be unconstitutional, neither Congress nor the president may simply undo the Court's ruling by issuing a contrary decision, even in the form of an executive order. Under the Constitution, the Court has the ultimate power of judicial review. See page 203.

3a. No. Hamilton's economic package included the proposal that the government raise revenue through protective tariffs, excise taxes, and the sale of bonds and public securities. His proposal concerning assumption of state debts was not an attempt to gain support for an income tax. See pages 205–206.

3b. Correct. In addition to his belief that assumption of state debts by the national government would help put the United States on a firm financial footing, Hamilton also believed such action would bind a particular group (holders of public securities) to the success of the national government. See page 205.

3c. No. Although some of the states felt the burden of their debts, it is incorrect to say that many were on the verge of bankruptcy. See page 205.

3d. No. One of the aims of Hamilton's proposal that the national government assume the debts of the states was to concentrate economic power in the hands of the central government. See pages 205–206.

4a. No. Madison did not argue that the assumption of state debts by the national government was unconstitutional. See page 205.

4b. No. Hamilton's plan did not have a favorable bias toward large states. However, the plan was more favorable to those states that had not paid their debts (such as Massachusetts) than to those that had (such as Virginia). See pages 205–206.

4c. Correct. Madison recognized that Hamilton's plan rewarded speculators who had bought debt certificates at a fraction of their face value, and he argued that the original holders of the certificates should be the ones to benefit from Hamilton's assumption plan. See page 205.

4d. No. Madison's argument against Hamilton's proposal was not based on the idea that it was unfair to merchants involved in interstate commerce. See page 205.

5a. No. Washington's reaction to the Whiskey Rebellion does not demonstrate governmental concern for the disadvantaged. See page 207.

5b. No. Washington believed that the Democratic-Republican societies were responsible for the Whiskey Rebellion. His reaction to the rebellion was an expression of his and the government's belief that an opposition group within a republic was subversive and a threat to the nation. See page 207.

Copyright © Houghton Mifflin Company. All rights reserved.

5c. Correct. By sending a force of over twelve thousand soldiers to quell the Whiskey Rebellion, Washington sent the message that the national government would not tolerate attempts to change national laws by violent means and that the national government would, when necessary, use power to enforce its laws. See page 207.

5d. No. The force used consisted of militia units from Pennsylvania and neighboring states. In the aftermath of the Rebellion, Washington did not believe that a permanent standing army was necessary. See page 207.

6a. Correct. Members of the Democratic-Republican societies believed that the Washington administration's economic policy and foreign policy indicated its hostility toward liberty and equality. Consequently, the societies sought to protect the people's liberties. See pages 209–210.

6b. No. The opposite is true. The Democratic-Republican societies strongly opposed the Jay Treaty. See pages 209–210.

6c. No. The Democratic-Republican societies believed that the United States should honor its treaty of alliance with France. See pages 209–210.

6d. No. Washington and Hamilton saw the Democratic-Republican societies as subversive organizations intent on overthrowing the government. In reality, these societies were the first in a long series of organized groups expressing loyal opposition to governmental policies. See pages 209–210.

7a. No. Analysis of the vote reveals that supporters came mainly from the New England and middle states. Strong merchant interests in both of those areas indicates that merchants supported the treaty. See pages 211–212.

7b. No. Analysis of the vote reveals that opponents of the treaty came mainly from the South. See pages 211–212.

7c. No. Analysis of the vote indicates a factional split between Federalists, who generally supported the treaty, and Republicans, who generally opposed the treaty. There is no indication that the two groups "put aside their differences." See pages 211–212.

7d. Correct. The fact that only 7 of 52 Republicans in the House voted in favor of the appropriations and only 3 of 47 Federalists voted against the funds indicates that partisanship was a force at work in American politics. See pages 211–212.

8a. Correct. A distinction that can be made between Republicans and Federalists is that Republicans attempted to involve more people in government and Federalists opposed such attempts. See pages 211–212.

8b. No. Republicans tended to be more optimistic and less fearful of potential internal and external enemies than Federalists. See pages 211–212.

8c. No. Republicans tended to be optimistic about the political and economic future of the United States. See pages 211–212.

8d. No. Since 90 percent of Americans in the 1790s lived in rural areas, it is a mistake to make an urban-rural distinction between Republicans and Federalists. See pages 211–212.

9a. No. England abided by the provisions of the Jay Treaty and evacuated its forts in the Northwest. See page 213.

9b. No. Such a provision was not part of the Jay Treaty. See page 213.

9c. Correct. France was angry and sought retaliation against the United States because the United States had abandoned the 1778 Treaty of Alliance with France and, through the Jay Treaty, had settled outstanding differences with the British. See page 213.

9d. No. Removal of the Spanish from the western territories was not a provision of the Jay Treaty. See page 213.

10a. Correct. The XYZ Affair caused a further deterioration of relations between the United States and France and led to the Quasi-War in the Caribbean between French and American vessels. This was the first undeclared war in which the United States was involved. See page 214.

10b. No. Although relations with Great Britain improved as relations with France deteriorated, the United States did not seek a military alliance with the British. See page 214.

10c. No. Although Republicans were convinced that President Adams was lying about the French response to the American commissioners sent to Paris to try to reach a settlement with France, Adams's accuracy was revealed when he turned over to Congress the secret dispatches concerning the incident. See page 214.

10d. No. The Directory government did not demonstrate through the XYZ Affair that it was willing to negotiate with the United States. See page 214.

11a. No. Although many Federalists *believed* that Republicans were subversive foreign agents and a threat to the country, this perception was inaccurate. See pages 214–215.

11b. Correct. The Federalists *believed* that Republicans were subversive foreign agents who had to be silenced. Therefore, the Federalist-controlled Congress passed the Alien and Sedition Acts to crush dissent and to destroy the Republican party. See pages 214–215.

11c. No. The text does not address the issue of public support for immigration restriction. Although the three "anti-alien" acts passed by Congress were clearly anti-immigrant, they did not actually "restrict" immigration. See pages 214–215.

11d. No. The United States naturalization law was on the books before the 1798 Naturalization Act was "effective" and required an immigrant to live in the United States for five years before being eligible for citizenship. See page 214.

12a. No. The Virginia and Kentucky resolutions were the response of the Republicans to the Alien and Sedition Acts and did not support the idea that federal law is superior to state law. See page 215.

12b. No. In their response to the Alien and Sedition Acts, the Republicans did not go so far as to support the idea of secession. See page 215.

12c. No. Although the Republicans opposed the Alien and Sedition Acts, they were loyal to the nation and did not support the idea that states could resist federal laws by armed force. See page 215.

12d. Correct. In their response to the Alien and Sedition Acts, the Republicans advanced the extreme states' rights position that a state has the power of judicial review and may declare an act of Congress unconstitutional. See page 215.

13a. No. In 1798, Congress had formally abrogated the Treaty of 1778. Adams's decision in 1800 to reopen negotiations with France led to the Convention of 1800 by which France officially recognized the abrogation of the treaty, freeing the United States of its only permanent alliance. See page 216.

13b. No. Political factions emerged as a result of disagreements over domestic and foreign policy and were clearly present by 1796, before Adams's decision to reopen negotiations with France. See page 216.

13c. Correct. Although the public did not learn the results of the Franco-American negotiations until after the election, Adams's decision to reopen negotiations, and thus defy the Hamiltonian wing of the Federalist party, so split the party that it cost Adams the election. See page 216.

13d. No. Adams's decision led to the Convention of 1800 and ended the Quasi-War with France. Far from creating unity within the Federalist party, Adams's decision caused a serious rift within Federalist ranks. See page 216.

14a. No. The United States did not experience a serious economic depression in the 1790s. See pages 219–220.

14b. No. The Second Great Awakening, an extension of the evangelical Christian movement of the 1740s and 1750s known as the First Great Awakening, grew from American rather than European roots. See pages 219–220.

14c. No. The effective use of revolutionary ideology by religious dissenters caused many states to dissolve their ties with churches or to drastically reduce monetary support for state churches. See page 219.

14d. Correct. The "volatile population mix" of the frontier created instability; and, in addition, migrants felt a sense of isolation. As a result, frontier men and women tried to create new communities to replace those left behind. One such "community" was that supplied by evangelical religion. See pages 219–220.

15a. No. As a result of heavy slave losses during the Revolutionary War, southern planters worked to replenish their depleted work force between 1783 and 1808. This effort led to the most massive influx of Africans into North America since the beginning of the slave trade. See page 219.

15b. Correct. Evangelists associated with the Second Great Awakening preached a message of universal salvation and harmony, which implied equality among all people. Furthermore, the ideas liberty and equality were also associated with the ideology of the American Revolution. Familiarity of slaves with these ideas heightened the fears of slaveowners about the likelihood of a slave rebellion and increased tensions between slaves and slaveowners. See pages 219–220.

15c. No. The Haitian revolution of the 1790s caused fear among southern slaveowners that white refugees from Haiti would bring their slaves, and ideas of revolution, into the South. Therefore, southern state legislatures passed laws forbidding white Haitian refugees from bringing their slaves with them. See page 219.

15d. No. After experiencing an economic downturn in the years immediately after the Revolutionary War, the southern economy expanded after the invention of the cotton gin in 1793. Although this growth led to the expansion of slavery and the slave labor system, it did not cause slaveowners to feel more secure in their control over blacks. See pages 219–220.

CHAPTER 9

Multiple-Choice Questions

1a. No. The failure of Republicans in the Senate to get the two-thirds vote necessary to convict Chase and remove him from office did not cause a split within Republican ranks. See page 229.

1b. No. Requiring annual mental-competency tests for judges was not a consequence of the Senate's failure to convict Justice Chase. See page 229.

1c. Correct. The Senate's failure to convict Justice Chase established that impeachment would not be used as a political tool. As a result, the independence of the Supreme Court from the executive and legislative branches was preserved. See page 229.

1d. No. There is no indication that the Senate's failure to convict Justice Chase caused widespread public disapproval. Furthermore, the Federalists did not regain control of the Senate in the next election. See page 229.

2a. No. The Court held that it did not have the power under the Constitution to compel the president or the secretary of state to appoint Marbury to the position of justice of the peace. See pages 229–230.

2b. Correct. In declaring that the Court, under the Constitution, did not have the power to issue a writ of mandamus, Chief Justice Marshall declared Section 13 of the Judiciary Act of 1789 unconstitutional. Thus the Court claimed the power to judge the constitutionality of acts of Congress. See pages 229–230.

2c. No. The Court held that it did not have the power under the Constitution to issue a writ of mandamus (a court order compelling Madison to appoint Marbury to the position in question). See pages 229–230.

2d. No. The Court was not dealing with state law in the case of *Marbury* v. *Madison*. See pages 229–230.

3a. Correct. Before becoming president, Jefferson advocated a "strict-constructionist" view of the Constitution. Adherence to such a view led to doubts about the legality of the Louisiana Purchase, doubts that Jefferson overcame by accepting the broad view of implied powers. See pages 230–231.

3b. No. Although it would be true to say that the treaty agreed to by Livingston and Monroe presented Jefferson with a dilemma, it is a misstatement to say that Jefferson was angry over the treaty. See pages 230–231.

3c. No. If Jefferson was right in his belief that the voters would accept or reject the purchase on election day in 1804, then they accepted the purchase by re-electing Jefferson to the presidency and by returning a larger majority of Republicans to Congress. See pages 230–231.

3d. No. It is true that Jefferson believed in a narrow interpretation of the Constitution. However, he did not confer with Chief Justice Marshall, a Federalist who accepted the broad-constructionist point of view, before agreeing to the Louisiana Purchase. See pages 230–231.

4a. No. Both eastern merchants and western farmers applauded the purchase because they would no longer have to worry about a hostile power controlling the port at New Orleans. See page 231.

4b. Correct. As a result of the Louisiana Purchase, the United States acquired 827,000 square miles of territory thus doubling the size of the United States. See page 231.

4c. No. Jefferson carried fifteen of seventeen states in the 1804 election for a total of 162 out of 176 electoral votes. See page 231.

4d. No. The Louisiana Purchase did not lead to increased animosity between the United States and Spain and did not lead to an Anglo-Spanish alliance. See page 231.

5a. No. Most states had outlawed dueling by 1804; and, even though New Jersey had not outlawed the practice, upon Hamilton's death Burr was charged with murder in both New Jersey and New York. These facts do not indicate that dueling was still common in the early nineteenth century. See page 234.

5b. No. Although divisions between Older and Younger Federalists did cause dissension within the Federalist party, the Burr-Hamilton duel is not an example of such dissension. See page 234.

5c. No. Although it may be true that Alexander Hamilton was an opportunist, the Burr-Hamilton duel does not provide evidence to support such an inference. See page 234.

5d. Correct. Animosity between Hamilton and Burr led Hamilton, a Federalist, to back an anti-Burr Republican faction in the 1804 New York gubernatorial race. As a result, Burr challenged Hamilton to a duel. These facts indicate that personal feelings prevented the emergence of true political parties. See page 234.

6a. Correct. British impressment of American sailors was an insult to the United States and an affront to American independence. To protest, Congress tried to put economic pressure on the British by passing the Non-Importation Act. See page 235.

6b. No. The text gives no statistics concerning the United States balance of payments in 1806. The Non-Importation Act was not an attempt to deal with a balance-of-payments deficit. See page 235.

6c. No. Congress did not pass the Non-Importation Act with the intention of spurring the development of domestic industry. The policy of "peaceable coercion" eventually led to passage of the Embargo Act, an act that *did* spur the development of domestic industry; but, even with the Embargo Act, this was not the outcome Congress intended. See page 235.

6d. No. The Non-Importation Act prohibited imports from Great Britain of certain cloth and metal articles; but these articles were not considered "decadent" and the act was not passed to protect American virtue. See page 235.

7a. No. Since many Republicans were uneasy about the act because of its use of federal power, it cannot be said that they enthusiastically began to support federal power. See pages 236–237.

7b. No. The Embargo Act did not have a dramatic adverse economic impact on Great Britain and actually helped some English merchants. Therefore, the act did not have the intended effect of pressuring the British either to respect America's rights as a neutral nation or to stop the practice of impressment. See pages 236–237.

7c. No. The Embargo Act was not intended to keep British ships out of the Gulf of Mexico, and, in any event, the United States did not have the naval power necessary to accomplish such a feat. See pages 236–237.

7d. Correct. The Embargo Act had more of an adverse impact on mercantile New Englanders than on the British and French. In addition, it had the unintended effect of helping American manufacturing by halting imports. See page 237.

8a. No. Prophet did not advocate that the Shawnees adapt to white American culture. See page 238.

8b. No. Prophet was the leader of a religious revival among the Shawnees, but he did not advocate acceptance of the Christian religion. See page 238.

8c. Correct. Prophet believed that the only way for American Indians to save themselves in the face of white encroachment was to return to traditional Indian ways. See page 238.

8d. No. Although Prophet did not advocate abandoning settled agriculture, he did not see the acceptance of settled agriculture as the means by which Indians could save their land and culture from white encroachment. See page 238.

9a. Correct. The vote in the House and Senate indicated that there was a regional split in the United States over the declaration of war against Great Britain. Representatives from the coastal states opposed the war; expansionists (War Hawks) from the South and West favored the war. See page 239.

9b. No. If interference with America's commercial rights as a neutral nation and impressment had been the main reasons for war, it is logical to assume that the nation's coastal shipping interests would have supported the war effort. But those interests did not support the war. See page 239.

9c. No. The New England area opposed war out of the belief that war with Great Britain would severely damage American shipping interests. See page 239.

9d. No. The vote in Congress indicated that Americans were divided concerning a declaration of war. See page 239.

10a. No. Although the Federalists gained some congressional seats in the 1812 election, President Madison, a Republican, won re-election against his Federalist opponent by 128 to 89 electoral votes. Therefore, the election cannot be classified as a "resounding Republican defeat." See page 244.

10b. No. Federalist opposition to the war ultimately worked against the party. For example, look at the consequences of the Hartford Convention. See pages 244–245.

10c. No. American actions leading to the war and then the war itself caused European imports to decline dramatically. As a result, the domestic production of manufactured goods increased. See page 244.

10d. Correct. By reaffirming American independence, the War of 1812 brought a wave of American nationalism and self-confidence. See page 244.

11a. No. Madison's veto of Calhoun's internal improvements bill indicates that Madison still clung to some Jeffersonian concepts about limited government. See page 245.

11b. Correct. By calling for military expansion and a program to stimulate economic growth, which included protective tariffs and the chartering of the Second Bank of the United States, Madison demonstrated his acceptance of some Federalist principles. See pages 245–246.

11c. No. Madison supported the first protective tariff in American history. This support indicates his acceptance of the Federalist belief that the central government should play an active role in the economic life of the state. See page 245.

11d. No. Madison supported the appropriation of funds to continue building the National Road to Ohio on the grounds that the project was a military necessity. See page 245.

12a. No. The information concerning the Court on page 246 and the information that directly refers to the *Fletcher* and *Dartmouth College* cases on page 246 clearly implies that the Court, especially under the leadership of Chief Justice Marshall, was unified and consistent in its view.

12b. No. The statement might be true in relation to the period between 1789 and 1801, when fifteen justices came and went, but this situation changed dramatically after John Marshall became chief justice in 1801. Evidence supportive of this conclusion may be found on page 246.

12c. No. In the *Fletcher* and *Dartmouth College* cases, the Court held that a state could not violate or revise contracts, including the Dartmouth College charter. See page 246.

12d. Correct. These cases, as well as the *McCulloch* case, are used to support the inference that the Court, under Chief Justice Marshall, upheld Federalist nationalism and Federalist economic views. See page 246.

13a. No. Some members of President Monroe's cabinet argued in favor of a British proposal that the United States and Great Britain issue a joint declaration against European intervention in the Western hemisphere. However, Secretary of State Adams rejected this approach in favor of a unilateral declaration. See page 248.

13b. No. Although the United States pledged not to interfere in Europe's existing New World colonies, the United States did not relinquish future territorial ambitions in North and South America. See page 248.

13c. No. The United States pledged not to interfere in Europe's existing New World colonies. See page 248.

13d. Correct. In addition to its demand that the nations of Europe not interfere in the affairs of independent Latin American states and to the pledge that the United States would not interfere in Europe's existing New World colonies, the Monroe Doctrine also called for noncolonization in the Western Hemisphere by European nations. See page 248.

14a. Correct. The Second Bank reacted to the Panic of 1819 by reducing loans, thus tightening the money supply. Many state banks, owing money to the national bank, failed. This caused economic hardships for indebted farmers, and they perceived the Second Bank as hostile to their interests. See page 248.

14b. No. President James Monroe ran unopposed in the 1820 election. Monroe received 231 electoral votes, with one vote being cast by a "stray" elector for John Quincy Adams. See page 248.

14c. No. The Panic of 1819 proved to be divisive. As a result, it is one reason for the re-emergence of sectionalism, and it sowed the seeds of the Jacksonian movement. See page 248.

14d. No. The government in 1819–1820 did not believe in the modern practice of federally sponsored public works projects. See page 248.

426 Answers

15a. No. Although the political balance between slave states and free states was definitely an issue in the Missouri debate, it was not the primary reason that people felt so deeply about Missouri's application for statehood. See pages 249–250.

15b. No. Although some politically astute northerners disliked the three-fifths compromise and believed that it gave the South more power in the House than it should have, there was no attempt in the Missouri debate to repeal this compromise that was part of the Constitution itself. See pages 249–250.

15c. Correct. By 1819 many northerners believed that slavery was morally wrong, a belief supported by evangelists associated with the Second Awakening. Therefore, the emotional attitudes of whites toward slavery made the issue more divisive than it otherwise would have been and explain why people felt so deeply. See pages 249–250.

15d. No. Few white Americans in the 1820s were concerned about the civil and political rights of African-Americans. Therefore, this was not a major issue in the debate over the admission of Missouri to the Union. See pages 249–250.

CHAPTER 10

Multiple-Choice

1a. Correct. While the South was investing most of its capital in slaves, the North was investing in canals and railroads and becoming the center of American commerce. See page 255.

1b. No. Congressional legislation did not increase the availability of money for investment in the North. See page 255.

1c. No. As is pointed out in the text, the natural orientation of the 1800 frontier was to the South. This pattern did not change until the 1820s and 1830s. See page 255.

1d. No. The fact that the South built fewer canals, turnpikes, and railroads was not a consequence of the southern terrain. See page 255.

2a. No. The building of the Erie Canal was a project undertaken by the state of New York and was not left to private initiative. See pages 256–257.

2b. Correct. The construction of the Erie Canal, which linked the Great Lakes with New York City and the Atlantic Ocean, was of primary importance in the reorientation of trade routes from their normal North-South pattern to the East-West pattern established in the 1820s and 1830s. See pages 256–257.

2c. No. Grain was carried from the west into markets in the East as a result of the opening of the Erie Canal. See pages 256–257.

2d. No. Throughout the first half of the nineteenth century, controversy continued to rage over the involvement of the federal government in the funding of internal improvements. See pages 256–257.

3a. No. Although there must be some concern about quality, this is not the most important factor in a market economy. See page 259. See also the discussion of the emergence of protests by New England millworkers on pages 271–272.

3b. No. In a market economy crops are grown and goods are produced for the marketplace rather than for the producers' own basic needs. Not only does such an economy encourage movement away from self-sufficient productive units, it encourages the growth of larger productive units as well. See page 259.

Copyright © Houghton Mifflin Company. All rights reserved.

3c. No. The information about boom-and-bust cycles and the impact of depressions on working-class families does not support the contention that a market economy closes the gap between rich and poor. See pages 259–260.

3d. Correct. As people began to concentrate on producing for the marketplace, they bought more items produced by other people. Therefore, as they became less self-sufficient, money became more of a necessity. This in turn led to specialization for the purpose of maximizing profits. See page 259.

4a. Correct. Adam Smith emphasized the idea that individuals should not be restricted in their economic activities by governmental regulations. If left to pursue their own self-interest, Smith believed, individuals would enrich themselves and, in turn, enrich the whole community. See page 261.

4b. No. Adam Smith believed that the role of government in the economic life of the state should be reduced. Therefore, he did not believe in government regulation of business and industry. See page 261.

4c. No. Although the text does not deal with this particular aspect of Adam Smith's philosophy, he believed in free trade among all nations and argued against protective tariffs. See page 261.

4d. No. Adam Smith was not primarily concerned with the development of a society in which all people were equal, and he never advocated the free distribution of land to individuals. See page 261.

5a. No. While Jefferson used the government to promote the economy, he continued to believe in the concept of limited government. See page 262.

5b. No. Jefferson and his fellow Republicans believed that government promotion of economic growth (e.g., the Louisiana Purchase) would provide economic opportunities for the masses. Therefore, such promotion is not evidence that Jefferson favored the rich and powerful. See page 262.

5c. Correct. Jefferson did not see limited government as an end in itself, and he believed that government should actively promote individual freedom by creating an economic environment in which opportunities abounded and in which the independence of the individual could flourish. See page 262.

5d. No. The evidence indicates that Jefferson had clear and definite beliefs about the role of government. See page 262.

6a. No. Although Jefferson and his fellow Republicans believed in government promotion of economic development, this belief did not include giving farmers the tools of their trade. To do so, it was believed, would destroy individual initiative and the competitive spirit of the free enterprise system. See page 262.

6b. No. Jefferson and his fellow Republicans believed that the invention of better farm implements should be left to individual creativity, and they attempted to create an economic environment in which this creativity could flourish. See page 262.

6c. No. Although the government disseminated horticultural information to farmers, active involvement in such things as irrigation projects was believed to be beyond the role of government. See page 262.

6d. Correct. The Jeffersonian Republicans realized that adequate transportation was crucial if individuals were to take advantage of opportunities in the western territories. Thus, they favored government-subsidized railroad construction to increase the economic choices open to free people. See page 262.

7a. No. Regulation of the banking industry was not an issue in the *Charles River Bridge* case. See page 263.

7b. No. The Court declared a state law unconstitutional for the first time in the *Ware* v. *Hylton* case in 1796. See page 263.

7c. No. In cases such as *Ware* v. *Hylton* (1796), the Court accepted the constitutionality of Section 25 of the Judiciary Act of 1789, which allowed appeals from state courts to the federal court system when certain types of constitutional issues were raised. See page 263.

7d. Correct. In speaking for the majority of the Court, Chief Justice Roger Taney focused on corporate privilege rather than on the right of contracts. In doing so, Taney ruled that ambiguous clauses in charter grants would be decided in favor of the public interest. See page 263.

8a. Correct. The major restraint on government promotion of the economy was financial rather than philosophical. See page 264.

8b. No. The philosophy of limited government did not severely limit government promotion of the economy. Even the Jeffersonian Republicans recognized that government promotion of the economy could create an environment in which there was more opportunity for individual freedom. See page 264.

8c. No. Jefferson and his fellow Republicans adopted a strict-constructionist view of the Constitution. However, the reality of governing caused Republicans to become more flexible and to modify this belief to some extent. Therefore, the Republicans' interpretation of the Constitution did not severely limit government promotion of economic development. See page 264.

8d. No. Financiers generally agreed on the goal of economic growth, realizing they would be strengthened as a result. Furthermore, as the private sector grew stronger, entrepreneurs looked less to government for financial support. See page 264.

9a. No. Although one of the initial goals of the owners of the Boston Manufacturing Company was to eliminate the problem of quality control inherent in the putting-out system, the owners did not organize their workers into "quality circles." Furthermore, their concern with quality control did not transform the manufacturing of textiles. See page 265.

9b. No. One of the major characteristics of the Boston Manufacturing Company was the use of a resident manager to run the mill. How did this change the relationship between the owner and the workers? See page 265.

9c. No. The owners of the Boston Manufacturing Company wanted to eliminate problems associated with the putting-out system. See page 265.

9d. Correct. In an effort to eliminate the problems associated with the putting-out system, the owners of the Boston Manufacturing Company combined all the manufacturing processes at a single location. See page 265.

10a. No. Since the machines were the key to the success of the Waltham system, the women who worked under the system did not learn domestic skills that would help them as wives and mothers. See page 265.

10b. Correct. Because of the shortage of available labor in Waltham, Massachusetts, Francis Lowell created the Waltham system to make his mill attractive to New England farm daughters. See page 265.

10c. No. Under the Waltham system, mill managers accepted responsibility for the virtue of the New England farm daughters employed by the mill. However, teaching virtue and morality to these young women was not the Waltham system's main purpose. See page 265.

10d. No. Although the amenities offered by the Waltham system, especially good pay, did offer a new sense of independence to rural women choosing to work in the mills, this was not the primary intent of the mill's owners. See page 265.

11a. Correct. Free banking made it easier for banks to incorporate but also imposed more restrictions on their practices, making bank failure less likely. The resulting increase in the number of new banks provided investors with the credit they needed and led to economic expansion. See pages 268–270.

11b. No. No longer did each new bank require a special legislative charter. As long as a proposed bank met certain minimum requirements, it automatically received a charter. Consequently, the chartering of each new bank was no longer a political decision. See page 270.

11c. No. Although free banking made it easier for banks to incorporate, more restrictions were placed on banking practices. See page 270.

11d. No. The free-banking movement stemmed from laws at the state level regulating the issuance of bank charters. These laws did not give the federal government more control over banking and credit. See pages 268–270.

12a. No. To say that the paternalism of the original Lowell system changed because of a change in the type of worker puts the cart before the horse. Furthermore, what is meant by the "type" of worker? To say that the worker changed the system implies that immigrant laborers caused the system to become more exploitive, which is not the case. See pages 268–270.

12b. Correct. The exploitive nature of mills by the 1830s and 1840s, characterized by the speedup, the stretchout, and the premium system, resulted from a "race for profits" on the part of the mill owners. See pages 268–270.

12c. No. Between 1836 and 1850 the number of spindles at the Lowell mills increased 150 percent and the number of looms 140 percent. Although it is reasonable to infer that this growth caused changes in the Lowell system, one must look deeper to find the primary reason for the change from paternalism to exploitation. See pages 268–270.

12d. No. The introduction of powered looms, both steam-powered and water-powered, undoubtedly changed the nature of the workplace and working conditions. However, this was not the reason for the changes that took place in the Lowell system. See pages 268–270.

13a. No. Most unions during this period were local and were composed of skilled craftsmen. Most members accepted the capitalist system and were not socialists and anarchists. See page 275.

13b. No. Organized labor was able to win a reduction in working hours in the 1850s, and the ten-hour day became standard. However, benefits such as pension plans were not won by workers until the twentieth century. See page 275.

13c. Correct. In an age when organized labor was weak because of divisions among workers, economic upheavals, and hostility from employers, the 1842 decision by the supreme court of Massachusetts that workers could legally organize and go on strike without violating conspiracy laws marks the major achievement of organized labor in the 1840s. See page 275.

13d. No. Workers during the 1830s and 1840s experienced many divisions among themselves. These divisions, whether sexual, ethnic, racial, or religious, were evidenced in the weakness of organized labor. See page 275.

14a. No. West-to-east transportation links led to the transporting of more grain from the Northwest into the Northeast. This increased competition in the grain market created problems for northeastern farmers that could not be solved by growing more grain. See pages 275–276.

14b. No. There was no more land open for cultivation in the Northeast. See pages 275–276.

14c. Correct. Many northeastern farmers realized they could not successfully compete with the Northwest in the production of wheat and corn. Therefore, they turned to vegetable and fruit production and to dairy farming. See pages 275–276.

14d. No. Because of the terrain of the Northeast, the farmers of that area could not take advantage of the new labor-saving farm implements of the 1830s. See pages 275–276.

15a. No. Pioneers began to settle the farming frontier before the introduction of farm machinery. See pages 281–282.

15b. Correct. The government granted land to war veterans, sold land on credit to civilians, reduced the minimum purchase from 640 acres to 80 acres, and reduced the price per acre. This evidence indicates that farm settlement was made possible by the availability of land and credit. See page 281.

15c. No. Cheap labor was not the key to the settlement of the farming frontier. See pages 281–282.

Copyright © Houghton Mifflin Company. All rights reserved.

15d. No. Tariffs were used by Congress in the early nineteenth century to promote economic growth, but tariffs helped domestic manufacturers rather than farmers. Therefore, high tariffs did not make farm settlement and the farming frontier possible. See pages 281–282.

CHAPTER 11

Multiple-Choice Questions

1a. No. The Old South was primarily engaged in staple-crop production and, since farms were far removed from each other, the population was thinly distributed. By 1860 there were only 18 people per square mile in the Old South state of Georgia. See pages 286–287.

1b. No. The South did not suffer from political instability between 1800 and 1860. See pages 286–287.

1c. Correct. Attracted by rich, fertile land, southern herdsmen, yeoman farmers, and slaveholders moved in successive waves into the undeveloped regions west of the southern Appalachians between 1800 and 1860. See page 286.

1d. No. Many of the yeoman farmers who moved into the regions west of the southern Appalachians acquired large tracts of land and became wealthy planters with slaves. Furthermore, a substantial number of the migrants were slaveholders who sought to profit from the cotton boom by buying more land and slaves and planting more cotton. See pages 286–287.

2a. Correct. Production of short-staple cotton was of limited profitability before the cotton gin because of the amount of labor required to remove the seeds from the cotton bolls. The cotton gin solved the problem, made this cotton salable, and made cotton production profitable. See pages 287–288.

2b. No. Innovative farming techniques were much slower in coming to the South than to the Northeast, in large part because of the South's reliance on a slave labor force. Such a labor force, which had to be kept busy, was not conducive to new and more efficient farming techniques. See pages 287–288.

2c. No. The McCormick reaper was a horse-drawn machine for the harvesting of grain and was not useful in the picking of cotton. See pages 287–288.

2d. No. Most areas of the South had rainfall adequate for the successful growing of cotton. See pages 287–288.

3a. No. Although immigrants came to the South in increasing numbers in the 1840s and 1850s, most immigrants were drawn to the urban areas of the North. Therefore, ethnic tension caused by the influx of immigrants is not a characteristic of the South between 1800 and 1860. See pages 290–291.

3b. No. Because of both the export orientation of the southern economy and the fact that southern planters invested their capital in slaves rather than in factories, southern cities remained smaller and less developed than Northern cities. See pages 290–291.

3c. No. The transportation revolution (the building of turnpikes, canals, and railroads) had more of an impact on the Northeast and Northwest than on the South. Therefore, the South was not characterized by the development of a regional transportation network between 1800 and 1860. See pages 290–291.

3d. Correct. Since agriculture and slavery continued to dominate the South's development between 1800 and 1860, the area remained predominantly rural. Furthermore, fewer immigrants, who sought urban areas, came to the South than to the North. As a result, low population density continued to characterize the South. See pages 290–291.

4a. No. In the discussion of the westward expansion of the South between 1800 and 1860, the text says: "Migration became almost a way of life for some yeoman families." See page 292.

4b. Correct. Most yeoman farmers had little connection with the market economy, lived an independent and self-sufficient existence on their isolated farms, and had little connection with slaveowners. See page 292.

4c. No. Since most yeoman farmers were far from the major market networks, they had little connection with the market economy. See page 292.

4d. No. Although most yeomen owned no slaves, they did not generally condemn the institution of slavery. Of the two examples offered in the text, John Flintoff, the aspiring yeoman, acquired slaves, while Ferdinand Steel, the more typical yeoman, does not seem to have been an "outspoken opponent" of slavery. See page 292.

5a. No. Although it is true that mulattos were recognized as a distinct class in cities like Mobile and New Orleans, this was the exception rather than the rule. In addition, even these mulattos did not have a status equal to that of whites. See page 295.

5b. No. Although free mulattos continued to suffer disadvantages, their status was generally higher than that of slaves, and they did not face harsher treatment than most slaves. See page 295.

5c. Correct. The free black mulattos of the cotton and Gulf regions are characterized in the text as "the privileged offspring of wealthy planters." One reason for such a characterization is that these blacks often received financial assistance from their white fathers. See page 295.

5d. No. Although there were instances of black overseers on plantations, this position was not one often held by the free mulattos in the cotton and Gulf regions. See page 295.

6a. No. Although it is true that slaveholders could be and often were harsh in dealing with their slaves, this question asks for the "best" description of the attitude of the wealthiest slaveowners. The evidence does not support "harsh" as the choice. See pages 296–297.

6b. No. We are told that slaveholders such as Paul Cameron "developed affectionate feelings" for their slaves. But the evidence does not support the conclusion that the "attitude" of the wealthiest slaveowners can 'best' be described as loving. See pages 296–297.

6c. Correct. Of the four descriptive words offered, "paternalistic" best describes the "attitude" of the wealthiest slaveholders. In their belief that they were superior to their slaves, they assumed they had the right to decide what was best for their "charges." See pages 296–297.

6d. No. If you have an accommodating attitude toward someone, you are willing to do favors for and help that person. This does not best describe the "attitude" of the wealthiest slaveholders toward their slaves. See pages 296–297.

7a. No. Women of the planter class were expected to keep their opinions about politics and society to themselves. Note, for example, the point of view expressed in articles published by southern men in the 1840s and 1850s. See pages 297–298.

7b. No. Although planter daughters in increasing numbers attended southern boarding schools, independence of thought was not the purpose of the education they received. See page 297.

7c. No. Upper-class southern women did not live a life of leisure and usually had many duties to perform in the home. See page 297.

7d. Correct. Upper-class southern women were to be subordinate to the men in their lives. They were to remain in their "proper" sphere of the home and not venture into politics and worldly affairs. They were to accept uncritically the rules of southern society. See pages 297–298.

8a. No. The fact that slave women did heavy field work alongside slave men indicates that slavery was not characterized by a "strict division of labor by gender." See page 300.

Copyright © Houghton Mifflin Company. All rights reserved.

8b. Correct. Reports from former slaves provide evidence that the lash was used frequently by slaveowners. See pages 300–301.

8c. No. Slave cabins were overcrowded and lacked proper sanitation. These conditions had a serious negative impact on the health of slaves. See page 300.

8d. No. The evidence indicates that slaveowners attempted to keep all slaves busy at all times. Therefore, jobs were assigned to the elderly and to children as well as to the young and middle-aged adults. See pages 300–301.

9a. No. Testimony from slaves indicates that physical abuse was part of the institution of slavery. However, the same testimony indicates that slaves considered something other than the pain from this abuse to be the worst evil of American slavery. See page 301.

9b. Correct. In commenting on their lives as slaves, former slaves emphasized the tyranny associated with physical cruelty as much as the pain. This evidence is the basis for the conclusion that the worst evil of slavery was "not its physical cruelty but the fact of slavery itself." See page 301.

9c. No. Hard work was central to the slave's existence, with most working from "sun to sun." However, slaves were often successful in slowing down the work pace. Even when the pace remained grueling, there was another factor associated with slavery that slaves considered a worse evil. See page 301.

9d. No. The attitude that slaves were expendable resources to be replaced after a certain period of time was much more prevalent in Latin America than in the United States. See page 301.

10a. No. The institution of slavery did not engender trust on the part of slaves toward whites. See pages 301–302.

10b. No. Slaves were considered property, with owners having virtual life-and-death powers over them. In addition, owners were paternalistic toward their slaves. These factors did not create an attitude of kindness and respect on the part of blacks toward whites. See pages 301–302.

10c. No. Without a doubt there were times when slaves showed gratitude toward whites; however, because of the nature of the institution, slavery did not engender an attitude of gratitude on the part of slaves toward whites. See pages 301–302.

10d. Correct. The characteristics associated with the institution of slavery (the paternalism of owners, unhealthy living quarters, grueling work routines, physical and mental abuse, and the fact of being owned) bred in slaves an attitude of antagonism and resistance toward whites. See pages 301–302.

11a. No. Although the African past faded from memory, remnants of African culture remained a part of African-American life, especially in dress and recreation. See pages 302–303.

11b. Correct. In choosing those elements of their African past and of their American present that they deemed useful for survival, blacks fashioned their own culture. This African-American culture was distinct and separate from white culture and gave slaves a sense of identity as a people. See pages 302–303.

11c. No. Blacks clearly recognized that whites believed themselves to be a superior people; however, African-American culture did not accept the idea of white superiority. See pages 302–303.

11d. No. In their interaction with whites, slaves often "displayed" a sense of loyalty, which was sometimes genuine but was often merely a survival technique. Moreover, loyalty to the master was not a part of slave culture, which stressed resistance to slavery and loyalty to fellow slaves. See pages 302–303.

12a. No. The evidence clearly indicates that slave families did exist. See pages 303–304.

12b. No. Slave families were not legally recognized, and masters sometimes chose to disrupt families by selling a spouse or a child. However, masters usually expected slaves to form families and have children since children added to the property holdings of owners. See pages 303–304.

12c. Correct. Slave families were central to the lives of blacks. The interpersonal relations within the family gave meaning to life, and the family was the slave's main source of support. See pages 303–304.

12d. No. The sexual division of labor may not have been the same within the slave family as it was within the white family, but it still existed. After work in the fields, for example, men usually performed "outdoor tasks" while women performed "indoor tasks." See pages 303–304.

13a. No. Most slaves were realistic and practical, and they realized that it was virtually impossible to overthrow the institution of slavery. Therefore, most slave resistance was not aimed at ending slavery. See pages 305–306.

13b. No. Demographic, geographic, and political factors made overthrow of the white power structure in North America virtually impossible, and most slaves recognized this fact. See pages 305–306.

13c. No. The goal of most slave resistance was not to get better housing. See pages 305–306.

13d. Correct. Most slaves were realistic and practical and realized that overthrowing slavery was virtually impossible. Therefore, the aim of resistance was to resist human bondage and at the same time survive. See pages 305–306.

14a. Correct. The existence of slavery in southern society led many whites to view certain types of labor as degrading and insulting Thus slavery led to the acceptance of an aristocratic value system in the South. See pages 307–308.

14b. No. Because of the association between manual labor and the work of slaves, many white southerners perceived manual labor as degrading. See pages 307–308.

14c. No. In the South, slaveowners wielded tremendous power, and they were very successful in using their power to silence slavery's critics. See page 307.

14d. No. Although there were signs of more conflict between slaveholding and nonslaveholding whites on the eve of the Civil War, the fact that southern society was rural, uncrowded, and mobile tended to prevent such conflicts from emerging. See pages 307–308.

15a. No. Due to Helper's thesis, many slaveowners saw the book as a challenge to their power and authority. See page 309.

15b. Correct. Helper attacked the institution of slavery on the grounds that it was detrimental to most southern whites and retarded the economic development of the South. This view was an indication of increasing tensions between whites who owned slaves and those who did not. See page 309.

15c. No. Helper was highly critical of the institution of slavery in his book. Therefore, his book did not indicate that nonslaveowning whites viewed the abolition of slavery as a threat to their independence. See page 309.

15d. No. Hinton Helper was a white nonslaveowner. His book was not an indication that free blacks were becoming more vocal in condemning slavery. See page 309.

CHAPTER 12

Multiple-Choice Questions

1a. No. Farm men and women seldom had the opportunity to travel to the city. Furthermore, even though the farm village was the center of rural life, it offered more of an outlet to farm men than to farm women. See pages 316–317.

1b. No. Farm men and women did not see having more children as a solution to the isolation of farm life. See pages 316–317.

1c. Correct. Although farm men had opportunities to go to the village and women gathered for sewing bees, farm families often gathered on each other's farms to engage in a community work project, play games, dance, and enjoy a communal meal. See pages 316–317.

1d. No. Since there were many farm tasks that had to be accomplished year round, farm families could not simply leave the farm and live in the city during the winter. Furthermore, this would entail having two residences, which most farm families could not afford. See pages 316–317.

2a. No. Most of the utopian communities were founded by people who wanted to live their lives in a way different from that offered by mainstream society, but these communities were not organized for the purpose of completely withdrawing from civilized society. See pages 317–318.

2b. No. Returning to a "state of nature" would mean abolishing all elements of organized society—its institutions and its government. A desire to return to a state of nature was not an objective shared by the founders of utopian communities. See pages 317–318.

2c. Correct. Whether one is dealing with the Shaker community, New Harmony, Brook Farm, or the Mormon community of saints, the characteristic common to these utopian experiments was the aim of establishing a cooperative rather than a competitive environment. See pages 317–318.

2d. No. A biblical orientation was not a characteristic of all of the utopian communities. See pages 317–318.

3a. No. Businessmen in the city did not assume the financial responsibility, through businessmen's associations, of constructing sewers. See page 321.

3b. Correct. Urban areas in the early nineteenth century did not have the taxing power to provide adequate services, such as sewers, to all citizens. Therefore, the city charged the cost of sewers to adjoining property owners. See page 321.

3c. No. Since urban areas in the early nineteenth century did not have the taxing power that cities have today, they did not have sufficient revenue to pay for the construction of citywide sewer lines. See page 321.

3d. No. State governments did not assume the financial responsibility of providing services, such as sewers, to urban residents. See page 321.

4a. No. Although Mann did not believe that direct religious indoctrination had a place in the school curriculum, moral education was retained. See page 321.

4b. No. Mann believed that the focus of education was too narrow and that it contained too much religious indoctrination. Therefore, Mann advocated a secular curriculum that he felt would be more suited to the needs of an industrial society. See page 321.

4c. Correct. Mann believed that children in a republic should be prepared for citizenship. To achieve that goal, he believed that free state education should concentrate on the abolition of ignorance, not on religious indoctrination. See page 321.

4d. No. Mann strongly believed in the importance of the family, but he did not believe the family could adequately carry the burden of educating the nation's children. Therefore, he advocated state-supported public schools. See page 321.

5a. Correct. Urban dwellers were often strangers to each other and found it difficult to find people with common interests. Therefore, middle- and upper-class urbanites often found like-minded people by joining clubs and associations. See page 323.

5b. No. Urban life was not conducive to the kind of neighborhood sports activities that were found in the neighborly gatherings associated with rural life. See pages 323–324.

5c. No. Although some people in the early nineteenth century sought to deal with the problems of urban life by joining utopian communities, it would be a mistake to say that middle- and upper-class urbanites often joined such communities. See page 323.

5d. No. Running for political office was not seen by most middle- and upper-class urbanites as a solution to their feeling of alienation in the city. See page 323.

6a. No. Although religious intolerance was associated with some of the riots, it was not a "common thread." See page 324.

6b. No. Although white racism was associated with some of the riots, it was not present in all and was, therefore, not a "common thread." See page 324.

6c. Correct. In all of the riots fearful people uncertain of their own future were striking out against scapegoats whom they *perceived* to be political and/or economic rivals. See page 324.

6d. No. Greed is not a "common thread" running through the urban riots of the 1830s and 1840s. See page 324.

7a. No. Although many Americans believed the popular myth that wealth was derived from hard work, most of those who held great fortunes in the 1840s and 1850s did not acquire their wealth in that manner. See pages 324–325.

7b. No. Parties like that attended by Philip Hone indicate that many of the upper-class elite displayed their wealth in an ostentatious manner. See pages 324–325.

7c. No. Rather than being part of an idle class, the upper-class elite "devoted energy to increasing their fortunes and power." See pages 324–325.

7d. Correct. Many Americans continued to believe the popular myth that wealth was derived from hard work, but for every person who acquired great wealth in that way, there were ten who built their wealth on money they inherited or married. See pages 324–325.

8a. No. Although it is true that some women, such as the New England farm daughters, found employment in the new factories, this was not true for most working-class women. See pages 327–328.

8b. No. Although it is true that most men had to acquire specialized work skills to compete successfully in the job market, this was not true for most working-class women in the early nineteenth century. See pages 327–328.

8c. Correct. Most working-class women of the early nineteenth century worked as domestic servants, seamstresses, cooks, laundresses, and the like. Therefore, they sold their domestic skills for wages. See pages 327–328.

8d. No. Some women did find employment as clerks and cash runners in urban department stores, but this was not true for most working-class women in the early nineteenth century. See pages 327–328.

9a. Correct. In the market economy, the family lost its importance in the production of goods, and more emphasis was put on the role of women as "housekeepers" and childrearers. This led to the idea that women were responsible for the educational, moral, and cultural functions of the family. See pages 328–329.

9b. No. The cult of domesticity supported the segregation of work tasks between men and women. See pages 328–329.

9c. No. The cult of domesticity relegated men to the world of the market economy as opposed to the world of the home. See pages 328–329.

Copyright © Houghton Mifflin Company. All rights reserved.

9d. No. The world of work outside the home was associated with men. See pages 328–329.

10a. Correct. More people began to view small families as desirable, and marriage manuals warned of the harmful effects of too many births on a woman's health. The evidence indicates that many married couples took the warnings of these manuals seriously and began to practice birth control to limit family size. See page 329.

10b. No. The world of work and of home did become more separate for men in the early nineteenth century. However, the fact that men left home to go to work did not preclude sex between husband and wife and was not the reason for the decline in family size in the early nineteenth century. See page 329.

10c. No. There is no evidence that sex education was better in early-nineteenth-century homes, and sex education was not offered in the schools. This was not a factor in the decline of family size during this period. See page 329.

10d. No. We are told that the birthrate declined in the early nineteenth century. This means that the number of children *born* declined. Therefore, we cannot conclude that an increase in infant mortality caused a decrease in family size. See page 329.

11a. No. Ireland in the early nineteenth century was one of the most impoverished European countries, and the potato blight of 1845–1846 caused widespread starvation. Most Irish immigrants left their homeland to escape desperate conditions and were not of the Irish middle class. See page 332.

11b. No. Most came from rural areas where conditions were desperate because of the 1845–1846 potato blight. See page 332.

11c. No. Although many young Irish women were able to find employment in American factories and households, the evidence indicates that finding such work was not always easy. See pages 332–333.

11d. Correct. Through an examination of the experience of Irish immigrants, one can see the ethnic and religious divisions that were part of American society in the early nineteenth century. See pages 332–333.

12a. No. Although the United States government appeared to accept Indian sovereignty by following international protocol in negotiating, signing, and ratifying treaties with Indian tribes, this was merely a facade. See page 334.

12b. No. Rather than showing a desire to protect Indian culture, the United States government usually showed disdain for that culture. See page 334.

12c. Correct. Although the United States seemed to recognize Indian independence by following international protocol in negotiating, signing, and ratifying treaties with Indian tribes, in fact treaty negotiations were used by the United States to acquire Indian land. See page 334.

12d. No. Treaty negotiations with Indian tribes, supposedly between equal nations, were carried out between victor and vanquished. This coercive atmosphere does not indicate that there was "an atmosphere of friendship and cooperation." See page 334.

13a. No. The Indian agency system was not designed to preserve Indian culture. In fact, while the government accepted this system, Congress passed a "civilization act" with the intent of teaching Indians to live like whites. See pages 334–335.

13b. Correct. Under the Indian agency system the government monopolized trade with the Indians in a certain area and "paid out the rations, supplies, and annuities they [the Indians] received in exchange for abandoning their land." As Indians became more dependent on these payments, they became more docile in treaty negotiations. See pages 334–335.

13c. No. Indians were not given land under the Indian agency system, and the system was not intended to make Indians economically independent. See pages 334–335.

13d. No. Under the Indian agency system the government paid out rations and supplies to Indians. This does not indicate that the system was an attempt to starve Indians into submission. See pages 334–335.

14a. No. Although General William Tecumseh Sherman often talked of "extermination," this was not President Monroe's policy. See page 335.

14b. No. The idea of federally sponsored job-training centers was outside the frame of reference of early-nineteenth-century Americans. See page 335.

14c. Correct. In his 1824 message to Congress, President Monroe advocated the settlement of all Indians to the west of the Mississippi. See page 335.

14d. No. President Monroe's policy did not call for the creation of the Bureau of Indian Affairs. He believed that the promise of a home free from white encroachment would be sufficient to win Indian acceptance. (The Bureau of Indian Affairs was not created until 1836.) See page 335.

15a. No. The federal government did not actively protect the rights of minority groups in the 1830s and 1840s. Not only is this apparent from the black experience, but from the experience of American Indians, Irish immigrants, and German immigrants. See pages 335–336.

15b. No. Evidence cited in the text does not lead to the conclusion that blacks turned to state governments for protection of their rights. See pages 335–336.

15c. Correct. Since the position of free blacks under federal law was uncertain, and since they were generally discriminated against politically, socially, and economically in both free and slave states, free blacks worked to help themselves by organizing strong, independent self-help societies. See pages 335–336.

15d. No. White institutions usually reflected the prevailing white-racist attitudes of most white Americans of the 1830s and 1840s. Therefore, as free blacks sought to improve their status in American society, they saw little reason to work through white institutions. See pages 335–336.

CHAPTER 13

Multiple-Choice Questions

1a. Correct. Leaders of the revival movement taught that perfection of earthly society would lead to the Second Coming. Therefore, evangelical Protestants became involved in reform movements that they believed were associated with the forces of good. See page 348–349.

1b. No. Although preachers of the Second Great Awakening taught that all people were sinners, they preached that anyone could achieve salvation. See page 348.

1c. No. The Second Great Awakening, based on evangelical Christianity, taught that God was an active force in the world. See page 348.

1d. No. Although the evangelists associated with this religious movement believed in the Second Coming and in the creation of God's kingdom on Earth, they preached neither that Jesus had already returned nor that the Last Judgment had begun. See page 348.

2a. No. This society, formed by concerned women, not only led the crusade against prostitution but extended aid to impoverished women and orphans as well. It was not antifeminist in its orientation. See page 349.

2b. No. The evidence does not support the conclusion that this society theologically supported the concept of women's rights. See page 349.

2c. Correct. At first the revival movement seemed to reinforce the traditional view of the role of women in a republican society. But the commitment of women to "spread the word" led to their involvement in reform organizations and to more involvement in the public and political arena. See page 349.

2d. No. Originally formed as an organization against prostitution, this organization was not antiforeign in its orientation. See page 349.

3a. No. The temperance movement gained widespread support and by the 1840s had brought a decline in the amount of alcohol consumed in the United States. See page 350.

3b. No. The key word in this choice is "regulate." The temperance movement was an attempt to prohibit the manufacture and sale of alcoholic spirits—whiskey, rum, and hard cider. Therefore, it went beyond a mere attempt to "regulate" hard liquor. See page 350.

3c. No. Women were at the vanguard of the temperance movement. See page 350.

3d. Correct. The habit of drinking could not be supported in the factory. As factory owners complained about workers taking "St. Monday" as a holiday, they supported the temperance movement. See page 350.

4a. No. Antimasonry did nothing to affect the electoral college. The electoral college is still in existence and is the mechanism by which the nation's president is elected. See pages 352–354.

4b. No. Andrew Jackson was a Mason and was opposed by the Antimasons, who supported John Quincy Adams in the 1828 election. See page 353.

4c. No. Antimasonry was turned into a moral crusade as church leaders and evangelicals joined the movement. It then crossed over into politics and was eventually absorbed by the Whig party. In the process, its crusading aspects helped to shape the political party system. See pages 353–354.

4d. Correct. At heart, Antimasonry was a reform movement that emphasized moral conduct and the rights of ordinary citizens. As a moral crusade, it attracted people in New England, the mid-Atlantic states, and Ohio. When it was then taken up by politicians as a device to win popular support, it became a bridge between reform and politics. See pages 353–354.

5a. No. Although there was dissension within the antislavery movement, it was over the women's rights question and over involvement of abolitionists in politics. Neither the Lovejoy murder nor the gag rule caused dissension within the movement. See page 356.

5b. Correct. Many northerners perceived the murder of Elijah Lovejoy, passage of the gag rule, and censorship of the mail in the South as a southern attack on the constitutional rights of abolitionists. As a result, many northerners became more supportive of the antislavery movement. See page 356.

5c. No. Neither the murder of Elijah Lovejoy nor the passage of the gag rule by the House of Representatives was related to the temperance movement. See page 356.

5d. No. Neither the Lovejoy murder nor the gag rule had any relation to government regulation of industry. See page 356.

6a. Correct. The women's movement was more controversial than other reform movements of the age. This was true in part because the movement questioned traditional ideas held by both men and women. As a result, the movement was not able to gain a broad popular base of support. See pages 356–357.

6b. No. The women's movement was very controversial. Most men actively opposed the movement, and the question of women's rights caused a serious split in the antislavery movement during the 1840s. See pages 356–357.

Copyright © Houghton Mifflin Company. All rights reserved.

6c.   No. In their re-examination of the position of women in American society, leaders of the women's movement were not concerned primarily with "moral" issues but with women's rights. Many of the other reform movements were more moralistic in their orientation. See pages 356–357.

6d.   No. Women did not have the right to vote and suffered legal disabilities and social restrictions. They did not have political and economic power. See pages 356–357.

7a.   No. The issues were secondary in a campaign that became a personal conflict between John Quincy Adams and Andrew Jackson. See page 359.

7b.   No. The election gave political reformers no reason to charge that the electoral college was obsolete. Jackson won 56 percent of the popular vote and won the electoral vote by a margin of 178 to 83. See page 359.

7c.   Correct. Jackson's victory was in large part due to his direct appeal to the voters through a well-organized and well-funded party organization. See pages 359–360.

7d.   No. The Jacksonian era is synonymous with the expansion of democracy and the advent of a more open political system, and the 1828 election did not lead to the adoption of literacy tests for voters. See pages 359–360.

8a.   Correct. Out of the belief that strong central government was the enemy of individual liberty, Jacksonian Democrats returned to the Jeffersonian notion of limited government. See page 360.

8b.   No. Jacksonian Democrats generally opposed the educational reform movement of the early nineteenth century. They believed that public education was too secular in its orientation and interfered with parental responsibilities. See page 360.

8c.   No. The Jacksonians rejected active government involvement in the economic life of the state because they believed such intervention benefited the wealthy. See page 360.

8d.   No. Jacksonian Democrats supported the idea of a strong chief executive who embodied the will of the people and acted on their behalf. See page 360.

9a.   No. The Union was dear to Daniel Webster, and he described it in glowing terms in his debate with Robert Hayne. See pages 360–361.

9b.   No. Robert Hayne and John C. Calhoun, supporters of states' rights, viewed the Union as a collection of sovereign, independent states. Daniel Webster did not share that view. See pages 360–361.

9c.   No. Although Daniel Webster probably believed that God smiled on the Union, he did not express the belief that the Union had been created by God. See pages 360–361.

9d.   Correct. Webster believed that the Union went beyond being merely a compact among sovereign states; he believed that it was an inviolable compact among the people of all of the states. See pages 360–361.

10a.   No. Jackson and Congress stood together in strongly advocating the supremacy of the federal government in the Constitution. See page 362.

10b.   No. South Carolina's nullification ordinance implied that the state would secede if the federal government attempted to enforce the Tariff of 1832. But other southern states did not formally accept either the theory of nullification or the more extreme idea of secession. See page 362.

10c.   Correct. In light of the outcome of the nullification crisis, which included Jackson's nullification proclamation, passage of the Force Act by Congress, and passage of a compromise tariff to appease South Carolina, one can logically conclude that neither side won a clear victory. See page 362.

10d. No. Although Jackson indicated his belief that the theory of nullification was repugnant to the Constitution and at odds with the preservation of the Union, he urged Congress to lower the tariff by choosing from among several compromise tariff bills under consideration. See page 362.

11a. No. Although Jackson's veto message was an emotional attack on the undemocratic nature of the bank, it also declared the bank unconstitutional. See page 363.

11b. Correct. Although Jackson declared the bank unconstitutional, his veto message focused on denouncing the bank as a symbol of special privilege and the undue concentration of economic power in the hands of the rich and powerful. See page 363.

11c. No. Although Jackson had certainly been known to attack his opponents on the personal level, he did not deliver a personal attack against the president of the Second Bank in his veto message. See page 363.

11d. No. Although the Second Bank had tightened credit considerably during the Panic of 1819 and generally followed a tight money policy after the depression ended in 1823, President Jackson's veto message did not focus on that policy. Furthermore, Jackson himself followed such a policy, as may be seen with the Specie Circular. See page 363.

12a. No. Social class was not the main determinant of party affiliation in the 1830s and 1840s. See page 365.

12b. Correct. Religion and ethnicity were the two major determinants of party affiliation in the 1830s and 1840s. See page 365.

12c. No. Since manufacturers, merchants, laborers, and farmers could be found in both parties, it cannot be said that occupation was the main determinant of party affiliation in the 1830s and 1840s. See page 365.

12d. No. Since only men could vote, gender was not a determinant of one's party affiliation in the 1830s and 1840s. See page 365.

13a. No. John Tyler was the first vice president to assume the office of the presidency because of the death of the president. Some questioned whether he should assume all the powers of the office, but Tyler did not question his right to do so and took the reins of presidential power firmly in his hands. See page 366.

13b. No. Tyler spoke out against South Carolina's nullification ordinance in 1832 when he was a senator from Virginia. However, he also opposed Jackson's nullification proclamation, a stand that caused him to resign his Senate seat and withdraw from the Democratic party in 1833. See page 366.

13c. No. Although John Tyler withdrew from the Democratic party in 1833, became a Whig, and ran as the Whig vice-presidential candidate in the 1840 election, at heart he was a strict constructionist and was devoted to the idea of limited government. See page 366.

13d. Correct. John Tyler withdrew from the Democratic party in 1833 in opposition to Jackson's use of executive power and his egalitarianism. Even though he joined the Whig party, he never accepted the Whig concept of an activist national government and opposed the Whig economic program. See page 366.

14a. No. Many Americans believed that foreign enemies, especially the British, posed a threat to the nation's security. Therefore, many supported expansionism in an effort to secure the nation's borders from this perceived threat. See pages 367–369.

14b. No. The depression of 1839 lasted until 1843, and the 1840s are considered to be a period of economic expansion. This expansion heightened national pride, which in turn was a reason for the expansionist sentiment of the 1840s. See pages 367–369.

14c. No. Spain was no longer a power in the North American West, having been ousted in 1821 as a result of the Mexican independence movement. See pages 367–369.

14d. Correct. One aspect of Manifest Destiny, and one of the reasons for the expansionist sentiment of the 1840s, was the idea that it was the mission of America to carry its superior civilization to inferior peoples. See pages 367–369.

15a. No. When Henry Clay first proposed the American System in 1824, he called for protective tariffs and federally funded internal improvements. With the rise of the Jacksonian Democrats, these proposals met with disaster. In 1844 the main campaign issue concerned expansion, not the American System. See page 371.

15b. No. Van Buren's stance in the 1844 presidential election did not decide the contest. See page 371.

15c. Correct. James G. Birney's presence on the ballot as the Liberty party's candidate drew enough votes away from Henry Clay in the state of New York to give the state and the election to James K. Polk. See page 371.

15d. No. Polk ran on a platform that called for the territorial expansion of the United States. He did not stand against the expansion of slavery into the territories. See page 371.

CHAPTER 14

Multiple-Choice Questions

1a. Correct. In his presidential campaign, one of Polk's slogans was "Fifty-four Forty or Fight." However, since war with Mexico seemed imminent, Polk was ultimately willing to accept the 49th parallel as Oregon's northernmost boundary in order to avoid a two-front war with Great Britain and Mexico. See pages 376–377.

1b. No. Polk gained widespread support in his presidential campaign through the use of the expansionist slogan "Fifty-four Forty or Fight." Therefore, in light of Polk's election, it was quite possible that a large segment of the American people would have supported a war with Great Britain over the Oregon Territory. See pages 376–377.

1c. No. Public disclosures by the Senate did not cause President Polk to accept British offers concerning the Oregon boundary. See page 377.

1d. No. Had the British accepted all of the American demands, there would have been no need for a negotiated settlement. By the settlement, the United States accepted the 49th parallel (rather than 54° 40′) as Oregon's northernmost boundary and agreed to perpetual free navigation of the Columbia River by the Hudson's Bay Company. See page 377.

2a. No. Although the expression of concern by Whigs that President Polk had engineered the war with Mexico demonstrates a fear of presidential power, no such fear was expressed in relation to the gag rule. See page 378.

2b. No. Those who opposed the Mexican War and the gag rule did not charge that "subversive foreign influence" was behind these acts. See page 378.

2c. Correct. It seemed to many northerners that the Mexican War was engineered by the Slave Power to acquire more slave territory. They also believed the Slave Power had placed free speech and civil liberties in jeopardy by passage of the gag rule in the House. See page 378.

2d. No. New Englanders were opposed to both the Mexican War and the gag rule. See page 378.

3a. No. Although the author and most supporters of the Wilmot Proviso did not believe that slavery was morally wrong and did not seek to abolish the institution in the slave states, neither did they advocate permitting slavery in the Utah and New Mexico territories. See page 379.

3b. No. David Wilmot did not propose the colonization of blacks in the territory acquired from Mexico. See page 379.

3c. No. David Wilmot, the author of the Wilmot Proviso, was not an abolitionist and neither believed in nor advocated equal rights for blacks in the Mexican cession territory. See page 379.

3d. Correct. In proposing the Wilmot Proviso, David Wilmot hoped to bar slavery from the Mexican cession territory and leave the area open to white opportunity only. The introduction of the proviso into the House transformed the debate over the Mexican War to a debate over the expansion of slavery. See page 379.

4a. No. William Lloyd Garrison did not believe that abolitionists should become involved in politics, and his stand on this issue caused a split in the abolitionist movement. In any event, Garrison could never have supported Taylor since Taylor was a slaveholder. See page 381.

4b. Correct. In the presidential election of 1848, both the Whig and Democratic parties tried to avoid the issue of slavery in the territories, but this was the main issue in the minds of many people. This issue caused many southern Democrats to vote for the Whig presidential candidate because he was a slaveholder. It was also this issue that caused antislavery Whigs, former members of the Liberty party, and some northern Democrats to organize the Free-Soil party and run a presidential candidate in 1848. These facts support the idea that the slavery issue caused fragmentation of the political parties in 1848. See page 381.

4c. No. Zachary Taylor, a slaveholder and the presidential nominee of the Whig party in the 1848 election, attempted to avoid the issue of the expansion of slavery into the territories. See page 381.

4d. No. Zachary Taylor was a Whig; James K. Polk was a Democrat. Polk did not endorse Taylor in the 1848 presidential election. See page 381.

5a. No. Although the Compromise of 1850 did not abolish slavery in Washington, D.C., it did abolish the slave trade. However, neither the failure to abolish slavery in D.C. nor the abolition of the slave trade in D.C. was a basic flaw of the compromise. See pages 381–382.

5b. No. California was admitted as a free state, but that was not a basic flaw in the Compromise of 1850 either. See pages 381–382.

5c. Correct. The statement concerning popular sovereignty was so vague that southerners explained it in one way while northerners explained it in another. Therefore, on this issue and the related issue of the expansion of slavery into the territories, the compromise settled nothing. See pages 381–382.

5d. No. The Missouri Compromise line applied only to the Louisiana Purchase Territory and was not extended to the Pacific Ocean. See pages 381–382 and the map on page 383.

6a. Correct. George Fitzhugh, a southern sociologist, argued that all societies should practice slavery because it was more humane than wage labor. See page 384.

6b. No. George Fitzhugh argued, instead, that wage labor was more inhumane than slavery. See page 384.

6c. No. In their defense of slavery, many southerners referred to biblical accounts of slaveholding. However, this was not true of the arguments expressed by George Fitzhugh. See page 384.

6d. No. Fitzhugh did not contend that slavery was morally wrong. Since the 1820s most southern leaders had consciously defended slavery as a positive good and were not willing to recognize it as a moral wrong. See page 384.

7a. No. By indicating that the question of slavery in Kansas and Nebraska would be left to the people living there, the Kansas-Nebraska Act accepted the concept of popular sovereignty. See page 386.

7b. No. The Kansas-Nebraska Act widened the division between the northern and southern wings of the Whig party and led to the party's demise. See page 386.

7c. No. Stephen Douglas believed that environmental and geographic conditions in Kansas and Nebraska would keep slavery out of the region. Because of this belief it cannot be said that he introduced the Kansas-Nebraska Act as a proslavery measure. See page 386.

7d. Correct. By adopting the concept of popular sovereignty in Kansas and Nebraska and thus allowing the people residing there to decide whether the region would be free or slave, the Kansas-Nebraska Act repealed the Missouri Compromise. See page 386.

8a. Correct. In its stand against the Slave Power and against the expansion of slavery into the territories, the Republican party stood on the belief that the future of the nation rested on the dignity of labor and the availability of economic opportunity. See pages 386–387.

8b. No. The Republican party's support of both internal improvements and a homestead bill indicates support for a strong and vigorous central government actively involved in the economic life of the state. See pages 386–387.

8c. No. Although Abraham Lincoln expressed the belief that slavery was morally wrong, the Republican party did not take a stand against slavery for moral reasons. Furthermore, the party did not call for an immediate end to the institution of slavery. See pages 386–387.

8d. No. The Republican party attempted to woo members of the anti-immigrant Know-Nothing party into its ranks and did so by sponsoring legislation that would postpone extending the right to vote to naturalized citizens. See pages 386–387.

9a. No. In their attempt to prevent conflict between the interests of the slaveowner and the nonslaveowner, southern Democrats did not promise to make slaves available to all white southerners. See page 389.

9b. Correct. In courting the support of the nonslaveowning white majority in the South, southern Democrats argued that all white men enjoyed liberty and social equality in a slave society *because* of the enslavement of blacks. See page 389.

9c. No. A homestead bill would give free land in the western territories to people who would use it. Southern Democrats' belief in a limited central government and their fear that a homestead bill would exclude slavery from the territories led them to oppose such a measure. See page 389.

9d. No. Southern Democrats believed in a limited central government. As a result, they did not support federally sponsored internal improvements. See page 389.

10a. No. The Democratic candidate, James Buchanan, carried five of sixteen free states and all of the slave states except Maryland. Although most of Buchanan's support came from the South, the fact that he carried some free states indicates that the Democratic party was not a purely sectional party. See pages 389–390.

10b. No. The Republican party had virtually no support in the South and carried no slave state. Maryland, the only slave state not to support Buchanan, went for Millard Fillmore, the Know-Nothing candidate. See pages 389–390.

10c. Correct. The Republican party carried eleven of sixteen free states. This evidence indicates that the Republican party had become the dominant party in the North. It also indicates that a massive polarization between North and South was under way. See pages 389–390.

10d. No. James Buchanan, who won the presidential election of 1856, had been ambassador to Great Britain during the controversy over the Kansas-Nebraska Act, and his views on territorial questions were not clear. See pages 389–390.

11a. No. The Court did not rule that property rights were subordinate to individual rights. See pages 391–392.

11b. No. Although the Court ruled against Scott's contention that he was free as a result of having been taken into free territory, it did not rule that slaves could not be freed by their owners. See pages 391–392.

Copyright © Houghton Mifflin Company. All rights reserved.

11c. Correct. The Court ruled the Missouri Compromise unconstitutional and in so doing ruled that Congress could in no way prohibit the movement of any kind of property, including slaves, into the territories. See pages 391–392.

11d. No. The Court ruled against Dred Scott's contention that he was free because he had been taken into free territory. See pages 391–392.

12a. No. Lincoln believed that the western territories should be open to free whites. See page 394.

12b. No. Lincoln hoped to confine slavery to the South, where it would die a natural death. But he did not advocate the immediate abolition of slavery. See page 394.

12c. No. Lincoln's belief that slavery should be barred from the territories indicates that he did not accept popular sovereignty as a way of dealing with the question of the expansion of slavery. See page 394.

12d. Correct. Lincoln believed that the Slave Power was attempting to impose its will on the Union and carry slavery into the territories and into all the states. Therefore, he saw the Slave Power as a threat to democracy and the free-wage labor system, and he saw slavery as a threat to all whites. See page 394.

13a. No. Douglas was attempting to find a stand that would help his political position in the North and not cause further erosion of his position in the South. Direct defiance of the Court's *Dred Scott* decision was not the route he chose. See page 395.

13b. Correct. Douglas attempted to revive the doctrine of popular sovereignty. He did so by asserting that although Congress could not prohibit slavery in the territories, a territorial legislature could do so by barring slavery or by doing nothing. See page 395.

13c. No. Douglas indicated in the Freeport Doctrine that, in spite of the *Dred Scott* decision, there was still a way to prohibit slavery in the territories. See page 395.

13d. No. Douglas did not assert in the Freeport Doctrine that slavery was morally wrong. See page 395.

14a. Correct. Some southern newspapers associated John C. Breckinridge, the presidential nominee of the southern wing of the Democratic party, with secessionists. In response, Breckinridge delivered a speech in which he publicly disavowed secession. See page 396.

14b. No. In the 1856 election, the Know-Nothing party ran on an anti-Catholic, anti-immigrant platform. By 1860, members of this party had joined either the Republican party or the Constitutional Union party, but its anti-Catholic rhetoric was not a major factor in the 1860 presidential election. See page 396.

14c. No. John C. Breckinridge, the presidential nominee of the southern wing of the Democratic party, did not call for military preparedness in the slave states. See page 396.

14d. No. In light of the fact that the Kansas-Nebraska Act repealed the Missouri Compromise, southerners generally supported it and supported the pro-slavery Lecompton constitution in 1857. This was also true of John C. Breckinridge, James Buchanan's vice president and the 1860 nominee of the southern wing of the Democratic party. See page 396.

15a. No. The results of the 1860 election indicated that most voters did not want extreme action and that compromise was still a possibility. See page 397.

15b. No. Although there were southern extremists who did not want compromise, southern leaders in the Senate demonstrated their willingness to accept the Crittenden Compromise under certain conditions. See page 397.

15c. No. The Union was very dear to northern leaders. They believed the South was bluffing when it threatened to secede and believed the pro-Union forces in the South would prevent secession. See page 397.

Copyright © Houghton Mifflin Company. All rights reserved.

15d. Correct. Lincoln had the political task of preserving the unity of the heterogeneous Republican party. To accomplish that task he believed it necessary to reject the Crittenden Compromise. This rejection caused southern leaders to reject the compromise as well, and the peace effort collapsed. See page 397.

CHAPTER 15

Evaluating and Using Information

C. Analysis of a Primary Source

The document is the journal of Lieutenant Colonel Alston, chief of staff for Confederate General John Hunt Morgan. According to the *New York Times* and part of the journal not quoted in the exercise, Alston was captured by Union pickets on July 5, 1863, taken to Lexington, Kentucky, where he learned of his side's defeat at Vicksburg, and then sent to Camp Chase, Ohio.

You should have circled 1, 2, 4, and 7.

Multiple-Choice Questions

1a. Correct. In 1861 about 90 percent of the blockade runners successfully penetrated the North's blockade, and by war's end some 50 percent were successful. Although these statistics indicate that the blockade gradually became more successful, they also indicate that the blockade was never a complete success. See page 406.

1b. No. Although the South made impressive gains in industrialization, especially in the production of small arms and ammunition, it never matched the North's industrial capacity. Therefore, although Confederate soldiers had weapons, they often did not have boots, uniforms, or blankets. See pages 406–407.

1c. No. There was never "mass starvation" throughout the South. Furthermore, the food shortages that existed were caused by a multiplicity of factors, such as destruction of food crops by advancing armies, a shortage of farm labor, hoarding of food, and inadequate transportation facilities. See pages 406–407.

1d. No. France never allied with the Confederacy and there is no mention of this in the text. See pages 406–407.

2a. No. Although the agrarian economy of the South was devastated by the war, cotton was still produced for export. See pages 406–407.

2b. No. Although the government forced factories to work on government contracts to supply government needs, businesspeople were not forced to extend loans to the army during the Civil War. See pages 406–407.

2c. Correct. Through the years the South advocated the states' rights philosophy. However, it became apparent, especially to Jefferson Davis, that centralization of power was necessary for the Confederacy to survive the Civil War. See pages 406–407.

2d. No. The evidence does not indicate that the Civil War changed southern society by forcing plantation owners to sell their estates. See pages 406–407.

3a. Correct. Managers of northern corporations were Hamiltonian in their ideology and believed that the government should actively aid business interests. On the other hand, they did not believe that government should protect consumers or workers by regulating business. See page 416.

3b. No. Managers of northern corporations did not believe in state regulation of business. See page 416.

3c. No. Managers of northern corporations would have viewed governmental regulatory commissions for industry as an unnecessary interference in their freedom of action and a threat to their property rights. See page 416.

3d. No. Managers of northern corporations generally did not believe workers had the right to organize and saw labor activism as a threat to the interests of private property. See pages 416, 417.

4a. No. There was a labor shortage in the western agricultural areas. This labor shortage resulted from (l) the food demands of the army and the industrial work force and (2) the drafting of men into the army. See pages 416–417.

4b. Correct. The shortage of labor in western agricultural areas caused increased reliance on labor-saving farm machinery. This in turn created a boom in the sale of agricultural machinery and increased the food supply for the growing urban work force. See page 416.

4c. No. The expansion of the northern urban work force and the need to feed the army caused the demand for farm products to remain constant and farm prices to remain high. See pages 416–417.

4d. No. Northern farm families turned increasingly to commercialized agriculture as the demand for farm products remained constant and farm prices remained high. The farm segment of the northern economy did not suffer depression during the war years. See pages 416–417.

5a. No. As one of the lines that linked Chicago and the Great Lakes region with the Northeast, the Erie Railroad clearly profited during the war years, with its stock increasing from $17 to $126 a share. However, of the groups listed, stockholders in this railroad did not make the highest profits during the war. See page 417.

5b. Correct. Many northern employers profited during the war years, but the highest profits and largest fortunes went to those who engaged in profiteering on government contracts. See page 417.

5c. No. Officers in the Union army did not amass large profits from war bonds. See pages 416–417.

5d. No. Western farm families did not suffer financially during the war because the demand for farm products remained constant and farm prices remained high. However, of the groups listed, farm families did not make the highest profits during the war. See pages 416–417.

6a. No. There is no indication that the shipbuilding program initiated by President Lincoln and approved by Congress was either unnecessary or unwise. See page 418.

6b. Correct. Although Congress later approved the shipbuilding program, the fact that it was initiated by Lincoln before Congress assembled indicates an increase in executive power. See page 418.

6c. No. There is no indication that the northern press influenced Lincoln's decision to support the shipbuilding program. See page 418.

6d. No. Lincoln had no Joint Chiefs of Staff. This advisory body was not created until 1942. See page 418.

7a. No. Lincoln never made such a promise. See pages 419–420.

7b. No. Lincoln made no such promise to the plantation elite of the South. See pages 419–420.

7c. Correct. Lincoln first mentioned the slavery issue in a major way in March 1862. He advocated (l) that Congress promise aid to any state that agreed to emancipate its slaves and (2) colonization of blacks outside the United States. See pages 419–420.

7d. No. Lincoln never offered federal aid to slaves who were able to escape to the North. See pages 419–420.

8a. No. Slavery was abolished by the Thirteenth Amendment, not by the Emancipation Proclamation. See pages 420–421.

8b. No. The Emancipation Proclamation allowed the border states (the slave states that had remained in the Union) to keep the institution of slavery. See pages 420–421.

8c. No. The Emancipation Proclamation did not provide for the gradual abolition of slavery in the Confederate states. See pages 420–421.

8d. Correct. The Emancipation Proclamation freed slaves only in those areas over which the Union had no control. It did not free slaves in any area of the Confederacy that had fallen under Union control and did not free slaves in the border states. See pages 420–421.

9a. No. The Emancipation Proclamation was far from being flawless as a legal document and, in fact, raised a number of legal questions. See page 421.

9b. No. The document was not religious in its intent or language and did not condemn slavery on religious or moral grounds. See page 421.

9c. Correct. The document raised legal questions, did not morally condemn slavery, and physically freed no slaves; however, it was nearly flawless as a political document. Both liberals and conservatives could accept it, and its ambiguity gave Lincoln the political flexibility he wanted. See page 421.

9d. No. The Emancipation Proclamation was not humanitarian in its intent or content. See page 421.

10a. No. The Conscription Act of 1862, passed by the Confederate Congress, allowed a young man eligible for the draft to hire a substitute. Not until passage of the Conscription Act of 1864, again passed by the Confederate Congress, was this practice ended. See page 422.

10b. No. Davis never supported the concept of "full equality" for blacks and never questioned the political, social, and economic discrimination of free blacks that was part of the fabric of southern society. See page 422.

10c. No. Although Davis and his men became desperate for Confederate recruits and even began using the army to round up deserters, the eligible age for recruits was never lowered to twelve. See page 422.

10d. Correct. Toward the end of the war, Davis realized that the only hope for the Confederacy was to increase the number of men in arms. Therefore, he proposed that slave soldiers be recruited and that the soldiers and their families be promised freedom. See page 422.

11a. Correct. As the Confederate government's powers increased, southern planters, committed only to their own selfish interests, increasingly resented and resisted the government's encroachment on their lives. See pages 428–429.

11b. No. Southern planters demonstrated little or no commitment to building a southern nation. They seemed committed only to their own selfish interests. See pages 428–429.

11c. No. Secession and war were bound to bring change to southern society. However, southern planters seemed not to recognize this fact and wanted a guarantee that their lives would remain unchanged and untouched. See pages 428–429.

11d. No. Southern planters had little sense of commitment to the war effort. See pages 428–429.

12a. Correct. Lincoln, unlike Davis, was at ease among common people and was able to communicate the sincerity of his feelings to them. He did not show the aloofness and austerity that were part of Davis's nature. See page 431.

12b. No. Lincoln was not quiet, shy, and retiring. See page 431.

12c. No. Davis, rather than Lincoln, was cold and aloof. See page 431.

12d. No. Lincoln and Davis appear to have been equally sincere in their beliefs. See page 431.

13a. No. Although France under Napoleon III was hostile toward the North, it never concluded an alliance with the Confederacy. See page 433.

Copyright © Houghton Mifflin Company. All rights reserved.

448 Answers

13b. Correct. Recognition of the Confederacy by European nations would hurt the Union cause in several respects; therefore, the Union's primary diplomatic goal was to prevent such recognition. See page 433.

13c. No. Although European loans to the Confederacy were certainly not in the North's best interest, the North's primary diplomatic goal was more all-encompassing than simply preventing such loans. See page 433.

13d. No. The North's industrial capacity was such that it could produce its own war materiel. See page 433.

14a. No. General Grant was not concerned with repatriation in 1863 and did not suggest this as an "innovative strategy." See page 434.

14b. No. General Grant did not attempt to organize Union loyalists in the South and did not adopt the strategy of guerrilla warfare on the part of such forces. See page 434.

14c. Correct. General Grant, with the goal of devastating the South economically and striking a decisive blow to southern morale, decided to use whole armies to conduct raids deep into the Confederacy. See page 434.

14d. No. Flexible response is a strategy associated with President John F. Kennedy, not with General Ulysses S. Grant. See page 434.

15a. No. It was clear to most people that federal control of the banking and transportation systems had been necessary because of wartime emergency and would end when that emergency passed. See page 439.

15b. No. It was generally accepted that women assumed roles outside the "proper sphere" because of the wartime emergency and that they would return to their traditional roles when the emergency passed. However, the new sense of confidence gained by many women could not be taken away. See page 439.

15c. No. It was clear in most people's minds that the federal government conscripted men into the service because of the wartime emergency and conscription would end when the emergency passed. See page 439.

15d. Correct. The question concerning the position of blacks in American society transcended the wartime emergency. At the end of the war this crucial question remained unanswered. See page 439.

CHAPTER 16

Evaluating and Using Information

The value of most of the Evaluating and Using Information exercises in this study guide lies in your working out interpretations for yourself and composing your own "answer"; therefore, the answer provided below is purposely incomplete.

What you see below is the essay's plan—for convenience sake, presented as a traditional outline—and a rough or working draft of one subsection of the body of the mock essay.

The plan represents the structure and sequencing of the whole essay suggested by the questions and the way they are grouped in the exercise. As you can see, Section I.A., which is more detailed than other sections of the outline, represents the part of the plan that you see developed in the illustrative partial "answer."

What follows the outline is an excerpt from a mock essay like the one you should now have in your Reader's Notebook. It is, of course, too long to serve as a quarter or a third of an essay written in an examination situation. When responding to such a broad essay question during a test, you would naturally drop the least important points and examples as well as some of the transitional devices. On the other hand, if the question on the test ended up being "What was the role of the presidency in influencing how and how far voting and other rights were extended during Reconstruction?," then including all of the points and examples in the excerpt below would be appropriate.

Outline

Thesis* _____

_____

_____

_____

I. Role of the federal government in the turmoil over voting rights
   A. Role of Presidents Lincoln, Johnson, and Grant
      1. Lincoln's attitudes about extending voting
      2. Johnson's attitudes about extending voting rights to particular groups
         a. Former Confederate officials and leaders
         b. African-Americans
      3. Johnson's actions supporting or hindering the extension of voting rights
         a. Former Confederate officials and leaders
         b. African-Americans
      4. Grant's attitude and actions regarding the extension of voting rights
   B. Role of Congress
   C. Role of the Supreme Court

II. Effect of public attitudes concerning the extension or possible extension of voting rights
   A. The degree to which voting rights were extended to particular groups
      1. Former Confederate officials and leaders
      2. African-Americans
      3. Women
      4. Immigrants
   B. Indicators of public attitudes about whether voting rights would be extended
      1. Indications of public attitudes in the South
      2. Indications of public attitudes in the North
   C. The relationship between public attitudes and the degree to which voting rights were extended during the period

Excerpt from a Mock Essay

(Development of Section I.A. in Outline)

During the Reconstruction era (1865–1877), Presidents Abraham Lincoln, Andrew Johnson, and Ulysses S. Grant encouraged the re-establishment of the voting rights of those who had been the Union's former enemies, the men who had led the Confederacy. In contrast, however, they hindered the extension of voting rights to African-Americans and, for all practical purposes, did not even consider extending voting rights to women.

Because he was killed before Reconstruction got under way, President Lincoln's role was more that of a vague background influence than as a real shaper of policy. As a part of his 10 Percent Plan for reconstruction following the war, Lincoln had recommended granting the right to vote to some African-Americans but to how many and under what conditions is not clear. The role of the presidency in the extension of voting rights during Reconstruction was thus left primarily to Presidents Johnson and Grant.

In the case of President Johnson, the only two groups whose voting rights were in question were former Confederate officials and leaders and African-Americans. From Johnson, neither group would have been justified

---

*Note—The statement of the thesis of the essay—its whole point about the nature of the changes in voting rights brought about by all the turmoil between 1864 and 1877—should precede the outline itself. In this case the statement of the thesis has been omitted because it is important that you compose your own thesis statement.

in expecting much support. Johnson had a long history of antipathy toward the planter class from which the Confederate leadership had come; and, although he said he favored African-American suffrage, he was in fact a white supremacist, as is indicated by his explanation of his veto of the Civil Rights Bill of 1866. He was also a states' rightist, which meant that he thought states—and to him the southern states were just that, states, not territories— rather than the federal government should decide who should vote. Of course, if it were left up to the old order in the former Confederate states, the right to vote would not be extended to African-Americans.

Johnson's actions promoted the quick re-establishment of voting rights for former Confederate officials and leaders but discouraged the extension of voting rights to African-Americans. Surprisingly, he was liberal in his granting of pardons, and that made many former Confederates eligible to vote for and/or be delegates to the state constitutional conventions. Furthermore, in defiance of the will of Congress, military officers in the South who were enforcing the provisions of the Reconstruction Act of 1867 that barred certain former Confederate leaders from voting were replaced by Johnson with officers who allowed such people to vote. As a result, the former Confederate leaders could exert major influence on the selection of delegates to the state constitutional conventions and the political leadership of the South. As for African-Americans, the sincerity of Johnson's declaration of support for black suffrage was not borne out in his actions. He opposed, and in fact vigorously campaigned against, ratification of the Fourteenth Amendment. That amendment granted citizenship to freedmen and, although it did not extend the right to vote to African-Americans, it did at least encourage southern states to do so by rewarding them with increased political representation in Congress if they did.

President Grant was another story. Unlike Johnson who said one thing and did another, Grant tacitly said one thing and actually did nothing. By supporting the Republican platform in the election of 1868, Grant tacitly said he supported black suffrage, at least in the southern states. In office, though, he did nothing to push it and very little to protect blacks' civil rights in general. Grant rarely used federal troops to back the Enforcement Acts of 1870 and 1871 or an anti-Klan law, even when military force was clearly called for, such as an 1875 Mississippi case. After the Greeley-Liberal Republicans' challenge in the election of 1872, Grant was, if anything, less willing to take action that would foster any extension of voting rights to African-Americans or to protect their civil rights.

Multiple-Choice Questions

1a. No. The federal government changed its policy toward enlistment of black volunteers in the Union Army, but it did so out of necessity rather than out of a commitment to equal rights. Unfortunately, evidence from the 1860s indicates that there were as few victories over racial discrimination at the federal level as at the state level. See page 446.

1b. No. There was an element within the Republican party committed to equality, but the Democratic party consistently fought against equality. See page 446.

1c. No. A faction in the Republican party was devoted to fighting racism, but the evidence does not support the conclusion that the racist attitudes of white northerners changed because blacks participated in the war. For example, what stand did the voters in Connecticut, Minnesota, and Wisconsin take in 1865 concerning black suffrage? See page 446.

1d. Correct. There were signs that wartime idealism had caused some questioning of racism and some movement toward racial equality. However, there was also evidence of continued racial prejudice within northern society. This leads to the conclusion that securing equality for blacks would be difficult. See page 446.

2a. No. Although Johnson demonstrated a considerable amount of sympathy toward the South, he did not go so far as to promise federal aid to rebuild the region. See pages 446–447.

2b. Correct. At first it appeared that Johnson's Reconstruction plan would prevent the prewar southern elite from returning to power. But Johnson freely gave pardons to ex-Confederates whom southerners had defiantly elected to Congress. This caused Congress to question Johnson's plan. See pages 446–447.

2c. No. Congress supported the requirement in Johnson's plan that the Confederate war debt be repudiated. Congress was angered when two southern states defiantly refused to abide by this requirement. See pages 446–447.

2d. No. The Johnson plan stipulated that most white southern males, including yeoman farmers, could gain the right to vote by swearing an oath of loyalty to the United States government. See pages 446–447.

3a. No. Although some of the southern states were reluctant to admit that slavery was a thing of the past, the black codes did not require that freedmen pay "freedom dues" to their former masters. See page 448.

3b. No. The black codes did not extend political rights to any freedmen. See page 448.

3c. Correct. The black codes, adopted by most southern state legislatures immediately after the war, were in large measure restatements of the old slave codes. Those responsible for enacting the codes intended permanently to relegate blacks to a subservient position in southern society. See page 448.

3d. No. The black codes did not indicate acceptance of the Thirteenth Amendment and did not protect the civil rights of the freedmen. See page 448.

4a. No. The Constitution stipulates that treaties must be ratified by the Senate, but Congress (the Senate and the House) did not base its claim that it had a right to have a voice in the Reconstruction process on this constitutional grant of power to the Senate. See pages 448–449.

4b. No. The Constitution does grant Congress the power to declare war, but this was not the basis for Congress's claim that it had a right to a voice in the Reconstruction process. See pages 448–449 and page A-11.

4c. Correct. Article IV, Section 4, of the Constitution states: "The United States shall guarantee to every State in this Union a republican form of government." It was on the basis of this statement that Congress claimed its right to have a voice in Reconstruction. See pages 448–449 and page A-13.

4d. No. The Preamble to the Constitution states that one of the purposes of the government is to "promote the general welfare," but this was not the section of the Constitution on which Congress based its claim to a voice in the Reconstruction process. See pages 448–449 and page A-9.

5a. No. Most conservative and moderate Republicans believed that voting was a privilege, not a right. They did not ally with the Radical Republicans out of the belief that full political rights should be extended to blacks. See page 449.

5b. No. Most conservative and moderate Republicans viewed property rights as sacred. They rejected the contention by the Radical Republicans that a redistribution of southern land was necessary. See page 449.

5c. Correct. All those who questioned Johnson's program, even conservatives and moderates, were labeled as "radical" by Johnson and the Democrats. Therefore, to make changes they thought necessary, conservative and moderate Republicans were forced into an alliance with the Radicals. See page 449.

5d. No. The Radical Republicans held views that most northerners rejected. For example, some Radicals went beyond advocating equality under the law for freedmen by advocating political, social, and economic equality as well. See page 449.

6a. No. The Fourteenth Amendment allowed the southern states to decide whether or not to extend voting rights to freedmen. If a state denied voting privileges to its black citizens, the state's delegation to the House of Representatives would be reduced proportionately. This provision was never enforced. See pages 450–451.

6b. No. Johnson condemned the Fourteenth Amendment. He actively worked against the amendment by urging northerners to reject it and southern state legislatures to vote against ratification. See pages 450–451.

6c. No. The Fourteenth Amendment ignored women. See pages 450–451.

6d. Correct. Conservative and moderate Republicans disagreed with Radical Republicans over extension of voting rights to freedmen. The second section of the Fourteenth Amendment clearly indicates a compromise favoring the conservative/moderate view on this question. See pages 450–451.

Copyright © Houghton Mifflin Company. All rights reserved.

7a. Correct. Only one southern state (Tennessee) had initially accepted and been reconstructed under the Fourteenth Amendment. However, under the Reconstruction Act of 1867 the southern states were required to ratify the amendment before returning to the Union. See page 451.

7b. No. Although most Radical Republicans called for redistribution of southern land, most people rejected the idea as being beyond the power of the federal government and as unwarranted interference in private property. See page 451.

7c. No. The act stipulated that the ten southern states to which it applied had to guarantee freedmen the right to vote in elections for state constitutional conventions and in subsequent state elections, but it did not guarantee freedmen the right to vote in federal elections. See page 451.

7d. No. The Reconstruction Act of 1867 did not stipulate a definite time period during which the Reconstruction process would take place. See page 451.

8a. No. Johnson's impeachment by the House and subsequent trial in the Senate rendered him almost totally powerless as president. See pages 452–453.

8b. Correct. The Radical Republicans who led the prosecution of Johnson in his Senate trial advanced the belief that impeachment was political in nature. The Senate's acquittal of Johnson was a rejection of that idea. See pages 452–453.

8c. No. The Senate fell only one vote shy of the two-thirds majority necessary to convict Johnson of the charges brought against him. This is not an indication that northern opinion toward Johnson and the South had softened. See pages 452–453.

8d. No. The Senate's failure to convict Johnson did not cause a rift between the House and the Senate. See pages 452–453.

9a. Correct. By eliminating property qualifications for voting, the new state constitutions made the South more democratic and brought the South in line with the rest of the nation. See page 455.

9b. No. Although these state constitutions extended more rights to women, women's suffrage, advocated by some black delegates, was considered radical and was not adopted. See page 455.

9c. No. The new constitutions did provide for public schools, but attendance to these schools was not compulsory. See page 455.

9d. No. Yearly reapportionment of legislative districts was not made mandatory by the new state constitutions. See page 455.

10a. Correct. Southern Republicans quickly restored the voting rights of former Confederates. This meant that the Republican party would face defeat if it could not gain white support. In courting the white vote, the Republican party abandoned its most loyal supporters—blacks. See pages 455–456.

10b. No. Although the southern Republicans appealed for support from a broad range of groups in the South, they were never able to build a broad popular base for the party. See pages 455–456.

10c. No. In the first place, southern Democrats were not more "liberal" than the southern Republicans. Furthermore, freedmen themselves supported restoration of the voting rights of former Confederates. See pages 455–456.

10d. No. The evidence does not indicate that congressional Republicans were embarrassed by the decision of southern Republicans to restore the voting rights of former Confederates. See pages 455–456.

11a. No. The evidence indicates that freedmen throughout the South, and especially those participating in Reconstruction governments, were very interested in participating in the political process and did so with great dignity and distinction. See page 457.

11b. Correct. Charges of "black domination" and "Negro rule" are examples of the racist propaganda used by white conservatives to discredit the Reconstruction governments. See page 457.

11c. No. Those blacks who participated in Reconstruction governments were practical and realistic in their approach to power. They extended the right to vote to former Confederates, did not insist on an integrated school system, and did not insist on social equality. See page 457.

11d. No. The evidence indicates that those blacks participating in Reconstruction governments were not vindictive toward their former masters. Their actions demonstrate their belief in "the Christian goal of reconciliation." See page 457.

12a. No. The evidence indicates that after 1867 the terrorist activities against blacks became more organized and purposeful, and the campaign of terror in Alamance and Caswell counties clearly fits this characterization. See pages 458–459.

12b. No. The campaign of terror in the North Carolina counties of Caswell and Alamance was organized by the wealthy and the powerful. See pages 458–459.

12c. Correct. Terrorist campaigns by the Klan were organized and purposeful after 1867. This was clearly the case in these North Carolina counties where the wealthy and powerful organized the campaign of terror for the purpose of regaining political control. See pages 458–459.

12d. No. Blacks and whites of the yeoman class were allies in Alamance and Caswell counties, and the Klan successfully used racism to destroy this coalition. See pages 458–459.

13a. No. Although the Reconstruction governments were able to effect some reform in the South, they chose not to demand redistribution of land. This decision is one of the main reasons that these governments were not able to alter the social structure of the region. See page 460.

13b. No. The success of the Klan's terrorist campaign in Alamance and Caswell counties in North Carolina is evidence that there was not a lasting alliance between blacks and whites of the yeoman class. See page 460.

13c. No. Blacks were given the right to vote, but it was naive to believe that the ballot was an adequate weapon in the struggle by African-Americans for a better life. See page 460.

13d. Correct. The Reconstruction governments did not demand and Congress did not bring about a redistribution of land in the South. As a result, blacks were denied economic independence and remained economically dependent on hostile whites. See page 460.

14a. Correct. John Campbell argued that the Fourteenth Amendment brought individual rights under federal protection by making the Bill of Rights applicable to the states. The Court disagreed and said that state citizenship and national citizenship were separate, with the former being more important. See page 468.

14b. No. The Court ruled that the Fourteenth Amendment protected only those rights that went along with national citizenship, and the Court narrowly defined those rights. See page 468.

14c. No. Although the Court later ruled that corporations were legal persons protected under the Fourteenth Amendment (the 1886 *Santa Clara* case), this was not its ruling in the *Slaughter-House* cases. See page 468.

14d. No. The Court ruled that, of the two, state citizenship was more important than national citizenship. See page 468.

15a. No. The monetary issue aroused a great deal of interest during the 1870s, especially among farmers, who tended to favor an inflationary policy. However, by the 1876 election a "sound money" policy had basically won out. See pages 469–470.

15b. No. William H. Seward was secretary of state from 1861 to 1869. His policies had no direct bearing on the outcome of the disputed presidential election of 1876. See pages 469–470.

Copyright © Houghton Mifflin Company. All rights reserved.

15c. Correct. The fact that both candidates in this disputed election favored removal of federal troops from the South and an end to Reconstruction indicates that the electorate had lost interest in Reconstruction. This is especially important in relation to the northern electorate. See pages 469–470.

15d. No. Since the end of the Civil War, the government had been injecting money into the economy and extending indirect aid to business interests. Most people favored a continuation of this practice, which had spurred industrial growth, especially in the North. See pages 469–470.